EVANGELICALS AND
DEMOCRACY IN AMERICA

EVANGELICALS AND DEMOCRACY IN AMERICA

VOLUME I: RELIGION AND SOCIETY

WILLOW INTERNATIONAL LIBRARY

STEVEN BRINT AND JEAN REITH SCHROEDEL

EDITORS

Russell Sage Foundation • New York

The Russell Sage Foundation

The Russell Sage Foundation, one of the oldest of America's general purpose foundations, was established in 1907 by Mrs. Margaret Olivia Sage for "the improvement of social and living conditions in the United States." The Foundation seeks to fulfill this mandate by fostering the development and dissemination of knowledge about the country's political, social, and economic problems. While the Foundation endeavors to assure the accuracy and objectivity of each book it publishes, the conclusions and interpretations in Russell Sage Foundation publications are those of the authors and not of the Foundation, its Trustees, or its staff. Publication by Russell Sage, therefore, does not imply Foundation endorsement.

Library of Congress Cataloging-in-Publication Data
Evangelicals and democracy in America / Steven Brint and Jean Reith Schroedel, editors.
     p.   cm. — (Religion and society ; v. 1)
  Includes bibliographical references and index.
  ISBN 978-0-87154-067-6 (alk. paper)
  1. Evangelicalism—United States. 2. Christianity and politics—United
  States. I. Brint, Steven G. II. Schroedel, Jean Reith.
  BR1642.U5E897 2009
  322'.10973—dc22

2009003543

The paper used in this publication meets the minimum requirements of American National Standard for Information Sciences—Permanence of Paper for Printed Library Materials. ANSI Z39.48-1992.

Text design by Suzanne Nichols.

RUSSELL SAGE FOUNDATION
112 East 64th Street, New York, New York 10065
10 9 8 7 6 5 4 3 2 1

Contents

About the Authors

Steven Brint is professor of sociology at the University of California, Riverside, director of the Colleges & Universities 2000 study, and associate dean of the College of Humanities, Arts, and Social Sciences.

Jean Reith Schroedel is dean of the School of Politics and Policy at Claremont Graduate University.

Nancy T. Ammerman is professor of sociology of religion in the School of Theology and the Department of Sociology at Boston University.

Prudence L. Carter is associate professor in the School of Education and the Department of Sociology at Stanford University.

John H. Evans is associate professor of sociology at the University of California, San Diego.

Philip S. Gorski is professor of sociology and religious studies and co-director of the Center for Comparative Research at Yale University.

John C. Green is senior fellow in religion and American politics at the Pew Forum on Religion & Public Life and director of the Ray C. Bliss Institute of Applied Politics and Distinguished Professor of Political Science at the University of Akron.

Michèle Lamont is the Robert I. Goldman Professor of European Studies and professor of sociology and African and African American Studies at Harvard University.

Paul Lichterman is professor of sociology and religion at the University of Southern California.

Jennifer Merolla is Mary Nicolai-George Blair Assistant Professor in the Department of Politics and Policy at Claremont Graduate University.

Gabriel Rossman is professor of sociology at University of California, Los Angeles.

David Sikkink is associate professor in the Department of Sociology at Notre Dame University, and fellow in the Center for the Study of Religion and Society at Notre Dame as well as at the Institute for Educational Initiatives.

Rogers M. Smith is Christopher H. Browne Distinguished Professor of Political Science at the University of Pennsylvania.

Scott Waller is graduate student in the Department of Politics and Policy at Claremont Graduate University.

W. Bradford Wilcox is associate professor of sociology at the University of Virginia and a member of the James Madison Society at Princeton University.

Robert Wuthnow is director of the Center for the Study of Religion and Gerhard R. Andlinger '52 Professor of Sociology at Princeton University.

Introduction

STEVEN BRINT AND JEAN REITH SCHROEDEL

I N THE thirty years since the rise of the Christian Right, evangelicals
have been at the center of a revived religious presence in America's
political life and social institutions. Their wealth and influence have
expanded dramatically, and they have reentered the halls of power.
Other religious conservatives—notably Catholics and Mormons but also
some mainline Protestants—have been drawn into the political and cultural alliance they lead. Nearly every sphere of American life has been
touched by the mobilization of religious conservatives. We explore the
causes and consequences of these developments.[1]

This volume focuses on social topics: the sources of evangelicals'
identity and growing prominence in American society, the relations
between evangelicals and other groups in American society, and the
influence of evangelicals on America's social institutions. A companion volume focuses on political topics: religious conservatives and
partisan politics, the mobilizing rhetoric of evangelicals, and the cycles and evolution of the movement as a force in American political
life.

In this introduction to volume 1, we sketch the historical events
that led to the reemergence and shaped the character of the evangelical movement in public life.[2] We also define the groups in which
the volumes are interested—evangelicals and the "traditionalist alliance"—because the first of these terms has been used in different
ways and the second requires careful specification. We situate the
volume in the context of the existing literature, and we discuss the
topics and themes that give the chapters in the volume coherence as a
whole.

Historical Contexts

The impress of activist Protestantism has rarely been absent in American history. Even before the Puritans set foot on the shores of America, John Winthrop evoked religious imagery in his depiction of their settlement: "We shall be a city on a hill; the eyes of all people are upon us" (Winthrop 1630/1931, 294–95). This vision of America as the new Israel, one with the mission to redeem its own people while providing a model for the rest of humanity, is an enduring legacy of America's Puritan fore-bears. Much of American history can be read through a biblical lens: the nation is especially blessed, but also continually challenged to fulfill its destiny.

Yet the history of Protestantism in the United States is also marked by divisions and cycles, periods of inward-looking subcultural concerns al-ternating with periods of outward-looking activism. A great gulf exists between the exclusive colonial Puritan establishment of the seventeenth century and the populist evangelicalism of the Second Great Awakening of 1790–1840. The Second Awakening virtually abandoned the stricter aspects of Calvinism, in particular the doctrines of predestination and innate human depravity, and established belief in the possibility of uni-versal salvation through personal faith and devotional service. Where traditional Calvinism had taught that election into heaven depended on the arbitrary will of a severe God, the evangelical Protestants of the Sec-ond Great Awakening preached that the regeneration and salvation of the soul depended on the individual's inner faith. Reconciliation with God still required living a morally good life, but salvation had been ef-fectively democratized.

Although the precepts of strict morality persisted as a cultural idiom among churchgoing Protestants, the outward-looking engagement with society fostered by mass revivals and the Arminian doctrine of salvation proved to be something new, dynamic, and unpredictable in American culture. We can see the offshoots of this outward-looking Protestantism in the enthusiasm of antebellum Northerners for voluntary associations of all types, in their support for common schools to teach both literacy and Protestant virtues, and in their advocacy of morality-infused social reform efforts, such as prison reform, reform of child labor laws, the abolition of slavery, and the Temperance movement. As the historian Daniel Walker Howe observed, "We remember [the evangelical move-ment's] morality as strict, and indeed it was. . . . But even its most prim-itive severity was redemptive in purpose. . . . [T]he converse of Victorian discipline was the proper development of human faculties. Education and self-improvement went along with discipline" (2007, 126).

This period of revivalism and social reform gave the nation a strongly evangelical flavor. The historian Mark Noll estimated that evangelical

Protestant denominations accounted for 85 percent of all U.S. churches in 1860 (2002, 170). The religious mainstream in the nineteenth century was comprised of large and medium-sized evangelical denominations and an evangelical wing of Episcopalians; nearly all of whom shared the dream that "some day the civilization of the country would be fully Christian" (Handy 1984, ix–x). Unlike today, most evangelical Protestants were post-millennialists, who believed that the Second Coming would only occur after society was fully Christianized.

During the Civil War, both Northerners and Southerners believed they were fighting for a Christian America. Northern clergy stressed the evils of slavery and the need for national redemption even as Southern ministers held that slavery was in keeping with God's plan for humanity and benefited both master and slave (Harlow 2007; Haynes 2002). Although few former Confederates recanted their beliefs about slavery, many accepted their loss on the battlefield as divinely mandated (Harlow 2007; Haynes 2002). In the postbellum era, both Northerners and Southerners returned to the mission of creating a Christian civilization—domestically and globally. Presbyterians, Lutherans, Episcopalians, Baptists, and Methodists all were deeply engaged in missionary work by the end of the nineteenth century.

A second gulf emerged during the early part of the twentieth century, when nearly all evangelical denominations were gripped by conflicts between modernists and fundamentalists (Marsden 2006, chaps. 16–21). The modernists tried to reconcile biblical truths with scientific developments, notably, Darwinian evolution, and conservatives emphasized a literal reading of the Bible. Long-standing tensions over the priority of social reform versus individual soul-saving fused onto this basic fault line. What we now refer to as the division between mainline and evangelical Protestants derives from this early-twentieth-century split, with today's liberal mainline Protestants descending from the modernists and today's conservative evangelicals descending from the fundamentalists. Of course, neither of the two camps was monolithic. Theologically conservative churches were divided by how much (or, more often, how little) of Darwin, internationalism, social reformism, and academic biblical scholarship they thought it permissible to accept.

Following the 1925 Scopes Monkey Trial, many theologically conservative Protestants withdrew from the public sphere. They retained their identification as fundamentalists and concentrated on creating and maintaining Bible-centered schools and colleges, Bible summer camps, Bible study groups, Christian radio programming, and strong local church communities. Others tried to accommodate to modern life. These people eventually emerged under the label neo-evangelicals. Both the founding of the National Association of Evangelicals in 1942 and the Billy Graham revivals of the 1940s and 1950s gave new life to the Second

Great Awakening's vision of an outward-looking, populist, and theologically conservative Protestantism.

Nevertheless, during the half century between 1925 and 1975, liberal historians and social commentators took it for granted that the era of Protestant cultural hegemony had ended with the Scopes trial and that cultural authority had definitively passed to science and secular institutions (see, for example, Cox 1965; Hofstadter 1955; Hodgson 1976; Leuchtenberg 1958; Parrington 1939). The nation's social and political elite was still overwhelmingly Protestant (Baltzell 1964), but few members of this elite saw religion as capable of addressing the problems of modern society. During this period, the so-called secular revolution dramatically reduced the numbers and influence of evangelical Protestants in the culture-producing institutions of higher education, science, publishing, and the arts (Smith 2003). Following the triumph of World War II, which seemed to validate the American creed of pluralistic tolerance, President-elect Dwight Eisenhower spoke of the "Judeo-Christian concept"—not Protestantism—as the "deeply religious faith" on which "our sense of government is founded" (quoted in Silk 1988). Urban, middle-class Americans who set the tone for the rest of society pointed to three important religious groups in American life—Protestants, Catholics, and Jews—not one (Herberg 1960). Religion was regarded by most as a private practice, not a public cause (Herberg, 73–74).

During the 1960s and 1970s, the cultural ground shifted again. The political and cultural upheavals of the period left many theologically conservative Protestants feeling besieged. In particular, the feminist and gay rights movements growing out of the 1960s threatened cornerstones of belief among fundamentalists and evangelicals: the centrality of men as community and family leaders and the strict biblical morality promulgated by theologically conservative churches. Mainline Protestant clergy often seemed to be at the forefront of countercultural protest (Hadden 1969), and only the theologically conservative evangelical congregations gave traditional religious answers to the challenges posed by the progressive movements of the day. Social resentments between progressives and religious conservatives sometimes boiled over. Grassroots protests broke out in West Virginia against literature textbooks used in the public schools and in Dade County, Florida, against a proposed gay rights ordinance (Wald 2003, 205–7). An organized protest against the Equal Rights Amendment also spread through states with large theologically conservative Protestant denominations (Wald 2003).

During the 1960s and 1970s, all forms of evangelical Protestantism experienced an upsurge in membership (Chaves 2004, 33; Hout, Greeley, and Wilde 2001), and Christian broadcast media helped to create a sense of common religious concerns crossing denominational lines. The distinctions between fundamentalists and neo-evangelicals grew less important, and religious groups, such as the Pentecostals and charismatics, whose members expressed their faith with greater emotion, became a more important part of the evangelical mix. Sensing a potential political windfall in the making, President Richard Nixon and the national Republican Party began to cultivate ties with theologically conservative Protestant church leaders and wealthy evangelicals (Martin 1996, 98).

However, as Rogers Smith shows in chapter 11, neither grassroots protests nor GOP networking precipitated the birth of the Christian Right; instead, the movement owes its origins to Internal Revenue Service (IRS) and court actions that seemed to threaten the tax-exempt status of Christian broadcasters and Christian private schools and universities. These were the triggering events that led to the mobilization of conservative Protestant ministers. Promoted and in some cases funded by national conservative movement activists, Christian Right organizations, such as the National Christian Action Coalition (founded in 1977), the Christian Voice (1978), the Moral Majority (1979), Concerned Women for America (1979), the Religious Roundtable (1979), the American Coalition for Traditional Values (1980), and the Family Research Council (1983), all formed in the wake of disappointments and anger with the IRS and the courts during the Carter administration.

As they focused on issues with appeal in evangelical communities, these organizations created a public identity and narrative for evangelicals to impel political action. Like other forms of identity politics, those of the Right emphasized the valuable qualities and central importance of a group unfairly marginalized by the dominant powers in society. But here the dominant powers were secular and progressive, not the conservative white males who figured so prominently in the identity politics of the Left. Social movement leaders heightened the salience of religious identities by focusing on the centrality of church communities and the threats to religious values posed by secular elites. Statements by Jerry Falwell before the 1980 election captured this emphasis: "We're not trying to jam our moral philosophy down the throats of others. We are simply trying to keep others from jamming their amoral philosophy down our throats" (quoted in William Greider, "Would Jesus Join the Moral Majority?" *Washington Post*, October 13, 1980, D1). In a separate statement from this period, Falwell called for a response: "The day of the silent church is passed. . . . Preachers, you need as never before to preach on the issues, no matter what they say or what they write about you" (quoted in Doug Willis, "Pastor Says God Opposes ERA," *Associated Press*, October 30, 1980).

Social movement leaders also developed a narrative about the perils facing American society and the role evangelicals could play in opposing these perils. This narrative drew on the long-standing theme in fundamentalist and evangelical discourse about the need to assert godly values to overcome a world in moral decline. This theme was given new energy by evangelicals' sense of a world turned upside down by sexual experimentation, gender equity, and an aggressive secularism that gave no quarter to religious sensibilities. A branch of the movement focusing on opposition to "secular elites" grew out of the organizing work of the Religious Roundtable and the Moral Majority, and a "pro-family" branch grew out of the Eagle Forum's organizing against the Equal Rights Amendment (Hudson 2008, 3–12, 62–65).

Early leaders began to speak not only of the need for spiritual renewal and the approaching end of times, but also of what believers could do to return morality to a society badly in need of it. As Nancy Ammerman writes in chapter 2 of this volume, "Evangelicals have never stopped believing that spiritual salvation is the key to long-lasting change, but did become convinced that they might lose the ability to preach that gospel and preserve their way of life if they did not also act politically." The sense of fighting an immoral power with only the force of divine favor and moral justice on one's side has, of course, deep roots in Christianity, and has regularly given rise to powerful movements for social change.

Evangelicals and the "Traditionalist Alliance"

The term *evangelical* can be confusing, because evangelicals have been defined in many ways. A basic difference between today's evangelical and mainline Protestants was captured by the sociologist Stephen Warner (1988). The contemporary two-party system of Protestantism is, he argued, based primarily on different understandings of Jesus. Mainline Protestants think mainly in terms of a "moral teacher who told disciples that they could best honor him by helping those in need," whereas evangelicals conceive of "one who offers (personal) salvation to anyone who confesses his name" (33–34). The mainline traditions are critical of selfishness and understand religious duty as sharing abundance. They rarely consider the Bible as the literal word of God but instead as containing important truths, together with ancient myths and legends. By contrast, evangelicals are much less interested in helping the needy than in saving souls. Their view of social reform tends to focus on the correction of individual moral failings. Moreover, evangelicals attribute religious authority to the Bible alone and accept it as the literal word of God. With these contrasts in mind, Lyman Kellstedt and Corwin Smidt defined four core beliefs of evangelicals as follows: the Bible is the literal word of God; salvation is possible only through personal acceptance of Jesus as savior; personal acceptance of Jesus as savior often occurs through the born-again experience, an intense event of spiritual renewal marking their life from that point on; and the obligation to witness one's beliefs to others.

Evangelicals can also be defined denominationally and by self-identification. Denominational definitions are appealing to social scientists, because social scientists are not in complete agreement about the core beliefs of evangelicals (see, for example, Greeley and Hout 2006, chap. 2), and most social surveys do not ask questions about all core beliefs of evangelicals. Moreover, the overlap between holding the core beliefs of evangelicals and affiliating with an evangelical denomination or religious tradition is considerable. The major evangelical religious traditions are the Baptist, the Pentecostal-Holiness, the Reformed-Confessional, and the Anabaptist. To these it is important to add evangelicals who worship at nondenominational churches or churches where denomination is de-emphasized. Some of these are large mega-churches with celebrity pastors, such as T. D. Jakes's Potter House Church in Dallas, Joel Osteen's Lakewood Church in Houston, and Rick Warren's Saddleback Church in Orange County, California. The Southern Baptists, claiming more than 16 million members in 42,000 churches (Southern Baptist Convention 2008), are in many ways the center of evangelical Protestantism in the United States. Smaller evangelical denominations include the Assemblies of God, the Missouri and Wisconsin Synod Lutherans, the Mennonites, the Nazarenes, and the Seventh-Day Adventists. Some branches of Methodism and Presbyterianism are also evangelical in orientation (see Steensland et al. 2000).

Definitions based on core beliefs yield the largest estimates of white evangelicals, more than 30 percent of the adult population in the United States, and self-identifications the smallest, usually less than 20 percent. Estimates based on denomination yield figures in between, around 25 percent (see Kellstedt and Smidt 1991; Wald 2003, 162–63). In the press, the most common estimates are based on denomination. Thus the proportion of white evangelicals in the U.S. adult population is commonly estimated at slightly more than 25 percent.

Readers may wonder why African American evangelicals are not treated at length in these pages. Many African Americans hold the same core beliefs as white evangelicals, as do many Latino and many Asian American Protestants. Moreover, black evangelicals are nearly as conservative as white on some moral-values issues, such as gay marriage (Loftus 2001). We focus on whites because blacks, despite their social conservatism, have few ties to white evangelicals or other white religious conservatives. Some tensions date from the days of racial segregation in the South; white evangelicals played either a complicit or active role in maintaining the institutions of Jim Crow. Although white evangelicals have made efforts to repent for the racial injustices of the past and to reach across racial lines, the success of these efforts remains in doubt, as Paul Lichterman and his colleagues show in chapter 6. Many remaining differences, of course, are based on the divergent political paths white and black evangelicals have taken. The latter are firmly anchored in the Democratic Party and embrace a political agenda focusing on increased equality and social justice. In this respect, African American Protestants, whether evangelical or not, are closer to mainline Protestant attitudes about helping the poor and sharing abundance. African Americans see the state as an ally, because of its antidiscrimination laws and programs to aid the poor. White evangelicals, by contrast, tend to see government programs as an inadequate and often wasteful substitute for individuals' commitment to living a well-directed and self-disciplined life.

White evangelicals have been at the center of the movement to restore traditional moral values, but they are not the only group involved in this project. Several chapters in this volume therefore branch out from the white evangelical core of the movement to talk about other white religious conservatives as well. The term *traditionalist alliance* is borrowed from the work of John Green and the composition of the alliance, as well as the commonalities and tensions within it, are analyzed in chapter 4 of this volume, which Green has written. The traditionalist alliance is defined by religious belief and practice, and includes the most religious members of several faith traditions: Mormons who are regular churchgoers (approximately 2 percent of the population), Catholics who are regular churchgoers (approximately 4.5 percent), mainline Protestants who are regular churchgoers (approximately 4.5 percent), and churchgoing evangelical Protestants (12.5 percent). It makes sense, we believe, to include evangelical Protestants who are not regular churchgoers (nearly 11 percent) as part of the alliance as well, because, like the other members, they are conservative on moral-values issues and a dependable part of the Republican Party coalition. Including them, more than 33 percent of the U.S. adult population is, nominally, a member of this traditionalist alliance. In 2004, these were the people who tended to say that moral values were very important in their voting decision, and they made up 60 percent of all voters for George W. Bush (see chapter 4, this volume).

The term *traditionalist* is used advisedly. Religious conservatives are not always traditional, even in matters of theology. In the born-again experience, evangelicals go through a life-changing event that leads many of them to reject their earlier religious upbringing. Pentecostals are especially open to life-changing events, however conservative or traditionalist they may be in theology. Moreover, religious conservatives accept many aspect of modernity—from the technology that helps knit their communities together to the consumerism so evident in the church-shopping experience. Even so, the term traditionalist seems preferable to possible alternatives. Traditionalist is not coterminous with traditional. The former is a self-conscious defense of tradition—an ideological outlook, not a set of unchanging practices—as well as a way of seeing self and community. Practices involved in asserting the defense of tradition can, ironically, involve abandonment of certain tenets of the tradition one seeks to defend. Assertive involvement in public life is, for example, one practice that stands at odds with religious traditions that once emphasized personal salvation over societal reform.

From a historical perspective, the creation of a working alliance among religious traditionalists is a great departure from earlier ethnoreligious patterns in American life. Throughout the nineteenth century, Protestants and Catholics were often at bitter odds. Protestants were suspicious of the dependence of Catholics on papal authority rather than that of the Bible. They found the easy forgiveness of the Catholic Church to foster indolent habits. Catholics, for their part, often resented the haughtiness and condescension of Protestant America. They also distrusted the extreme individualism of Protestant culture, which clashed with the more communitarian norms of Catholic ethnic neighborhoods. Differences in ethnicity and social status created a sense among Catholics that they were outsiders to the mainstream of American culture. Theological orientations were also a factor; for Catholics, God's kingdom was not of this world, and no human programs of conversion or social reform could usher in the millennium (Kleppner 1979). If anything, fiercer tensions existed between Protestants and Mormons because of the "heretical" principles and practices of Mormonism, including polygamy and the proclamation of Joseph Smith as a prophet of God. These were and remain large barriers to overcome.

Sociologists became aware of the possibility of an alliance in the making more than two decades ago, when Robert Wuthnow published his pioneering study *The Restructuring of American Religion* (1988). In Wuthnow's view, old divisions between Protestants, Catholics, and Jews were breaking down and new divisions based on levels of religiosity within faith communities were taking their place. The new structure built on interfaith contacts that had developed in the postwar period and shared concerns about the diminished role of religion as a moral guide. In a society marked by higher levels of education and secular culture-producing institutions, religious conservatives from all traditions felt imperiled by those within their own communities who had weaker attachments to faith and stronger attachments to nonreligious sources of moral guidance. Shortly after the publication of Wuthnow's book, another sociologist, James Davison Hunter, published another influential study, *Culture Wars*, arguing that a cultural divide was growing between people who believed in transcendental, typically religious, sources of moral authority, and others who embraced progressive ideals and human interactions as the primary sources of moral authority (1992).

The restructuring both Wuthnow and Hunter predicted has not come to pass—at least not completely. Faith traditions continue to matter. The proportion of Catholics and mainline Protestants who identify as religious right or take conservative positions on moral-values issues are much smaller than the proportion of evangelicals who do so. Part of this has to do with the lower proportion of very religious people in these faith traditions. Mainline Protestants, in particular, have drifted leftward in recent years, and Catholics continue to be hesitant about allying with evangelicals. Some old biases against Catholics remain in white evangelical communities, including assertions that Catholics do not think for themselves and that the rosary is a superstition (Greeley and Hout 2006, chap. 12). Such views are particularly common among Pentecostals (Greeley and Hout 2006). Historical tensions between evangelicals and Mormons also have not been overcome in spite of Mormon strongly allied views on moral-values issues and partisan identification. The most recent indicator is the sharp backlash among evangelicals against the presidential bid of the Mormon former governor of Massachusetts, Mitt Romney. The continuation of the traditionalist alliance as a major force in American society and politics consequently remains an open question. Historically, alliances among religious conservatives have been relatively short-lived in American society, and, as Peter Dobkin Hall shows in chapter 8 of volume 2, frequently subject to dissolution along sectarian lines.

One important reason to expect continued cultural divisions between social conservatives and the less religious is that social conservatives are joined, in large measure, through their opposition to a common foe: secular people or, more pointedly, secular humanists. Seculars, consequently, stand as an important, if background, presence in the volume. They have become the defining moral other for members of the traditionalist alliance. For religious conservatives, they are guilty of a fundamental fault: they believe in the moral authority of humanity, not of God (for a discussion of secular elites as moral other, see Rhys Williams, volume 2, chapter 5).

Religious conservatives are undoubtedly right that seculars' influence on culture-producing industries belies their small numbers in the population. At the heart of the identity politics of religious conservatives, therefore, lies the story of a real, if often exaggerated, conflict in American society. Even so, the culture war idea has been more useful as a mobilization tool than as a depiction of social reality. The number of people who claim no religious affiliation is growing, to be sure, but still falls at around 15 percent of the population. Moreover, in the United States, few of these people are entirely without religious belief. About nine out of ten Americans, for example, say that they believe in God and eight out of ten say that they pray. Estimates for the proportion of atheists in the United States run between 3 and 7 percent (Zuckerman 2005).

Background to the Volume

To consider the topics of conservative religion and social identity, intergroup relations, and religiously motivated change in secular social institutions, we assembled a group of leading scholars from several academic disciplines. As might be expected in a volume that includes chapters written by scholars trained in sociology, political science, history, and religious studies, the methods used range from aggregate data analysis and ethnographic research to archival research and close textual analysis. Our motivation for bringing this distinguished group together was to address weaknesses in the existing literature and to build, if we could, a more comprehensive and fully integrated understanding of the interplay between religious conservatives and American society.

In our view, the most important weakness of the popular literature has been its polemical character. Much of the public discussion of theologically conservative Protestants has been closely tied to dramatic images of conflict. Mass mailings from groups, such as the Traditional Values Coalition and Concerned Women of America, rally supporters by raising the specter of control of the policy agenda by secular humanists who, they allege, support the degradation of American culture, hedonistic lifestyles, and a range of irreligious and anti-American values from advocacy of abortion and homosexuality to atheism and pacifism. Similarly, liberal groups have demonized Christian conservatives as an army on the march whose theocratic leaders are intent on dismantling barriers to the separation of church and state. Vivid images of powerful extremists have proven an effective part of the machinery used to raise donations for political campaigns, and they have seeped into that of other milieus where strong narratives and epic confrontations matter greatly— namely, daily journalism. Culture wars issues are much more popular in the press than discussion of the many issues on which Americans see eye to eye. According to Lexis-Nexis, for example, stories on culture wars issues, such as abortion and gay marriage, have outnumbered stories on interfaith dialogues by a factor of ten in recent years.

Less polemical journalistic commentators, though they lower the volume of the rhetoric somewhat, do not always provide a clear understanding of the motivations of conservative Protestants and values voters. For example, in his best-selling book *What's the Matter with Kansas*, the liberal social critic Thomas Frank advanced an interpretation of the Christian Right that rests ultimately on economic class conflict (2004). For Frank, the Republican Party, with the help of allied Christian conservative leaders, has been able to direct resentments arising from economic insecurity into the cultural arena. White working- and middle-class anger has been directed toward culturally alien secular elites rather than where, according to Frank, the anger should be directed—against the economic polities of the Republican Party. Frank fails to take seriously the possibility that religious beliefs can be a decisive motivation for social and political action in their own right.

A vibrant scholarly literature now exists on evangelicals, religious conservatives, and American democracy (in social science, see, for example, Ammerman 2005; Chaves 2004; Greeley and Hout 2006; Green et al. 1996; Layman 2001; Leege et al. 2002; Lindsay 2007; Marsden 2006; Smith 1998, 2000; Wolfe 2003). Nevertheless, taken as a whole, the scholarly literature has failed to surmount three limitations. The first is that much of the most widely cited literature is now dated. The second is that the literature has neglected some key questions, or has not addressed these questions fully. The third is that the literature has tended to develop in piecemeal, relatively unconnected to a broad, balanced, and well-integrated view of evangelicals and their place in American society and politics.

Work on evangelicals and the Christian Right has not always kept up with the evolution of the movement or its ties to other religious groups in American society. Social mobility, including higher levels of education, has encouraged many more evangelicals to feel a sense of belonging in the upper reaches of American society. The movement has accordingly evolved in important ways. Its elastic orthodoxy, to use Michael Lindsay's phrase (2007), allows it to engage with members of other faith traditions while maintaining core positions on social issues. As evangelicals have moved into the halls of power, culture war imagery has faded; the language of moral rectitude has given way to the language of expanded rights and freedoms (Moen 1995). Evangelicals are adapting to new issues, too; many now include environmental and poverty issues as moral-values issues, without necessarily abandoning their earlier commitments to fighting abortion and gay marriage. Encouraged by an increasingly moderate National Association of Evangelicals, younger evangelicals have been particularly interested in exploring these new directions.

Important gaps also exist in the literature. Social scientists have, as yet, failed to investigate as completely as they might how the distinctive cultural capital and mobilization strategies of evangelicals have contributed to their advance. These issues are addressed in part I of this volume. Relations between evangelicals and other religious groups remains inadequately investigated as well, hindered by stereotypes of the culture wars alliance of the orthodox, of evangelicalism as racism by another name, and of mainline Protestants as a disappearing liberal voice in society. Part II of this volume challenges these stereotypes and illuminate the complexities of relations among evangelicals and their putative friends and foes.

Perhaps the most important gap in the literature, however, has been the failure of social scientists to consider the interaction between evangelicals and America's nonreligious social institutions: the family, education, mass media, and the law. Evangelicals have been active in efforts to reshape social institutions, both through the creation of separate subcultural institutions and through their efforts to influence the culture and structure of mainstream institutions. To what extent have they succeeded? Very few assessments exist of the consequences of these efforts, or, just as important, of the accommodations religious conservatives have made to secular social institutions. The chapters in part III of this volume go a long way toward bridging this gap.

We believe the two volumes in this series realize our hope for a deeper, more balanced, and better integrated portrait of the evangelical movement and the traditionalist alliance than has so far been available. The volumes combine a sophisticated view of religious doctrines and organizations with a sharp sense of the distinctiveness of the American context, and an awareness of the dependence of religious actors on well-supported secular institutions and the broader political coalitions in their environment.

The authors suggest that there is something very different about the role conservative religion plays in American society from the one it has played elsewhere. In the United States, theologically conservative Protestantism has often served to stimulate, rather than to prevent, social activism—and structurally similar moralistic styles are characteristic of "traditionalist" and "progressive" activists alike, however different the policies they advocate. While religiosity has been an important influence on cultural understandings of middle-class respectability in American society, it has not stopped the progress of equality for groups whose self-presentation fits within the broad confines set by the norms of middle-class respectability. Though struggles for equality have often taken decades, social activists seeking equality for marginalized groups have gained acceptance by presenting themselves as non-violent, conformity-seeking aspirants to middle class status. This is one important reason why the most right-wing elements of the traditionalist alliance have not prevented egalitarian social change. Another has to do with the counter-mobilizations of progressives they have encouraged. Another—and perhaps most important of all—is that secular social institutions and culture-producing industries have much firmer foundations in the United States than political progressives themselves sometimes credit.

This leads us to the other term in the title of this volume—democracy in America. Indeed, the great work of the same name by Alexis de Tocqueville is an explicit reference point in many of the chapters. Following de Tocqueville, we define democracy not only as active citizen participation in political life, but also as egalitarian social relations. De Tocqueville considered the latter the great distinction of American society in the nineteenth century. For him, equality of conditions was the master key that unlocked many of the mysteries of America's character: the active participation of its citizens in public affairs, the efflorescence of voluntary organizations of all types, as well as the informal manners of its inhabitants and the grandiose themes of its writers and rhetoricians. Religion for de Tocqueville played an important role in the background. It served as a restraint against the potential for social conflict inherent in the liberties Americans had and have:

> Nature and circumstances have made the inhabitants of the United States bold, as is sufficiently attested by the enterprising spirit with which they seek for fortune. If the mind of the Americans were free from all hindrances, they would shortly become the most daring innovators and the most persistent disputants in the world. But the revolutionists of America are obliged to profess an ostensible respect for Christian morality and equity, which does not permit them to violate wantonly the laws that oppose their designs. . . . Hitherto no one in the United States has dared to advance the maxim that everything is permissible for the interests of society, an impious adage which seems to have been invented in an age of freedom to shelter all future tyrants. Thus, while the law permits the Americans to do what they please, religion prevents them from conceiving, and forbids them to commit, what is rash or unjust. (1835/1961, 362)

The concerns of the authors in this volume are in the tradition of de Tocqueville, but the conclusions they reach differ from those of de Tocqueville on several counts. These authors see the spirit of equality itself as a product not only of the similar economic circumstances shared by Americans, but also of the religious beliefs that were becoming dominant in American society at the time of de Tocqueville's study. The emotional pietism and Arminian views of salvation of the Second Great Awakening created a spirit of equality, perhaps to a greater degree than the widespread distribution of small property holdings that de Tocqueville emphasized. They also observe that de Tocqueville missed the extent to which evangelical religion was a primary generator of the voluntary associations he correctly saw as a distinctive feature of American society.

Nor are the authors inclined to interpret conservative religion as simply a check on the passions liberty allows. Although the strict morality of theologically conservative Protestantism has created many inhibitions and prohibitions throughout American history, the outward-looking reformism of evangelical Protestantism in the antebellum North stimulated, rather than restrained, the moral passions. The entrepreneurialism fostered by the capitalist marketplace was mirrored by the organizational dynamism of evangelical Protestantism to which it was so often wedded. These cultural emphases continue to be influential sources of populist optimism and, indirectly, of the expectation of social and economic opportunity.

Some of the authors in this volume continue to see conservative religion as an important restraint in an otherwise liberal and pleasure-seeking society, but most emphasize that case law and norms of public reason are far more important restraints today. Indeed, according to most of the authors, the secular revolution of the early twentieth century effectively reduced conservative religion to the role of another interest in society, albeit an interest strongly associated with norms of middle-class respectability. This reduction of the role of religion has led to a number of changes that de Tocqueville could not have foreseen. In the context of a far more pluralistic society than the one de Tocqueville knew, the mobilization of traditional religion leads to the countermobilization of the forces it opposes. The moralistic style, subcultural communalism, and media savvy it favors is, not surprisingly, mirrored in the moralistic style, subcultural communalism, and media savvy of its foes.

For the authors, the political involvement of evangelicals and other religious conservatives has strengthened participatory democracy in the United States by bringing new voices into the public arena, but it has simultaneously exacerbated tensions and divisions in a diverse population—abetted, of course, by ambitious politicians and a conflict-loving mass media. Under these changed conditions, conservative religion is perhaps less a support to egalitarian social relations than an impediment to the equality of women, gays, and lower-income citizens. Yet it has not proven to be an insurmountable barrier to the counter-mobilizations it stimulates and the secularism of America's social institutions. The authors also observe that the network-building properties de Tocqueville attributed to voluntary associations may be limited in the theologically conservative churches today. These limitations derive from the failures of churches to practice sufficiently sophisticated "bridging" interactions (to use Robert Putnam's phrase) across class and racial lines and by the tendency of evangelicals to adopt the sloganeering discourse of modern media-based politics, rather than serious, if sometimes painful, dialogues about social differences. As John Evans observes in chapter 7, mainline Protestants provide an instructive counterexample because they tend to avoid the media glare while pursuing consensus moral causes, such as poverty reduction and medical improvements in the developing world.

Because conservative religion has become a powerful and contested interest in American society, some of the authors in volume 2 suggest that the social and moral reforms favored by evangelicals will flourish only if the movement becomes less wedded to achieving its ends through partisan means. All agree that partisanship has not as yet yielded many of the policy changes that evangelicals hoped to see. Indeed, the authors see the policy influence of religious conservatives as severely circumscribed, due to the strong currents of egalitarianism and liberal consumerism in American society, and to the restraining influence of secular institutions and nonreligious public-good norms of political discourse. American society is first of all an arena of pluralistic competition, legal authority, and a consumer marketplace. Religious conservatives are shaped by these realities more than they have been able to shape them. Consequently, as they have entered the political mainstream, religious conservatives have found it necessary to appeal for change on nonreligious grounds using secular political philosophies and social science research as tools.

Overview of the Chapters

These, then, are the major concerns and perspectives that unite the work in this volume. But each of the chapters also provides new research and insights on the specific topics it covers. We therefore conclude with a brief overview of the chapters, showing their relation to one another.

The first set of issues, discussed in part I, address why evangelicals returned to the public arena in the 1970s and have remained so prominent in American society and politics over the last thirty years. Earlier scholars described the rise of a politicized evangelical movement as the "politics of lifestyle concern" or the "politics of cultural defense" (see, for example, Guth 1983). This research showed how the movement gained force as a response to potential regulatory challenges to evangelicals' school and broadcast institutions, as well as the threats represented by the various countercultural movements of the 1960s. However, the continued prominence of the movement, during periods of social turmoil and relative social quiet alike, requires explanation.

The chapters in part I provide new ways of thinking about this issue. In chapter 1, Robert Wuthnow analyzes the cultural capital of evangelicals—the set of beliefs and practices that not only form the central components of an identity, but also represent a type of currency that can be used to activate social networks and help evangelicals achieve their aims. Unlike those who see cultural capital as the marker of upper-class taste in the arts, Wuthnow's broadened understanding of the concept makes it usable as a way to understand both the status conflict among subcultural forms of cultural capital and the ways that cultural capital can serve as an engine of collective mobility.

In chapter 2, Nancy Ammerman emphasizes the improved social standing of evangelicals and, more important, the power of the narrative they have devised to create a permanent campaign against secular and liberal agents of moral decline:

> This is a movement that gained momentum as it learned to tell a new story about what is wrong with American culture and what they must do about it. In the 1970s, leaders such as Jerry Falwell and Pat Robertson began speaking not just of the approaching End Times, but also of what believers can do in the meantime 'while He tarries'. . . . Evangelicals have never stopped believing that spiritual salvation is the key to long-lasting change, but they became convinced that they might lose the ability to preach that gospel and preserve their way of life if they did not also act politically. They came to see their own families as endangered and the privileged place of America in the world at risk.

Ammerman also situates white evangelicals in the variegated religious landscape of twenty-first century America and emphasizes the extent to which they represent a minority voice in a religiously diverse society.

In chapter 3, Philip Gorski provides an important interpretation of the resurgence of evangelicals by looking at conservative Protestantism in the United States in comparative perspective. For Gorski, the recurring prominence and activism of evangelicals in the United States is a function of characteristics that have made evangelicalism in the United States distinctive. In Gorski's telling, these characteristics include the early disestablishment of a state church; the early linking of Protestantism to American nationalism through the idea that America is God's chosen instrument of civilization; extreme pluralism in religious competition attributable in large part to mass immigration; development of an evangelical subculture in reaction to modernist movement in the mainline Protestant churches; a history of frontier revivals and overseas missions that kept evangelical beliefs in wide circulation and served as training grounds for leaders; and, most recently, the ongoing partisan mobilization of evangelicals by the Republican Party and its allied organizations.

Wuthnow's focus on cultural capital and Ammerman's focus on narrative add up to a new perspective on the identity politics of the Right. Like the identity politics of the Left, evangelicals have found ways to highlight the salience of the characteristics they share as a community, and have found a unifying narrative to justify continuous struggle against ostensibly powerful foes. Gorski's historical institutionalism broadens these interpretations to show the underlying conditions that made the resurgence of evangelicals' identity politics possible—and indeed likely—given the right precipitating conditions.

The second set of issues, addressed in part II, concerns the relationship between evangelicals and their interlocutors. Rethinking these relations has become necessary because much of the early work on evangelical intergroup relations is now dated. It is no longer a foregone conclusion that evangelicals can make common cause with other religious conservatives. Nor are once-popular arguments that evangelicalism is racism by another name plausible any longer in light of the many evangelical race-bridging efforts. Similarly, it no longer seems reasonable to attribute the quiescence of mainline Protestants, once the dominant religious voice in the United States, to tensions between liberal ministers and their more conservative congregations, because mainline Protestants themselves have become increasingly liberal on these issues (Manza and Brooks 1997).

In chapter 4, John Green provides a new assessment of relations within the traditionalist alliance. Although he finds impressive sources of attachment among members of the alliance—including religiosity, similar positions on social issues, and traditions of civic engagement—he also finds sources of disunity. These sources include ecumenical orthodoxy and divergent views on issues outside the moral-values domain. Moreover, the current attachment to the alliance of evangelicals who are irregular churchgoers may decline in the future, if the restructuring trends that Wuthnow found for other religious groups begin to influence the evangelical community. Green's analysis raises important questions about the long-term durability of the alliance.

Evangelicals and other members of the traditionalist alliance have defined themselves, in large measure, by their opponents: feminists and gays, as well as secular elites. In chapter 5, Jennifer Merolla, Jean Reith Schroedel, and Scott Waller assess the impact of evangelical strength on the opportunities of women and gays. Controlling for a variety of economic and demographic covariates, they show that states in which evangelicals make up a large proportion of the population are significantly less likely to elect women and gays to political office. However, the proportion of women and gays who hold elected office has grown over time even in states where evangelicals do make up a large proportion of the population. The chapter suggests that American society's movement toward equality is difficult to turn back, even in states where religious traditionalism is most prevalent.

Evangelicals have been far more open to race-bridging than they have been to accepting women's and gay rights. The shift of evangelicals away from the racist past is evident in the Southern Baptist Convention's repudiation of its role in perpetuating segregation and of such interracial evangelical groups as Promise Keepers. Survey data, too, shows that people committed to religion for its intrinsic value are least likely to hold prejudiced views of African Americans (Wald 2003, 185).

In chapter 6, Paul Lichterman, Prudence Carter, and Michèle Lamont provide the most comprehensive account available of evangelicals' race-bridging efforts. The results of their study are discomfiting. Evangelicals base race-bridging efforts on a Christ-centered approach in which everyone is considered equal in the eyes of Jesus. Lichterman and his colleagues find that this approach often fails to address frankly the unequal social circumstances of whites and blacks, leaving both sides feeling uncomfortable with one another in spite of their sincere efforts to achieve greater racial harmony.

Democracy depends on the active engagement of all important interests in society. For this reason, democratic theorists generally applaud the increased civic engagement of evangelicals and other religious conservatives (see, for example, Gutmann 1998; Putnam 2000; Shields 2007). However, in the face of highly mobilized interests, democracy sometimes also depends on the strength of countervailing powers. Mainline Protestants were once the most important voice on moral-values issues in the United States, but today they represent for some observers the missing counterweight. In chapter 7, John Evans takes up the mystery of the disappearing mainline Protestant public voice. Evans concludes that the declining numbers of mainline Protestants are only part of the explanation. Other parts are the tendency of mainliners to move toward supporting consensus issues, such as improving health care in the developing world, and their lack of interest in stirring the pot on the contentious culture war issues that attract media attention. Mainline Protestants are active on values issues, but not on the issues that excite evangelicals, progressive secular people, and the media.

In the popular press, a common reading has been that evangelicals and other religious conservatives are highly united and, thanks to their numbers and political influence, can drown out more liberal voices on moral-values issues. The chapters in part II present a more complex picture. In these chapters, we see important cracks in the traditionalist alliance. We see evangelicals reaching out across racial lines, but not always succeeding on the human level. We also see the slow but steady advance in the representation of women and gays, even in states dominated by evangelicals, and another continent of moral-values issues in which moderate and liberal voices continue to play an important role outside the media glare.

Evangelicals and their religious allies have attempted to transform American institutions in a direction that creates more space for traditional family and religious values. The chapters in part III suggest that, with the partial exception of the family, America's secular social institutions have exercised much more influence on evangelicals than evangelicals have on them. The dominant theme of the chapters is accommodation to mainstream secular institutions and norms of public discourse, and the inability of evangelicals to effect change except as a part of broader political coalitions.

In chapter 8, Bradford Wilcox discusses evangelicals' advocacy of the traditional family as a response to the decline of marriage and the increase in family instability during the 1960s and 1970s. The conservative Protestant family is distinctive; men are the heads of families, though discussion is the norm, and children are raised with both discipline and affection. Wilcox shows that some elements of this model have been more successful than others. Evangelical fathers, for example, are, according to some indicators, more involved in their children's lives than fathers from other religious traditions. However, divorce rates remain high among evangelicals and little evidence exists that evangelical families have been able to control teenage sexuality any better than families with other religious traditions. In the policy domain, evangelicals have been at the head of experiments to deepen marriage commitments and to educate others on the benefits of marriage, as well as of efforts to control teen sexuality through such means as abstinence education and virginity pledges. Although many of these policy interventions have failed to show positive results, evangelicals have succeeded in helping change the discourse about marriage and family, but have done so only with the help of secular social scientists who have called attention to the effects of single parenthood on children's well-being.

As we move from the family to schooling, we find evangelicals considerably more accommodating to secular norms. In chapter 9, David Sikkink shows that among evangelicals only the "spirit-filled" groups (Pentecostals and charismatics) tend to be adamantly opposed to the public system. Evangelical parents have often encouraged schools in their communities to allow for the teaching of religious traditions, alternatives to evolutionary theory, and school prayer. But even here evangelicals are far from united in their policy preferences, and partly for this reason have experienced limited success influencing the curriculum and practices of the public schools. Sikkink's chapter also looks inside private Protestant schools and finds that they closely resemble the organization and curriculum offered in public schools. Students have opportunities to study about democracy and pluralism, to participate in student government, and to discuss public affairs. They also volunteer more often than students in public schools. Only in reading about public affairs do they seem to fall below students in other sectors.

Accommodation is perhaps even higher in relations between religious conservatives and the mass media. In chapter 10, Gabriel Rossman shows that most conservative Christians stick with the popular media in spite of their expressed objections to salacious content. Although most voice efforts, such as filings with the Federal Communications Commission to protest indecency, are unsuccessful, Rossman shows that some campaigns to put pressure on advertisers have scored at least limited successes. Rossman also charts the growth of alternative Christian media and notes the extraordinary mobilizing tool that Christian broadcasting has become, capable of generating hundreds of thousands of telephone calls against bills that popular broadcasters oppose. Although evangelical Protestant media has grown with the movement, its market share is but a small fraction of the mainstream media. Rossman concludes that conservative Christians have established themselves as a viable market niche in an industry committed both to a mass market and to product differentiation. Christian media also sometimes serve, to borrow a phrase from major league baseball, as a farm system for the mainstream media; talented performers can prove themselves in the niche market before crossing over to the mass market.

Law is another institutional arena in which religious conservatives have achieved only limited success. In chapter 11, Rogers Smith shows that though religious conservatives have won important changes in prevailing constitutional doctrines governing state-church and state-society relations, the changes have been far less than activists have hoped for. In cases involving the religious establishment clause of the First Amendment, they have had most success when they have argued for equal treatment of religious and secular groups. In cases involving the free exercise of religion clause of the First Amendment, their greatest success has come when they have joined religious claims to broader free speech claims. Smith shows that the political challenge of defining positions that can win the support of broader coalitions of citizens means that religion is unlikely ever to receive special recognition, protection, or privileges in U.S. constitutional law.

Taken together, these chapters show that secular norms dominate public institutions and constrain the reforms desired by religious conservatives. The deference of American society to academic scholarship and constitutional language severely limits the extent to which religious conservatives have been able to transform the schools or the courts. This work also shows that the freedoms offered by liberal culture frequently override the restraints advocated by Christian morality. Teenage sex and divorce are as common among evangelicals as in any other group, and the enticements of the popular media apparently only a little less appealing. Evangelicals and religious conservatives are an important interest group in American society, but they are embedded within a secular state and liberal culture that, to reverse de Tocqueville, greatly limits their influence. These chapters indicate that religious conservatives have had the most influence when they are able to make common cause with broader coalitions of actors and to couch their arguments in secular terms.

Notes

1. These volumes are the product of a conference held in New York in April 2007 at the Russell Sage Foundation. We are grateful to the Foundation, and particularly to Eric Wanner, for generous support of the conference. We would also like to thank the Center for Ideas and Society at the University of California, Riverside for providing funds to help with conference organizing. Seth Abrutyn played an important role in the success of the conference by creating the conference website and facilitating conference arrangements for participants.

2. Supplemental materials available at: http://www.russellsage.org/publications/ EvangelicalTimelines.

References

Ammerman, Nancy T. 2005. *Pillars of Faith: American Congregations and their Partners, Building Traditions, Building Communities*. Berkeley: University of California Press.

Baltzell, E. Digby. 1964. *The Protestant Establishment: Aristocracy and Caste in America*. New York: Random House.

Chaves, Mark. 2004. *Congregations in America*. Cambridge, Mass.: Harvard University Press.

Cox, Harvey G. 1965. *The Secular City: Secularization and Urbanization in Theological Perspective*. New York: Macmillan.

de Tocqueville, Alexis. 1835/1961. *Democracy in America*, vol. 1. New York: Schocken Books.

Frank, Thomas. 2004. *What's the Matter with Kansas? How Conservatives Won the Heart of America*. New York: Henry Holt.

Greeley, Andrew, and Michael Hout. 2006. *The Truth about Conservative Christians: What They Think and What They Believe*. Chicago: University of Chicago Press.

Green, John C., James L. Guth, Corwin E. Smidt, and Lyman A. Kellstedt. 1996. *Religion and the Culture Wars: Dispatches from the Front*. Boulder, Colo.: Rowman & Littlefield.

Gutmann, Amy. 1998. *Freedom of Association*. Princeton, N.J.: Princeton University Press.

Guth, James L. 1983. "The Politics of the Christian Right." In *Religion and the Culture Wars: Dispatches from the Front*, edited by John C. Green, James L. Guth, Corwin E. Smidt, and Lyman A. Kellstedt. Boulder, Colo.: Rowman & Littlefield.

Hadden, Jeffrey K. 1969. *Gathering Storm in the Churches*. Garden City, N.Y.: Doubleday-Anchor.

Handy, Robert T. 1984. *A Christian America? Protestant Hopes and Historical Realities*. New York: Oxford University Press.

Harlow, Luke E. 2007. "Slavery, Race, and Political Ideology in the White Christian South Before and After the Civil War." In *Religion and American Politics*, 2nd ed., edited by Mark A. Noll and Luke E. Harlow. New York: Oxford University Press.

Haynes, Stephen R. 2002. *Noah's Curse: The Biblical Justification of American Slavery*. New York: Oxford University Press.

Herberg, Will. 1960. *Protestant, Catholic, Jew*. Garden City, N.Y.: Anchor Books.

Hofstadter, Richard. 1955. *The Age of Reform: From Bryant to F.D.R.* New York: Vintage.

Hodgson, Geoffrey. 1976. *America in Our Time*. Garden City, N.Y.: Doubleday.

Hout, Michael, Andrew Greeley, and Melissa J. Wilde. 2001. "The Demographic Imperative in Religious Change in the United States." *American Journal of Sociology* 107(2): 468–500.

Howe, Daniel Walker. 2007. "Religion and Politics in the Antebellum North." In *Religion and American Politics*, 2nd ed., edited by Mark A. Noll and Luke E. Harlow. New York: Oxford University Press.

Hudson, Deal W. 2008. *Onward, Christian Soldiers: The Growing Political Power of Catholics and Evangelicals in the United States*. New York: Simon and Schuster Threshold Editions.

Hunter, James Davison. 1992. *Culture Wars: The Struggle to Define America*. New York: Basic Books.

Kellstedt, Lyman A. and Corwin W. Smidt. 1991. "Measuring Fundamentalism: An Analysis of Different Operational Strategies." In *Religion and the Culture Wars: Dispatches from the Front*, edited by John C. Green, James L. Guth, Corwin E. Smidt, and Lyman A. Kellstedt. Boulder, Colo.: Rowman and Littlefield.

Kleppner, Paul. 1979. *The Third Electoral System, 1853–1892: Parties, Voters, and Political Cultures*. Chapel Hill: University of North Carolina Press.

Layman, Geoffrey. 2001. *The Great Divide: Religious and Cultural Conflict in American Party Politics*. New York: Columbia University Press.

Leege, David C., Kenneth D. Wald, Brian S. Krueger, and Paul D. Mueller. 2002. *The Politics of Cultural Differences: Social Change and Voter Mobilization Strategies in the Post-New Deal Period*. Princeton, N.J.: Princeton University Press.

Leuchtenberg, William E. 1958. *The Perils of Prosperity, 1914–1932*. Chicago: University of Chicago Press.

Lindsay, D. Michael. 2007. *Faith in the Halls of Power: How Evangelicals Joined the American Elite*. New York: Oxford University Press.

Loftus, Jeri. 2001. "America's Liberalization in Attitudes toward Homosexuality, 1973 to 1998." *American Sociological Review* 66(5): 762–82.

Manza, Jeff, and Clem Brooks. 1997. "The Religious Factor in U.S. Presidential Elections, 1960–1992." *American Journal of Sociology* 103(1): 38–81.

Marsden, George M. 2006. *Fundamentalism and American Culture*, 2nd ed. New York: Oxford University Press.

Martin, William C. 1996. *With God on Our Side: The Rise of the Religious Right in America*. New York: Broadway Books.

Moen, Matthew C. 1995. "From Revolution to Evolution: The Changing Nature of the Christian Right." In *The Rapture in Politics*, edited by Steve Bruce, Peter Kivisto, and William Swatos. New Brunswick, N.J.: Transaction Books.

Noll, Mark A. 2002. *America's God: From Jonathan Edwards to Abraham Lincoln*. New York : Oxford University Press.

Parrington, Vernon L. 1939. *Main Currents in American Thought*. New York: Harcourt-Brace.

Putnam, Robert L. 2000. *Bowling Alone: The Collapse and Revival of American Community*. New York: Simon and Schuster.

Shields, Jon A. 2007. "In Praise of the Values Voter." *The Wilson Quarterly* 31(4)(Autumn): 32–38. Available at: http://www.wilsoncenter.org.

Silk, Mark. 1988. *Spiritual Politics: Religion in America Since World War II*. New York: Simon and Schuster.

Smith, Christian S. 1998. *American Evangelicalism: Embattled and Thriving*. Chicago: University of Chicago Press.

———. 2000. *Christian America? What Evangelicals Really Want*. Berkeley: University of California Press.

———. 2003. *The Secular Revolution: Power, Interest, and Conflict in the Secularization of American Life*. Berkeley: University of California Press.

Southern Baptist Convention. 2008. "About Us—Meet the Southern Baptists." Available at: http://www.sbc.net.

Steensland, Brian, Jerry Z. Park, Mark D. Regnerus, Lynn D. Robinson, W. Bradford Wilcox, and Robert D. Woodberry. 2000. "The Measure of American Religion: Toward Improving the State of the Art." *Social Forces* 79(1): 291–318.

Wald, Kenneth D. 2003. *Religion and Politics in the United States*, 4th ed. Boulder, Colo.: Rowman & Littlefield.

Warner, R. Stephen. 1988. *New Wine in Old Wineskins: Evangelicals and Liberals in a Small-town Church*. Berkeley: University of California Press.

Winthrop, John. 1630/1931. "A Modell of Christian Charity." *Winthrop Papers*, vol. 2. Boston: Massachusetts Historical Society.

Wolfe, Alan. 2003. *The Transformation of American Religion: How We Actually Live Our Faith*. New York: Free Press.

Wuthnow, Robert. 1988. *The Restructuring of American Religion*. Princeton, N.J.: Princeton University Press.

Zuckerman, Phil. 2005. "Atheism: Contemporary Rates and Patterns." In *The Cambridge Companion to Atheism*, edited by Michael Martin. Cambridge: Cambridge University Press.

PART I

EVANGELICALS' IDENTITY AND ACTIVISM

Chapter 1

The Cultural Capital of American Evangelicalism

Robert Wuthnow

T HE FOCUS of this chapter is evangelical Protestantism as religion, which I consider through the lens of cultural capital. This is not the language that evangelical Protestants themselves would use. Nor is it a concept that lends itself readily to the study of evangelical Protestantism without some clarification. Among sociologists of culture, whose view of culture has necessarily been broadened enough to include all kinds of beliefs and values, the concept of cultural capital has been a convenient way of focusing on the high-status culture that still matters most to academics. In operational terms, cultural capital means graduating from college, gaining an advanced degree, reading books, going to art galleries and the opera, and having fine taste in consumption of art and music. Cultural capital, then, is simply haute couture. It consists of skills, talents, and experiences that get people into the higher echelons of society—into the right universities, professions, and clubs. There is little room for ordinary people in the study of cultural capital except insofar as they mimic elite culture in such small ways as buying books for their children or enrolling them in ballet classes. Among secular scholars, evangelical Protestants are more likely to be considered the benighted heirs of snake handlers and faith healers.

The reason for focusing here on cultural capital is precisely that it is odd for academics to think that evangelical Protestants even have any. To move in the direction of making this a credible argument, we need to remember two important qualifications that have been made to the concept of cultural capital in recent years. The first is that Pierre Bourdieu's rarified emphasis on aesthetic taste has had to be broadened even in studying elites (1984). As Michele Lamont's work has shown, money and especially morality are important markers of status as well as taste (1992). The other is that cultural capital is context specific. Especially in pluralistic societies like the United States, people living in different racial, ethnic, and regional subcultures have their own forms of cultural capital and their own standards of performance in relation to these status rankings. Black workers who pride themselves on being more honest than their white counterparts (Lamont 2000), and Latino immigrants with loyalties to *la raza*, are examples. Evangelical Protestants have cultural capital as well that serve as symbols of status within their own subculture. In addition, and an important part of my argument, evangelical Protestants' cultural capital includes characteristics that help them pursue—and, indeed, attain—their aims in the wider society. In this respect, cultural capital is less about status and more about identity. Evangelical culture currently gives evangelicals a unifying identity, engages them in common practices, helps them attract resources, and mobilizes them to be involved in the wider society.

The cultural capital of evangelical Protestants, though, is not only about identity. They have found ways of being who they are—of being faithful members of their churches and adhering to what they regard as authentic Christian beliefs—and to get along without much difficulty in the same largely secular society as everyone else. They do this by subtly adapting their distinctive beliefs to the pluralistic context in which they live, both to make these beliefs more attractive to potential recruits and to make them less offensive to adherents of other religions or of no religion. Believing in Jesus as a divine savior, having had a born-again experience, and regarding the Bible as the literal word of God are thus not nearly as strange in the real world as academics sometimes imagine them to be. At the same time, there is a pecking order among evangelical Protestants, just as there is among bearers of other kinds of cultural capital. Knowing the Bible well and being active in one's church, for example, are ways of earning prestige among fellow evangelical Protestants. And that prestige has been shown to translate into greater self-confidence and, in some instances, greater capacity to do well academically and professionally (Mooney 2005; Lindsay 2007).

Money, power, and organizational resources are impressive elements in contemporary evangelical Protestantism (see, for example, Lindsay 2007; Wuthnow and Lindsay 2006). However, evangelical Protestantism cannot be understood by looking only at organizations and money. This approach misses the cultural elements that propel the success of evangelical Protestantism in American society. The cultural capital of evangelical Protestantism lies in its teachings and practices, its worship, and its spiritual experiences—in short, in what makes it religion. Each aspect of evangelical Protestantism has adapted to American culture in ways that retain evangelicalism's distinct identity and yet permit its adherents to engage actively in nearly all realms of cultural life.

Jesus in American Evangelicalism

If evangelicals were asked what lies at the heart of their faith, the majority would probably say Jesus. In a national survey conducted in 2003, 66 percent of adults in the United States said they believed that "Jesus was the only divine son of God who died and rose again to save us from our sins" (Wuthnow 2003a). Among members of evangelical Protestant denominations, 85 percent believed it and an additional 9 percent said, "Jesus embodied the essence of divine love and showed us how to attain spiritual union with God." In another national survey, 94 percent of respondents affiliated with evangelical denominations agreed that "God has been fully revealed to humans in Jesus Christ" (Wuthnow 1999). Believing in the divinity of Jesus is hardly unique to evangelicals, but it does provide evangelical culture with a unifying core. The cultural capital of collectivities involves being able to agree about something and having a symbol to represent that agreement. If infant baptism, eschatology, or speaking in tongues were central, there would be far less agreement among evangelicals. One of the feats of Billy Graham and Campus Crusade for Christ was to refocus the evangelical movement around the figure of Jesus in a way that cut across denominational lines. In both, the essential feature of the Christian gospel was inviting Jesus into one's life. "Jesus is Lord," explained a member of an evangelical church that has been growing since it decided to focus less on its distinctive denominational heritage. "That's the primary statement of faith. How you understand that should not be a hindrance to being in community together."[1] Evangelicals can agree that people around the world should see the *Jesus Project*, a film about the life of Jesus, which has been distributed in video and audiocassettes across the globe. They can embrace *The Passion of the Christ* as a special witness to their beliefs, even though the movie's imagery is more traditionally Catholic. Moreover, Jesus is less about belief, creed, or doctrine in contemporary evangelicalism (even though those remain important) and more about narratives and symbols. The Jesus film is not about the teachings of Jesus, but the life story of Jesus. Warner Salman's many paintings of what he imagined Jesus to be like were some of the twentieth century's most widely circulated popular art (Morgan and Promey 2001).

"Jesus is a friend, is a friend next to you," sang the children during a summer program at an evangelical church. "We look to him," said a member of a Christian and Missionary Alliance church. "No matter what your problems are, whether it be with children, or your marriage, or your neighbor, whatever it is. He will show you the way. He'll give you the answers." Qualitative research shows that evangelicals frequently speak about Jesus in intimate terms like these. Although God may also be personal, God is more likely to be viewed as wholly other, pure, conceptually separate from humans, and indeed spiritually separated from humans who are sinful or at least unrepentant. Indeed, the distance between God and humans is one of the distinguishing features of evangelical grassroots theology, setting evangelicals apart from theologically liberal Protestants and Catholics, who view God as more of an essence of life or as a mystery. The figure of God is also less distinctly associated with evangelicals, because Catholics, Jews, and Muslims all worship God. In contrast, Jesus is both God and human and thus identifies with human pain and provides comfort. "I believe Jesus walked and lived on this earth," said a member of a charismatic church. "He lived here, he lived among people, he loved people." For evangelicals, the special status is confirmed in the idea that only Jesus can bridge the considerable gap that exists between sinful people and a perfect God. An evangelical Presbyterian said, "The Lord tried to reach down and touch us and talk to us and help us and guide us. Christ was the ultimate effort." "He lived and he died that we could be reconciled back to God," a Church of Christ member echoed.

The extent to which Jesus has become "our buddy," as one evangelical put it, has been criticized as an accommodation to the therapeutic emphasis in contemporary culture (Hunter 1983). There is probably some warrant for this criticism. The rhetoric of separation from God is sometimes framed in language about alienation, estrangement, and even loneliness. Jesus solves that problem by lending a comforting ear, just as a therapist might. However, viewed as cultural capital, the emphasis on Jesus is a considerable asset. Jesus not only offers eternal salvation, but also provides a companion who gives people strength to believe they can overcome their problems. In a society that values self-help as much as America does, that is indeed a considerable asset. It means having a powerful friend, a source of divine strength. It is as much a kind of cultural capital as being a member of Alcoholics Anonymous or having a good psychiatrist is. The highly personalized relationship with Jesus, moreover, gives flexibility in how one chooses to follow Jesus. The popular question, "What would Jesus do?" can be answered in many ways, depending on one's circumstances. A person can have a moral compass, but adapt to new situations.

Evangelicals' belief in Jesus lends itself to mobilization as well. In her research among Pentecostal women, Marie Griffith observed that a woman who experiences "boundless and unconditional love from her 'daddy' [God] makes her feel she can never be lonely again" and, in return, feels "constant praise and gratitude for such generosity, and the perpetual desire to obey God's will in all circumstances" (1997, 137). In my research among recipients of caregiving from churches and faith-based organizations, I observed who many regarded it as their right to receive assistance, and caregivers agreed that having one's needs met was a basic human right (Wuthnow 2004). However, among evangelicals it was more common to draw parallels between the assistance given and the love God showed the world in sending Jesus. As one pastor explained, "It's the love that we read about in the New Testament that God has toward all mankind. And when Jesus dies on the cross, he dies for the sins of all mankind from the whitest lie to the darkest, horrific action anyone has taken. Without conditions. We aspire to mirror that as best we can." One might assume that if a gift is given unconditionally, there is no reason to pay it back. Yet the response from recipients was quite different. If the assistance received was an instance of unconditional love, then overwhelming gratitude was the appropriate response. "The more I'm helped, the more I want to help others," said one recipient. One of the most obvious ways of helping was to do volunteer service work. Those who received assistance from congregations were especially likely to say they had done service work in response. In short, the belief that Jesus had helped them became a form of cultural capital that the leaders of their churches cashed in to build up their churches.

The Meaning of Biblical Literalism

According to the General Social Survey, 24 percent of Americans believed in a literal interpretation of the Bible. Among members of evangelical Protestant denominations, this figure was 57 percent. Over the past twenty years, biblical literalism has dropped by 14 percent in the population at large but has held almost constant among evangelicals. Does this mean that evangelicals are increasingly out of step with the culture? With better survey data and qualitative interviews, we can say what all this means and see more clearly how the Bible serves as cultural capital for evangelicals. One possible interpretation is that biblical literalists are believers in what fundamentalist theologians term *inerrancy*. Inerrantists believe that the Bible is perfect, just as God is, and thus is free of mistakes, including assertions that might be false historically or scientifically. Belief in inerrancy does go with biblical literalism, but the relationship is by no means perfect. In one national survey, 30 percent of biblical literalists agreed that "the Bible may contain historical or scientific errors" and another 12 percent were unsure (Wuthnow 1999). Nor does biblical literalism mean that evangelicals regard the Bible simply as a book of factual truths. Eighty-four percent of evangelicals and 71 percent of biblical literalists agreed that there is "a lot of music and poetry in the Bible." Another view of biblical literalism is that it means looking only to the Bible for divine truth, and thus, in the view of critics, being insufferably narrow and dogmatic. However, this interpretation describes only a minority of biblical literalists: 37 percent thought that "God's truth is fully revealed only in the Bible," whereas 60 percent said that "the Bible is one of many ways in which God's truth is revealed." Among biblical literalists more agreement can be found for the view that "the Bible is a detailed book of rules that Christians should try to follow." Ninety percent agreed. Like stories and artistic depictions of Jesus, the Bible is also a tangible symbol for many evangelicals. It is a book, a sacred object that reminds them of their families and their congregations. Seventy-one percent of evangelicals said they had a special Bible that belonged to them or their family while they were growing up (Wuthnow 1999).

From qualitative information, it appears that biblical literalism indeed means that a person takes the Bible seriously and regards it as an important practical guide, not as a text that one examines systematically for consistency or scientific facts. An incident that occurred while I was monitoring interviews being conducted for a recent survey of mine was revealing. As the interviewer began reading the standard question about the Bible, the respondent stopped her in the middle of the literalism option and said, "That's me. That's what I believe." The interviewer politely insisted that she needed to read all three options. The respondent cut her off again: "That's what I believe. I just believe in the Bible." In in-depth interviews, evangelicals are often unsure what it means to say that the Bible is free of errors, but they regard it as God's unique revelation to humankind. It is unique because it tells the story of Jesus. "It's the story of how [God] revealed himself to people over time," a Southern Baptist said. In telling about Jesus and other biblical characters, the Bible thus provides practical guidance. "It's a guide book for how to live," an evangelical Reformed-Confessional member said. "It's not the same as any other book." A Missouri-Synod Lutheran expressed a similar view: "The Bible to me is a constant reminder of how we should live our lives. It's definitely a fact."

If the Bible is an instruction book for life, taking it seriously is an important cultural asset. In an era of uncertainty and ambiguity, having one source of practical wisdom is highly reassuring. That there is a demand for such guidance is evident in the fact that megachurch pastor Rick Warren's *Purpose-Driven Life*, which distills biblical wisdom into succinct easy-to-digest lessons, has sold 20 million copies. At the same time, when biblical literalism means taking the Bible seriously, rather than regarding it as a radical departure from common sense, evangelicals can adapt more easily to contemporary culture. For instance, in the General Social Survey, biblical literalism, though negatively associated with higher levels of education, is more weakly associated now that it was twenty years ago (Wuthnow 2007).

The mobilizing potential of biblical literalism is evident in the fact that evangelicals not only believe things about the Bible, but also organize individual and group activities around it. Some 75 percent of evangelical Protestants say they read the Bible in their daily life at home at least once a week, 62 percent say that participating in small Bible study or prayer groups has been very important to their spiritual growth, and an additional 22 percent say that this participation has been fairly important. Bible study groups were one of the keys to Baptist and Methodist growth in the nineteenth century, and are currently one of the most common small group activities in the United States. Research shows that between 35 and 40 percent of U.S. adults are involved in a small group that meets regularly and provides caring and support for its members (Wuthnow 1994). Fifty-six percent of the members of any kind of small group have said that their group activities include study or discussion of the Bible. Forty-four percent described their group as a Bible study. For evangelicals, and indeed for many nonevangelicals, Bible study groups are an important source of social capital. People make friends, support one another within the group, but also become more involved in their congregations, and do volunteer work in their communities. For some members of Bible study groups, participation also exposes them to wider issues: 70 percent said their group discusses social issues or politics; 33 percent said their group has caused them to be more interested in peace or social justice (Wuthnow 1994).

In some circles, being able to quote the French literary theorist Jacques Derrida is a form of cultural capital. It suggests to anyone who might be listening that one is an intellectual. In many more communities, being able to talk about the Bible has even more cache. It shows that a person is good and decent, moral, trustworthy. But it has to be done right. A flaming zealot who claims unique knowledge of divine truth may have a following, but it will be a limited following. That is not how most evangelical Protestants view the Bible. For them, it is a source of guidance that also requires discernment.

The Born-Again Experience

In recent national surveys, 40 to 45 percent of Americans claimed to have had a born-again experience. Among members of evangelical Protestant denominations, this figure was 83 percent (Wuthnow 1999). Among self-identified evangelicals actively involved in Protestant congregations, it rose to 89 percent. Historically, the born-again experience was interpreted differently in traditions that did or did not teach that God's elect were already chosen from the beginning of time. For those that did, being born again was a sign or moment of affirmation of one's foreordained election. For those that did not, the born-again experience acquired greater urgency as the time when a person decided to become a believer in Jesus and thus gain entry into the kingdom of heaven. The latter understanding gained popularity during the nineteenth century and was thus the one that helped define the evangelical movement of the twentieth century. Baptist worship services notably included an "altar call," during which a person who wished to be born again could walk to the front of the church and publicly "receive Christ." The Billy Graham crusades that began in the 1950s exposed viewers to thousands of examples of people "going forward" to be born again.

The idea that a born-again experience is required to secure a place in heaven for one's soul after death remains strong, but has been modified by other understandings that emphasize the feelings associated with the moment of conversion and especially the sense of being strengthened, uplifted, or set on a new path. The following account, told by a former Episcopalian who now attends a nondenominational evangelical congregation, is typical. "I was married but not very happy, struggling with two little children, and [Jesus] came and met me at the point of my need. I was sitting in church on an Easter morning and He just said, 'Do you want your will for your life or my will for your life?' I sat there thinking that my will has not been doing a very good job, so I said, 'I'll take your will.'" She said that she was "converted" in that instant and now has a "personal relationship with the Lord Jesus Christ."

Viewed sociologically, the born-again experience is a significant aspect of the cultural capital of American evangelicals. It defines symbolic boundaries separating insiders from outsiders and elevates a person's status within the evangelical community. It also punctuates ordinary time with a special moment that is charged with emotion, associated with collective rituals, and filled with power (Collins 2004). The same woman continued, "This shower of joy just fell all over me. I'm sitting in there with this huge grin on my face, with God's presence just coming all over me." Emile Durkheim would have viewed this as an experience of empowerment: "The man who has obeyed his god and who, for this reason, believes the god is with him, approaches the world with confidence and with the feeling of an increased energy" (1973, 172).

Recent work in cognitive psychology also helps interpret the significance of the born-again experience. Schemas emphasizing emotion and the self produce memories that are among the most long-lasting of all experiences (DiMaggio 1997). A person remembers a born-again experience because it was a kind of peak experience, involving a flood of joy or feelings of release, and because it marked a transition in one's personal identity. A born-again experience thus becomes a pivotal point in an individual's personal narrative. As believers reconstruct their life stories, a typical pattern is to emphasize problems before the born-again experience, such as depression, loneliness, a lack of focus, or substance abuse, and then to describe the postconversion life as one of greater peace, emotional strength, and moral stability. Having had such an experience becomes cultural capital, then, in two respects: it provides a story of one's self that both incorporates faith and makes sense of one's life in a compact memorable format, and it is the kind of scripted narrative that can be shared as a marker of being a member of the evangelical community.

The born-again experience must also be understood, not as a one-time event, but as an experience that either recurs or symbolizes additional possibilities for personal transformation. The word that best captures this aspect of the born-again experience is hope. A person who feels pulled down by an addiction or a failed marriage is inspired to believe that he or she can move on, start over, embark on a new life—in short, be born again. Griffith's study of Pentecostal women's prayer groups shows that stories about one's past and present life are common (1997). In telling their stories, members create frameworks that conceptualize complex events in familiar ways and that often follow examples of characters in the Bible. The stories include expressions of hope that the past can be set aside and a new life begun. Prayer, Griffith argued, is not simply uttering petitions to God, but "operates as a climactic moment in an endlessly repeatable pattern of spiraling downward and ascending to victory yet again. [It] provides a woman with the courage to look within herself and request a change, whether a return to the purer selfhood of a younger age or the abolition of all former pretenses in favor of a new authenticity" (78).

Patterns of Worship

Worship services in evangelical Protestant churches vary widely in style and content. In the National Congregations Study, variation among congregations classified as "white conservative, evangelical, or fundamental" was evident especially in styles of music (Chaves 2004). Although nearly all (98 percent) included congregational singing, about half featured singing by a soloist, about one-quarter used drums and electric guitars, half used an organ, and three-quarters used a piano. Relatively few (18 percent) had celebrated communion at their most recent service. And fewer than half (44 percent) included a time during the service especially for children. The variation, though, should not obscure the importance of worship as a common, unifying experience among evangelical Christians. Worship is a weekly ritual that draws adherents out of their homes, engages them in corporate prayer and singing, and exposes them to sermons about the Bible. In qualitative interviews, participants typically associated worship with the strength of their personal faith and often remarked about their sense of worshipping with fellow Christians even when attending churches other than their own and outside of the United States.

One of the distinguishing features of evangelical Protestant worship is its emphasis on congregational participation, often through structured informality and sometimes with a relatively high level of emotion. In addition to congregational singing, services usually include a time when people greet each other by shaking hands (84 percent) and many churches (65 percent) include a time for silent prayer or meditation, consider it acceptable for people to call out "amen" or other expressions of approval (81 percent), and encourage laughter (72 percent) or applause (62 percent). These figures are significantly higher for evangelical Protestant churches than for mainline Protestant and Catholic churches, and resemble, but are lower than those for African American churches.

Worship is thus similar in some respects to the born-again experience in that both are sacred times set apart from everyday life by an emotionally memorable encounter with God. Although biblical preaching is important, the ambience of the service is equally significant. Evangelical praise music is notably meditative, setting the mood for worshippers to listen attentively and submissively to the sermon, and reinforcing the sense of intimacy with Jesus (Wuthnow 2003b). Analysis of evangelical sermons shows that they frequently begin by emphasizing the chaotic complexity of contemporary society and then move toward solutions that can be framed in simple language, such as "God loves you" or "Jesus is the answer" (Witten 1993). The narrative structure of the sermon includes anecdotes that establish the pastor's authority by showing the pastor answering questions presented by interlocutors and that draw sharp distinctions between the gathered faith community and the secular world.

The other notable feature of evangelical Protestant worship is its repetitiveness. This aspect is often overlooked by observers who associate repetitiveness with more highly ritualized liturgical traditions. Repetition, however, is also an important feature of evangelical worship. Services typically occur at the same time of day on the same day each week. They occur in the same space with many of the same people present and the same person or persons officiating. Although the hymns are likely to vary from week to week, they are usually sung at the same time during the service and take up the same amount of time. Familiar hymns are sung again and again. Scripture readings and the sermon always focus on the same book, which is revered as having canonical significance. These practices structure expectations, provide an experience of continuity in a world where many other things appear to be changing, and give people a common identity as fellow Christians.

As cultural capital, it is difficult to overestimate the significance of evangelical worship services. Churches in general are one of the few places where Americans engage in choral singing (Chaves 2004). As many adults say they sang in a church choir while they were growing up as sang in a choir at school (Wuthnow 2003b). There are twenty times more congregations in the United States than performing arts organizations. In total, Americans make about 3 billion visits to their places of worship each year—at least three times the number of visits to art museums, plays, musical performances, historical sites, and arts and craft fairs combined. Evangelicals typically attend religious services more often than members of other denominations. Half of evangelicals say their congregation has sponsored a music performance other than during worship and half say this about sponsoring a drama or skit. One-quarter of members report that their congregations hold an annual art festival or craft fair.

It would be inaccurate, though, to suggest that evangelical cultural capital consists mainly of providing alternative venues for the arts. The central feature of evangelical worship is worship. Evangelical churches are by no means the only places in which worship happens, but they are among the nation's most numerous and most frequented. Evangelicals believe they are preaching the authentic Bible and adapting worship to contemporary culture as effectively as Saint Gregory did in his day or Martin Luther did in his. They also believe that there is "power in the Word." They would not say "magical," but they do argue that God's spirit enters into the biblical and spoken word and works mysteriously in "hearts" to "convict" people. Susan Harding's account of how dramatically she, as a secular anthropologist, was influenced by the words of an evangelical preacher during a lengthy interview is gripping evidence of what evangelicals regard as spiritual power (2000).

Integration of Faith and Life

In cultural sociology, it has long been recognized that people divide their lives into separate domains. Peter Berger and Thomas Luckmann, following Alfred Schutz, termed these spheres of relevance (1966). In more recent parlance, these spheres are sometimes called schemata (DiMaggio 1997). They organize enough of one's experience to accomplish certain tasks, such as going to the grocery store or playing tennis, but they also bracket extraneous considerations that would complicate focusing on the task at hand (a reason why talking on cell phones while driving is prohibited in some states). It is this need for compartmentalization that has led recent sociologists of culture to argue that culture is fragmented. However, there also appears to be a countervailing desire for coherence. A person somehow has to decide whether to spend a morning shopping for groceries or playing tennis. And that person, as a person, is likely to understand that he or she is both a grocery shopper and a tennis player and that these are part of but do not exhaust his or her identity. This desire for coherence can be fulfilled in various ways. At one extreme, coherence may be found through such scripts as "I go with the flow," "I am just a bundle of roles," "I don't think much about the big questions in life," or "I like diversity and am good at multitasking." At the opposite extreme are people who believe that one dominant characteristic or interest infuses their entire life. For instance, my neighbor, a physicist, has told me that she is "a scientist, and being a scientist I take a scientific approach to everything I do, whether it's working in my lab, doing my taxes, buying groceries, or cleaning house."

Evangelicals are like my neighbor, only they emphasize that their faith should be the integrating feature of their life. In a 2005 survey of church members, 94 percent of evangelical Protestants said it was extremely or very important to them as an adult to grow in their spiritual life and 40 percent, versus only 25 percent of mainline Protestants and Catholics, said they had devoted a great deal of effort in the past year to their spiritual life (Wuthnow 2005b). Working on their spiritual life involves attending worship services, participating in small groups, reading the Bible, and praying. All of these activities help evangelicals define themselves in relation to their faith. They also believe in spreading their faith, meaning that they expend energy that helps their congregations grow. In the same survey, 85 percent said that it is very important for Christians to share their faith with people who are not Christians and 95 percent agreed that "Christians in the United States should work harder to spread their faith throughout the world." Although evangelicals seldom engage in conversations with Muslims, Hindus, Buddhists, or Jews with the aim of converting them, approximately 65 percent said that they have talked with someone—usually a person who does not attend church—to encourage them to become a Christian (Wuthnow 2005a, 200).

Integration of faith and life manifests itself in all sorts of organized evangelical endeavors. One of the most notable in recent years is the Christian dieting movement, which applies the same born-again logic to bodies as evangelicals do to the soul. The Christian dieting phenomenon, which is largely directed toward evangelical women, includes self-help groups, diet books, and exercise regimens. It is the evangelical counterpart to the wider interest in health foods, weight loss, and fitness (Griffith 2004). Other examples of efforts to bring evangelical spirituality into various realms of life include integration of faith and learning statements at church-related colleges, where enrollments have been rising in recent years; evangelical feminist groups; and Christian crossover music, such as holy hip hop.

The point is not that evangelicals consistently behave in ways that correspond with their convictions or that differ from the lives of other

Americans. It is rather that evangelicals like to believe that there are connections between their faith and their lives and thus engage in social activities that reinforce this belief. Although they are no more likely to do volunteer work in their communities than mainline Protestants and Catholics, they do volunteer more at their churches and argue that service is best provided under religious auspices (Wuthnow 2004). They also want churches and church leaders to be involved in politics and in other ways to speak out on social issues. In a 2004 survey conducted nationally, only 24 percent of evangelical Protestants said it made them uncomfortable when political candidates discuss faith; 87 percent said it is important that a president have strong religious beliefs (Green 2004). The survey also showed that 84 percent of evangelical Protestants thought organized religious groups should stand up for their beliefs and only 35 percent thought that they should stay out of politics.

Putting Faith in Practice

Evangelicals are thus predisposed to think that their faith should matter in any and all spheres of life. They are not content to say that some realms simply should not be influenced by faith, even though they drive on the same roads and use the same ATM machines as everyone else. For our considerations about cultural capital, this poses two problems. One is that evangelicals have to live in the same world as nonevangelicals and yet feel that their faith is not irrelevant. A focus on emotions is the way they do this. Faith governs how they feel about their world, they said, even if it does not have distinctive consequences (Wuthnow 1998). The other is how to determine what the hot button issues are that are worth becoming especially involved in. On many issues, evangelicals are divided or do not differ much from nonevangelicals. But they have gravitated toward a few issues, largely those with a predisposition toward involvement. Ziad Munson has shown that people become involved in pro-life advocacy, less because of strong convictions and more through being in harm's way at a meeting or rally that energizes them into further involvement (2002). This is where organized leadership becomes important. Pat Robertson's enormous wealth, the late Jerry Falwell's television audience, and James Dobson's Focus on the Family reach large numbers of people in these ways.

It is important, though, to understand that the relationship between evangelicals and public issues is constructed and is a way in which evangelical identity is reaffirmed. Examples include journalists writing about evangelical influence in politics, even when it is difficult to determine where the influence lies. A *Boston Globe* writer, for instance, observed that George W. Bush had "happily ceded huge swaths of his domestic and international policy" to Christian fundamentalists, even using "his global AIDS initiative, his foreign aid policy, and his war on terror to please religious radicals" (Kaplan 2005, 13). In a more sympathetic view, a *Wall Street Journal* article suggested that "interest in global issues" had "galvanized" among evangelical Christians and led to greater involvement in efforts to curb international sex trafficking and promote peace in southern Sudan (Peter Waldman, "Evangelicals Give U.S. Foreign Policy an Activist Tinge," May 26, 2004). Evangelical leaders themselves have embraced these statements about their influence. Richard Cizik, vice president of government affairs for the National Association of Evangelicals, for instance, has stated, "We represent conservative evangelicals who are the mainstay of the GOP coalition that's running both ends of Pennsylvania Avenue" (Susan Page, "Christian Right's Alliances Bend Political Spectrum," *USA Today*, June 14, 2005). The reality is more complex. Alan Hertzke showed that evangelicals played a role in international religious freedom and sex trafficking legislation, but Jews also did, and so did high-ranking public officials (2005). Similar arguments have been made about evangelicals' influence in the 2000 and 2004 presidential elections and in the Bush administration's decision to invade Iraq. Yet it is difficult to establish that evangelicals played the decisive role in these events. A better interpretation may be that publicity about evangelicals' political role is itself a form of cultural capital. News stories about evangelicals reinforce the symbolic prominence of the evangelical identity and convey the idea that this is a segment of U.S. religion with particular clout.

Conclusion

Evangelical Protestants have cultural capital that maintains their distinctive identity and yet makes it possible for them to adapt to the wider society. Part of the story is the symbolic distance from "the world" that comes from imagining themselves as being embattled (Smith 1998). But this is more than simply a gesture without substance. It depends on the cultural practices that maintain evangelical identity. Part of the story is accommodating to the culture (Hunter 1983; Wolfe 2003). But it is not enough simply to declare culture the winner and evangelicals neutered in the process. In emphasizing cultural capital, I have argued that evangelicals have beliefs about Jesus and the Bible, experiences of personal transformation and worship, and understandings about their faith's relevance to individual life and the world—all of which make their religious commitment attractive to them and capable of mobilizing them to join groups, seek converts, and engage in political action. Their cultural capital not only makes them feel good, as critics might argue; it also helps them get what they want, whether that is clarity about serving God by making money in business, organizing large churches that provide training for children and care for the needy, or mobilizing political movements.

It is worth emphasizing that many of the characteristics of evangelical Protestants are not unique to them. Many mainline Protestants and Catholics share the same Christian beliefs and practices. These other religious traditions also have repetitive rituals and emotionally charged experiences, and their adherents do volunteer work and sometimes participate in social advocacy. In examining the cultural capital of evangelicals, one need not argue that their beliefs and practices are necessarily more attractive or powerful than those of other faith traditions (or of those with no faith). The point is rather that evangelical Protestantism is one of the viable ways in which people in an otherwise secular world continue to find faith commitments meaningful. Given their prominence in American history, it should not be surprising that evangelicals' forms of religious expression generate cultural capital.

Evangelical Protestants' continuing place in the American culture-scape, I suggest, lies in more than numbers and can hardly be understood by characterizing them as backwoods folks who are naively misinterpreting their class interests or being duped by political leaders. Like many other groups, evangelicals sometimes feel that their position in society is not what it once was or should be. Many do believe that they have found the answer to a happy life and wish to share that answer with others. They have a stake in believing that they do—or should—have cultural and political influence. One of the reasons they are as influential as they are is that they have a rich tradition distinctive enough to help maintain their identity, and yet not so distinct that they are incapable of participating in the wider society.

Note

1. The verbatim quotes included in this chapter are from qualitative interviews with lay members and pastors conducted according to a quota design that maximized denominational and demographic factors—age, race, gender, and region (further information about the interviews are included in Wuthnow 2005a, 2007).

References

Berger, Peter L., and Thomas Luckmann. 1966. *The Social Construction of Reality: A Treatise in the Sociology of Knowledge*. Garden City, N.Y.: Doubleday.

Bourdieu, Pierre. 1984. *Distinction*. Cambridge, Mass.: Harvard University Press.

Chaves, Mark. 2004. *Congregations in America*. Cambridge, Mass.: Harvard University Press.

Collins, Randall. 2004. *Interaction Ritual Chains*. Princeton, N.J.: Princeton University Press.

DiMaggio, Paul. 1997. "Culture and Cognition." *Annual Review of Sociology* 23(1997): 263–87.

Durkheim, Emile. 1973. *On Morality and Society*. Chicago: University of Chicago Press.

Green, John C. 2004. "Religion and the 2004 Election: A Pre-Election Analysis." Washington, D.C.: Pew Forum on Religion & Public Life. http://www.pew forum.org/publications/surveys/green-full.pdf.

Griffith, R. Marie. 1997. *God's Daughters: Evangelical Women and the Power of Submission*. Berkeley: University of California Press.

———. 2004. *Born Again Bodies: Flesh and Spirit in American Christianity*. Berkeley: University of California Press.

Harding, Susan Friend. 2000. *The Book of Jerry Falwell: Fundamentalist Language and Politics*. Princeton, N.J.: Princeton University Press.

Hertzke, Alan D. 2005. *Freeing God's Children: The Unlikely Alliance for Global Human Rights*. Lanham, Md.: Rowman & Littlefield.

Hunter, James Davison. 1983. *American Evangelicalism: Conservative Religion and the Quandary of Modernity*. New Brunswick, N.J.: Rutgers University Press.

Kaplan, Esther. 2005. *With God on Their Side: How Christian Fundamentalists Trampled Science, Policy and Democracy in George W. Bush's White House*. New York: New Press.

Lamont, Michele. 1992. *Money, Morals, and Manners: The Culture of the French and the American Upper-Middle Class*. Chicago: University of Chicago Press.

———. 2000. *The Dignity of Working Men*. Cambridge, Mass.: Harvard University Press.

Lindsay, D. Michael. 2007. *Faith in the Halls of Power: How Evangelicals Joined the American Elite*. New York: Oxford University Press.

Mooney, Margarita. 2005. "Religion, College Grades, and Satisfaction among Students at Elite Colleges and Universities." Princeton, N.J.: Princeton University, Office of Population Research.

Morgan, David, and Sally M. Promey, eds. 2001. *The Visual Culture of American Religions*. Berkeley: University of California Press.

Munson, Ziad. 2002. *Becoming an Activist: Believers, Sympathizers, and Mobilization in the American Pro-Life Movement*. Ph.D. diss., Harvard University.

Smith, Christian. 1998. *American Evangelicalism: Embattled and Thriving*. Chicago: University of Chicago Press.

Witten, Marsha G. 1993. *All Is Forgiven: The Secular Message in American Protestantism*. Princeton, N.J.: Princeton University Press.

Wolfe, Alan. 2003. *The Transformation of American Religion: How We Actually Live Our Faith*. New York: Free Press.

Wuthnow, Robert. 1994. *Sharing the Journey: Support Groups and America's New Quest for Community*. New York: Free Press.

———. 1998. *After Heaven: Spirituality in American Since the 1950s*. Berkeley: University of California Press.

———. 1999. *Arts and Religion Survey Codebook*. Princeton, N.J.: Princeton University, Department of Sociology.

———. 2003a. *Religion and Diversity Codebook*. Princeton, N.J.: Princeton University, Department of Sociology.

———. 2003b. *All In Sync: How Art and Music Are Revitalizing American Religion.* Berkeley: University of California Press.

———. 2004. *Saving America? Faith-Based Activism and the Future of Civil Society.* Princeton, N.J.: Princeton University Press.

———. 2005a. *America and the Challenges of Religious Diversity.* Princeton, N.J.: Princeton University Press.

———. 2005b. *Global Issues Survey Codebook.* Princeton, N.J.: Princeton University, Center for the Study of Religion.

———. 2007. *After the Baby Boomers: How Twenty- and Thirty-Somethings Are Shaping the Future of American Religion.* Princeton, N.J.: Princeton University Press.

Wuthnow, Robert, and D. Michael Lindsay. 2006. "The Role of Foundations in American Religion." Princeton, N.J.: Princeton University, Center for the Study of Religion.

Chapter 2

American Evangelicals in American Culture: Continuity and Change

NANCY T. AMMERMAN

O BSERVERS OF American religion in the early twenty-first century, like observers two centuries earlier, are often struck by this country's religious abundance and diversity (de Tocqueville 1835). With at least one in four adult Americans attending religious services on a given weekend, religious participation in one of the country's more than 350,000 local congregations provides a broad populist base for social engagement. Every weekend, about 58 million American adults go to religious services at their local church or synagogue, mosque, or temple.[1] In addition to this dedicated core of weekly attenders, nearly another 100 million are connected enough to a religious tradition to attend a few times a year, put their names on the rolls of a local congregation at least some time in their lives, and tell pollsters that they believe in God and say their prayers with some regularity. Most do not actually know very much about the traditions they identify with (Prothero 2007), but to a striking degree Americans think of themselves in religious terms.[2]

What those terms are, however, requires a thick dictionary of definitions. With literally hundreds of denominations and faiths to choose from, no single religious tradition can claim anything like a majority of the population. The number and range of religious groups here is unprecedented. Religion is one of the ways American citizens organize and identify themselves (Warner 1999). Although these myriad group and individual identities are often highly salient, it is also possible to map the patterns within America's religious complexity in ways that allow a clearer picture of how the traditions are related to each other, to American history, and to today's public arena.

This volume draws attention to the "evangelical" territory, but it is important to place that portion of the map in its proper location. A little more than a generation ago, Will Herberg described American religion as having three variants—"Protestant, Catholic, Jew"—but there is more to it today (1960). I begin by identifying eight, rather than three, major territories within the current American religious landscape and then asking how the evangelicals came to occupy the place they inhabit today.[3]

Today's Religious Map

The largest single denomination in the United States is the Roman Catholic Church. If we were to locate them on a literal map, we would shade in all the borders and highlight the cities, because Catholics are far more numerous there than in the rural heartland (Gaustad and Barlow 2001, 161).[4] Still, midwestern cities like St. Louis and Chicago and Milwaukee are Catholic strongholds no less than New York or Los Angeles. Having arrived in the western territories even before other Europeans arrived on the eastern shores, Catholics have very deep roots in North American soil. Although they have been the largest religious group in the United States for almost 150 years, Catholics were not seen as fully American by the Protestant majority until after World War II, when they began to emerge from their ethnic enclaves into the middle-class mainstream (Dolan 1987; McGreevy 2003). Today they constitute roughly a quarter of the U.S. population, and as the recipient communities for many of the most recent immigrants, they remain emblematic of the mix of old and new, tension and welcome, that has long characterized America's local religious gatherings.

Jews were the other non-Protestant part of Herberg's triangle. Having first arrived in 1654, Jews joined the American experiment in voluntary religion in its earliest days (Sarna 2004). They remain a visible and distinct voice in the religious chorus, even though they constitute less than 2 percent of the American population. The various Jewish denominations have established the model for bringing non-Christian traditions into the American mix. Because they are very unevenly distributed around the country, the Jewish presence is quite visible in some places, but barely apparent in others (Kotler-Berkowitz et al. 2003). In some parts of Brooklyn, for example, the sidewalks look as much like Jerusalem as New York, whereas in Boise or Birmingham, the Jewish population is hard to find.

Outnumbering Jews today are the combined forces of the various other world religions that have since 1965 been increasingly present here—Muslims, Hindus, Baha'is, Buddhists, and the like. Together they constitute perhaps 4 percent of the population. When earlier accounts of American religion were written, there were too few to justify more than a mention, but they have now substantially altered the American landscape and are rapidly organizing what will become their equivalent of denominations and local congregations. Especially since September 11, 2001, it has become increasingly impossible to speak about religion in America without including these diverse new voices. The Pluralism Project at Harvard now has more than 5,000 listings for worship centers of faiths other than Christianity and Judaism.[5] They are more likely to be in the cities with the largest immigrant populations, but every corner of the country is included in this new pattern of diversity.

Neither Jews nor adherents of the other world religions have any doubt that they are a minority in a country dominated by Christians. And neither they nor Catholics fail to recognize that Protestants (collectively) remain the most numerous and culturally dominant American religious tradition. Protestants account for a little more than half the adult population, and Protestant assumptions about individual religious choice and local congregational organizing pervade religious traditions far beyond Protestantism itself (Warner 1993). Within Protestantism, however, there are three points on the compass, three distinct and particular ways of expressing the Protestant vision.

The theologically moderate to liberal Protestant denominations make up the so-called mainline and total about 15 percent of the adult population. Included here are most of the original colonial groups—Congregationalists, Presbyterians, Episcopalians, and the like, as well as the Methodist, Lutheran, and Disciples of Christ groups that joined the mainline in the nineteenth century. Churches in this territory are more likely to read the Bible critically, to have an inclusive view of who will get to heaven, and to expect individuals to make their own choices in matters of theology and morality (Hoge, Johnson, and Luidens 1994; Roof and McKinney 1987; Wellman 2002). They are held together as much by their very acceptability as by shared theology. Congregationalist and Presbyterian and Episcopal and Methodist and Lutheran remain among the most recognizable and respectable religious identities in U.S. society. They are respectable in part because their members have been disproportionately middle class for several generations, and they expect both clergy and members to be well educated and able to participate in public life. These groups think of themselves as publicly engaged citizens, with a responsibility for the well-being of their communities; and they have, in fact, consistently been overrepresented in board rooms and corridors of political power (Davidson, Pyle, and Reyes 1995).

No less engaged but with a very different relationship to American culture are the historic African American churches—three black Baptist denominations, three black Methodist denominations, and the rapidly growing Church of God in Christ, in addition to thousands of independent churches. These black and independent churches have their own distinct places on the American religious map (Lincoln and Mamiya 1990). We really have no good count of the membership or number of churches, but the Pew Religious Landscape Project placed African American Protestants at 7 percent of the population (2008). A long history of enforced separation has resulted in distinctive worship traditions and ways of organizing. Black churches share the evangelical piety of their white evangelical counterparts, but they combine that evangelicalism with a concern for this-worldly community engagement. Not every black Church is led by a Martin Luther King Jr., but it is no accident that King emerged from and gained support through the Protestant churches that have been shaped by the African American experience of exile and exodus (Franklin 1994). Black churches are still disproportionately located in the South, but wherever there is an African American population, there are churches whose way of being Protestant is their distinct creation.

White Evangelical Protestants are the third and currently largest location on the Protestant map. With between 25 and 30 percent of the U.S. adult population, the combined forces of the dozens of denominations in this camp actually exceed the number of Roman Catholics. Their geographic distribution, on the other hand, is almost the mirror opposite of the Catholic coastline and borderland presence. Evangelicals are an overwhelming presence in the South and ubiquitous in the Midwest, and have a strong presence in small towns and suburbs in every corner of the country. Denominational traditions within the Baptist, Holiness, and Pentecostal families belong here, as do the conservative offshoots of many of the mainline denominations—the Lutheran church, Missouri Synod, for instance, or the Wesleyan churches. The biggest single denomination among them is the Southern Baptist Convention, at 16 million members and counting. Although there is immense variation within this territory, which we will explore in more detail, evangelicals recognize each other by their emphasis on individual conversion and disciplined personal piety. Churches in this territory are serious about teaching the Bible and preaching about the saving blood of Jesus.

Most of the American religious landscape is covered by these six religious traditions—three kinds of Protestants, Catholics, Jews, and the new-to-the-United-States other world religions. Almost always overlooked or lumped into other categories, however, are the homegrown

American religious inventions: Latter-Day Saints, Jehovah's Witnesses, and Christian Scientists. Together, they are at least as numerous as either the Jews or the other world religions. They are Christian in heritage, but add their own unique prophets, doctrines, scriptures, and practices (for the Latter-Day Saints, see Shipps 1985; for the Jehovah's Witnesses, see Penton 1997; for Christian Science, see Gottschalk 1973). These are the groups that have most often tested the legal limits of religious tolerance, defining the boundaries of acceptable practice in American religion. There is, of course, a very clear Mormon territory radiating out from Salt Lake City, but all three groups can be found throughout the country. Indeed, Mormons and Jehovah's Witnesses can often be found on neighborhood doorsteps, given that they actively seek converts here and abroad.

There is a final part of the landscape to be accounted for, and that is the growing segment of American society that finds no organized religious tradition to their liking, what sociologists have dubbed the *nones* (Hout and Fischer 2002). About one in six Americans claims no religious preference, and at least that many more claim a preference but almost never attend worship services (Marler and Hadaway 1993). Very few of these people are nonbelievers—most still say they believe in some sort of higher power—and it does not appear that the ranks of unbelief are growing. Still, roughly one-third of the population are effectively nonobservant; at most they are religious (or spiritual) in their own ways.

Evangelicals, then, are not the whole story. Nor are they a single story. The 25 percent or so of Americans who inhabit the evangelical world share among themselves a devotion to the Bible as their primary source of authority, but they differ widely on exactly what the Bible tells them to do. They share a devotion to Jesus as their savior, but the Pentecostal branch adds an equal measure of devotion to the Holy Spirit. They share a commitment to living a Christ-like life, but it is no longer assumed, for instance, that Christ would require them to avoid drinking and dancing. Most of them are evangelistic and think they should tell others about their faith, but some conservative Protestants focus on sacraments and creeds rather than witnessing and conversion.[6] Black and white traditions share a love of Jesus and the Bible and personal piety, but they have strikingly different community activities and worship styles that bear the marks of their long separation. Bill Clinton, Jesse Jackson, and Jerry Falwell might all have been able to join in a chorus of "Blessed Assurance, Jesus is Mine," but their differing ways of living out that assurance of salvation highlight the breadth of the evangelical territory.

Thus, no one way of being religious (or irreligious) can claim a monopoly or even dominance within American culture today (for a numerical breakdown of the major religions and Protestant denominations from 1780 through 2000, see table 2.1). Evangelicals, collectively, are among the most visible and numerous, but must compete with a wide and varied array of other religious voices as they enter the public square. As has always been the case, the most salient social fact about American religion is its diversity (Greeley 1972). Although one or another religious group may, at any given time, enjoy a certain cultural privilege or public visibility, all traditions are forced by legal disestablishment to gain that privilege and visibility by their own effort. If evangelicals are a prominent force in American culture and politics today, we will need to understand their prominence as emerging from some combination of their own cultural and organizational strength and the particular political and cultural climate of this time in our history.

Evangelical Roots

Understanding today's situation may be easier if we take a look back in history, both for the continuities and for the changes that have made it possible. The diversity of today's evangelical communities, as well as the differences that separate them from other communities of faith and those with no faith, find their roots in the fertile soil of America's experiment in religious voluntarism.[7] Both the lively agnosticism of American society and its vibrant religious diversity are points of continuity with the past.

The Europeans who came to this country early on brought with them a bewildering array of convictions about what God demands of humanity and enough differences over how to live out those convictions to make the colonial era a time of persistent religious struggle. Attempts at religious establishment—both Puritan and Anglican—vied with experiments in religious liberty. Revivals challenged colonists to live more deeply godly lives, while equal numbers of colonists welcomed the chance to strike out into a frontier devoid of doctrinal and church restraints. Jews found a place, even if sometimes tenuous, almost from the beginning, but the array of Christians only seemed to get wider with each boat that arrived and each preacher with a new message.

By the time a constitution was being written, no single religious group or clergy elite held enough sway to make an argument for an official state church. Congregationalists, Anglicans, and Presbyterians were clearly the dominant groups (see table 2.1), collectively claiming about 55 percent of the churchgoing population, but fewer than 15 percent of the population were officially affiliated with any church (Holifield 1994). The (Puritan) Congregationalists managed to retain the right to their establishment status in various New England states, but that, too, eroded by the early nineteenth century, declined precipitously in the years that

Table 2.1   Changes in Number and Types of Congregations, 1780 to 2000

	1780[a]	1850[b]	1935[c]	2000
Congregationalists	750	1706	6129	5,923
Anglican-Episcopalian	400	1459	7529	7,364
Presbyterians	475	4824	13263	11,178
Cumberland Presbyterian & Presbyterian Church in America[d]			1288	2,237
Baptists (→ Northern→ American)	450	9375	7694	5,756
Southern Baptists & miscellaneous other white conservative Baptists			31499	@60,000[e]
African American Baptists			33400	@37,500
Dutch & German Reformed (→ Reformed Church in America & Christian Reformed Church)	325	668	1010	1,578
Lutheran (→ Evangelical Lutheran Church in America)	225	1217	10125	10,816
Lutheran Church, Missouri and Wisconsin Synods			4224	6,150
Quaker	75	726	660	1,100
Roman Catholic	50	1221	18242	19,500
Eastern Orthodox			@750	2,400
Jews		31	3118	@3,500

Mennonites, Moravians, Brethren, and European pietists	495	2129	4,358
Methodists (→ United Methodist Church)	13280	49828	35,469
African Methodist Episcopal, AME, Zion & Christian Methodist Episcopal		15568	@10,593
Restorationists (→ Disciples of Christ)	859	8118	3,781
Churches of Christ		6226	15,000
Adventists (→ Seventh-Day Adventists)		2912	4,989
Holiness (Wesleyan, Nazarene, Church of God, Salvation Army, and so on)		6802	12,331
Pentecostal (Assemblies of God, Church of God in Christ, and so on)		6068	41,053
Nondenominational evangelical			@35,000
Church of Jesus Christ of Latter-Day Saints	9	1927	12,798
Jehovah's Witnesses		@3000	11,636
Christian Science		2132	@2,000
Other world religions			@5,000

Source: Authors' compilation.

a 1780 data from Gausted and Barlow (2001, 8). Although there were a few Methodists, Jews, and Eastern Orthodox Churches, as well as substantial numbers of Mennonite, Moravian, Brethren, and pietist churches, no counts are provided for them.

b 1850 data from DeBow (1854). Note that both the Baptists and Methodists had already split into Northern and Southern branches in the mid-1840s, but the Census did not pick up that distinction. Nor are data provided for any African American groups and many other denominations that were already growing.

c Data for 1935 and 2000 come primarily from the American Religion Data Archive (2006). Many very small denominations are not included. Data for Eastern Orthodox churches are from Diana Eck, 2007, http://www.pluralism.org Krindatch (2006), and estimates for other world religions come from The Pluralism Project.

d Groups shown below and to the right are conservative offshoots of the historical group they follow. Gray shading indicates an evangelical group.

e All figures here are estimates, but some more so than others (marked by "@"). Baptists, for instance, comprise dozens of small decentralized denominations that do not always keep records or report to anyone.

followed (Finke and Stark 1992). Some of the Founders were convinced that religious faith was a helpful prerequisite to the sort of democratic citizenship the new nation would need, but they were content to leave the population free to find their own version of that faith (Washington 1796).

The new nation had, then, left both its geographic and religious frontiers open to expansion. With an officially secular state in place, the religious arena was open and unregulated. In this new democratic experiment, citizens were entrusted to choose their political representatives, but also to organize as they wished in the religious realm. The expression "a new life" took on numerous meanings in this new land, and evangelicalism meshed remarkably well with a New World in which one could reinvent oneself. Here fate was not set at birth or even sealed by a string of good luck or bad behavior. Sinners could repent and turn their lives around, just as peasants could become citizens. The evangelical message and the evangelical way of organizing that developed in the early nineteenth century were well suited to the emerging American republic.

Evangelicalism was not, of course, entirely new or uniquely American. The term *evangelical* was adopted from European religions, in which it was essentially synonymous with *protestant*, but it began to take on its distinctly American character in the early years of the republic. The foundation for American evangelical religion was laid by colonial Puritans and Baptists, with their insistence on the obligation of each individual to study the scriptures and live a prudent, sober, and godly life. The experiential dimension of faith was deepened by the preachers of the First Great Awakening, and again by the Methodist movement launched by John Wesley, all urging believers to be attuned to the feelings of the heart as well as the thoughts of the mind. Baptists combined the emphasis on a life-changing experience of conversion with an intensely egalitarian form of church life. The localized leadership of ordinary believers allowed Baptists to spread throughout the frontier and deeply into slave communities. By the early nineteenth century, it was the Baptists and Methodists who were the dominant face of American religion, having far outpaced the colonial establishment churches.

Over the course of the nineteenth century, the denominational landscape became increasingly dense as new movements were formed out of each new interpretation of scripture and tradition. At the end of the century, still another addition to the evangelical family came in the form of Pentecostalism. Pious believers had already begun to talk about the "baptism with the Holy Ghost," and by mid-century, some began to include miraculous healings and dramatic "gifts of tongues." These new manifestations of the spirit spread from Maine to Kansas and finally to Los Angeles. The now famous Azusa Street revival, led by African

American evangelist William Seymour, began in Los Angeles in 1906; and in short order tens of thousands of Pentecostal converts could be found throughout North America (Wacker 2001). Over the course of the next century, Pentecostalism became the single most dynamic movement in global evangelicalism, combining from its very beginning indigenous traditions of miracles and healing with more orthodox forms of conservative Christianity (Martin 2002; Cox 1995).

Throughout the nineteenth century, those who preached a gospel of salvation through Jesus were very likely to be public advocates for social as well as personal change. Evangelicals are often associated, of course, with the temperance movement, but they were also central to the crusade to end slavery and, later, to secure female suffrage.[8] Reform impulses from within evangelicalism led at least some of its most passionate believers to seek this-worldly change. The postmillennial bent of most nineteenth-century Protestantism meant that utopian dreams of reformed societies were not unusual.[9] Immoral societies needed to be called to repentance and remade as civilizations in which virtuous souls can flourish.

Persuading people to change requires, of course, both a convincing message and a good organization for getting it delivered; and evangelicals excelled at both. Their evangelistic desire to spread the gospel, set in the context of an open American religious "market," spawned a nineteenth-century organizing frenzy. They were free to promote religious values, and they organized to do it. Religious impulses were turned into voluntary benevolent action (Hall 1998). Not only were evangelicals consistent in creating new congregations to follow pioneering populations past the Eastern Seaboard, they also used—and invented—all the organizational tools a voluntary religious system made both possible and necessary. They founded colleges and hospitals and orphanages, but also created benevolent societies and publishing societies and reform societies for every possible cause. What Protestants accomplished during this period was the invention of a vast and ever-changing organizational world, freely formed by citizens allowed to express at will their religious preferences and their benevolent goals.

Rolling all these impulses for changing the world into one global effort, the missionary movement gained momentum as the nineteenth century progressed. American missionaries traveled into Asia, Africa, Latin America, and the Middle East, combining pleas for conversion with practical instruction in living a good life on earth. They preached the virtues of democracy, mixing in education, health care, and hygiene along the way. Although they offered salvation in the next world, they were convinced that their message would change this world as well.[10]

All these voluntary organizations provided, in turn, opportunities for their creators and members to practice precisely the democratic and entrepreneurial skills the American context called forth. Women especially found their organizational niche in this work. By the end of the nineteenth century, American Protestant women were running multi-million dollar mission and benevolent enterprises with work in dozens of countries around the world.[11]

This work of missions and benevolence was, throughout the century, as much the domain of Presbyterians and Lutherans and Episcopalians as of Baptists or Methodists (Hutchison 1987; Hempton 2005). Although there was enormous diversity in doctrine and practice across American Protestantism, much of what we now recognize as conservative or evangelical actually characterized virtually all the Protestant world. Protestant entrepreneurs like John D. Rockefeller built businesses, but they also built churches (Riverside Church in New York) and colleges (the University of Chicago). Whether Baptist (like Rockefeller) or Episcopalian (like the Astors), whether Presbyterian or Methodist, the Christian gospel was understood to require both personal piety and public responsibility, both spiritual transformation and improvements in the conditions of this world. Methodist Frances Willard began her career as an educator, became a temperance crusader, and eventually led the Women's Christian Temperance Union toward advocacy on prison reform, sex education, minimum wages and woman suffrage (Scott 1993). Similarly, the thriving missions movement was as concerned with education and medicine as it was with building churches (Hutchison 1987; Robert 1997). In short, nineteenth-century American Protestantism, across nearly every denomination, was what we would call today both evangelical and liberal at the same time (Dayton 1976). Today's evangelical wedding of religious piety with social activism in pursuit of a better world is in clear continuity with this earlier period in our history.

Twentieth-Century Transformations

It is not, however, a continuity without interruption. Religious piety and social activism suffered a bitter divorce in the early-twentieth-century upheavals that we have come to call the fundamentalist-modernist controversies (Marsden 1980). The university-educated modernists who emerged in the late nineteenth century introduced critical readings of the Bible, using the scientific lenses of history and archeology, and celebrated the possibility of unity among followers of the world religions as brothers under one universal god.[12] Fundamentalists insisted that the Bible needed no special scientific explanations and that Jesus' sacrificial blood was the only key to salvation. Theirs was not just a reassertion of tradition, however. Fundamentalism was as much about an innovative theological understanding of the End Times as about a return to the bible (Ammerman 1991). Dispensational premillennialism, a theology that had emerged earlier in the nineteenth century, posited an imminent return of Jesus to rescue believers from an increasingly sinful world (the Rapture), and it found fertile ground in the new challenges—social, theological, and intellectual—of late nineteenth- and early twentieth-century America.

In the ensuing conflicts, denominations were divided between conservative and liberal, but just as important, the terms of today's cultural debates began to take hold. Believers came to see their opponents as godless and determined secular foes. On the other side, those who thought of themselves as enlightened and progressive saw their opponents as Bible-thumping rednecks who would stop the progress of science and liberty, if given the chance.[13]

Nowhere was the divide more dramatically enacted than in Dayton, Tennessee, in the famous 1925 Scopes Trial about the teaching of evolution. As Clarence Darrow debated William Jennings Bryan, the stage for twentieth-century cultural battles was set. Assisted by the vivid prose of H. L. Mencken and, later, the acting prowess of Spencer Tracy in *Inherit the Wind*, images were proffered that captured the public imagination. In spite of the legal outcome (Darrow lost), the death of Bryan before he could even leave town gave the story its narrative arc. Both sides agreed: an aggressive secularism was on the march and destined to be triumphant, but believers, however futilely, would resist (Harding 2000).

And so the sorting began, with conservatives largely disappearing from public view for the next half-century. Liberal religionists shunned the evangelistic and missionary activity of their forebears and focused on both intellectual respectability and liberal social causes (Hutchison 1976). Those on the fundamentalist side shunned the reformist concerns of their forebears to concentrate on evangelism. For fifty years, revivalist Dwight Moody's philosophy became the watchword of many American evangelicals: "I look upon this world as a wrecked vessel. God has given me a lifeboat and said to me, 'Moody, save all you can.'" (as quoted in William G. McLoughlin's *Revivals, Awakenings, and Reform* [1978, 144]).

That did not mean, however, that evangelicals were inactive. In the decades following the Scopes trial, they went right on starting new churches, founding new schools and colleges, and sending missionaries. They also founded innovative youth and campus ministries, added new publishing and broadcast ministries, and began the network of manufacturing and retail outlets from which the Christian Booksellers Association would be formed (Carpenter 1997). By the 1960s, always ready to use new technologies and try out new organizational forms, American evangelicals had built a formidable network of churches and "parachurch" organizations. Even inside many of the liberal denominations conservative caucuses were organized, sometimes resisting the changes denominational leaders wanted to make (Roozen and Nieman 2005; McKinney and Finke 2002).

Although the twentieth century brought discontinuity in the ideological landscape, rhetorically dividing Protestantism between conservative and liberal and altering the evangelical place in the culture, there was, then, continuity in the organizational impulses and strategies they had long used. To those on the outside, evangelicals seemed marginal and withdrawn. Only occasionally, as when Billy Graham routinely filled huge stadiums, did cultural elites notice the burgeoning organizational strength of the movement.

This organizational strength was not, however, built on theological single-mindedness. Most ordinary churchgoers at mid-century were unconvinced by the hardest version of the fundamentalist gospel, even if they were likely to describe themselves as believing the Bible. They were clearly not committed to the liberal account of scripture, either, meaning that the chasm between the two warring camps was actually wellpopulated by a very large middle.[14] Even in the 1970s and 1980s, Americans were more likely to tell survey researchers that they think of the Bible as the "inspired word of God" (48 percent) than either to say it is literally true (36 percent) or merely a book of fables (15 percent). Conservative views were more prominent in the South, liberal ones in the New England and Pacific regions, but nowhere did the most secular view (a book of fables) garner more than the 28 percent found in New England.[15]

By the end of the century, much of the American cultural elite had rejected biblical religion, but the population had not. Protestantism of a fairly conservative sort still had a solid base, even in denominations not always thought of as conservative. The language of belief remained a powerful cultural idiom. Evangelicals could draw on familiar religious language and images even beyond their own theological base. With a formidable organizational network to produce and disseminate those images, evangelicalism entered its current era of prominence.

An Era of Growing Influence

Evangelicalism is also an increasingly well-placed competitor. Evangelicals are today found in cultural locations that allow them a visible social base from which to wield influence. In addition to their stronghold in places like the Southern Baptist Convention and the Assemblies of God, two of the largest American denominations, there are also conservatives across the denominational spectrum. Indeed, many conservative believers are not in church at all. Hout and Greeley document the prevalence of conservative beliefs among the "nones," and Farnsley provides a vivid portrait of the biblical literalists who populate flea markets on

Sunday morning rather than going to church (Farnsley 2006). To assume that all the evangelicals are in a small array of evangelical denominations is to miss the pervasiveness of their presence.

But the presence of "flea market believers" should not lead us to assume that evangelicals are primarily uneducated or rural. At the moment when the Moral Majority and Jimmy Carter—each in very different ways—first began to remind the country that evangelicalism was not dead, it was still true that supporters of Jerry Falwell were slightly more likely than political liberals to lack a college education, live in the South, and belong to the working class.[16] But the gaps were already closing. By the mid-1990s, when the sociologist Christian Smith surveyed the American population's religious identities, those who called themselves evangelicals had an average of 14.2 years of schooling, compared to the 14.3 among the mainline Protestants; and only 15 percent were in the lowest income categories (less than $20,000), compared to 13 percent of mainline Protestants (1998). The upward mobility that had begun in the postwar era had brought evangelicals to a level of near parity. Using different measures, Andrew Greeley and Michael Hout found some of class and education differences remaining, but cautioned that "all these characteristics are shades of difference—matters of degree, not kind" (2006, 91).

Evangelicals, in other words, are thoroughly middle class and have made middle-class consumer culture their own. Pious believers of all sorts have always enshrined their devotions in material objects—from Bible verses on a wall plaque to saint statues in the garden (McDannell 1995). The commercial explosion of the last three decades, however, may be unprecedented. Sales at Christian bookstores run into the billions, and every media genre has its evangelical counterpart, often entertaining enough to attract nonevangelical audiences. The *Passion of the Christ* was but the most controversial of recent film offerings, and *The Chronicles of Narnia* more easily drew wide and diverse movie audiences. Both were heavily marketed to and consumed by evangelicals. Evangelical buying power has forced the American market to recognize them as a consumer demographic worth catering to (Hendershot 2004). Isolated and nonmainstream they are not (see chapter 10, this volume).

This is one of the several cultural shifts that exemplify the growing prominence of evangelicals. Until the 1980s, evangelicals had poured their considerable organizational energy into the construction of a parallel cultural universe, trying to insulate believers from the dangers of the secular world (Ammerman 1987). The separateness of that evangelical culture, however, has eroded in more recent years. Older generations may have shunned or been unable to afford elite universities, but Yale and UC Berkeley are today full of evangelicals who have learned to engage secular philosophies rather than avoiding them.[17] They are supported by the same campus organizations that have always provided a home—Campus Crusade, Intervarsity, and the like—but the activities and speakers today may include tips on getting a job in government or a casual chat with a Fortune 500 CEO. Nor are those campus groups the anglo enclaves they might have been fifty years ago. Indeed today, the evangelical presence on many elite campuses and in many denominations has a decidedly Asian look (Warner 2005; Kim 2006). The evangelical presence in American culture today is, in fact, as much about Asian Yalies as about Southern preachers. Through both economic mobility and deliberate influence strategies, evangelicals have achieved a place in American culture that makes them hard to ignore (Lindsay 2007).

But are there actually more of them today than in days past? The sight of booming megachurches certainly makes it look as if there are, and some of those new churches seem to be garnering net increases of new conservative believers (Perrin, Kennedy, and Miller 1997). But a long history of research on membership in conservative churches casts doubt on whether the larger picture is one of substantial growth. To the extent that the number of conservatives is growing, it is largely through higher birth rates, not because mainline members (or others) are switching (Hout, Greeley, and Wilde 2001). Indeed, because many conservative churches have no incentive to prune their rolls of members long gone, the soaring numbers supplied by some denominations may not reflect the reality on the ground.[18] Reginald Bibby has carefully analyzed Canadian survey data over more than twenty years and describes what he calls "circulating saints" (1999). New members in one church are very likely to have left a similar church to join.

The question of numbers and growth, then, is an extremely difficult question to answer. There is no religious census in the United States, and each national survey tends to ask religion questions in its own way. The General Social Survey (GSS) is an excellent source of data on the American population, but its questions about religious beliefs and affiliations are blunt instruments at best. As with most other surveys, the religious categories deduced from GSS data are based on denominational affiliation, so they misclassify the liberal Southern Baptist as well as the conservative Episcopalian. Still, with a consistent set of questions over nearly forty years, the GSS offers us a reasonable guess about the trends. In their recent book, Greeley and Hout (2006) created a sensible category of white evangelicals from the data and track their percentage in the population over four decades. They show that the category grew from 22 percent to 26 percent between the 1970s and 1980s, but has remained steady since. The 2008 Pew Forum Religious Landscape Survey similarly found 26.3 percent with an evangelical Protestant affiliation (2008). There is simply no strong evidence to suggest that evangelicals are a more substantial part of the American population today than in the years when they were less visible. The real shifts in the American religious landscape are the decline in the Protestant mainline, the growth of nonaffiliation, and the steady increase in numbers outside Judaism and Christianity. Whatever has made evangelicals more visible, it is not primarily a matter of growth.

Evangelicals have, however, increased their apparent presence by finding common cause with other conservative religionists whose theologies might have kept earlier generations apart. One can hardly imagine more different theological traditions than Roman Catholicism, the Church of Jesus Christ of Latter-Day Saints (LDS), Orthodox Judaism, and evangelical Christians. Yet common concerns for family and morality have helped forge alliances across those doctrinal lines. At the 2007 Values Voter Summit, sponsored by Focus on the Family, among others, the long list of evangelical speakers was joined by Roman Catholic priest Frank Pavone and prominent Catholics Bill Bennett, Robert Bork, and Rick Santorum, along with Rabbi Daniel Lapin and Jewish commentators Ben Stein and Mark Levin. Latino (Catholic) film star Eduardo Verastegui and African American preachers and politicians joined in calling for cultural and political values that reflected their moral concerns. All the Republican presidential candidates made appearances, as well.[19]

Although Mormons are less visible in such national gatherings, the convergence of evangelical and Mormon opinions on family issues is striking. Both groups are much more likely than other Americans to say that homosexuality should be discouraged not tolerated (64 percent and 68 percent, respectively, versus 40 percent of the population as a whole). The two groups also agree, again in contrast to the rest of the population, that abortion should be illegal in most or all cases (61 percent and 70 percent, versus 43 percent) (Pew Forum on Religion and Public Life 2008). Mitt Romney's difficulties in the 2008 Republican primaries demonstrated, however, that it is not easy to convert this issue agreement into political cooperation. The theological tension between evangelicals and the LDS Church was too strong for many to ignore.

Growing evangelical-Catholic cooperation is difficult in its own way. Although Catholics are a visible presence in Right to Life and other traditionalist coalitions, the Catholic population as a whole is much more divided on these issues than their leaders might wish. They mirror the national population in being about evenly split on abortion, for instance; and they are as relatively liberal on homosexuality as mainline Protestants (Pew Forum 2008). Ziad Munson's study of the Right to Life movement revealed, in fact, that many Catholic activists are frustrated at not being able to use their parishes as an organizing base because the issue is too divisive (2005). Instead, those Catholic activists are likely to join forces with like-minded evangelicals in a vigil outside an abortion clinic.

The ancient animosities that made it necessary for John Kennedy to explain himself to the Baptist ministers of Texas have nearly disappeared. In an increasingly multicultural America, the lines of division may be inside religious traditions, rather than between them.[20]

That multicultural sensibility has also added African American, Hispanic, and Asian voices to the evangelical chorus. Asian Christians, those who emigrate as Christians as well as those who convert here, are very likely to be evangelical, even if they belong to Methodist or Presbyterian denominations. Latino and Latina Protestants, of whom there are at least 8 million, are most likely to be Pentecostal and conservative on sexual morality issues, though not necessarily on other political questions. In Stephen Warner's words, American religion as a whole is being "de-europeanized," and that is most apparent among Catholics and evangelicals (2005). Immigrant evangelicals often resonate with the rhetoric about moral values that has dominated white evangelical political involvement. Concern for traditional moral values and for the future of the family seems to be a ground on which concerned white evangelicals are meeting some populations of color. Citing both their moral concerns and their enthusiasm for George W. Bush's faith-based initiatives, some prominent African American pastors have begun to break ranks with the Democratic party as well (Chaves 1999). Although black churches are still overwhelmingly in the Democratic camp, the color line no longer defines evangelical boundaries in quite the way it once did.

By the 1990s, in fact, evangelicalism was increasingly integrated, even in the South. Attending an integrated religious congregation—evangelical or otherwise—is still the exception, not the rule. Michael Emerson and Rodney Woo found that only about 7 percent of all U.S. congregations have an ethnic mix that exceeds 80-20, whatever the 80 happens to be (2006). But evangelical Protestant churches are as likely to be in that exceptional 7 percent as liberal Protestant ones are. Even in the South, congregations in expanding urban regions are increasingly likely to attract a mixed membership that would have astounded a previous generation. And on the West Coast, the ethnic salad bowl is celebrated in dozens of highly visible, culturally hip multicultural evangelical megachurches (Marti 2005).

Evangelicals today simply have a different place in the culture than the one they occupied at mid-century. They may not claim a bigger portion of the population, but their decreasing insularity has made interethnic and interreligious cooperation possible. (John Green's chapter in this volume analyzes cooperation and tensions in the traditionalist alliance.) Their climb up the income and status ladder has made them more visible as well. Still, if they had not entered the political arena, the question of their prominence in American life would surely not have gained such urgency.

Accounting for Activism

How should we explain that move into American public life? Since the late 1970s, evangelicals have mobilized a visible social movement and have gained a sense of their own voice and entitlement. Social movement theories, then, can offer useful ways to understand the activism of today's evangelicals.

Some of the earliest social movement theories relied on status discontent to explain how movements emerge. The thought was that people who are disadvantaged, either in absolute or relative terms, have good reason to rise up in opposition to the status quo. But evangelicals are no longer a disadvantaged or marginal group in American society. They may occupy somewhat lower rungs on the status ladder, but most are solidly middle class. Their movement may have taken much of its shape in 1920s antimodernist crusades, but today evangelicals are as thoroughly modern as the next iPod user. In the earliest days of the movement, status discontent explanations seemed plausible. The status gaps were there, and the decade of the 1960s provided a vivid set of cultural forces to oppose. As early as the 1980s, however, Michael Wood and Michael Hughes showed that status discontent could not account for the growing movement for moral reform (1984). By the early 1990s, political scientists consistently found that the demographic variables— education, income, place of residence—failed to tell them very much about who supported conservative political activism (Green, Rozell, and Wilcox 2003).

Nor is this a movement whose political aims are racism by another name. We have already noted its own growing ethnic diversity, but that cannot overcome lingering suspicions about the links among region, race, and religion. The shift of southern whites (most of them admittedly evangelical) into the Republican Party began, however, before Falwell and company emerged on the scene and stopped long enough for those southern evangelicals to vote for one of their own in 1976. Throughout the 1980s and 1990s, the racial undertones that accompanied Republican gains were as appealing to nonsouthern (and nonevangelical) whites as they were to southerners. Catholics in the north were as likely to be swayed by racial resentment as were evangelicals in the south (Leege and Kellstedt 1993).

If evangelical political activism is not easily located in discontent or demography, it can be found in a group of identifying issues and the rhetoric surrounding them.[21] This is a movement that gained momentum as it learned to tell a new story about what is wrong with American culture and what they must do about it. In the 1970s, leaders such as Jerry Falwell and Pat Robertson began speaking not just of the approaching End Times, but also of what believers can do in the meantime "while He tarries." Such rhetoric created, as Harding argued, new ways to envision oneself and one's world (1994). To name themselves the Moral Majority and to claim this time before the End Time as a time for God to work miracles opened up a space in the story for political action in this world. Evangelicals have never stopped believing that spiritual salvation is the key to long-lasting change, but did become convinced that they might lose the ability to preach that gospel and preserve their way of life if they did not also act politically. They came to see their own families as endangered and the privileged place of America in the world at risk. Abortion, gay marriage, and what their children were learning in the classroom spoke of threats to the moral core of the nation. Drawing on their own religious traditions, they adapted the story for a new day.

They also learned to use the new political frames coming from the very secular enemies they opposed. Drawing on the lessons of the civil rights movement, they learned to speak of the rights of minorities. Drawing on postmodern and feminist themes, they painted themselves as an embattled minority, fighting a hegemonic culture. The believers versus secularists narrative frame has been present since the 1920s, but took on new content and nuance as a cadre of new leaders sought to mobilize a movement.

The links between the early movement entrepreneurs and the Republican Party were actually quite weak at first (Liebman 1983). But in the election cycles that followed, the Republican Party became increasingly adept at framing party identity with the story of moral threat followed by potential moral restoration. Although there has been much debate about what the exit polls on moral values really mean, those who say that moral values are important to their voting decisions are very likely to mention some sort of conservative social policy, including abortion (28 percent), gay marriage (29 percent) or simply "traditional values" (17 percent) (Keeter 2007, 87). As Sunshine Hillygus noted after the 2004 election, "a subset of voters cared about moral issues and . . . the Bush campaign was able to use direct mail, phone calls, and personal canvassing to emphasize issues like abortion and gay marriage for that subset of voters" (2007, 66). David Campbell and Quin Monson argued that "the president did not need to talk much about gay marriage to cement his opposition in the minds of voters. . . . Having spent a generation building an infrastructure within the evangelical community and courting support from traditionalist Catholics as well, the Republican Party is widely identified as the party of social conservatism" (2007, 127). In today's political discourse, *moral values* has a Republican brand label, and evangelical voters have learned to recognize that label (for an analysis of moral-values politics as a cultural and organizational phenomenon, see Steven Brint and Seth Abrutyn, volume 2, chapter 4).

The foreign policy part of this new political story is less visible, but no less important. Two distinctive evangelical legacies shape the issue agenda. The first of these is unstinting support for Israel (Ammerman 1988). Geoffrey Layman and Laura Hussey reported 2004 National Election Study data showing that evangelicals who attend church frequently are significantly more supportive of Israel than other white Christians (2007). The attachment of evangelicals to the Holy Land and its role in their understanding of the End Times accounts for the importance of this issue on their list of concerns. The same study by Layman and Hussey shows that dedicated evangelicals are also distinctive for their hawkish support of the war on terror, the war in Iraq, and militarism in general. Perhaps this is a natural extension of the strong anti-communist stance they took during the cold war, a stance that can largely be explained by their conviction that the United States has a unique role to play in salvation history and in sustaining a worldwide missionary enterprise. Like the Puritan city on a hill, they see the United States as an evangelical light to the nations.

Political candidates need not share an evangelical theology of missions or of the End Times to evoke evangelical identification with them. They can do so by waving the flag and talking about family values or a strong America. Nor are evangelicals the only Americans for whom such images resonate. Evangelicals simply put their own content into those rhetorical symbols and use them in identifying which candidates share their concerns.

Even more important than the concrete issues is the sense of mutual identification that defines any social movement (Polletta and Jasper 2001). People who are mobilized to action have to learn to recognize each other as part of a collective "we." For a significant minority of Americans, mutual recognition as born-again children of God may be more important than class- or ethnic-based group identities in shaping political decisions. American politics has always been more about culture than class, and the reality that religion might trump other interests and identities is not new. Catholics were disproportionately likely to vote for John Kennedy in 1960, and southern evangelicals got over their discontent with the Democrats long enough to vote overwhelmingly for Jimmy Carter, at least in 1976 (Leege et al. 2002). In both cases, religiously based mutual identification played a significant political role, just as it did again in 2000 and 2004. Whatever other issues or interests may be at play in any given election, people vote for people they recognize as like themselves. To the extent that an evangelical identity has become a salient political identity, being born again counts.

Indeed, it may count a great deal. This is a community that brings a good deal of mobilizing strength to the table. Social movement theories have taught us to look for mutual identification and the framing of a shared narrative of change, but they have also taught us to pay attention to the ways in which groups mobilize key resources in their struggle for change (McCarthy and Wolfson 1996). For evangelicals, one of those resources is the level of commitment they invest in their religious communities. Evangelicals simply believe more fervently and go to church more often than other Americans do.[22] Evangelical congregations (white and black) are more likely than mainline Protestant or Catholic ones to become communities of political discourse, not so much because of what is preached from the pulpit as because of what is talked about at the pot luck or in the Bible study group (Wald, Owen, and Hill 1988). Some do provide direct political messages, but the effects of a strong culture amplify both direct and indirect appeals (Beyerlein and Chaves 2003; Regnerus, Sikkink, and Smith 1999).

Recent research has made it clear, in fact, that conservative political activism is strongest among those evangelicals who are the most frequent church attenders (Hillygus 2007). The most committed and traditionalist members of all religious traditions tend to provide fertile ground for Republican appeals, but the picture is dramatic among evangelicals, with nearly 90 percent of the most committed among them reporting a 2004 vote for George W. Bush (Green et al. 2007). Since 1970, the proportion of Republican identifiers among faithful evangelicals has steadily increased (Layman and Hussey 2007), and it is therefore likely that evangelical church communities now reflect that dominance. It is likely, in turn, that evangelicals not inclined toward Republican politics may seek out other places to worship, reinforcing through this sorting effect increasingly homogeneous religio-political congregational cultures.[23]

Beyond vigorous local congregations, evangelical life also continues to be strengthened by the organizational and cultural entrepreneurship of its members. Evangelicals reentered the political arena on the strength of a century and a half of energetic institution-building. In the fifty years between the Scopes trial and the Moral Majority, those institutions sustained a parallel subculture. As the boundaries around that culture have softened, one of the points of connection is a growing network of political organizations and a growing literature on political engagement. Today's Christian bookstores are full of political tomes alongside the Bibles, and training camps for organizers have taken their place alongside the summer revival. Creating political action committees and prayer fellowships on Capitol Hill are but the latest instance of the organizational skills evangelicals bring to a movement for moral reform (for an analysis of the influence and beliefs of socially and politically prominent evangelicals, see Michael Lindsay, volume 2, chapter 10).

Today's activism, then, is sustained by the organizational resources and religious commitment of evangelical believers. It is given its direction by the new framing narrative of moral reform that developed in the 1980s and increasingly linked to Republican Party identification. As long as evangelical activists find that story convincing—as long as they see their families, churches, and national character threatened and their public participation making a difference—they are likely to stay involved. As long as Republican candidates can convincingly tie their agendas to the evangelical moral narrative, large majorities of engaged evangelicals will continue to vote Republican. But no story is without the possibility of new chapters and shifting plots.

The Long View, Again

We began with the reminder that white evangelical Protestants constitute less than 30 percent of the American population, a substantial minority, but one that is not a uniform political bloc any more than it is a uniform theological community. The differences between Pentecostals and conservative Presbyterians, between Southern Baptists and Mennonites, make conservative Protestant a very broad tent. Not nearly all deserve the evangelical label we typically use to describe them, because not all attempt to encourage religious awakenings in others. Nor are all of them politically mobilized. Although the most frequent attenders in the most conservative churches may be highly involved, they do not constitute the whole. They include, in fact, only about 12 percent of the adult population.[24] The remainder of those who might be called evangelicals either attend church less often or are in denominations where a conservative political agenda may be less often reinforced. The core of evangelicalism may be very strong, bolstered by a powerful institutional infrastructure and important networks linking them to centers of political and cultural influence, but the periphery is broad and diffuse. There are at least as many whose commitments are marginal as there are mobilized true believers.

Nor is it helpful to exaggerate the passion at work here. Most evangelicals are not "culture warriors." In the United States, only the tiniest of a radical fringe advocates violence in service of God's mandates. The vast majority of those who believe abortion is murder, for instance, nevertheless believe that the American political system allows them enough space to pursue their convictions through normal avenues of persuasion (Munson 2005). From his survey of American evangelicals, Christian Smith was convinced that they would rather offer a quiet good example with their lives than force their beliefs on others (2000). They are, in other words, as committed to living civilly as are more liberal Americans.[25] It is important to remember, as well, that there is no institutionalized religious establishment lurking within evangelicalism, no church longing to take over the American state. The ecclesial pluralism and diversity within this movement is far too great to pose a credible threat to the U.S. Constitution.

Like their nineteenth-century abolitionist forebears, many evangelicals have become morally outraged. As in that earlier era, they are acting as citizens trying to persuade their fellow citizens to act. American politics has always been as much about moral convictions and a sense of destiny as about economic or political ideology. The argument over which moral convictions and sense of destiny will guide the nation is one that is likely to remain at the heart of American politics, and evangelicals are likely to remain in the debate. The connection of evangelicals to powerful narratives about sources of moral decline and their connection to important power centers in American society make it likely that they will continue to have influence as well. Yet the history of evangelicalism in the United States is full of cross-currents. How evangelicals express their public moral voice is less certain than that their presence is no longer easy to ignore.

Notes

1. These figures, as well as religious preference percentages in the following section, have been calculated from the General Social Survey, using pooled data from annual surveys since 1995 (National Opinion Research Center 2001).
2. Small portions of this essay have been adapted from my article "Deep and Wide: The Real Evangelicals" (Ammerman 2006).
3. This description of American religious traditions is elaborated in more depth in my book *Pillars of Faith* (Ammerman 2005).
4. Maps showing the geographic distribution of American denominations can also be found at American Religion Data Archive (available at: http://www.thearda.org). There are also many smaller Catholic groups, as well as the various Eastern Orthodox churches that are neighbors to Roman Catholics in the American religious ecology.
5. Diana L. Eck and Harvard University, "The Pluralism Project." Available at: http://www.pluralism.org.
6. I use the terms *evangelical* and *Conservative Protestant* fairly interchangeably in this chapter, although one could easily write another essay on what the proper terminology ought to be.
7. This account of early U.S. religious history follows closely the arguments made by Jon Butler (1990) and Nathan Hatch (1989).
8. Michael Young provided a brilliant analysis of the links between revivalist confession and moral reform in the early national period (2002).
9. Postmillennialists believed that the millennium of Christ's reign on earth would come as the culmination of the Christianization of the planet, as all humankind came to live as God originally wished them to live.
10. The lingering effects of missionary institution building can be seen throughout the world. Robert Woodberry and Timothy Shah argued that where mission schools were most prevalent, democracy is today most stable (2004).

11. Dana Robert has provided the definitive history of women's involvement in the mission movement (1997). For an account of women's organizational prowess, see also Yohn 2000.
12. These universalist impulses were always described in masculine language.
13. Christian Smith provided an illuminating account of the secularist movement that undertook this transformation (2003).
14. The reality of a middle between the sides in the presumed culture war has been amply demonstrated (Davis and Robinson 1996; DiMaggio, Evans, and Bryson 1996; Wolfe 1998).
15. Figures compiled by the author from the General Social Survey, cumulative surveys prior to 1990 (National Opinion Research Center 2001).
16. Clyde Wilcox provided a careful analysis of the early social sources of support for the Moral Majority (1992).
17. Michael Lindsay's study of elite evangelicals made this quite clear, as have some earlier reports (2007; Laurie Goodstein and David Kirkpatrick, "On a Christian Mission to the Top," New York Times, May 22, 2005; Bramadat 2000).
18. Among Southern Baptists, for instance, the number of resident members is always significantly lower than the total numbers reported to the public. And even those numbers have begun to slip in recent years (Associated Press, "Ranks of Southern Baptists are Still Growing Thinner," New York Times, April 25, 2008).
19. A complete list of speakers is available at the Values Voter Summit website (available at: http://www.frcaction.org/get.cfm?i=PG08B01&load=WX07 C08).
20. A Southern Baptist leader once observed to me that he felt more at home with conservative Catholic activists than with the (now defunct) liberal wing of his own denomination.
21. Here I follow social movement theories that point to framing, narratives, and other cultural symbols as keys to the collective work that turns nascent troubles into public issues (for example, Davis 2002; McAdam, McCarthy, and Zald 1996; Mische 2003).
22. The Pew Forum's Religious Landscape Survey reported that 90 percent of evangelicals were "absolutely certain" they believe in God, compared with 72 percent of mainline Protestants and 73 percent of Catholics (2008). Seventy-nine percent said religion is very important in their lives, versus 52 percent and 56 percent, respectively, of mainliners and Catholics. More than half (58 percent) claimed to attend services once a week or more, versus 34 percent and 42 percent in the other two groups.
23. There is a growing literature on racial homophily in American congregations (Emerson and Smith 2000; Christerson and Emerson 2003). I am convinced that political attributes are also among the signals that churchgoers pick up as they explore a new congregation. The extent to which the signals are strong or the churchgoer is politically committed may be a factor in decisions about membership and commitment. For a similar argument about the culture as a whole, see The Economist, "The Big Sort," 387(June 19, 2008): 41–42.
24. Calculated from pooled General Social Survey data on attendance and religious preference (National Opinion Research Center 2001).

25. Smith's conclusions are echoed in Alan Wolfe's assessment of the evangelical community (2003).

References

Ammerman, Nancy T. 1987. *Bible Believers: Fundamentalists in the Modern World.* New Brunswick, N.J.: Rutgers University Press.

———. 1988. "Fundamentalists Proselytizing Jews: Incivility in Preparation for the Rapture." In *Pushing the Faith,* edited by Frederick E. Greenspahn and Martin E. Marty. New York: Crossroad.

———. 1991. "North American Protestant Fundamentalism." In *Fundamentalisms Observed,* edited by Martin E. Marty and R. Scott Appleby. Chicago: University of Chicago Press.

———. 2005. *Pillars of Faith: American Congregations and Their Partners.* Berkeley: University of California Press.

———. 2006. "Deep and Wide: The Real Evangelicals." *The American Interest* 2(1): 25–34.

Beyerlein, Kraig, and Mark Chaves. 2003. "The Political Activities of Religious Congregations in the United States." *Journal for the Scientific Study of Religion* 42(2): 229–46.

Bibby, Reginald. 1999. "On Boundaries, Gates, and Circulating Saints: A Longitudinal Look at Loyalty and Loss." *Review of Religious Research* 41(2): 149–64.

Bramadat, Paul A. 2000. *The Church on the World's Turf: An Evangelical Christian Group at a Secular University.* New York: Oxford University Press.

Butler, Jon. 1990. *Awash in a Sea of Faith.* Cambridge, Mass.: Harvard University Press.

Campbell, David E., and J. Quin Monson. 2007. "The Case of Bush's Reelection: Did Gay Marriage Do It?" In *A Matter of Faith: Religion in the 2004 Presidential Election,* edited by David E. Campbell. Washington, D.C.: Brookings Institution Press.

Carpenter, Joel A. 1997. *Revive Us Again: The Reawakening of American Fundamentalism.* New York: Oxford University Press.

Chaves, Mark. 1999. "Religious Congregations and Welfare Reform: Who Will Take Advantage of 'Charitable Choice'?" *American Sociological Review* 64(6): 836–46.

Christerson, Brad, and Michael O. Emerson. 2003. "The Costs of Diversity in Religious Organizations: An In-Depth Case Study." *Sociology of Religion* 64(2): 163–81.

Cox, Harvey. 1995. *Fire from Heaven: The Rise of Pentecostal Spirituality and the Reshaping of Religion in the Twenty-first Century.* Reading, Mass.: Addison-Wesley.

Davidson, James D., Ralph E. Pyle, and David V. Reyes. 1995. "Persistence and Change in the Protestant Establishment, 1930–1992." *Social Forces* 74(1): 157–75.

Davis, Joseph E. 2002. *Stories of Change: Narrative and Social Movements.* Albany: State University of New York Press.

Davis, Nancy J., and Robert V. Robinson. 1996. "Are the Rumors of War Exaggerated? Religious Orthodoxy and Moral Progressivism in America." *American Journal of Sociology* 102(3): 756–87.

Dayton, Donald W. 1976. *Discovering an Evangelical Heritage*. New York: Harper & Row.

DeBow, J. D. B. 1854. *Statistical View of the United States: Compendium of the Seventh Census*. Washington, D.C.: Senate Printer.

de Tocqueville, Alexis. 1835. *Democracy in America*. Translated by George Lawrence. Garden City, N.Y.: Doubleday.

DiMaggio, Paul, John Evans, and Bethany Bryson. 1996. "Have Americans' Social Attitudes Become More Polarized?" *American Journal of Sociology* 102(3): 690–755.

Dolan, Jay P., ed. 1987. *The American Catholic Parish: A History from 1850 to the Present*. New York: Paulist Press.

Emerson, Michael O., and Christian Smith. 2000. *Divided by Faith: Evangelical Religion and the Problem of Race in America*. New York: Oxford University Press.

Emerson, Michael O., and Rodney M. Woo. 2006. *People of the Dream: Multiracial Congregations in the United States*. Princeton, N.J.: Princeton University Press.

Farnsley, Arthur Emery II. 2006. "Flea Market Believers." *Christianity Today* 50(October): 114–21.

Finke, Roger, and Rodney Stark. 1992. *The Churching of America*. New Brunswick, N.J.: Rutgers University Press.

Franklin, Robert Michael. 1994. "The Safest Place on Earth: The Culture of Black Congregations." In *American Congregations: New Perspectives in the Study of Congregations*, edited by James P. Wind and James W. Lewis. Chicago: University of Chicago Press.

Gaustad, Edwin Scott, and Philip Barlow. 2001. *New Historical Atlas of Religion in America*. New York: Oxford University Press.

Gottschalk, Stephen. 1973. *The Emergence of Christian Science in American Religious Life*. Berkeley: University of California Press.

Greeley, Andrew M. 1972. *The Denominational Society*. Glenview, Ill.: Scott-Forsman.

Greeley, Andrew, and Michael Hout. 2006. *The Truth About Conservative Christians: What They Think and What They Believe*. Chicago: University of Chicago Press.

Green, John C., Mark J. Rozell, and Clyde Wilcox, eds. 2003. *The Christian Right in American Politics: Marching to the Millennium*. Washington, D.C.: Georgetown University Press.

Green, John C., Lyman Kellstedt, Corwin Smidt, and James Guth. 2007. "How the Faithful Voted: Religious Communities and the Presidential Vote." In *A Matter of Faith: Religion in the 2004 Presidential Election*, edited by David E. Campbell. Washington, D.C.: Brookings Institution Press.

Hall, Peter Dobkin. 1998. "Religion and the Organizational Revolution in the United States." In *Sacred Companies*, edited by N. Jay Demerath III, Peter D. Hall, Terry Schmitt, and Rhys H. Williams. New York: Oxford University Press.

Harding, Susan. 1994. "The Politics of Apocalyptic Language in the Moral Majority Movement." In *Accounting for Fundamentalisms*, edited by Martin E. Marty and R. Scott Appleby. Chicago: University of Chicago Press.

————. 2000. *The Book of Jerry Falwell: Fundamentalist Language and Politics.* Princeton, N.J.: Princeton University Press.

Hatch, Nathan G. 1989. *The Democratization of American Christianity.* New Haven, Conn.: Yale University Press.

Hempton, David. 2005. *Methodism: Empire of the Spirit.* New Haven, Conn.: Yale University Press.

Hendershot, Heather. 2004. *Shaking the World for Jesus: Media and Conservative Evangelical Culture.* Chicago: University of Chicago Press.

Herberg, Will. 1960. *Protestant-Catholic-Jew.* Garden City, N.Y.: Anchor Doubleday.

Hillygus, D. Sunshine. 2007. "Moral Values: Media, Voters, and Candidate Strategy." In *A Matter of Faith: Religion in the 2004 Presidential Election*, edited by David E. Campbell. Washington, D.C.: Brookings Institution Press.

Hoge, Dean R., Benton Johnson, and Donald A. Luidens. 1994. *Vanishing Boundaries: The Religion of Mainline Protestant Baby Boomers.* Louisville, Ky.: Westminster/John Knox.

Holifield, E. Brooks. 1994. "Toward a History of American Congregations." In *American Congregations: New Perspectives in the Study of Congregations*, edited by James P. Wind and James W. Lewis. Chicago: University of Chicago Press.

Hout, Michael, and Claude Fischer. 2002. "Why More Americans Have No Religious Preference: Politics and Generations." *American Sociological Review* 67(2): 165–90.

Hout, Michael, Andrew Greeley, and Melissa J. Wilde. 2001. "The Demographic Imperative in Religious Change in the United States." *American Journal of Sociology* 107(2): 468–500.

Hutchison, William R. 1976. *The Modernist Impulse in American Protestantism.* New York: Oxford University.

————. 1987. *Errand to the World: American Protestant Thought and Foreign Missions.* Chicago: University of Chicago Press.

Keeter, Scott. 2007. "Evangelicals and Moral Values." In *A Matter of Faith: Religion in the 2004 Presidential Election*, edited by David E. Campbell. Washington, D.C.: Brookings Institution Press.

Kim, Rebecca Y. 2006. *God's New Whiz Kids? Korean American Evangelicals on Campus.* New York: New York University Press.

Kotler-Berkowitz, Laurence , Steven M. Cohen, Jonathon Ament, Vivian Klaff, Frank Mott, and Danyelle Peckerman-Neuman. 2003. *NJPS 2000–01 Report.* New York: United Jewish Communities.

Krindatch, Alexei D. 2006. *Research on Orthodox Religious Groups in the United States.* Hartford, Conn.: Hartford Institute for Religion Research. Available at: http://hirr.hartsem.edu/research/orthodoxsummary.html.

Layman, Geoffrey C., and Laura S. Hussey. 2007. "George W. Bush and the Evangelicals: Religious Commitment and Partisan Change among Evangelical Protestants, 1960–2004." In *A Matter of Faith: Religion in the 2004 Presidential Election*, edited by David E. Campbell. Washington, D.C.: Brookings Institution Press.

Leege, David C., and Lyman A. Kellstedt. 1993. *Rediscovering the Religious Factor in American Politics.* Armonk, N.Y.: M. E. Sharpe.

Leege, David C., Kenneth D. Wald, Brian S. Krueger, and Paul D. Mueller. 2002.

The Politics of Cultural Differences: Social Change and Voter Mobilization Strategies in the Post-New Deal Period. Princeton, N.J.: Princeton University Press.

Liebman, Robert. 1983. *The New Christian Right: Mobilization & Legitimation.* New York: Aldine de Gruyter.

Lincoln, C. Eric, and Lawrence H. Mamiya. 1990. *The Black Church in the African American Experience.* Durham, N.C.: Duke University Press.

Lindsay, D. Michael. 2007. *Faith in the Halls of Power: How Evangelicals Joined the American Elite.* New York: Oxford University Press.

Marler, Penny Long, and C. Kirk Hadaway. 1993. "Toward a Typology of Protestant 'Marginal Members'." *Review of Religious Research* 35(1): 34–54.

Marsden, George M. 1980. *Fundamentalism and American Culture.* New York: Oxford University Press.

Marti, Gerardo. 2005. *A Mosaic of Believers.* Bloomington: Indiana University Press.

Martin, David. 2002. *Pentecostalism: The World Their Parish.* Malden, Mass.: Blackwell Publishers.

McAdam, Doug, John D. McCarthy, and Mayer N. Zald. 1996. *Comparative Perspectives on Social Movements: Political Opportunities, Mobilizing Structures, and Cultural Framings.* New York: Cambridge University Press.

McCarthy, John D., and Mark Wolfson. 1996. "Resource Mobilization by Local Social Movement Organizations: Agency, Strategy, and Organization in the Movement Against Drinking and Driving." *American Sociological Review* 61(6): 1070–88.

McDannell, Colleen. 1995. *Material Christianity.* New Haven, Conn.: Yale University Press.

McGreevy, John T. 2003. *Catholicism and American Freedom.* New York: W. W. Norton.

McKinney, Jennifer, and Roger Finke. 2002. "Reviving the Mainline: An Overview of Clergy Support for Evangelical Renewal Movements." *Journal for the Scientific Study of Religion* 41(4): 771–83.

McLoughlin, William G. 1978. *Revivals, Awakenings, and Reform: An Essay on Religion and Social Change in America, 1607–1977.* Chicago: University of Chicago Press.

Mische, Ann. 2003. "Cross-Talk in Movements: Reconceiving the Culture-Network Link." In *Social Movements and Networks: Relational Approaches in Collective Action,* edited by Mario Diani and Doug McAdam. London: Oxford University Press.

Munson, Ziad. 2005. "Fighting for the Sanctity of Life: Juggling God, Democracy, and Abortion in the American Pro-Life Movement." In *Taking Faith Seriously,* edited by Mary Jo Bane, Brent Coffin, and Richard Higgins. Cambridge, Mass.: Harvard University Press.

National Opinion Research Center. 2001. *GSSDIRS General Social Survey: 1972–2000 Cumulative Codebook.* Chicago: University of Chicago. Available at: http://www.norc.org/GSS+Website/.

Penton, M. James. 1997. *Apocalypse Delayed: The Story of Jehovah's Witnesses,* 2nd ed. Toronto, Ont.: University of Toronto Press.

Perrin, Robin, Paul Kennedy, and Donald E. Miller. 1997. "Examining the Sources of Conservative Church Growth: Where Are the New Evangelical

Movements Getting Their Numbers?" *Journal for the Scientific Study of Religion* 36(1): 71–80.

Pew Forum on Religion and Public Life. 2008. *U.S. Religious Landscape Survey*. Washington, D.C.: Pew Forum on Religion & Public Life. Available at: http://religions.pewforum.org/pdf/report-religious-landscape-study-full.pdf.

Polletta, Francesca, and James Jasper. 2001. "Collective Identity and Social Movements." *Annual Review of Sociology* 27(2001): 283–305.

Prothero, Stephen. 2007. *Religious Literacy: What Every American Needs to Know— And Doesn't*. San Francisco: HarperOne.

Regnerus, Mark D., David Sikkink, and Christian Smith. 1999. "Voting with the Christian Right: Contextual and Individual Patterns of Electoral Influence." *Social Forces* 77(4): 1375–401.

Robert, Dana L. 1997. *Women in Mission: A Social History of Their Thought and Practice*. Macon, Ga.: Mercer University Press.

Roof, Wade Clark, and William McKinney. 1987. *American Mainline Religion*. New Brunswick, N.J.: Rutgers University Press.

Roozen, David, and James Nieman, eds. 2005. *Church, Identity, and Change: Theology and Denominational Structures in Unsettled Times*. Grand Rapids, Mich.: William B. Eerdmans.

Sarna, Jonathan D. 2004. *American Judaism: A History*. New Haven, Conn.: Yale University Press.

Scott, Ann Firor. 1993. *Natural Allies: Women's Associations in American History*. Urbana: University of Illinois Press.

Shipps, Jan. 1985. *Mormonism: The Story of a New Religious Tradition*. Urbana: University of Illinois Press.

Smith, Christian. 1998. *American Evangelicalism: Embattled and Thriving*. Chicago: University of Chicago Press.

———. 2000. *Christian America? What Evangelicals Really Want*. Berkeley: University of California Press.

———, ed. 2003. *The Secular Revolution: Power, Interests, and Conflict in the Secularization of American Public Life*. Berkeley: University of California Press.

Wacker, Grant. 2001. *Heaven Below: Early Pentecostals and American Culture*. Cambridge, Mass.: Harvard University Press.

Wald, Kenneth D., Dennis E. Owen, and Samuel S. Hill. 1988. "Churches as Political Communities." *American Political Science Review* 82(3): 531–48.

Warner, R. Stephen. 1993. "Work in Progress Toward a New Paradigm for the Sociological Study of Religion in the United States." *American Journal of Sociology* 98(5): 1044–93.

———. 1999. "Changes in the Civic Role of Religion." In *Diversity and Its Discontents: Cultural Conflict and Common Ground in Contermporary American Society*, edited by N. J. Smelser and Jeffrey C. Alexander. Princeton, N.J.: Princeton University Press.

———. 2005. "The De-Europeanization of American Christianity." In *A Church of Our Own: Disestablishment and Diversity in American Religion*, edited by R. Stephen Warner. New Brunswick, N.J.: Rutgers University Press.

Washington, George. 1796. "Farewell Address to the People of the United States, September 17." *Archiving Early America*. Available at: http://www.earlyamerica.com/earlyamerica/milestones/farewell/text.html.

Wellman, James A. 2002. "Religion Without a Net: Strictness in the Religious Practices of West Coast Urban Liberal Christian Congregations." *Review of Religious Research* 44(2): 184–99.

Wilcox, Clyde. 1992. *God's Warriors: The Christian Right in 20th Century America.* Baltimore, Md.: John Hopkins University Press.

Wolfe, Alan. 1998. *One Nation, After All.* New York: Viking.

———. 2003. *The Transformation of American Religion.* New York: Free Press.

Wood, Michael, and Michael Hughes. 1984. "The Moral Basis of Moral Reform: Status Discontent vs. Culture and Socialization as Explanations of Anti-Pornography Social Movement Adherence." *American Sociological Review* 49(1): 86–99.

Woodberry, Robert D., and Timothy S. Shah. 2004. "The Pioneering Protestants." *Journal of Democracy* 15(2): 47–61.

Yohn, Susan M. 2000. "'Let the Christian Women Set the Example in Their Own Gifts': The 'Business' of Protestant Women's Organizations." In *More Money, More Ministry: Money and Evangelicals in Recent North American History*, edited by Larry Eskridge and Mark Noll. Grand Rapids, Mich.: William B. Eerdmans.

Young, Michael P. 2002. "Confessional Protest: The Religious Birth of U.S. National Social Movements." *American Sociological Review* 67(5): 660–88.

Chapter 3

Conservative Protestantism in the United States? Toward a Comparative and Historical Perspective

PHILIP S. GORSKI

F OR MANY of those who observe it closely, the current state of con- servative Protestantism in the United States is a source of consid- erable shock. For political liberals, the shock derives from the strength of the movement (Habermas 2006; Taylor 2006). They wonder why the United States is not a normal country, like, say, England or Holland, countries in which religious belief is much quieter, and churchgoing much rarer. For religious conservatives, on the other hand, it is the weakness of conservative Protestantism that is the source of shock. They wish the United States could become a Christian nation once again, a country aware of the providential link between public morality and national greatness (Barton 1992; Rushdoony 1978; DeMar 1995; Kennedy and Newcombe 2005). How can two sets of observers arrive at such disparate assessments of the same phenomenon? My goal in this chapter is to critique and move beyond these assessments by placing the folk theories and the phenomenon itself within a com- parative-historical context.

Any comparative and historical analysis necessarily takes a particular set of comparisons and a particular period of history as its starting point, and that starting point inevitably influences the questions that arise and the answers that result. This chapter is no exception to that rule, so I would like to be clear about my starting point, which is the Reformation era in western Europe, a period I studied intensively before becoming interested in modern America. Against that background, the title of this chapter is transformed into a question, even a perplexity: conservative Protestantism in the United States?

Why the perplexity? There are several reasons. One is that the two traditions that constitute the theological and organizational core of conservative Protestantism at the moment—the Reformed and the Baptist— are typically categorized as radical or even revolutionary within the early modern historiography (Baylor 1991; Hill 1962, 1975; Williams 1992). And not without reason: Calvinists have been variously credited with inventing capitalism, fomenting revolution, and promoting democracy (Camic, Gorski, and Trubek 2005; Gorski 1999, 2001, 2006; Marshall 1980, 1982; Walzer 1968); Max Weber accordingly described the Calvinist ethos as one of world mastery and world transformation, terms one does not immediately associate with political conservatism (Weber 2001; Weber, Gerth, and Mills 1964). As for the Baptists, they were tried and convicted of a variety of radical misdeeds, including antinomianism and free love and, later, of pacifism and sectarianism. How then, one wonders, does one start from the Puritan radicals of Cambridge, Massachusetts, in the seventeenth century and arrive at their theological descendants, the conservative Presbyterians of J. Gresham Machen's Westminster Seminary? Or start from the German Anabaptist revolutionary Thomas Müntzer and arrive at the American Baptist conservative Billy Graham?

If the notion that some denominations of American Protestants are both theologically and politically conservative is one source of puzzlement, another is that conservative Protestantism should have come to be seen as something specifically and peculiarly American. In this case, we need only think back a century or so to see just how surprising this state of affairs really is. In 1900, when many of their European counterparts were still desperately clinging to the "marriage of throne and altar," American Protestants had long accepted the separation of church and state, at least as it was then understood (Gaustad 2003; Handy 1991; Rémond 1999). In some countries, such as Norway and the Netherlands, conservative Protestants were going so far as to organize political parties to protect their churches, their schools, and their families against the twin onslaughts of secularism and liberalism (Dunk 1975; Skillen and Carlson-Thies 1982); in Germany, on the other hand, to be Protestant was to be ipso facto conservative. Meanwhile, the temperance movement and other moral crusades championed by many Protestants in the United States attracted equal or greater amounts of support in certain parts of Europe (Gusfield 1986; Hurd 1994, 1996; Young 2006). It was not at all obvious then that the United States would eventually become the global center of conservative Protestantism. This raises an important question, the central question of this chapter: how and in what sense or senses did the majority of American Protestants come to see themselves as conservative?

These are not easy questions to answer. What makes them so slippery is that the terms *conservative* and *Protestant* are not analytical or theoretical categories whose meaning can be fixed by definitional fiat. Rather, they are practical and political terms whose meanings are themselves sources and sites of conflict (Bourdieu 2000). Even within the narrower confines of recent American history, conservative is a polysemous concept, that is, contains multiple dimensions and layers of meaning not necessarily consistent with one another: small government and strong defense, conservation and free markets, strict constructionism and law and economics, biblical literalism and confessionalism, traditional values and libertarianism, and neoconservatism and isolationism. And the meanings become even more varied if we look at the longer sweep of American history. The boundaries of Protestantism have themselves been the subject of ongoing dispute. The old Protestant mainliners, dominated by the New England establishment, were hesitant to accept the holiness and Pentecostal movements of the late nineteenth and early twentieth centuries into their confessional family. Today, the denominations to which these movements gave birth (for example, Nazarenes and Assemblies of God) are at the core of a new and conservative Protestant establishment (Roof and McKinney 1987).

This is not to deny that terms such as conservative and Protestant can acquire relatively stable and widely shared meanings within a given context or community, nor that the words *conservative Protestantism* can serve as a rallying cry or source of solidarity amongst these groups. It is simply to emphasize that shared understandings of the term, to the extent they exist, are the result of considerable symbolic and organizational work, that the resulting constructions are not necessarily logically coherent or politically enduring, and that partisan attempts to project present meanings into the historical past should not be uncritically accepted.

It is not possible to trace these shifts and accretions exhaustively or systematically in a single chapter. I instead enumerate several of the key turning points in the story and identify a few of the key mechanisms that underlie them. In so doing, I invoke cross-national comparisons, for the most part between the United States and the (predominantly) Protestant countries of northern Europe. For reasons of space, these comparisons will necessarily be rather brief and stylized. My goal, then, is modest: I do not pretend to provide definitive answers but instead to sharpen questions and develop hypotheses.

My first task is to construct the object I wish to explain—conservative

Protestantism. To do that, I first need to deconstruct two folk constructions of it.

Deconstructing the Object: Two Tropes of Conservative Protestantism

The sociologist Pierre Bourdieu warned against the dangers of what he
called preconstructed objects of analysis, that is, ones defined before scientific analysis and outside the scientific field (Bourdieu et al. 1991). Conservative Protestantism is a paradigmatic example of such an object. In assessing it, we need to be skeptical of the descriptions given by aggressive
and upbeat salespeople (conservative Protestant leaders) or their disgrun-
tled and resentful neighbors (secularist intellectuals), even, or perhaps especially, if this means being critical of our own preconceptions.

The Covenant-Apostasy-Revival Trope

I begin with the account of conservative Protestantism that the conservative Protestants themselves favor, what I call the covenant-apostasy-
revival trope (CART). The CART recounts American history, and indeed
any history, as a story in three acts: a primordial golden age of religious
faith and social order (covenant), which is followed by a period of religious apostasy and social decline, necessitating an age of religious revival and social restoration. The golden age begins with a founding
agreement between the Christian God and the American people. When
the people fall away from the covenant, God punishes them by with-
drawing his blessings and unleashing his wrath. To win back God's
grace, the people must return to the covenant. The trope is old and enduring. It is rooted in the Old Testament, played a pivotal role in the development of European nationalism, was inserted into the Mayflower
Compact, and has remained a fixture of Protestant narratives about
America ever since (Akenson 1991; Anthony Smith 2003; Tuveson 1968;
Walzer 1985). Today, it can be found in history texts for Christian home-
schoolers, in the jeremiads of Christian nationalist clergymen, and even
in the writings of some conservative Christian historians (Brewer 1905;
DeMar 1995; Kennedy and Newcombe 2005; McDowell and Beliles 1991;
Reed 1996; Rosin 2007; Stevens 2001). It is even accepted by many liberal
secularists, at least insofar as it suggests that conservative Protestantism
is the remnant of a premodern tradition.

The CART generates a number of rather serious problems, which
conservative Protestant authors are often at great pains to resolve—or
conceal. One is political and derives from the claim that America is a
Christian nation. Obviously, this is not simply a statement of sociologi-

cal fact; it is also the enunciation of a political program, a radical program for what is called the re-Christianization of America (Diamond 1995, 1998; Goldberg 2006; Hedges 2006), which is premised, not only on a specific vision of America, but also on a very specific understanding of Christianity, a vision and an understanding that is rejected not only by secular humanists and liberal Protestants, but also by a good number of evangelicals (Boyd 2005; Carter 2000; Hart 2006). Christian nationalists often attempt to gloss over this problem by eliding the distinction between the descriptive and prescriptive senses of the words *Christian* and *nation*. They imply that true Americans are conservative Christians and vice versa.

Where the founding of America as a Christian nation is concerned, the problems are empirical. If the founding is located in Puritan New England, for instance, what are we to make of the middle and southern colonies, especially insofar as they were founded on commercial charters rather than religious covenants? The colonists of early America were not all religious refugees; they included a good many economic opportunists, such as John Smith, and more than a few political radicals, such as Thomas Paine, and this pattern obtains for post–Revolutionary America as well. If the founding is located in the Revolution, a different set of problems arises. There is, first, the simple fact that many of the Founding Fathers can hardly be described as Christians, much less orthodox Christians, whether by contemporary or historical standards (Allen 2006; Holmes 2006; Kramnick and Moore 2005). Nonetheless, a veritable army of amateur historians has mined the words of the founders in search of theistic language—*creation, providence,* and so on—which they present as proof of Christian orthodoxy.

A second and related problem concerns the influence of liberal political philosophy on the laws and institutions of the United States (Bailyn 1992; Wood 1992). If the United States was founded on liberal principles, perhaps more than Christian principles, in what sense can it be considered a Christian nation? Conservative Protestant writers attempt to circumvent this problem by arguing that because liberal theorists like John Locke and Montesquieu were practicing Christians, their philosophies are not liberal but Christian. This is not an argument that liberal political philosophers—aware of the commercial imagery of the social contract—are inclined to embrace, for obvious reasons.

What, finally, of the covenant? To suggest that it was closely observed until 1963 taxes the imagination. What, do we make of Indian removal, the slave trade, and Jim Crow, to name only the most infamous breaches (Bellah 1992)? One could, of course, argue that the 1960s represent only the latest violation, which some more historically informed writers have done (Reed 1996). But what is one to make of the civil rights movement and the desegregation laws? Although some southern Protestants of an earlier generation—the late Jerry Falwell, for example—might have suggested that these laws were of a piece with Roe v. Wade, few of them would be willing to defend such a position today (compare Weisman 1989).

These anomalies have not deterred conservative Protestant social critics from asserting a close connection between the breaking of the covenant and various indicators of social breakdown—illegitimate births, divorce, crime, and so on (Boyd 2005; Kennedy and Newcombe 2005; Pay 1990). Some of this literature uses a prophetic mode of historical interpretation in which obscure events become signs of the times and hidden conspiracies abound. Perhaps the most important feature of these works—and the thing that puts them most sharply at odds with the work of professional historians, religious or secular—is their assumption that the lines of historical and eschatological time must move in parallel with one another, and that the main task of historical interpretation is to divine the connection between them. It might be imagined that this makes such narratives less convincing to their readers. In fact, the opposite is probably true. For an audience familiar with literalist forms of biblical exegesis, and schooled in prophecy seminars, history written in the CART is undoubtedly quite resonant and probably more convincing than the work of professional historians (Boyer 1992).

Whatever its weaknesses as a historiographical schema of early America, the CART provides a strong framework for conservative Protestantism. Like any good social movement frame, it identifies a problem—social decline, its causes—religious apostasy, and its solution—evangelical revival (Snow 1999; Snow et al. 1986). Further, it uses a language of covenant and an interpretation of prophecy that is deeply inscribed in, and highly resonant with, a large segment of the American population (Boyer 1992). Finally, it has built-in bridgeheads to other conservative frames. For example, its emphasis on American exceptionalism and national greatness can easily be bridged with the neoconservative emphasis on unilateralism and militarism. Similarly, its emphasis on individual morality as the true solution to moral problems is compatible with the neoliberal celebration of free market solutions to policy problems as well as with libertarian antistatism, with *personal accountability* the bridging phrase (Budziszewski and Weeks 2006; Gay 1991). Even less effort is required to bridge the conservative version of the CART with the concerns of (secular and Catholic) values conservatives insofar as it emphasizes the importance of natural law and moral absolutes (First Things 2006; George 2001). Last, the quasi-Jeffersonian vision of the real America of small towns and private property resonates strongly with sectional resentments that pit the rural areas of the Heartland, and especially the South, against the secular cultural elites of the big cities and the coasts.

Through the lens of the CART, the current strength of conservative Protestantism needs no explanation. From this perspective, conservatives Protestants are the true heirs and the best guardians of the religious and national traditions of America, and it is foreordained that they should rise again. For them, the real puzzle is their (supposed) weakness. And the villains in the story, naturally, are secular humanists and their liberal and nominally Christian fellow travelers.

The Tradition-Modernity-Secularity Trope

I call the second trope the tradition-modernity-secularity trope (TMST). It should be familiar because it is the dominant narrative in learned and liberal discourse about religion.[1] It frames most academic and progressive discussions, not only of conservative Protestantism, but also of global fundamentalisms (Marty, Appleby, and American Academy of Arts and Sciences 1991). For that reason, some readers may be surprised to see the TMST presented as a folk theory with the same epistemological status as the CART. But the TMST enjoyed a long career as a political slogan that antedates its recent promotion to the rank of a scientific theory (Lübber 2003). A brief review of its changing meanings is enough to illustrate this point. During the Middle Ages, *secular* was a residual term and referred to those things that were not of religion or the church, as in secular education or secular rulers. Its properly political career begins in the Reformation era, albeit under a slightly altered name, when the term *secularization* was used to denote expropriation, specifically, the seizure of church property by the state. During the epic church-state battles of the late nineteenth century, these two meanings were combined and secularization came to mean the removal of various functions or institutions from the control of the church, particularly education and the schools. Secularization, then, was an integral part of the development of the modern research university and the class of worldly priests who inhabit it, and indeed for the autonomy of other fields of cultural production as well (art, literature, music and so on), all of which had been subject to clerical authority and ecclesiastical patronage to one degree or another (Brown 2001; Howard 2006; Marsden 1994; Monod 2002; Ozouf 1963; Reuben 1996; Christian Smith 2003). Academic theories of secularization and modernization were, among other things, an effort to present this outcome as natural and inevitable, which it most assuredly was not. Like the CART, the TMST is therefore an interested account that must be deconstructed and critiqued before a genuinely scientific account of processes of secularization (and religious persistence) can begin.

The arc of the plot inscribed in the TMST is simple enough: it begins with traditional society, which is suffused with religion, and it concludes with modern society, which is thought to be inherently secular. The plot development is driven by an irreconcilable tension between religion and modernization, which is gradually but inevitably resolved in favor of the latter, and irreversibly so. The narrative is flexible, because its key categories—traditional, modern, and secular—are elastic and can be filled with a variety of different contents. For example, the terms *traditional* and *tradition* are often associated or equated with notions like small, simple, unified, community, oppression, supernatural, and irrational. The terms *modern* and *modernity*, on the other hand, are then associated or equated with a series of opposed notions like growth, complex, diverse, individual, freedom, scientific, and rational. The terms refer to two forms or states of social life, which define the beginning and the end of a historical process. That process, the process that drives the plot, is modernization. It too is a highly elastic concept that is typically filled with some subset: economic growth, social differentiation, individualism, liberation, scientific revolution, and industrial revolution. *Secularity*, finally, refers to the consequences of modernization for religious life. It is normally defined as involving one or more of the following: differentiation of church and state, loss of social functions-power, privatization of individual belief-practice, and decline of aggregate levels of belief-practice. It tends to be conceived in negative terms as an absence, a contraction, shrinkage, or a decline.

Because of the rich stock of conceptual elements it contains, the TMST allows for many different opening scenes and chapter headings in the narrative. Some accounts of secularization begin before the birth of Christ, others in the early twentieth century, and many others somewhere in between, with the Protestant Reformation, say, or with one revolution or another—the Copernican, the French, the Industrial, or the Darwinian (Berger 1969; Chadwick 1990; Gilbert 1980; Martin 1978). These historical events can also serve as chapter headings in a multistage account, as can social processes such as urbanization, democratization, or industrialization. Modernization can thus be emplotted around key turning points as well as around cumulative processes.

The TMST is perhaps somewhat less flexible than the CART with regard to plot sequencing. In the CART, reversals and rebellions are an expected and integral part of the plot dynamics. They serve moral renewal and revival and bring the plot closer to a resolution. In the TMST, by contrast, there is no obvious place for backsliding and prodigal sons. It is a triumphalist narrative in which modernization and secularization are expected to move forward together irreversibly.

This is one reason, albeit not the only reason, why the seemingly sudden emergence of the Christian Right caught so many academic observers and political liberals off guard: it violated the plot sequence. Literalist, supernaturalist, traditionalist religion had been slated for extinction. Suddenly, it was back from the grave. What's more, it had company—rude company. The Moral Majority was established in 1978. It was followed by the Iranian Revolution in 1979—a furious one-two punch that threatened to topple the TMST for good.

What to do about this unexpected anomaly? Some concluded that the TMST was fatally flawed. Others sought to stabilize it. They deployed two main lines of argument. The first might be called American anomalism, a variety of American exceptionalism. According to this argument, America is, and always has been, different from Europe, either socially or culturally. Thus we should not be surprised if America diverges from Europe along this dimension (Bruce 1996; Norris and Inglehart 2004). The second evokes a backlash against modernity. According to this argument, modernization can spark counterreactions if it proceeds so rapidly that "backward" and traditional segments of the population do not have enough time to adjust to its demands (Gellner 1994; Wallace 2003).

The first argument contains an element of truth—the relative strength of conservative Protestantism in America does, of course, stem from certain differences in its social and cultural starting point and trajectory. It homogenizes American history, however. It ignores the ebbs in the tides of American religion—the skeptical decades between the Revolution and the Second Great Awakening (Finke and Stark 1992), for instance, or the religious depression of the 1930s and 1940s (Handy 1960; Lankford 1964). It also ignores the unchurched and even irreligious character of the eighteenth-century frontiers and the antebellum South—and thus the anomalous coincidence of tradition and irreligion (Heyrman 1997; Isaac 1982). America was not always and everywhere more religious than Europe.[2]

The second argument—fundamentalism as backlash—also contains an element of truth: conservative Protestantism is partly a reaction to social change. But the concept of modernization is far too blunt an instrument to parse and describe these changes. Conservative Protestantism and other forms of global fundamentalism are not reactions against modernity *tout court*. Their relationship to modern technology, for example, is often positive. And they often embrace more individualistic and textual forms of religiosity (Roy 2004). Indeed, the success of these movements is largely the result of their adept and innovative uses of modern communications technologies (Carpenter 1997; Diamond 1998; Martin 1996). Similarly, many forms of modern political organization and tactics, including political parties, voluntary associations, transnational networks, and single-issue movements, appear to have been invented by religious activists (Kingdon 2000; Koenigsberger 1971; Stamatov 2006; Young 2006).

Given its manifest empirical and conceptual weaknesses, one wonders why the TMST has survived so long and been defended so vigorously. This is all the more puzzling given that modernization theory was jettisoned from most accounts of political and economic development long ago. One answer, I believe, is that it has enabled liberal secularists to conceal the political content of secularization from others and, not least, from themselves, by portraying it as an inevitable and impersonal process, driven by scientific truth rather than as political program driven by group interests (Gorski 2005; Christian Smith 2003). This strategy has been all the more effective to the degree that secularization is conceived as the evacuation of religion from the secular realm, rather than the displacement of one form of sacralization (the religious) by another (the secular). But as a number of social theorists, political philosophers, and postmodern theologians have forcefully argued, secularity is itself a religious formation, albeit an antitranscendental and inner-worldly one, insofar as it invests certain objects (the individual, reason, science, and so on) with a sacred status (Asad 1993; Davis, Milbank, and Zizek 2005; Milbank 2006; Owen 2001; Schmitt 2005). One need not be a cultural relativist to see that the definition of legitimate truth is not the only thing at stake. Also at stake is the distribution of cultural power. When conservative Protestants rage against the power of cultural elites and secular humanists who, they believe, would destroy tradition and religion but offer nothing to replace them, they are only half wrong.

This is not the only thing that perpetuates the TMST, however. Another is the CART. As should be clear by now, they are mirror images of one another. Both agree that modernity is at odds with religion. What they disagree about is the solution. One proposes the recovery of tradition, the other an embrace of secularity. Whatever one may think about the normative issue that is at stake—namely, the proper place of religion in public life—it should be evident that moving out of this hall of mirrors is an important first step toward a clearer understanding of conservative Protestantism. The next section is a first move in this direction.

Reconstructing the Object: Putting Conservative Protestantism in its Space

In the underlying ontology of the CART, conservative Protestantism is tacitly conceived as an unchanging set of religious ideas (a tradition) or a self-reproducing group of religious adherents (a community). It is an unchanging entity that moves through historical time. In the underlying ontology of the TMST, by contrast, conservative Protestantism is represented either as an aged organism that has outlived its normal lifespan or as an anomalous by-product of nonreligious forces that affect some societies and not others. As we have just seen, neither set of assumptions is historically adequate. Contrary to the CART, the ideology and sociology of conservative Protestantism have changed substantially over time.

Conservative Protestantism is not a monad. Neither, however, is it an organism or an epiphenomenon. It does not have a predetermined lifespan. Nor can it be described or explained from a purely externalist perspective. Religious ideas and communities have their own logics and structures.

To address the manifest limitations of the CART and the TMST, what is needed is a conceptual framework that attends to continuity and discontinuity in the history of conservative Protestantism and gives both religious and nonreligious dynamics their due. To this end, I propose that we think of conservative Protestantism as a location within social space through which various religious, social, and political groups and ideas flow. I argue that the size and composition of this flow will be determined, not only by struggles within the religious field, but by the way in which those struggles intersect with dynamics in other fields.

We need to look at conservative Protestantism from three distinct but complementary perspectives: statically as an alliance between certain positions and principles in the religious, political, economic, and demographic spheres of social life; dynamically as an ever-changing flow of socioreligious agents and principles through this location in social space; and comparatively to better understand the reasons why this flow took the shape that it did in the United States. It is to these three tasks that I now turn.

Conservative Protestantism in the United States: A Static View

I begin with the post-1980 portrait of conservative Protestantism in the United States. Let us begin by looking at the sociodiscursive space of interest in religious terms, meaning theological and denominational terms. Although there is naturally some disagreement about who is and is not a true conservative Protestant, among both observers and participants—and inevitably so—theological orthodoxy is stable enough at the moment that the disagreement is not really that great. On my reading, which is in line with most others, one can define an orthodox conservative Protestant as someone who agrees with most (if not necessarily all) of the following three claims (see, for example, Bebbington 1989; Smith and Emerson 1998). First is biblical literalism, namely, that the Bible is a divinely inspired text; to be read literally and historically, not allegorically or mythologically; and thus the creation story in Genesis is a factual description of real events. Second is Arminan soteriology, which maintains that salvation is made possible by Jesus's atonement, freely available to all who choose to accept Christ as their personal savior, and only available to those who experience being born again. Third is premillennialist eschatology, which holds that at the end of days true Christians will be raptured into heaven, those left on earth will undergo a period of tribulation, and Jesus will then return to rule the earth. A heterodox conservative Protestant can be described as someone who has doubts about more than a few of these claims, but also adopts many of them. The term *evangelicals* has become synonymous in popular usage with conservative Protestants, but it requires an additional element of belief and practice, namely, actions to convince others to make a (deeper) commitment to Jesus. For a discussion of the cultural capital of evangelicals, see chapter 1, this volume.

The denominational core of conservative Protestantism is Baptist. Other key constituents include conservative breakaways from mainline or liberal Protestantism (for example, the Missouri Synod of the Lutheran Church or the Presbyterian Churches of America), churches rooted in the holiness tradition (such as Churches or Assemblies of God), Pentecostals, and Mormons (Steensland et al. 2000).[3]

Conservative Protestantism can also be defined in political terms to include all Protestants who espouse a certain political orientation regardless of their theology or affiliation. Here, too, the orthodox meaning of conservative Protestantism is relatively stable at the moment, though not uncontested (Greeley and Hout 2006; Smith 2000; Wilcox and Larson 2006). As is well known, conservative Protestantism is strongly associated with opposition to gay marriage and abortion and, conversely, with support for the traditional family. Conservative Protestants are also typically Republican. As regards economic policy, the results are paradoxical. On the one hand, the individual voting behavior of (denominationally) conservative Protestants is more strongly influenced by their attitudes toward economic inequality than that of other groups. On the other hand, taken as a group, conservative Protestants are more averse to government-led efforts to reduce inequality than other groups (Greeley and Hout 2006). The overlap between religion and politics is far from complete. Politically conservative Protestants can be found in mainline and even liberal denominations. Conversely, politically liberal Protestants, though relatively few in number, can be found in evangelical and fundamentalist denominations.

We can also characterize conservative Protestantism socioeconomically, that is, in terms of class position. The results will depend on whether we begin with a denominational or theological definition. If the former, then conservative Protestants have levels of education, income, and occupational attainment that are lower than most other groups (Greeley and Hout 2006). If the latter, however, the results become decidedly more mixed and ambiguous (Smith 2000). The likely reason is that denominations labeled evangelical or fundamentalist have a sociodemographic profile that skews downward, leading some individuals with conservative Protestant theologies to join mainline and liberal churches with higher social status.

A fourth and final field in which we can fruitfully situate conservative Protestantism is the nation, understood as both a geographical and a discursive space. The distribution of conservative Protestants across geographical space is hardly random. They are most heavily concentrated in the South. Their distribution in discursive space is also skewed. They are not simply more apt to be proud of America than other groups; they are also more apt to be proud of America's political and military influence throughout the world, and to believe that America has a mission to transmit its values and institutions to others. In other words, they are not simply more nationalistic or patriotic; their vision of the nation is one that emphasizes power and influence (Greeley and Hout 2006). Conservative Protestants favor a state that enforces morality and projects power, and oppose a state that redistributes wealth.

Conservative Protestantism in the United States: Dynamic Views

I now look at conservative Protestantism dynamically, emphasizing four episodes of change. These episodes provide substance to my contention that conservative Protestantism is a constructed and historically developing discursive and social space, rather than a timeless monad.

Theology and Class Conflict: The Strange Triumph of Arminianism   Most of what social scientists read and write about the theology of conservative Protestants takes the rise of Protestant fundamentalism as its starting point, and identifies the publication of *The Fundamentals* and the drama of the Scopes trial as the seminal events (Ammerman 1994; Carpenter 1997; Marsden 2006). The key feature of conservative Protestant theology, the object in need of explanation, then becomes its literalist hermeneutics, creationist cosmology, and premillennialist eschatology—the issues that set it apart from the liberal Protestant theology that gradually took hold during the nineteenth century (Dorrien 2001). This framing of the question contains its own answer: conservative Protestantism is portrayed either as a backlash against modernity, the dominant approach and the one favored by less sympathetic observers (Ammerman 1987), or as an act of self-defense in a war on religion, a heterodox approach favored by some more sympathetic observers (Marsden 2006). Both accounts can easily be folded into the overarching narratives of the TMST and the CART.

But if we push the temporal parameters back to the colonial era, the most striking transformation in American Protestantism is a different one: the strange triumph of Arminianism (Conkin 1995; Holifield 2003).

Developed by the seventeenth-century Dutch theologian Jacobus Arminius, and elaborated by John Wesley and others, Arminianism is the view that God's grace is offered to all but accepted by only some. Its triumph is strange, because its universalist and voluntarist soteriology is so radically at odds, not only with the predestinarian theology of the orthodox Calvinists who dominated early New England, but also with the institutionalist and even sacramentalist soteriology of the Anglicans who came to dominate the Middle Colonies. Orthodox Calvinists have not disappeared from the scene, of course. But they have become a small minority. Ironically, they are now a part of an evangelical community dominated by Arminians.

How might we explain this strange triumph? We certainly cannot explain it as a backlash against modernity. After all, what could be more modern than personal transformation and individual choice? It would be more plausible to explain it as a product or even a progenitor of modernity (Turner 2001). A more fruitful line of analysis, however, and one more consonant with the approach developed here, would focus on struggles in the religious field, both within and between the clergy and the laity (Hatch 1989; Heclo et al. 2007; Noll 2002). Simplifying greatly, one could argue that the voluntarism and individualism of Arminian theology was a potent weapon in the hands of heterodox fractions of the clergy and subordinate members of the laity, who allied with one another in a struggle against what came to be called the New England Way and of later coalitions of social, clerical, and sectional elites, such as the northern, liberal Protestantism of the late nineteenth century, the eventual target of the fundamentalist rebellion. One outcome of these struggles is clear: if we understand democracy in the Tocquevillian sense, as egalitarianism in social interaction and cultural norms, then Arminianism has been a democratizing ideology par excellence.

The Arminianization of American Protestantism, and especially of American evangelicalism, is an important chapter in the story of conservative Protestantism and American conservatism more generally. By rejecting the importance of hierocratic mediation and even of divine grace to achieving personal salvation, and highlighting the centrality of individual choice and self-expression, it paved the way toward the current alliance of conservative evangelicals with laissez-faire liberals and anti-statist libertarians.

Cotton Mather Meets the Market: From Moral Economy to Milton Friedman
In his bestselling book, *What's the Matter with Kansas?*, the liberal commentator Thomas Frank argued that the political allegiances of the Republican base are founded on a dubious quid pro quo (2004). Heartland proletarians renounce their material interests in good jobs, good wages, and social welfare; in exchange, politicians reward them with vicious

attacks on so-called cultural elites and high-sounding rhetoric on symbolic issues. In a phrase, the rhetoric focuses not on economic policy, but on "God, guns, and gays." The only real beneficiary, Frank concluded, is corporate capital. The irony was inescapable: what could be more incongruous than an alliance between Jesus's Sermon on the Mount and Milton Friedman's *Free to Choose*?

But compelling as it might seem to liberal secularists, Frank's account would be unconvincing to many conservative Protestants. For them, free markets are not at odds with Christian religion; indeed, although critical voices are by no means absent (Clapp 1996), many religious conservatives would argue that Christianity and capitalism go hand in glove (Budziszewski and Weeks 2006; Gay 1991; Johnson 1990; Novak 1982; Sacks 2000; Stark 2005). Max Weber noted the historical affinity between the Protestant ethic and the utilitarian ethic more than a century ago (2001). This affinity has not disappeared. Consider the similarities between mainstream neoliberal economics and contemporary evangelical theology. Both emphasize the selfish instincts of natural man, both are suspicious of government, and both emphasize that an individual's ultimate fate is and ought to be the result of personal choices. All that separates evangelicalism and utilitarianism, one might argue, is the matter of pleasure.

To assert such affinities between evangelicalism and neoliberalism is not to deny tensions as well. In colonial New England, it was precisely the tensions that were emphasized. There, the ideal was not unfettered capitalism but what was known as the godly commonwealth, a society in which church and state were jointly responsible for regulating economy and morality, and the untrammeled commercialism that prevailed in other parts of the New World was viewed with suspicion and even horror (Appleby 2001; Bushman 1967; Innes 1995; Wuthnow and Scott 1997). The economic world envisioned by Cotton Mather was governed, not by the laws of supply and demand, but rather by norms of fair wages and just prices.

The real question, then, is not Frank's question—why benighted heartlanders sacrificed their interests for their religion—but Weber's, namely, how and why conservative Protestant thinkers reconciled their theology with the market. The answer is not, as some charge, that conservative Protestants have ceased to care about social and economic justice. Indeed, there is evidence that they care more about these issues than most liberals do (Brooks and Wilson 2007; Davis and Robinson 1999, 2001). Instead, the question is why they have come to reject government-led solutions to them. The answer has multiple strands, including the triumph of Arminianism. Another may be the fundamentalist-modernist split during the Progressive era in the choice of conservative Protestants to concentrate on the saving of individual souls against the choice of liberal Protestants to embrace the communalism of the social gospel movement. Another part of the answer no doubt lies in the expansive interpretations of separation of church and state developed by the American judiciary beginning with the incorporation of the Fourteenth Amendment in 1940 and building toward the IRS action against Bob Jones University in the early 1970s. These actions directly threatened the conservative Protestant subculture that had grown up following the Scopes trial, which indirectly threatened the place of Protestantism in public culture more generally.

Denominations and Parties: Congregationalists and Baptists Trade Spaces
No two denominations provide more instruction concerning the denominational instability of conservative Protestantism than the Congregationalists and the Baptists. Both have been mobile, one leftward, the other rightward. Indeed, one could say that they have traded sociodiscursive spaces, at least in the United States. The Baptists began as an upstart heterodoxy with affinities for political radicalism both in the colonial period and during the early Republic (McLoughlin 1971). Today, they are the core denomination of the Christian Right (Ammerman 1990). The Congregationalists took the reverse trajectory. Having begun as the established orthodoxy, at least within New England, they evolved into a bulwark of liberal heterodoxy, with strong affinities for the left (Youngs 1998).[4]

I cannot provide a full accounting for the political mobility of Baptists and Congregationalists here. What I can do is suggest mechanisms that would figure prominently in any such accounting. One is partisan realignment around new issues (Formisano 1971; Formisano and Burns 1984; Kleppner 1970, 1987; Manza and Brooks 1997; Swieringa 1990). Here, one naturally thinks of the role of social welfare and economic redistribution in the New Deal coalition and its capture of liberal Protestants. Another is the entry of new groups into the religious and cultural fields. Here, one thinks of the way in which the rapid expansion of nonclerical and nonreligious intellectuals (the scientific, managerial, and professional elites) had on the theological dispositions of upper-crust Protestant clergymen in the late nineteenth and early twentieth centuries, particularly in the intellectual centers of the Northeast.

This narrative, in turn, fits into the larger epoch of regional and partisan realignments: the GOP, once dominant in and dominated by the North and especially the Northeast, comes to be dominant in and dominated by the South, with the reverse development for the Democratic Party. The epoch is a complex one, of course, with many plots and players. There is the racial subplot, involving the movement of African Americans into the Democratic Party, and the movement of southern whites out of it. There is the economic subplot, involving the deindustrialization of the North and migration to the Sun Belt. But the religious subplot just outlined is an important one as well, and one which has received far less attention. And if the organizational strength and demographic vigor of the Southern Baptists and other conservative Protestants is one reason for the ascendance of a Republican South, then certainly the demographic weakness and internal decline of mainline Protestantism is one reason for the decline of a Republican North and political liberalism more generally.[5]

Thus, chapter headings in a narrative about the rightward drift of Baptists—especially Southern Baptists—might include abolition, the Fundamentals, and civil rights (Kleppner 1981; Swieringa 1990) Those for the Congregationalist story might include industrialization, the social gospel, liberal theology, and the New Deal (Carter 1971; Conn 1950; Gorrell 1988; Hopkins 1982). The cover of such a book might juxtapose two images: McCain-Palin lawn signs in a Texas RV park and Obama-Biden lawn signs in front of a Greenwich mansion.

Nationalism and Sectionalism: New England and the Old South Trade Places
Shortly after George W. Bush's victory in the 2004 presidential election, a remarkable map began to circulate depicting a new country, BlueUSA, that covered the states of the Northeast, the Upper Midwest, and the West Coast that had voted for John Kerry. For at least a few weeks, there was even some talk, however unserious, about secession (Jack Hitt, "Neo-Secessionism." *New York Times Magazine*, December 12, 2004).[6] The irony was intentional, and it was hard to miss. The new map of red and blue states was remarkably similar to the old map of Confederate and Union states, but with sectional and national symbolism reversed. The sectional South had become the heart of the heartland, the most nationalist part of the nation. Old New England, meanwhile, had gone from being the most unionist part of the Union, the most Protestant part of a Protestant nation, to become its most cosmopolitan and secular region.

What explains this remarkable reversal? To the extent they have addressed it, social scientists have emphasized the conflicts of the Vietnam era and the realignments of the Reagan era. By this account, the conquest of the Democratic Party by cosmopolitan liberals—also known as the McGovernites—was the chief cause of the migration of working-class patriots—first labeled the Silent Majority and later the Reagan Democrats—to the Republican Party (Phillips 1970, 2006).

Although there is certainly some truth to this explanation, it places too great an onus on the 1970s. Most important, at least for us, it fails to explain how and when southerners became patriots. It wasn't always so. The South has long had a strong regional identity, but this identity was originally sectionalist rather than nationalist. This identity was rooted in a religion of the Lost Cause, a Protestant-influenced civil religion with its own rituals and symbols, its own monuments and martyrs, a religion marked, furthermore, by a deep ambivalence toward the Union that was not fully overcome until at least the Spanish-American War (Foster 1987; Stout 2006; Wilson 1983). During World War I, many conservative Protestant evangelicals advocated isolationism and pacifism; it was the liberals who wrapped themselves in the flag (Marsden 2006). It was the heat of World War II that fused Christianity, democracy, and patriotism in the evangelical mind, and the chill of the cold war that hardened the new compound (Heclo et al. 2007). And it was the civil rights movement and Vietnam protest that completed the process as Northerners and mainliners completed their transformation into antimilitarists and cosmopolitans (Friedland 1998).

Conservative Continuities: Religious Nationalism, Calvinist Moralism, Public Activism   So far, I have highlighted a series of discontinuities in the historical trajectory of conservative Protestantism. Naturally, there are continuities as well, some of which stretch back to the colonial era—and beyond.

One is Christian nationalism. By this I mean a blending of Christian and patriotic narratives and iconography that blurs or erases the line between religious and political community and identity. Sometimes it takes a relatively diffuse form, as when Christian and American symbols (such as a cross and a flag) are juxtaposed with one another, establishing an implied equivalence (for example, good Christian = good American). At other times, it takes a more explicit one, as in the common claim that America has been chosen to play a leading role in the eschatological drama, that it has a special mission to spread Christianity and democracy to the rest of the world (Smith 1994; Tuveson 1968). It has taken liberal scholars and commentators a long time to notice the prevalence of Christian nationalism among conservative Protestants. Perhaps that is why they often claim that it is new. They are mistaken. Although Christian nationalism may have experienced a resurgence of late, it has certainly not been an instance of emergence. Christian nationalism has been around for a very long time and has been a robust feature of American political discourse (Cherry 1998). It is in fact older than the Republic. The notion that the American people are a chosen people and the New World a New Israel is implicit in the language of the Mayflower Compact, which speaks of the Puritan emigration as an "errand in the wilderness" and famously urges the settlers to construct a "city on a hill."[7]

A second area of continuity is a strong emphasis on—indeed, an obsession with—sexual morality. There is nothing specifically American about this obsession, however much European and Europhile intellectuals like to believe that there is. But there is definitely something quite Calvinist about it (Gorski 2003). Virtually all Christian communities have regulated sexuality to one degree or another, as, for that matter, have most non-Christian religions. Still, the Geneva Calvinists and their sectarian offspring were more concerned with disciplining sexuality than their confessional competitors, and that Puritan strain in conservative Protestant ethics has remained to this day.

Cross-denominational public activism is a third area of continuity that deserves emphasis. American Protestants have excelled in creating activist, cross-denominational organizations to promulgate their ideals in public life. These skills have enabled them to exert greater influence in the political process. Although much has been said about the role such organizations have played in the rise of the post-1960s Christian Right—from the Moral Majority through the Christian Coalition to Focus on the Family—commentators have often failed to notice that the only thing new about these organizations is their name. From the missionary societies through the abolitionist crusade to the temperance movement, cross-denominational, single-purpose organizations have been staples of Protestant politics in the United States—and not only in the United States (Young 2006). Nor is congressional lobbying by religious conservatives new. Protestant activists played a major role in the invention of lobbying over 100 years ago (2002; for an historical analysis of cross-denominational activism, see Peter Dobkin Hall, volume 2, chapter 8).

Conservative Protestantism in the United States: Comparative Views

One of the puzzles about conservative Protestantism in the United States is how it has come to have the shape it has. I have discussed some of the ways in which the sociological occupants and ideological contents of conservative Protestantism have, and have not, shifted. I also identified some of the mechanisms and conjunctures that produced these shifts and helped give conservative Protestantism the specific form it has today. Some of the most important mechanisms include competition between clergy for followers and resources, partisan mobilization and electoral realignments, political alliances between religious and secular movements and groups, and sectional rivalries and identities. Key conjunctures—moments when these mechanisms aligned to produce significant change—include the 1920s and the 1870s as well as the 1960s.

The other puzzle is why conservative Protestantism is so much stronger in the United States than in other historically Protestant countries. It is tempting to conclude that the United States has always been different in this regard—tempting, but mistaken. If we look back to the second half of the nineteenth century, we find that conservative Protestants were a powerful force in many northern European polities. In England, the Liberal Party was dominated by Protestant dissenters who used it to push an aggressive agenda of social and moral reform. In imperial Germany, conservative Protestants were aggressive champions of military spending, national greatness and colonial expansion, initially through liberal parties and later through conservative ones. In the Netherlands, Abraham Kuyper's Calvinistic Anti-Revolutionary Party aggressively opposed the secularization of public education and championed what are now called family values. In Sweden, evangelical Protestants were an important fraction within the Social Democratic Party, which proved an aggressive champion of temperance. Nor have these movements disappeared, but they have shrunk—drastically—as has organized Christianity more generally. If we wish to understand why conservative Protestantism is so strong in the United States, then we must first try to understand why organized Christianity in general is so strong in the United States. That is the task I take up in this final section.

I follow the lead of several prominent historians and sociologists, especially David Martin (1978) and Hugh McLeod (1997, 2000), who direct our attention to competitive and cooperative relations between Christian churches, state elites, and social classes. I also go beyond them by emphasizing other factors as well, including global geopolitics, political parties, national identity, and demography. Together, these factors can help us account for the particular patterns of unchurching found in northern Europe, and consequently provide a valuable lens through which to understand the distinctiveness of American Protestantism. Rather than beginning with a long list of hypotheses or predictions based on the values of variables, I offer a series of case studies *en miniature*, which better allow me to highlight the role of interactions between institutions and groups in society and the timing of these interactions. These interactions and sequences are at the heart of my approach.

Sweden

Let us begin with what is, from our perspective, a particularly extreme case: Sweden. Today, Sweden is the most unchurched country in the Christian world. For most of the twentieth century, conventional Christian belief and practice among Swedes have declined across cohorts as well as within cohorts through time (Hamberg 1991). The historical evidence suggests that the de-Christianization of Sweden began in the late eighteenth century amongst educated liberals and spread to the urban working classes in the late nineteenth century (Bäckström 1984; Lenhammar 1998). Today, surveys consistently find that fewer than 50 percent of Swedes believe in God, and that only 3 or 4 percent attend church regularly (Hamberg 2003; Tomasson 2002). Most do still belong to the Church of Sweden, however, and most Swedish children are still confirmed by the church. Interestingly, the only social groups that still display significant degrees of individual piety are immigrants (Hamberg and Runblom 1999). In summary, the typical pattern in contemporary Sweden is well captured in the phrase "belonging without believing."

In Sweden, as in the other Nordic lands, the state has exerted an extraordinary degree of administrative control over the Swedish church ever since the Reformation (Murray 1961; Ryman 2005). Swedes did not have the sort of individual religious freedoms granted to Americans by the First Amendment until the 1950s (Alwall 2000), and the Swedish church was not formally disestablished until 2000 (Gustafsson and Swensson 2003; Wångmar 2004). Until quite recently, church officials were essentially civil servants. They were not only appointed and paid by the state; they also served as de facto state administrators at the local level. There was also considerable overlap between the clerical and social elites, a pattern that continued until well into the twentieth century (Nilsson 2005). The result was that evangelical and progressive segments of the Swedish population, both bourgeois and working-class, became increasingly estranged from the Swedish church, which was perceived as a bulwark of clerical domination and political conservatism (Gustafsson 1953; Thyssen 1969). This estrangement took a variety of forms. Some established pietistic, lay circles within the church; others joined evangelical, free churches outside it; and still others broke with Christianity altogether (Hansson 1960; Kjellberg 1994).

This hardly explains the belonging without believing pattern. It does not explain why the evangelical movement withered. Nor does it explain why so many Swedes remained formal members of the church. There were other mechanisms and conjunctures that were critical in producing the Swedish outcome. One is emigration (Ljungmark and Westerberg 1979). The evangelical movement in Sweden was never as large as its sister movements in the United Kingdom and the United States, partly because the Swedish church and the Swedish state put so many obstacles in its way, at least until the 1870s. Its ranks were further depleted by emigration, which included many Swedish dissenters, both leaders and the rank and file (Wikén 1984). Another was the religious policy of the Social Democrats toward the Church of Sweden, which followed the *Godfather* maxim: "hold your friends close, hold your enemies closer." By holding the Church of Sweden very close, by refusing to grant it full autonomy, and by maintaining a tight hold over religious life more generally, the Social Democrats were able, not only to prevent the Church of Sweden from becoming a serious political rival, but also to stunt the growth of a Christian subculture outside it (Gustafsson and Dahlgren 1985; Murray 1961). At the same time, they succeeded in keeping their (religious) friends close by favoring liberals and liberal theology within the Church of Sweden and perhaps also by adhering to the ethical precepts of liberal Christianity. A third factor is the link between Swedish Lutheranism and national identity. However irrelevant it may be for the everyday life of most Swedes, the Church of Sweden is still widely regarded as an important source of the national character (Blückert 2000; Harmati 1984). As such, it remains a moral authority of sorts, but one consulted only in times of collective crisis or tragedy. Although contemporary Sweden is certainly unchurched, it is not necessarily anti-Christian. The dominant attitude is indifference, not hostility. The fourth and final factor is overseas missions or, rather, the lack thereof. Sweden's era of empire ended in the seventeenth century. It therefore had no natural mission fields. And insofar as the mission fields of empires served as the training grounds for inner missions to burgeoning urban populations, Sweden was not well equipped to transplant Christianity into the industrial era. Most of Sweden's missionary energies were spent in raising the flag on the Great Plains of the United States rather than planting crosses in Africa or in the great cities of the homeland. Taken together, these mechanisms and conjunctures go far toward explaining the Swedish situation of belonging without believing, and unchurching without anti-Christianity.

A summary comparison of Sweden with the United States highlights the importance of each of these factors for the reproduction of churchly Christianity. The contrast between the two cases is a sharp one. Consider church-state-society relations. Even in New England, establishment was relatively short lived. And though the relationship between the New England elite and the "Presbygational" and Unitarian clergy was tight, the authority of the clerical establishment was under constant challenge from uneducated prophets and entrepreneurial ministers. Consequently, the history of American Christianity has been, among other things, a history of sectarian schisms and individual questing, that resulted in an unprecedented level of religio-cultural pluralism even before mass immigration from central, southern, and eastern Europe. As regards immigration, it not only increased religious pluralism; it increased religious vitality as well, and for two reasons. First was that some immigrants came for religious reasons. Second was that immigrants generally tend to become more religious once they arrive in the United States, in part because churches provide a uniquely rich source of sociability, respectability, and social capital for immigrants, and in part because belonging often leads to believing. Missions and revivals are also a central part of the American story. America has never lacked for missions fields: first was the frontier, then the rest of the world. Expertise and personnel developed in these external missions provided an invaluable resource for internal missions. Although fin-de-siècle missionaries often bemoaned the religious state of the nation's cities, the truth is that they had little to complain about. Their jeremiads may have had motivational value, but not descriptive (Butler 1997).

Of course, there are parallels between Sweden and the United States, too. Like the Swedes, many Americans weave a religious strand into their national identity. The strand has grown larger if fuzzier over time: first it was Protestant, then Christian, and now Judeo-Christian. The strand does not spin itself, of course. Rather, it is spun by religious and political activists, who use it to tie together otherwise diverse groups and identities into a tight partisan bundle—in recent years, a Republican one. There are few abstractions capable of catching so many people— *freedom* and *prosperity* are perhaps the other ones—but probably none that can bind them so tightly.

Germany

An approach focusing on interactions and timing also gives considerable purchase on other cases. Take Germany, for instance. Aggregate levels of Christian observance in Germany are somewhat greater than in Sweden, though considerably lower than in the United States. The difference between Germany and Sweden is largely, if not entirely, due to greater levels of observance among German Catholics. For German Protestants, the story is similar, if not identical, to the Swedish. The similarity lies in the area of church-state-society relations. Following the Reformation, Germany became a multiconfessional society, embracing not only Catholics and Lutherans, but various other types of Protestants as well, particularly Calvinists and Baptists (Schilling 1988). But most of the post-Reformation polities were religiously homogeneous—and became more so over time—and Germany as a whole (including Austria) was relatively evenly divided between Protestants and Catholics. This situation changed in the 1870s when Prussia politically unified Germany to the exclusion of Catholic Austria and religiously unified German Protestants under Berlin.

From this point on German Protestants found themselves in much the same situation as their Swedish coreligionists: confronted with a state church that was closely allied with conservative social elites and tolerated little dissent from within or without. The result was much the same as well: the state church lost the hearts of the reformist bourgeoisie and the urban working classes beginning in the late nineteenth century. The difference lay in the relationship between religious movements, political parties, and the Bismarck regime. As is well known, Otto von Bismarck staged the *Kulturkampf* to shore up support for the new German state and for his conservative regime. By demonizing Catholics and Social Democrats as enemies of the nation and the state, he forged a coalition between middle-class Protestants, economic liberals, and conservative agrarians.

As a result of his policies, the German trajectory diverged from the Swedish in at least three, closely interrelated, and highly consequential ways. First was the emergence of a tight-knit, Catholic subculture with a strong regional anchoring, such as Bavaria, and eventually to the formation of a Catholic political party, the Center Party (Gross 2004; Lönne 1986). Second was a deepening of anticlerical currents amongst political progressives, and a deep and long-lasting rupture between the Social Democrats and the Christian Churches (Hölscher 1989). Third was a tight bond between conservative Protestant and ultranationalist organizations that mutated in an anti-Semitic direction, such as Adolf Stoecker's Christian Social Party, and persisted into the Nazi era (Dreyfus 1996; Pulzer 1988). If, and to what degree, Bismarck's policies set the German state in the direction of the Nazi Party is, of course, much debated (Groh 1983; Hobson 1989; Kocka 1988). What is certain is that the failure of the Third Reich dealt a mortal blow to German nationalism and dissolved its bond with German Protestantism, which came to be dominated by theological and political liberals during the post–World War II era (Heimerl 1990; Vollnhals 1989).

The Netherlands

In the Netherlands and England, organized Christianity survived much longer, but collapsed more precipitously, beginning in the 1960s (Knippenberg 1992). The reasons it survived longer are similar to the reasons it still survives in the United States: pluralism, immigration, missions, and nationalism. In the Netherlands, the Reformation settlement yielded a high degree of religious diversity and a system of partial disestablishment (Israel 1995). The Dutch Reformed Church did enjoy some legal privileges and was closely allied with the House of Orange (Deursen 1974, 1991). But its position was much weaker than that of the Protestant churches of Germany and Sweden. The urban patriciate—the socially and politically dominant class in most of the Netherlands—tended to be suspicious of the Reformed clergy, whom they regarded as busybodies and reactionaries (Kaplan 1995). De facto religious tolerance and economic opportunity drew many refugees and immigrants to the Netherlands up to the nineteenth century, further diversifying an already pluralistic religious landscape (de Vries 1984; Lucassen 1987; Lucassen and Penninx 1997). The Netherlands also had a strong tradition of missions and revivals as well, because of both its overseas empire and its pietistic heritage (Kluit 1970). And the socioeconomic transformations of the nineteenth century were, in any event, less disruptive to religious life in the Netherlands than elsewhere, because the Netherlands urbanized long before it industrialized (Vries and Woude 1997). There, industrial revolution did not necessitate the kinds of mass resettlements it precipitated in other countries. Dutch democratization also reinforced organized Christianity. The dominance of liberalism among the country's social and political elites sparked a populist counterreaction that took a religious form, first Protestant, then Catholic (Kroef 1948; Langley 1995). These defensive movements quickly gave rise to political parties, and the Protestant and Catholic parties went on to dominate Dutch politics until World War I. This made it impossible for Dutch socialists to claim the populist mantle all for themselves, and prevented the fusion of radicalism and anticlericalism that emerged elsewhere in northern Europe, particularly in Wilhelmine Germany. The parties, however, were merely the parliamentary arms of self-contained, sociocultural milieux that encompassed everything from newspapers and radio stations to soccer clubs and choral societies (Blom and Talsma 2000; Groot 1992; Lijphart 1968). They were full-service organizations, megachurches writ large, which bound their members together by interest as much as by ideology.

Precisely why this "pillarized" or "consociational" system collapsed during the 1960s is a matter of some dispute, but collapse it did, as did organized Christianity shortly thereafter. From the perspective developed here, three developments appear to have been key. First was the increasing secularization of social provision, which removed a major material incentive for membership in a religious community (Lechner 1996). Second was the emergence of new political parties, which destabilized the consociational system and weakened the religious parties. Third was the spread of more individualistic and expressive values in the wake of the counterculture, which challenged the communitarian ethos of the pillarized society (Ester, Halman, and Moor 1993). In sum, the strength of the Dutch churches derived from the strength of the Dutch pillars, and when the pillars crumbled, the fate of the churches was sealed.

England

Finally, I briefly consider the British case. The pattern of unchurching in the United Kingdom is similar to, if less extreme than, the pattern in the Netherlands—late and precipitous, though less so in both respects (Currie, Gilbert, and Horsley 1977). Much the same might be said of Britain's Reformation settlement: more establishment and less pluralism. The privileges of the Church of England were greater, its position less contested, the number of sectarians smaller, the number of Catholics smaller still, at least outside of Ireland. But disaffection from the Anglican church was counterbalanced by several factors, all quite powerful.

One was the existence of a large and dynamic evangelical sector, well-schooled in missionary work through the British Empire, and well-versed in revivalist techniques, which it helped invent and then perfect (Lewis 1986; McIlhiney 1988; Stout 1991). Another was the close connection between ethnic, political and religious identity in Scotland and, even more so, in Ireland (Claydon and McBride 1998; Pope 2001). Last was immigration, particularly of Irish Catholics to English cities, which not only increased religious diversity but strengthened the Catholicism of the immigrants (Gallman 2000).

For these reasons, nineteenth-century England did not experience the degree of unchurching that Sweden and Germany did. But the English churches did not fare as well as the Dutch churches. One important reason is that England never experienced pillarization. Religion and party were, of course, related. Protestant dissenters and Irish Catholics tended to vote for the Liberals and, later, for Labor; Anglicans, on the other hand, were typically Tories (Lawrence and Taylor 1997). Although the parties did have ancillary organizations, they did not give rise to self-contained subcultures of the Dutch variety.

An Analytical Framework on Processes of Unchurching

Having illustrated my approach to the problem of unchurching in a narrative form, let me now restate it in more analytical terms. I begin by making explicit its two major assumptions, reproduction and reinforcement.

Consider reproduction. Whereas secularization theorists assume that organized religion naturally declines, I assume the reverse, namely, that organized religion naturally reproduces itself, all else equal. But I also assume that religious reproduction is a social process that occurs through a variety of mechanisms: parents and families, social networks and ritual communities, religious leaders and churches, and so on. My explanations for unchurching therefore focus on social changes that disrupt the operation of such mechanisms (such as urbanization, industrialization, state formation, democratization, and so on), but also on the organizational capacities of religious communities to respond effectively to such disruptions (for example, through missions and revivals). From this perspective, we would expect that variations in religious observance would be positively related with the degree of social disruption, on the one hand, and negatively related to the degree of organizational capacities.

The concept of reinforcement directs our attention to the way in which religious interests (for example, in otherworldly salvation) and identities can become intertwined with, or opposed to nonreligious interests (for example, economic, cultural, or political) or identities (for example, ethnic, national, or regional). The assumption here is that religious observance is strengthened by positive associations with nonreligious interests and identities and weakened by negative oppositions to them.

This approach does not generate any general laws of religious change that would be valid for all times and places, because I do not believe that such laws exist (Gorski 2008). But it does direct our attention to certain mechanisms of unchurching that may be operating across relatively wide swaths of historical reality. The findings of the case studies indicate several of the most important of these mechanisms:

- The church-state-society mechanism. In democratizing and democratic societies, close ties between religious, political, and social elites tend to generate popular disaffection from the dominant religious institutions and, if there are no alternatives to these institutions, from organized religion per se. The more powerful the dominant religious institution and the more complete its monopoly, the more powerful this mechanism will be.

- The church-party-society mechanism. In democratic polities with partisan competition, participation in organized religion will be strengthened by the integration of churches with ancillary organizations and political parties that provide nonreligious goods. The more expansive and the more centralized the subcultural milieu, the stronger its hold.

- The ethno-regional identity mechanism. Religious observance will be strengthened if, and to the degree that, religious identities are perceived to align with nonreligious identities such as region, race, ethnicity, and nation, and weakened to the degree that such identities fail to align. Clearly, this is one area in which strategic, symbolic work by elites or individuals can be particularly consequential. This mechanism explains the positive effects of immigration on religious observance.

- The urbanization-industrialization-class-formation mechanism. Orthodox secularization theory has rightly insisted that the socioeconomic transformations of the nineteenth century tended to disrupt the reproduction of organized Christianity. But it has not been attentive enough to variations in the degree of disruption, which would be greater when urbanization, industrialization, and proletarianization occurred rapidly and concomitantly, as in Germany, than when they did not, as in the Netherlands.

- The empire-missions-revivals mechanism. One key determinant of how effectively churches responded to these disruptions was previous experience with missionary work, whether on the frontier, in the empire, or both, given that the lessons learned and the people trained in such work can be redeployed to the metropole. Here, too, timing could be critical: Germany's overseas missions in the early twentieth century were of little use in addressing the disruptions of the late nineteenth; the damage had already been done.

Against this background, the peculiar strength of conservative Protestantism and organized religion in the contemporary United States is not at all hard to understand. Indeed, it can be largely accounted for in just a few phrases: early disestablishment of a state church, extreme pluralism in religious competition, mass immigration, development of an evangelical subculture, frontier revivals, overseas missions, Christian nationalism, and partisan mobilization.

Conclusion

I conclude with a final observation about the term *conservative Protestantism*. However different their historical narratives of American history may be, the CART and the TMST do share one fundamental assumption, namely, that conservative Protestantism conserves tradition. But does it? Is conservative Protestantism really conservative? And, if so, in what sense is it conservative?

There is no definitive, scientific answer to the first question. The issue is one for conservative intellectuals and pundits to debate. But it is possible to suggest how the conservativism of contemporary conservative Protestants differs from other articulations of conservatism. We can thereby perform a kind of negative political theology in which we seek to disclose what conservative Protestantism is by noting the things that it is not. In that spirit, I argue that most conservative Protestants do not defend inherited class privilege, advocate authoritarian forms of government, or reject freedom of conscience. On the contrary, their religious forebears played no small role in establishing the relatively egalitarian, democratic, and liberal sociopolitical order that prevails within the former domains of western Christendom. Indeed, it could be argued—rightly, in my view—that this order would not exist without their contribution.

What separates conservative Protestants from political liberals and even from certain conservatives is their understanding of what sustains this order. Generally speaking, conservative Protestants point to individual virtue and divine favor, whereas liberals, religious and secular, are more apt to emphasize institutional structures and human goodness. There are some deep and nonnegotiable disagreements here, as regards the reality of divine Providence and the goodness of human nature. But there is also an area of rapprochement, which any good sociologist should immediately spot: the synergy between good institutions and human virtue, which are, after all, two sides of the same coin. Whether the areas of disagreement or rapprochement become primary, however, is a question of political praxis, not social analysis.

Notes

1. The origins of the secularization paradigm are to be found in the work of Auguste Comte (see Comte and Lenzer 1998). The definitive overviews are Olivier Tschannen's "The Secularization Paradigm: A Systematization" and *Les théories de la sécularisation* (1991, 1992). For historical and theoretical critiques, see Philip Gorski (2005), John Milbank (2006), and Christian Smith (2003).
2. The argument also distorts certain similar elements of European history. For the sake of brevity, consider France, which has a special significance in the American debate. One of the few things that liberal secularists and conservative Christians would probably agree on is that the French Revolution destroyed French Catholicism and hastened the triumph of secularism in Europe. In truth, this is a highly anachronistic and tendentious reading of French history. The post-Revolutionary era witnessed a remarkable efflorescence of French Catholicism, which remained a powerful force in French society until well into the twentieth century (Cholvy 1994, 1995; Cholvy and Hiliare 1986; Gibson 1989; Larkin 1995; Sowerwine 2001).
3. Note that the theological and denomination definitions are not wholly congruent. For example, insofar as they remain orthodox Calvinists, conservative Presbyterians would reject the Armenian soteriology of most evangelical denominations. Baptists, on the other hand, may be skeptical of Pentecostal soteriology insofar as it insists on baptism in the Holy Spirit. Further, many conservative Protestants do not regard Mormons as Christians. This list of divisions could easily be expanded, and the potential for discord based on these divisions should not be underestimated.
4. Since Richard Niebuhr (1929), the changing political orientations of American denominations have usually been explained in terms of an escalator effect (Roof and McKinney 1987). It is an escalator with three steps: a new denomination arises out of a subordinate (social) stratum; as a result of their moral discipline and communal solidarity, members of the domination gradually become more prosperous; and, as a result of their increased prosperity, they eventually become more (politically) conservative. Unfortunately, the escalator mechanism does not account for the trading spaces dynamic. It can explain how a Baptist becomes a Whig (or how a Pentecostal or a Mormon becomes a Republican). But it cannot tell us why a Congregationalist stops being a Federalist (or a why an Episcopalian becomes a Democrat). There are two fundamental problems with the escalator model: economism and reductionism. Social stratification is not limited to the economic field; the religious subfield and cultural and political fields also have their own forms of inequality. Nor can political orientation be reduced to

socioeconomic position; partisan alignment is also influenced by forces from the other subfields. I discuss how one overcomes these deficiencies later.

5. For analysis of the role of demography in the vitality of conservative Protestantism, see chapters 2 and 7, this volume.

6. http://www.nytimes.com/2004/12/12/magazine/12NEO.html.

7. The salience and content Christian nationalism have varied over time. It has been more prominent in certain times of trial, such as the early decades of the Republic, the time of the Civil War, and the early decades of the twentieth century. And its content has evolved as well (Bellah 1992). For example, until recently, it was virulently anti-Catholic (Higham 1965). That has changed in recent years as conservative Protestants have joined forces with conservative Catholics in the battle against secular humanists (Colson 1994). The claims that Americans are God's new chosen people are also heard less frequently. Perhaps this is a concession to the sensitivities of conservative Jews. Nor has Christian nationalism always been the monopoly of conservatives. Until quite recently, it was also a staple of progressive rhetoric—as anyone who has read the speeches of Josiah Strong, William Jennings Bryan, or, for that matter, Woodrow Wilson well knows (Cherry 1998; Tuveson 1968).

References

Akenson, Donald H. 1991. *God's People: Covenant and Land in South Africa, Israel, and Ulster*. Montreal: McGill-Queen's University Press.

Allen, Brooke. 2006. *Moral Minority: Our Skeptical Founding Fathers*. Chicago: Ivan R. Dee.

Alwall, Jonas. 2000. "Religious Liberty in Sweden: An Overview." *Journal of Church and State* 42(Winter): 147–71.

Ammerman, Nancy T. 1987. *Bible Believers: Fundamentalists in the Modern World*. New Brunswick, N.J.: Rutgers University Press.

———. 1990. *Baptist Battles: Social Change and Religious Conflict in the Southern Baptist Convention*. New Brunswick, N.J.: Rutgers University Press.

———. 1994. "North American Protestant Fundamentalism." In *Fundamentalisms Observed*, edited by Martin E. Marty and R. Scott Appleby. Chicago: University of Chicago Press.

Appleby, Joyce O. 2001. "The Vexed Story of Capitalism Told by American Historians." *Journal of the Early Republic* 21(1):1–18.

Asad, Talal. 1993. *Genealogies of Religion: Discipline and Reasons of Power in Christianity and Islam*. Baltimore, Md.: Johns Hopkins University Press.

Bäckström, Anders. 1984. "Nattvardssedens förändring under 1800-talet som uttryck för den religiösa och sociala omvälningen." *Kyrkohistorisk Årsskrift* 140.

Bailyn, Bernard. 1992. *The Ideological Origins of the American Revolution*. Cambridge, Mass.: Belknap Press of Harvard University Press.

Barton, David. 1992. *The Myth of Separation*. Aledo, Tex.: Wallbuilders.

Baylor, Michael G. 1991. *The Radical Reformation*. Cambridge: Cambridge University Press.

Bebbington, David W. 1989. *Evangelicalism in Modern Britain: A History from the 1730s to the 1980s*. London: Unwin Hyman.

Bellah, Robert Neelly. 1992. *The Broken Covenant: American Civil Religion in Time of Trial*. Chicago: University of Chicago Press.

Berger, Peter L. 1969. *The Sacred Canopy: Elements of a Sociological Theory of Religion*. Garden City, N.Y.: Doubleday.

Blom, J. C. H., and J. Talsma. 2000. *De verzuiling voorbij: Godsdienst, stand en natie in de lange negentiende eeuw*. Amsterdam: Het Spinhuis.

Blückert, Kjell. 2000. *The Church as Nation: A Study in Ecclesiology and Nationhood*. New York: Peter Lang.

Bourdieu, Pierre. 2000. *Pascalian Meditations*. Cambridge: Polity.

Bourdieu, Pierre, Jean C. Chamboredon, Jean Claude Passeron, and Beate Krais. 1991. *The Craft of Sociology: Epistemological Preliminaries*. New York: Walter de Gruyter.

Boyd, Gregory A. 2005. *The Myth of a Christian Nation: How the Quest for Political Power Is Destroying the Church*. Grand Rapids, Mich.: Zondervan.

Boyer, Paul S. 1992. *When Time Shall Be No More: Prophecy Belief in Modern American Culture*. Cambridge, Mass.: Harvard University Press.

Brewer, David J. 1905. *The United States, A Christian Nation*. Philadelphia, Pa.: Winston.

Brooks, Arthur C., and James Q. Wilson. 2007. *Who Really Cares: The Surprising Truth About Compassionate Conservatism—America's Charity Divide—Who Gives, Who Doesn't, and Why It Matters*. New York: Basic Books.

Brown, Callum G. 2001. *The Death of Christian Britain: Understanding Secularisation, 1800–2000*. London: Routledge.

Bruce, Steve. 1996. *Religion in the Modern World: From Cathedrals to Cults*. Oxford; New York: Oxford University Press.

Budziszewski, Jay, and David L. Weeks. 2006. *Evangelicals in the Public Square: Four Formative Voices on Political Thought and Action*. Grand Rapids, Mich.: Baker Academic.

Bushman, Richard L. 1967. *From Puritan to Yankee: Character and the Social Order in Connecticut, 1690–1765*. Cambridge, Mass.: Harvard University Press.

Butler, Jon. 1997. "Protestant Succes in the New American City, 1870–1920: The Anxious Secrets of Rev. Walter Laidlaw, Ph.D"." In *New Directions in American Religious History*, edited by D. G. Hart and Harry S. Stout. New York: Oxford University Press.

Camic, Charles, Philip S. Gorski, and David M. Trubek. 2005. *Max Weber's Economy and Society: A Critical Companion*. Stanford, Calif.: Stanford University Press.

Carpenter, Joel A. 1997. *Revive Us Again: The Reawakening of American Fundamentalism*. New York: Oxford University Press.

Carter, Paul Allen. 1971. *The Decline and Revival of the Social Gospel; Social and Political Liberalism in American Protestant Churches, 1920–1940*. Hamden, Conn.: Archon Books.

Carter, Stephen L. 2000. *God's Name in Vain: The Wrongs and Rights of Religion in Politics*. New York: Basic Books.

Chadwick, Owen. 1990. *The Secularization of the European Mind in the Nineteenth Century*. New York: Cambridge University Press.

Cherry, Conrad. 1998. *God's New Israel: Religious Interpretations of American Destiny*. Chapel Hill: University of North Carolina Press.

Cholvy, Gérard. 1994. "Sociologists, Historians and the Religious Evolution of France from the 18th Century to the Present." *Modern and Contemporary France* 2(3) : 257–67.

———. 1995. "Déchristianisés? Les ouvriers en France (XIXeme–XXeme siècles)." *Historiens et Géographes* 86:311–19.

Cholvy, Gérard, and Yves-Marie Hiliare. 1986. *Histoire religieuse de la France contemporaine, volume II: 1880–1930.* Paris: Bibliothèque Historique Privat.

Clapp, Rodney. 1996. "Why the Devil Takes VISA." *Christianity Today* 40(11): 18. http://www.christianitytoday.com/ct/1996/october7/6tb018.html.

Claydon, Tony, and Ian McBride. 1998. *Protestantism and National Identity: Britain and Ireland, c. 1650–c. 1850.* New York: Cambridge University Press.

Colson, Charles W. 1994. "Evangelicals & Catholics Together: The Christian Mission in the Third Millennium." *First Things: A Monthly Journal of Religion, Culture, and Public Life* 1994(May): 15–22.

Comte, Auguste, and Gertrud Lenzer. 1998. *Auguste Comte and Positivism: The Essential Writings.* New Brunswick, N.J.: Transaction Publishers.

Conkin, Paul Keith. 1995. *The Uneasy Center: Reformed Christianity in Antebellum America.* Chapel Hill: University of North Carolina Press.

Conn, Howard. 1950. *Congregationalism and the Social Gospel: A Statement of Personal Point of View.* Minneapolis, Minn.: Plymouth Congregational Church.

Currie, Robert, Alan D. Gilbert, and Lee Horsley. 1977. *Churches and Churchgoers: Patterns of Church Growth in the British Isles Since 1700.* Oxford: Clarendon Press.

Davis, Creston, John Milbank, and Slavoj Zizek. 2005. *Theology and the Political: The New Debate.* Durham, N.C.: Duke University Press.

Davis, Nancy J., and Robert V. Robinson. 1999. "Their Brothers' Keepers? Orthodox Religionists, Modernists, and Economic Justice in Europe." *The American Journal of Sociology* 104(6): 1631–665.

———. 2001. "Theological Modernism, Cultural Libertarianism and Laissez-Faire Economics in Contemporary European Societies." *Sociology of Religion* 62(Spring): 23–50.

DeMar, Gary. 1995. *America's Christian History.* Powder Springs, Ga.: American Vision.

Deursen, Arie Theodorus van. 1974. *Bavianen en Slijkgeuzen: kerk en kerkvolk ten tijde van Maurits en Olde[n]barnevelt.* Assen: Van Gorcum.

———. 1991. *Plain Lives in a Golden Age: Popular Culture, Religion, and Society in Seventeenth-Century Holland.* Cambridge: Cambridge University Press.

Diamond, Sara. 1995. *Roads to Dominion: Right-Wing Movements and Political Power in the United States.* New York: Guilford Press.

———. 1998. *Not by Politics Alone: The Enduring Influence of the Christian Right.* New York: Guilford Press.

Dorrien, Gary J. 2001. *The Making of American Liberal Theology: Idealism, Realism, and Modernity, 1805–1900.* Louisville, Ky.: Westminster John Knox Press.

Dreyfus, François-Georges. 1996. "Religion, nation et nationalisme dans le monde allemand de 1850 a 1920 " *Revue d'Allemagne* 28:17–30.

Dunk, Hermann Walter von der. 1975. "Conservatisme in vooroorlogs Nederland." *Bijdragen en Mededelingen betreffende de Geschiedenis der Nederlanden* 90:15–37.

Ester, Peter, Loek Halman, and Ruud A. de Moor. 1993. *The Individualizing Society: Value Change in Europe and North America.* Tilburg, Netherlands: Tilburg University Press.

Finke, Roger, and Rodney Stark. 1992. *The Churching of America, 1776–1990: Winners and Losers in Our Religious Economy.* New Brunswick, N.J.: Rutgers University Press.

Formisano, Ronald P. 1971. *The Birth of Mass Political Parties, Michigan, 1827–1861.* Princeton, N.J.,: Princeton University Press.

Formisano, Ronald P., and Constance K. Burns. 1984. *Boston, 1700–1980: The Evolution of Urban Politics.* Westport, Conn.: Greenwood Press.

Foster, Gaines M. 1987. *Ghosts of the Confederacy: Defeat, the Lost Cause, and the Emergence of the New South, 1865 to 1913.* New York: Oxford University Press.

Frank, Thomas. 2004. *What's the Matter with Kansas? How Conservatives Won the Heart of America.* New York: Metropolitan Books.

Friedland, Michael B. 1998. *Lift Up Your Voice like a Trumpet: White Clergy and the Civil Rights and Antiwar Movements, 1954–1973.* Chapel Hill: University of North Carolina Press.

Gallman, J. Matthew. 2000. *Receiving Erin's Children: Philadelphia, Liverpool, and the Irish Famine Migration, 1845–1855.* Chapel Hill: University of North Carolina Press.

Gaustad, Edwin S. 2003. *Church and State in America.* New York: Oxford University Press.

Gay, Craig M. 1991. *With Liberty and Justice for Whom? The Recent Evangelical Debate over Capitalism.* Grand Rapids, Mich.: W. B. Eerdmans.

Gellner, Ernest. 1994. *Conditions of Liberty: Civil Society and Its Rivals.* London: Hamish Hamilton.

George, Robert P. 2001. *The Clash of Orthodoxies: Law, Religion, and Morality in Crisis.* Wilmington, Del.: ISI Books.

Gibson, Ralph. 1989. *A Social History of French Catholicism, 1789–1914.* London: Routledge.

Gilbert, Alan D. 1980. *The Making of Post-Christian Britain: A History of the Secularization of Modern Society.* New York: Longman.

Goldberg, Michelle. 2006. *Kingdom Coming: The Rise of Christian Nationalism.* New York: W. W. Norton.

Gorrell, Donald K. 1988. *The Age of Social Responsibility: The Social Gospel in the Progressive Era, 1900–1920.* Macon, Ga.: Mercer University Press.

Gorski, Philip S. 1999. "Calvinism and Democracy: Populism, Pacification and Resistance in the Dutch Republic, 1555–1787." In *Breakup, Breakdown, Breakthrough: Germany's Torturous Path to Modernity,* edited by Carl Lankowski. New York: Berghahn.

———. 2001. "Calvinism and Revolution: The Walzer Thesis Re-Considered." In *Meaning and Modernity: Religion, Polity and Self,* edited by Richard Madsen, Ann Swidler, and Steven Tipton. Berkeley: University of California Press.

———. 2003. *The Disciplinary Revolution: Calvinism and the Rise of the State in Early Modern Europe.* Chicago: University of Chicago Press.

———. 2004. "The Poverty of Deductivism: A Constructive Realist Model of Sociological Explanation." *Sociological Methodology* 34(1): 1–33.

———. 2005. "The Return of the Repressed: Religion and the Political Unconscious of Historical Sociology." In *Remaking Modernity: Politics, History and Sociology*, edited by Julia Adams, Elisabeth Clemens, and Ann Shola Orloff. Durham: Duke University Press.

———. 2006. "The Little Divergence: The Protestant Ethic and Economic Hegemony in Early Modern Europe." In *The Protestant Ethic Turns 100: Essays on the Centenary of the Weber Thesis*, edited by Lutz Kaelber and Richard Swatos. Boulder, Colo.: Paradigm.

———. 2008. "Social 'Mechanisms' and Comparative-Historical Sociology: A Critical Realist Approach." In *Frontiers of Sociology*, edited by Björn Wittrock and Peter Hedström. Leiden: Brill.

Greeley, Andrew M., and Michael Hout. 2006. *The Truth About Conservative Christians: What They Think and What They Believe*. Chicago: University of Chicago Press.

Groh, Dieter. 1983. "Le "Sonderweg" de l'histoire allemande: Mythe ou realité?" *Annales: Economies, Sociétés, Civilisations* 38(5): 1166–187.

Groot, Frans. 1992. *Roomsen, rechtzinnigen en nieuwlichters: verzuiling in een Hollandse plattelandsgemeente, Naaldwijk 1850–1930*. Hilversum: Uitgeverij Verloren.

Gross, Michael B. 2004. *The War Against Catholicism: Liberalism and the Anti-Catholic Imagination in Nineteenth-Century Germany*. Ann Arbor: University of Michigan Press.

Gusfield, Joseph R. 1986. *Symbolic Crusade: Status Politics and the American Temperance Movement*. Urbana: University of Illinois Press.

Gustafsson, Berndt. 1953. *Socialdemokratien och kyrkan, 1881–1890*. Stockholm: Svenska kyrkans diakonistyrelses bokförlag.

Gustafsson, Göran, and Curt Dahlgren. 1985. *Religiös förändring i Norden 1930–1980*. Malmö: Liber.

Gustafsson, Göran, and Gerd Swensson. 2003. "Church-State Separation Swedish Style." *West European Politics* 26(1): 51–72.

Habermas, Jürgen. 2006. "Religion in the Public Sphere." *European Journal of Philosophy* 14(1): 1–25.

Hamberg, Eva M. 1991. "Stability and Change in Religious Beliefs, Practice, and Attitudes: A Swedish Panel Study." *Journal for the Scientific Study of Religion* 30(1): 63–80.

———. 2003. "Christendom in Decline: The Swedish Case." In *The Decline of Christendom in Western Europe, 1750–2000*, edited by Hugh McLeod and Werner Ustorf. Cambridge: Cambridge University Press.

Hamberg, Eva M., and Harald Runblom. 1999. "Invandrare i ett sekulariserat samhälle: Religiös förändring bland sverigeungrare." *Kyrkohistorisk Årsskrift* 71.

Handy, Robert T. 1960. "The American Religious Depression, 1925–1935." *Church History* 29(1): 3–16.

———. 1991. *Undermined Establishment: Church-State Relations in America, 1880–1920*. Princeton, N.J.: Princeton University Press.

Hansson, Sven. 1960. "Kyrko-och Ambetsfrågan vi den inre Missionens Framträdande i Sverige vid Mitten av 1800-Talet." *Kyrkohistorisk Årsskrift* 60:98–126.

Harmati, Bela. 1984. *The Church and Civil Religion in the Nordic Countries of Europe*. Geneva: LWF Studies.

Hart, Darryl G. 2006. *A Secular Faith: Why Christianity Favors the Separation of Church and State*. Chicago: I. R. Dee.

Hatch, Nathan O. 1989. *The Democratization of American Christianity*. New Haven, Conn.: Yale University Press.

Heclo, Hugh, Mary Jo Bane, Michael Kazin, and Alan Wolfe. 2007. *Christianity and American Democracy*. Cambridge, Mass.: Harvard University Press.

Hedges, Chris. 2006. *American Fascists: The Christian Right and the War on America*. New York: Free Press.

Heimerl, Daniela. 1990. "Evangelische Kirche und SPD in den fünfziger Jahren." *Kirchliche Zeitgeschichte* 3(1): 187–200.

Heyrman, Christine Leigh. 1997. *Southern Cross: The Beginnings of the Bible Belt*. New York: Alfred A. Knopf.

Higham, John. 1965. *Strangers in the Land; Patterns of American Nativism, 1860–1925*. New York: Atheneum.

Hill, Christopher. 1962. *Puritanism and Revolution: Studies in Interpretation of the English Revolution of the 17th Century*. London: Mercury Books.

————. 1975. *The World Turned Upside Down: Radical Ideas During the English Revolution*. New York: Penguin Books.

Hobson, Rolf. 1989. "Slutten på den tyske Sonderweg? Keiserrikkets Historiografi og forbundsrepublikken går nye veier." *Historisk Tidsskrift* 68: 303–32.

Holifield, E. Brooks. 2003. *Theology in America: Christian thought from the age of the Puritans to the Civil War*. New Haven, Conn.: Yale University Press.

Holmes, David L. 2006. *The Faiths of the Founding Fathers*. New York: Oxford University Press.

Hölscher, Lucian. 1989. *Weltgericht oder Revolution: Protestantische und sozialistische Zukunftsvorstellungen im deutschen Kaiserreich*. Stuttgart: Klett-Cotta.

Hopkins, Charles Howard. 1982. *The Rise of the Social Gospel in American Protestantism, 1865–1915*. New York: AMS Press.

Howard, Thomas A. 2006. *Protestant Theology and the Making of the Modern German University*. New York: Oxford University Press.

Hurd, Madeleine. 1994. "Liberals, Socialists, and Sobriety: The Rhetoric of Citizenship in Turn-of-the-Century Sweden." *International Labor and Working-Class History* 45(March): 44–62.

————. 1996. "Education, Morality, and the Politics of Class in Hamburg and Stockholm, 1870–1914." *Journal of Contemporary History* 31(4): 619–50.

Innes, Stephen. 1995. *Creating the Commonwealth: The Economic Culture of Puritan New England*. New York: W. W. Norton.

Isaac, Rhys. 1982. *The Transformation of Virginia, 1740–1790*. Chapel Hill: University of North Carolina Press.

Israel, Jonathan Irvine. 1995. *The Dutch Republic: Its Rise, Greatness, and Fall, 1477–1806*. New York: Oxford University Press.

Johnson, Paul. 1990. "The Capitalism and Morality Debate." *First Things: A Monthly Journal of Religion, Culture, and Public Life* 1990(March): 18–22.

Kaplan, Benjamin J. 1995. *Calvinists and Libertines: Confession and Community in Utrecht, 1578–1620*. New York: Oxford University Press.

Kennedy, D. James, and Jerry Newcombe. 2005. *What If America Were a Christian Nation Again?* Nashville, Tenn.: Thomas Nelson.

Kingdon, Robert M. 2000. "The Protestant Reformation as a Revolution: The Case of Geneva." *Journal of the Historical Society* 1(2–3): 101–8.

Kjellberg, Knut. 1994. *Folkväckelse i Sverige under 1800-talet: uppkomst och genombrott*. Stockholm: Carlsson Bokförlag.

Kleppner, Paul. 1970. *The Cross of Culture: A Social Analysis of Midwestern Politics, 1850–1900*. New York: Free Press.

———. 1981. *The Evolution of American Electoral Systems*. Westport, Conn.: Greenwood Press.

———. 1987. *Continuity and Change in Electoral Politics, 1893–1928*. New York: Greenwood Press.

Kluit, Marie Elisabeth. 1970. *Het Protestantse réveil in Nederland en daarbuiten 1815–1865*. Amsterdam: Paris.

Knippenberg, Hans. 1992. *De religieuze kaart van Nederland: omvang en geografische spreiding van de godsdienstige gezindten vanaf de Reformatie tot heden*. Assen: Van Gorcum.

Kocka, Jürgen. 1988. "German History before Hitler: The Debate About the German 'Sonderweg.'" *Journal of Contemporary History* 23(1): 3–16.

Koenigsberger, Helmut G. 1971. *Estates and Revolutions: Essays in Early Modern European History*. Ithaca, N.Y.: Cornell University Press.

Kramnick, Isaac, and R. Laurence Moore. 2005. *The Godless Constitution: A Moral Defense of the Secular State*. New York: W. W. Norton.

Kroef, Justus M. van der. 1948. "Abraham Kuyper and the Rise of Neo-Calvinism in the Netherlands." *Church History* 17(4): 316–34.

Langley, McKendree R. 1995. "Emancipation and Apologetics: The Formation of Abraham Kuyper's Anti-Revolutionary Party in the Netherlands, 1872–1880." Ph.D. diss., Westkminster Theological Seminary, Philadelphia.

Lankford, John. 1964. "The Impact of the Religious Depression Upon Protestant Benevolence, 1925–1935." *Journal of Presbyterian History* 42(2): 104–23.

Larkin, Maurice. 1995. *Religion, Politics, and Preferment in France Since 1890: La Belle Epoque and Its Legacy*. New York: Cambridge University Press.

Lawrence, Jon, and Miles Taylor. 1997. *Party, State, and Society: Electoral Behaviour in Britain Since 1820*. Aldershot, Hampshire: Scolar Press.

Lechner, Frank J. 1996. "Secularization in the Netherlands?" *Journal for the Scientific Study of Religion* 35(3): 252–64.

Lenhammar, Harry. 1998. "The Christianization of America and the De-Christianization of Europe, Particularly of Sweden, in the 19th and 20th Centuries." *Kirchliche Zeitgeschichte* 11:41–50.

Lewis, Donald M. 1986. *Lighten their Darkness: The Evangelical Mission to Working-Class London, 1828–1860*. New York: Greenwood Press.

Lijphart, Arend. 1968. *Verzuiling, pacificatie en kentering in de Nederlandse politiek*. Amsterdam: J. H. de Bussy.

Ljungmark, Lars, and Kermit B. Westerberg. 1979. *Swedish Exodus*. Carbondale: Southern Illinois University Press.

Lönne, Karl-Egon. 1986. *Politischer Katholizismus im 19. und 20. Jahrhundert*. Frankfurt-am-Main: Suhrkamp.

Lübber, Hermann. 2003. *Säkularisierung. Geschichte eines ideenpolitischen Begriffs*. Munich: Verlag Karl Alber Freiburg.

Lucassen, Jan. 1987. *Migrant Labour in Europe, 1600–1900: The Drift to the North Sea*. London: Croom Helm.

Lucassen, Jan, and Rinus Penninx. 1997. *Newcomers: Immigrants and Their Descendants in the Netherlands 1550–1995*. Amsterdam: Het Spinhuis.

Manza, Jeff, and Clem Brooks. 1997. "The Religious Factor in U.S. Presidential Elections, 1960–1992." *American Journal of Sociology* 103(1): 38–81.

Marsden, George M. 1994. *The Soul of the American University: From Protestant Establishment to Established Nonbelief*. New York: Oxford University Press.

———. 2006. *Fundamentalism and American Culture*. New York: Oxford University Press.

Marshall, Gordon. 1980. *Presbyteries and Profits: Calvinism and the Development of Capitalism in Scotland, 1560–1707*. New York: Oxford University Press.

———. 1982. *In Search of the Spirit of Capitalism: An Essay on Max Weber's Protestant Ethic Thesis*. New York: Columbia University Press.

Martin, David. 1978. *A General Theory of Secularization*. New York: Harper & Row.

Martin, William C. 1996. *With God on Our Side: The Rise of the Religious Right in America*. New York: Broadway Books.

Marty, Martin E., R. Scott Appleby, and American Academy of Arts and Sciences. 1991. *Fundamentalisms Observed*. Chicago: University of Chicago Press.

McDowell, Stephen K., and Mark A. Beliles. 1991. *America's Providential History*. Charlottesville, Va.: The Providence Foundation.

McIlhiney, David Brown. 1988. *A Gentleman in Every Slum: Church of England Missions in East London, 1837–1914*. Allison Park, Pa.: Pickwick Publications.

McLeod, Hugh. 1997. *Religion and the People of Western Europe, 1789–1989*. New York: Oxford University Press.

———. 2000. *Secularisation in Western Europe, 1848–1914*. New York: St. Martin's Press.

McLoughlin, William Gerald. 1971. *New England Dissent, 1630–1833: The Baptists and the Separation of Church and State*. Cambridge, Mass.: Harvard University Press.

Milbank, John. 2006. *Theology and Social Theory: Beyond Secular Reason*. Malden, Mass.: Blackwell Publishing.

Monod, Jean-Claude. 2002. *La querelle de la sécularisation: théologie politique et philosophies de l'histoire de Hegel à Blumenberg*. Paris: Vrin.

Murray, Robert. 1961. *A Brief History of the Church of Sweden: Origins and Modern Structure*. Stockholm: Diakonistyrelsens bokforlag.

Niebuhr, H. Richard. 1929. *The Social Sources of Denominationalism*. New York: Henry Holt and Co.

Nilsson, Ulrika Lagerlöf. 2005. "The Bishops in the Church of Sweden: An Elite in Society During the First half of the 20th Century." *Scandinavian Journal of History* 30(3-4): 308–19.

Noll, Mark A. 2002. *America's God: From Jonathan Edwards to Abraham Lincoln*. New York: Oxford University Press.

Norris, Pippa, and Ronald Inglehart. 2004. *Sacred and Secular: Religion and Politics Worldwide*. New York: Cambridge University Press.

Novak, Michael. 1982. *The Spirit of Democratic Capitalism*. New York: Simon and Schuster.

Owen, J. Judd. 2001. *Religion and the Demise of Liberal Rationalism: The Foundational Crisis of the Separation of Church and State.* Chicago: University of Chicago Press.

Ozouf, Mona. 1963. *L'École, l'Église et la République, 1871–1914.* Paris: A. Colin.

Pay, Marty. 1990. *Downfall: Secularization of a Christian Nation.* Green Forest, Ariz.: New Leaf Press.

Phillips, Kevin P. 1970. *The Emerging Republican Majority.* Garden City, N.Y.: Anchor Books.

———. 2006. *American Theocracy: The Peril and Politics of Radical Religion, Oil, and Borrowed Money in the 21st Century.* New York: Viking.

Pope, Robert. 2001. *Religion and National Identity: Wales and Scotland c. 1700–2000.* Cardiff: University of Wales Press.

Pulzer, Peter G. J. 1988. *The Rise of Political Anti-Semitism in Germany & Austria.* London: P. Halban.

Reed, Ralph. 1996. *Active Faith: How Christians are Changing the Soul of American Politics.* New York: The Free Press.

Rémond, René. 1999. *Religion and Society in Modern Europe.* Malden, Mass.: Blackwell Publishers.

Reuben, Julie A. 1996. *The Making of the Modern University: Intellectual Transformation and the Marginalization of Morality.* Chicago: University of Chicago Press.

Roof, Wade Clark, and William McKinney. 1987. *American Mainline Religion: Its Changing Shape and Future.* New Brunswick, N.J.: Rutgers University Press.

Rosin, Hanna. 2007. *God's Harvard: A Christian College on a Mission to Save America.* Orlando, Fl.: Harcourt.

Roy, Olivier. 2004. *Globalized Islam: The Search for a New Ummah.* New York and Paris: Columbia University Press and the Centre d'Etudes et de Recherches Internationales.

Rushdoony, Rousas John, and Intercollegiate Society of Individualists. 1978. *This Independent Republic: Studies in the Nature and Meaning of American History.* Fairfax, Va.: Thoburn Press.

Ryman, Björn. 2005. *Nordic Folk Churches: A Contemporary Church History.* Grand Rapids, Mich.: William B. Eerdmans.

Sacks, Jonathan. 2000. "Markets and Morals." *First Things: A Monthly Journal of Religion, Culture, and Public Life* 2000(August): 23–28.

Schilling, Heinz. 1988. "Die Konfessionalisierung im Reich: Religiöser und gsellschaftlicher Wandel in Deutschland zwischen 1555 und 1620." *Historische Zeitschrift* 246:1–45.

Schmitt, Carl. 2005. *Political Theology: Four Chapters on the Concept of Sovereignty.* Chicago: University of Chicago Press.

Skillen, James W., and Stanley W. Carlson-Thies. 1982. "Religion and Political Development in Nineteenth-Century Holland." *Publius* 12(3): 43–64.

Smith, Anthony D. 2003. *Chosen Peoples: Sacred Sources of National Identity.* Oxford: Oxford University Press.

Smith, Christian. 2000. *Christian America? What Evangelicals Really Want.* Berkeley: University of California Press.

———. 2003. *The Secular Revolution: Power, Interests, and Conflict in the Secularization of American Public Life.* Berkeley: University of California Press.

Smith, Christian, and Michael Emerson. 1998. *American Evangelicalism: Embattled and Thriving*. Chicago: University of Chicago Press.

Smith, Tony. 1994. *America's Mission: The United States and the Worldwide Struggle for Democracy in the Twentieth Century*. Princeton, N.J.: Princeton University Press.

Snow, David A. 1999. "1998 PSA Presidential Address: The Value of Sociology." *Sociological Perspectives* 42(1): 1–22.

Snow, David A., E. Burke Rochford Jr, Steven K. Worden, and Robert D. Benford. 1986. "Frame Alignment Processes, Micromobilization, and Movement Participation." *American Sociological Review* 51(4): 464–81.

Sowerwine, Charles. 2001. *France Since 1870: Culture, Politics and Society*. New York: Palgrave.

Stamatov, Peter. 2006. "The Religious Origins of Modern Long-Distance Humanitarianism: England, 1780–1880, in Comparative Perspective." Ph.D. diss., Yale University.

Stark, Rodney. 2005. *The Victory of Reason: How Christianity Led to Freedom, Capitalism, and Western Success*. New York: Random House.

Steensland, Brian, Jerry Z. Park, Mark D. Regnerus, Lynn D. Robinson, W. Bradford Wilcox, and Robert D. Woodberry. 2000. "The Measure of American Religion: Toward Improving the State of the Art." *Social Forces* 79(September): 291–324.

Stevens, Mitchell L. 2001. *Kingdom of Children: Culture and Controversy in the Homeschooling Movement*. Princeton, N.J.: Princeton University Press.

Stout, Harry S. 1991. *The Divine Dramatist: George Whitefield and the Rise of Modern Evangelicalism*. Grand Rapids, Mich.: William B. Eerdmans.

———. 2006. *Upon the Altar of the Nation: A Moral History of the American Civil War*. New York: Viking.

Swieringa, Robert P. 1990. "Ethnoreligious Political Behavior in the Mid-Nineteenth Century: Voting, Values, Cultures." In *Religion and American Politics*, edited by Mark Noll. New York: Oxford University Press.

Taylor, Charles. 2006. "Religious Mobilizations." *Public Culture* 18(2): 281–300.

Thyssen, Anders Pontoppidan. 1969. *Väckelse och kyrka i nordiskt perspektiv*. Copenhagen: G. E. C. Gad.

Tomasson, Richard F. 2002. "How Sweden Became So Secular." *Scandinavian Studies* 75(1): 61–88.

Tschannen, Olivier. 1991. "The Secularization Paradigm: A Systematization." *Journal for the Scientific Study of Religion* 30(4): 395–415.

———. 1992. *Les théories de la sécularisation*. Genève: Droz.

Turner, Bryan S. 2001. "Cosmopolitan Virtue: On Religion in a Global Age." *European Journal of Social Theory* 4(2): 131–52.

Tuveson, Ernest Lee. 1968. *Redeemer Nation: The Idea of America's Millennial Role*. Chicago: University of Chicago Press.

Vollnhals, Clemens. 1989. *Evangelische Kirche und Entnazifizierung, 1945–1949*. München: R. Oldenbourg.

Vries, Jan de. 1984. *European Urbanization, 1500–1800*. Cambridge, Mass.: Harvard University Press.

Vries, Jan de, and A. M. van der Woude. 1997. *The First Modern Economy: Success,*

Failure, and Perseverance of the Dutch Economy, 1500–1815. New York: Cambridge University Press.

Wallace, Andy. 2003. "Reason, Society and Religion." *Philosophy & Social Criticism* 29(5): 491–515.

Walzer, Michael. 1968. *The Revolution of the Saints: A Study in the Origins of Radical Politics*. New York: Atheneum.

———. 1985. *Exodus and Revolution*. New York: Basic Books.

Wångmar, Erik. 2004. "Sambandet mellan kyrklig och kommunal indelning 1863-1999 [The relationship between the church and municipal division]." *Kyrkohistorisk Årsskrift* 104: 61–81.

Weber, Max. 2001. *The Protestant Ethic and the Spirit of Capitalism*. London: Routledge.

Weber, Max, Hans Heinrich Gerth, and C. Wright Mills. 1964. *From Max Weber: Essays in Sociology*. New York: Oxford University Press.

Weisman, Charles A. 1989. *America: Free, White & Christian*. Apple Valley, Minn.: Weisman Publications.

Wikén, Erik. 1984. "New Light on the Erik Janssonists' Emigration, 1845–1854." *Swedish-American Historical Quarterly* 35(July): 221–38.

Wilcox, Clyde, and Carin Larson. 2006. *Onward Christian Soldiers? The Religious Right in American Politics*. Boulder, Colo.: Westview Press.

Williams, George Huntston. 1992. *The Radical Reformation*. Kirksville, Mo.: Sixteenth Century Journal Publishers.

Wilson, Charles Reagan. 1983. *Baptized in Blood: The Religion of the Lost Cause, 1865–1920*. Athens: University of Georgia Press.

Wood, Gordon S. 1992. *The Radicalism of the American Revolution*. New York: Alfred A. Knopf.

Wuthnow, Robert, and Tracy L. Scott. 1997. "Protestants and Economic Behavior." In *New Directions in American Religious History*, edited by Harry S. Stout and D. G. Hart. New York: Oxford University Press.

Young, Michael P. 2006. *Bearing Witness Against Sin: The Evangelical Birth of the American Social Movement*. Chicago: University of Chicago Press.

Youngs, J. William T. 1998. *The Congregationalists*. Westport, Conn.: Greenwood.

PART II

EVANGELICALS AND INTERGROUP RELATIONS

Chapter 4

Exploring the Traditionalist Alliance: Evangelical Protestants, Religious Voters, and the Republican Presidential Vote

JOHN C. GREEN

M ANY JOURNALISTS and pundits rediscovered the political impact of religion in the 2004 presidential election. For one thing, they noted a strong vote for George W. Bush from white evangelical Protestants. But at the same time they found a strong backing for the Republicans from voters who reported attending worship services once a week or more often, a phenomenon called the religion gap or God gap. Both these patterns appeared to be central to Bush's campaign strategy (Green 2007, chap. 1). A *New York Times* report explained it this way:

> The Republicans used their [national] convention to court deeply religious voters among two different, traditionally Democratic groups, Roman Catholics and Jews, by holding rallies for supporters of each faith yesterday.... Although Evangelical Protestants have become a core part of the Republican base over the last three decades, pollsters say *traditionalists* among all faiths are likely to support the Republicans' stance on social issues, if the party can speak to them on their own terms. In a close election, no minority is too small to pursue, not even the small Orthodox Jewish minority. ("Republicans Court Catholics and Jews," September 3, 2004, emphasis added)

Observers saw clear evidence of these voting patterns when they poured over the 2004 exit polls. Table 4.1 illustrates what they found,

Table 4.1   **Religious Groups and the Two-Party Presidential Vote, 2004**

	Bush	Kerry
White Evangelical Protestants, weekly worship attenders	82.5	17.5
White Evangelical Protestants, less observant	71.9	28.1
White Catholics, weekly worship attenders	61.8	38.2
Other Christians, weekly worship attenders	60.3	39.7
White Mainline Protestants, weekly worship attenders	57.3	42.7
White Catholics, less observant	53.2	46.8
White Mainline Protestants, less observant	52.3	47.7
ALL	**51.6**	**48.4**
Other Christians, less observant	40.4	59.6
Unaffiliated, nonattenders	26.9	73.1
Other Faiths, weekly worship attenders	24.1	75.9
Other Faiths, less observant	19.6	80.4
African American Protestants, weekly worship attenders	16.9	83.1
African American Protestants, less observant	8.5	91.5

Source: Author's compilation based on National Election Pool 2004.

listing the key religious groups in the order of the Bush vote.[1] Bush did indeed enjoy strong support from white evangelical Protestants, but he also won large majorities of weekly attending white Catholics, mainline Protestants, and a composite category of other Christians—the most traditionally religious elements of these religious communities. In fact, weekly worshippers voted more Republican than the less observant in every one of these religious categories, including the strongly Democratic groups of African American Protestants and a composite category of other faiths. This attendance gap in the vote was evident even among white evangelicals, with Bush doing especially well among the most traditionally religious, the weekly attenders (Olson and Green 2008).

Taken together, white evangelical Protestants and the weekly attenders in all the other religious affiliations accounted for 50.2 percent of all Bush's 2004 ballots; adding in less observant evangelicals swelled the total to 60.7 percent of the Republican vote. In contrast, the combination of the less observant religious groups and the unaffiliated accounted for 66.3 percent of all the Democratic ballots. These figures were especially impressive given the closeness of the 2004 vote (see table 4.1). It is small wonder then that numerous observers saw in the 2004 results evidence of a new kind of faith-based politics in the United States focused on moral values (Rozell and Das Gupta 2006). White evangelical Protestants certainly played a major role in Bush's reelection, but they were just one part of a broader coalition based on traditional expressions of faith.

This chapter explores the characteristics of this traditionalist alliance at the ballot box, with a special emphasis on the relationships among the potential allies among religious groups. These groups share traditional religiosity, high levels of civic engagement, and a focus on cultural issues. In addition, the alliance extends beyond voters to political activists and leaders. But at the same time, the potential allies display some religious particularism, related social insularity, and diverse political views on noncultural topics. In addition, the alliance does not extend much beyond white Christian communities and all the allies report an unwillingness to compromise on principle. The traditionalist alliance is fundamentally a political alliance, and like many such alliances it can be strong, as in 2004 (and 2000). It also faces significant limitations, as revealed in the 2008 presidential election, when the alliance was weaker (Pew Forum on Religion and Public Life 2008).

Origins and Nature of the Traditionalist Alliance

The presidential vote of religious groups illustrated in table 4.1 may have surprised journalists and pundits, but the development of these groups over the previous thirty years has been well documented by social scientists (Kohut et al. 2000; Layman 2001; Green 2007). Beginning in the 1970s, traditional religious practices and beliefs—apart from affiliation with a religious tradition—began to have an impact on the presidential vote. This pattern was a major change. Religious traditions defined in part by ethnicity and race had been key elements of the major party coalitions throughout most of American history (McCormick 1974). Perhaps the best-known example is from the New Deal era (Kellstedt, Green, et al. 2007), when the Republicans were an alliance of various kinds of mainline Protestants (particularly in the Midwest and Northeast), and the Democrats were an alliance of Catholics, Jews, and evangelical Protestants (especially in the South).

By the late 1980s, the new political impact of traditional beliefs and practices had begun to receive systematic attention from scholars. Robert Wuthnow described these patterns as a restructuring of American religion (1988, 1996), and because disputes over cultural issues (such as abortion and homosexuality) were central to this new structure, James Hunter referred to them as culture wars (1991, 1994). Both accounts identified rival camps within the major religious communities defined by differences in practices and beliefs, with conservatives, orthodox, or traditionalists arrayed against liberals, progressives, or modernists. Thus older religious divisions based on religious traditions, such as between

Catholics and evangelicals, were supplemented by new divisions based on beliefs and practices, such as among the most and least traditionally religious Catholics and evangelicals (Layman and Green 2005).

As a consequence, the major party coalitions were restructured as well: the Republicans began to receive support from the most tradition-ally religious voters in former Democratic constituencies, such as white Catholics, and the Democrats gained among the least traditionally reli-gious voters in former Republican constituencies, such as white main-line Protestants (Green 2009; Layman 2001). By the beginning of the twenty-first century, mainline Protestants had been replaced as the an-chor of the GOP coalition by evangelical Protestants, who were charac-terized by high levels of traditional practice and belief, and in the Demo-cratic coalition Catholics had been superseded by the unaffiliated population, who were characterized by low levels of traditional religios-ity (Green and Dionne 2008).

This traditionalist alliance was one part of a new connection between religion and the presidential vote that developed during the last third of the twentieth century.[2] The Reverend Jerry Falwell described an early vi-sion of this alliance in the Moral Majority: "We are Catholics, Jews, Protes-tants, Mormons, Fundamentalists—blacks and whites. . . . We are Ameri-cans from all walks of life united in one central concern: to serve as a special interest group providing a return to moral sanity in these United States of America" (reprinted in Neuhaus and Cromartie 1987, 113).

Two decades later, Governor Mitt Romney described a slightly differ-ent version of the alliance during his bid for the 2008 Republican presi-dential nomination:

> I love the profound ceremony of the Catholic Mass, the approachability of God in the prayers of the evangelicals, the tenderness of spirit among the Pentecostals, the confident independence of the Lutherans, the ancient tra-ditions of the Jews, unchanged through the ages, and the commitment to frequent prayer of the Muslims. . . . It is important to recognize that while differences in theology exist between the churches in America, we share a common creed of moral convictions. . . . They are not unique to any one denomination. They belong to the great moral inheritance we hold in com-mon. They are the firm ground on which Americans of different faiths meet and stand as a nation, united.[3]

Survey evidence suggests that Falwell's vision was far from a reality in the heyday of the Moral Majority (Wilcox 1992), but, as presented in table 4.1, Romney's vision had more of a factual basis.

The development of this traditionalist alliance raises a number of questions. How far does the alliance extend across America's diverse reli-gious traditions? How much contact do the potential allies have with each other in religious and civic venues? How much do the allies agree politically? Does the alliance extend beyond voters to political activists and leaders? And what are its future prospects? The scholarly literature offers mixed evidence on these questions. Some scholars argue that the alliance is strong and broad, and will eventually grow to include traditionalists in all religious communities. Other are skeptical of many of these conclusions, seeing the alliance as weaker, narrower, and episodic.[4]

Assessing the Traditionalist Allies

To investigate these questions, table 4.2 presents a more precise measure of the potential allies than table 4.1. It lists six categories based on affiliation: the four largest Christian religious traditions in the country and two composite categories. The four Christian groups are white evangelicals, white mainline Protestants, African American Protestants, and white Catholics. The two composite groups are other Christians (which include Mormons, Eastern Orthodox, ethnic and racial minorities among Catholics, evangelical and mainline Protestants) and other faiths (which include Jews, Muslims, Hindus, and Buddhists). These six categories were then divided, using a number of simple measures of religious practice and belief, into traditionalists (respondents with the most traditional practices and beliefs) and the less traditional. The less traditional categories were quite diverse in religious terms but, along with the unaffiliated, serve as a point of comparison with the traditionalists (see the appendix for a detailed description of how these categories were defined). It is worth noting that the traditionalists exist within all religious traditions, and that this label is not a judgment about religious traditions as a whole.

The first column of table 4.2 indicates the size of these religious groups as a percentage of the adult population using the 2004 National Survey of Religion and Politics (see appendix for details). All of these religious categories were relatively small, reflecting in part the great diversity of American religion. The traditionalist groups are a relatively large portion of the religious categories, ranging from more than 50 percent of African American Protestants to about 40 percent of white evangelicals to roughly 25 percent of white Catholics. Taken together, all these groups accounted for about 30 percent of the adult population. A case can be made that less traditional evangelicals should also be included in size estimates of the traditionalist alliance because their voting behavior often resembles their traditionalist coreligionists. If included, the size of the alliance would expand to more than 40 percent of the adult population. But it is important to note that not all evangelicals are traditionalists and that religious variation among them is considerable.

The next three columns of table 4.2 report simple religious measures used to define the traditionalist groups: weekly worship attendance,

Table 4.2   Measuring Religious Traditionalists, 2004

Practice or Belief	Percent Population	Weekly Worship	Religion Important	Believe in Personal God	Preserve Tradition	My Religion True Faith*	Religious Diversity Bad**
Traditionalists							
White Evangelical Protestants	9.8	93.6	79.6	92.6	77.8	49.2	26.4
White Catholics	3.9	90.3	70.3	58.1	69.9	22.5	6.8
Other Christians	4.6	94.5	82.9	79.8	76.1	54.2	16.7
White mainline Protestants	4.2	78.1	57.4	75.1	64.2	27.6	18.2
Other faiths	2.9	46.5	62.4	23.9	60.3	26.2	22.2
African American Protestants	4.8	88.8	78.6	79.1	53.5	41.2	16.4
Less traditional							
White Evangelical Protestants	14.1	40.9	42.6	55.3	46.5	21.9	12.7
White Catholics	11.9	35.4	21.6	22.9	17.6	8.8	8.5
Other Christians	9.0	35.2	38.4	26.3	37.5	26.4	18.8
White mainline Protestants	11.5	17.7	21.8	20.0	21.9	7.7	6.1
Other faiths	3.4	14.7	20.6	2.2	22.9	6.0	10.3
African American Protestants	4.5	32.7	55.1	30.1	28.9	24.8	18.7
Unaffiliated	15.4	0.8	5.3	4.4	*	0.0	15.8
ALL	**100.0**	**43.3**	**41.0**	**40.0**	**43.7**	**23.7**	**14.5**

Sources: Author's compilation based on National Survey of Religion and Politics 2004 (N = 4,000); U.S. Religious Landscape Survey 2007b (N = 35,000); Religion and Diversity Study 2002–2003 (N = 2,910).
Note: * 2007 U.S. Religious Landscape Survey; ** 2002–2003 Religion and Diversity Study.

high religious salience, and certain belief in a personal God. In five of the six traditionalist groups, a majority reported all three measures. The one exception was the other faiths composite group. It could be that worship attendance and theistic belief do not apply as well to the non-Christians in this category, but the relatively high level of religious salience is noteworthy.

Thus the five groups of traditionalist Christians shared a high level of traditional religiosity measured in these basic ways. Nevertheless, some variation existed among the traditionalists. For instance, the composite category of other Christians reported the highest level of weekly worship attendance (94.5 percent), and traditionalist mainline Protestants were markedly lower (78.1 percent). Likewise, traditionalist evangelicals were the most likely to report certain belief in a personal God (92.8 percent), and traditionalist Catholics scored lower (58.1 percent). There was also some variation among the less traditional groups, with the less traditional evangelicals scoring highest on these measures, but still much lower than the traditionalist evangelicals.

The fourth column of table 4.2 offers a modest validation of these categories using a measure not used in their creation: the percentage of each group who agreed that their church or denomination should strive to preserve its traditional beliefs and practices (as opposed to adapting its tradition to current circumstances or adopting new traditions). Majorities of the traditionalist categories agreed with this statement and majorities of the less traditional categories did not. Hence most of the traditionalists were proponents of preserving the traditional practices and beliefs of their faith—evidence of cognitive traditionalism. But here, too, the data show considerable variation among the groups, with traditionalist evangelicals scoring the highest (77.8 percent) and traditionalist African American Protestants the lowest (53.5 percent).

The final two columns of table 4.2 report on two attitudes often associated with traditional religiosity. The first question is a measure of religious particularism, the percentage of each group who agreed that "my religion is the one, true faith leading to eternal life" (as opposed to "many religions can lead to eternal life"). Most traditionalists disagreed with this statement, with just two groups, traditionalist evangelicals and other Christians, having as many as half in agreement. Large majorities of the less traditional groups also disagreed with the statement.[5] One must be careful not to overinterpret these results, given that the question does not tell us how the respondents defined either *religion* or *many faiths*. The results do suggest, however, that the elements of the traditionalist alliance are not strongly committed to an exclusive view of their own particular religion.

The second question is a measure of opposition to religious pluralism, the percentage of each group who saw such pluralism as a bad thing, disagreeing with the statement "religious diversity has been good for America." Only small minorities of any of the traditionalist groups held a negative view of religious pluralism. The low points come with traditionalist evangelicals and traditionalist other Christians, but even there only about 25 percent disagreed. These results must be viewed with caution as well because general support for the idea of religious pluralism may mask intense dislike of particular religious minorities (Wuthnow 2005).[6] Nevertheless, these data suggest that the elements of the traditionalist alliance have a relatively high degree of comfort with religious diversity.

Ecumenical Orthodoxy and the Traditionalist Alliance

The combination of traditional religiosity and less exclusionary views of religion fits well with the appearance of ecumenical orthodoxy among some conservative intellectuals and activists, including evangelical and mainline Protestants, Catholics, and Eastern Orthodox (Oden 2003; see also Hunter 1991, 97–103). On the one hand, this perspective affirms ancient Christian practices and doctrines that have been regarded as orthodox in all these traditions, while respecting the historic diversity among them. On the other hand, it rejects secular orthodoxies that raise doubts about the roots of the Christian traditions and opposes the erosion of religious distinctiveness in the name of pluralism. In this regard, the Eastern Orthodox churches, the present-day keepers of the "grand tradition" of foundational Christian beliefs, have been influential in these efforts, and so has the Roman Catholic Church, the strongest proponents of natural law.

Ironically, the proponents of ecumenical orthodoxy are hostile to modern ecumenism, as embodied by the National Council of Churches and the World Council of Churches. But in some respects, the National Association of Evangelicals, having followed a middle path between fundamentalism and modernism among evangelicals, is a model for ecumenical orthodoxy.[7] Indeed, Thomas Oden noted the importance of evangelicals in these developments, singling out para-church ministries such as Prison Fellowship, World Relief, World Vision, the Billy Graham Evangelistic Association, and Samaritan's Purse as well as journals in which Evangelical intellectuals are prominent, such as *First Things*, *Pro Ecclesia*, *Touchstone*, and *Faith and Freedom* (2003, 63).

Ecumenical orthodoxy has been fostered principally by intellectuals and activists outside of formal denominational structures. An excellent example is *Evangelicals & Catholics Together: Toward a Common Mission* (Colson and Neuhaus 1995, see also 2002), an effort to find common ground among traditional evangelicals and Catholics. Among the key participants were Richard John Neuhaus, a former Catholic priest and editor of *First Things*; Charles Colson, an evangelical writer and founder of the Prison Fellowship; George Weigel, a Catholic writer and official biographer of Pope John Paul II; and James I. Packard, a conservative Anglican theologian. There is evidence of similar religious developments within Judaism (Freedman 2000) and perhaps in a return to tradition in other faiths as well (Jay Tolson, "A Return to Tradition," *U.S. News and World Report*, December 3, 2007).

Ecumenical orthodoxy may seem to be an oxymoron, given the general understanding of the orthodox as the most committed to the particulars of their faith and the ecumenical as the least committed to them (Evans 2006). Indeed, the engagement of evangelical Protestants with ecumenical orthodoxy may be especially puzzling because of the sectarian character of the tradition (Green 2005). In fact, evidence is considerable that religious particularism persists among the most committed evangelical Protestants (Smith et al. 1998), especially among its subtraditions (Wilcox 1992), and also among Catholics (Davidson et al. 1997) and mainline Protestants (Wuthnow and Evans 2002)—not to mention smaller Christians traditions, such as Mormons (Bloomberg and Robinson 1997).[8] Similar internal religious differences are found within American Judaism and Islam.[9]

Social Insularity and the Traditionalist Alliance

Such religious particularism may well set limits on the strength and scope of the traditionalist alliance, and one such limit could be social insularity. Robert Putnam has found that religious communities are an important source of social capital, but that they are more likely to generate bonding social capital, trust and cooperation within religious groups, than bridging social capital, trust and cooperation between religious groups (2000, chap. 4; Bolin et al. 2004). Traditionalists appear to be more involved in bonding capital than bridging capital.

A good illustration of relationships that create bonding social capital is the number of friends within a person's congregation. A 1996 survey found that a majority of all the traditionalist groups reported that half or more of their friends were members of their congregations.[10] In contrast, large majorities of the less traditional groups reported that half or more of their friends were outside their congregation. Here, traditionalist other Christians and traditionalist evangelicals were the most likely to report friendship networks concentrated within their congregations, and traditionalist other faiths were the least likely. These patterns are supported by evidence on joint worship services from the 1998 National Congregations Study, where most respondents reported few such activities involving congregations from a different religious tradition.[11] In a 2000 survey, only a minority of evangelicals and Catholics claimed to have had in-depth conversations with each other or to understand the other's beliefs very well[12] (on the relatively low level of contact between Christians and non-Christians, see Wuthnow 2005, 212–29).

Table 4.3 illustrates this pattern of social insularity with survey data on the religious affiliation of the respondent's personal confidants.[13] More than 70 percent of the confidants of traditionalist evangelicals and mainline Protestants were also Protestants, roughly 10 percent were Catholics, and about 10 percent from all other faiths combined. For traditionalist African American Protestants, 80 percent of the confidants were also Protestants. Unfortunately, these data do not distinguish the various kinds of Protestants among the respondent's confidants, but given the patterns of friendship indicated earlier it seems likely that most were from the same religious tradition as the respondent. Traditionalist Catholics reported a somewhat wider network of confidants, with 74 percent Catholic, about 15 percent Protestants, and roughly 10 percent from all other faiths. Among the four largest Christian traditions, the less traditional members showed more diversity in their confidants than their traditionalist counterparts.

These patterns for friends and confidants fit reasonably well with evidence on interfaith marriage and religious change.[14] Overall, both the traditionalists and nontraditionalists were likely to have a spouse who belongs to the same religious tradition, but the figures were higher for traditionalists. For example, more than 75 percent of traditionalist evangelicals had an evangelical spouse versus about 65 percent among less traditional evangelicals; for white Catholics, the comparable figures were 40 percent and 60 percent, respectively.

However, a more complex pattern holds for reported change in religion since childhood. Traditionalist evangelical and mainline Protestants were more likely to have changed from their childhood religion than their less traditional coreligionists, and were more likely to have changed than Catholics or the other groups. But, overall, most members of all groups belonged to the religious tradition in which they were raised. In addition, these patterns fit with evidence on changing residential patterns that are concentrating like-minded people in the same neighborhoods, based in part on religious traditionalism (Bishop 2008, 176–78).

Evidence on the psychological distance between the traditionalist groups reinforces these patterns. Table 4.4 reports a proximity measure, listing the percentage of each religious group who reported feeling "very close" or "close" to the major traditions.[15] As one might expect, most respondents reported feeling close to their own group. For example, 62 percent of traditionalist evangelicals felt close to evangelical Protestants and the same proportion of traditionalist mainliners felt close to mainline Protestants. Interestingly, only 40 percent of traditionalist African Ameri-

Table 4.3 Exploring the Traditionalist Alliance: Personal Confidants, 2004

	Protestants	Catholics	Jews	Other Religions	Not Religious	Total
Traditionalists						
White Evangelical Protestants	76	9	0	8	7	100
White Catholics	15	74	0	2	9	100
Other Christians	48	39	0	9	4	100
White mainline Protestants	78	10	5	2	5	100
Other faiths	25	18	15	27	15	100
African American Protestants	80	10	0	10	0	100
Less traditional						
White Evangelical Protestants	66	16	1	8	9	100
White Catholics	20	60	5	6	9	100
Other Christians	28	43	2	11	16	100
White mainline Protestants	56	18	2	9	15	100
Other faiths	16	16	36	16	16	100
African America Protestants	72	7	1	12	8	100
Unaffiliated	26	25	3	10	36	100
ALL	**43**	**29**	**4**	**9**	**15**	**100**

Source: Author's compilation based on General Social Survey 2004 (N = 959).

can Protestants felt close to the black Protestants. These figures may reflect the internal denominational diversity of the Protestant traditions. In contrast, 84 percent of traditionalist Catholics reported feeling close to the Roman Catholics. In all cases, however, the traditionalists felt closer to their own religious tradition than their less traditional counterparts, and in the case of the Protestant groups, markedly so.

The most revealing pattern in table 4.4 is the relatively low level of proximity felt by members of religious groups toward those from other faith traditions. For example, just 13.9 percent of traditionalist evangelicals reported feeling close to Roman Catholics and just 14.4 percent of traditionalist Catholics reported feeling close to evangelical Protestants. All of the Protestant traditionalists felt closer to the Protestant traditions than to the other religious traditions, but these figures never reached 50 percent of any group. Even fewer of the less traditional groups claimed to feel close to other religious traditions. By this measure, social insularity is actually a bit lower among the traditionalists than nontraditionalists, despite being relatively high overall.

Was this social insularity reinforced by demographic differences among the traditionalists groups? To address this question, table 4.5 presents the percentage of each group who were female and above the median age, education, and income for the nation as a whole.[16] This evidence shows a mixed pattern, with some demographic factors reinforcing religious differences and others providing a basis for unity between the traditionalist groups. Overall, a majority of traditionalists were female, the largest percentage among traditionalist mainline Protestants, followed by African American Protestants, and then the composite category of other faiths. In all cases, the traditionalists included more women than their less traditional counterparts. So the potential allies in the traditionalist alliance were united in part by gender.

Larger differences appeared among the traditionalists on age, education and income. For instance, the oldest traditionalist groups were mainline Protestants and Catholics (about 70 percent above the median age) and the youngest were the composite categories of other Christians and other faiths (about 30 percent each). With the exception of the other faiths, the traditionalists were always older than their less traditional counterparts. So the potential allies in the traditionalist alliance were united in part by generation.

Traditionalist mainline Protestants and Catholics were the best educated, and the least so were African American Protestants. Interestingly, traditionalist mainline Protestants and Catholics were better educated than their less traditional counterparts, and the two composite categories of other Christians and other faiths were less educated than their counterparts. White evangelicals and black Protestants showed essentially no educational differences by traditionalism. The potential allies in the traditionalist alliance, then, were divided in part by educational attainment.

Table 4.4   Exploring the Traditionalist Alliance: Closeness to Religious Groups

Percent Close, Very Close	Evangelical Protestants	Mainline Protestants	Black Protestants	Catholics	Jews	Not Religious
Traditionalists						
White Evangelical Protestants	62.0	45.5	42.9	13.9	26.7	19.8
White Catholics	14.4	18.5	17.0	84.3	21.4	14.8
Other Christians	26.5	29.0	27.5	36.5	26.5	6.2
White mainline Protestants	39.1	62.4	27.5	21.5	18.5	13.6
Other faiths	14.5	12.3	23.8	24.1	35.7	50.6
African American Protestants	39.2	12.8	40.0	8.4	37.4	18.7
Less traditional						
White Evangelical Protestants	28.9	29.3	19.8	13.5	17.8	13.8
White Catholics	8.3	12.5	9.5	70.6	14.6	9.7
Other Christians	17.8	8.6	11.6	50.9	16.4	11.2
White mainline Protestants	13.3	43.2	17.9	20.1	15.5	17.3
Other faiths	2.1	11.7	6.4	8.0	54.0	51.6
African American Protestants	24.6	9.3	34.6	6.3	22.1	32.1
Unaffiliated	2.1	7.9	7.8	13.0	11.8	49.4
ALL	**22.3**	**25.5**	**20.4**	**29.5**	**20.2**	**22.1**

Source: Author's compilation based on National Survey of Religion and Politics 2000 (N = 3,000).

Table 4.5   Exploring the Traditionalist Alliance: Basic Demography, 2004

	Percent Female	Percent Above Median Age	Percent Above Median Education	Percent Above Median Income
Traditionalists				
White Evangelical Protestants	57.4	56.9	45.0	50.7
White Catholics	57.1	70.0	59.4	56.5
Other Christians	56.7	34.2	43.8	46.3
White mainline Protestants	73.2	70.1	62.2	55.9
Other faiths	60.0	34.1	53.3	46.2
African American Protestants	70.9	48.4	38.6	34.6
Less traditional				
White Evangelical Protestants	51.5	55.5	44.7	44.8
White Catholics	45.5	56.0	56.0	59.4
Other Christians	55.3	30.9	52.8	42.1
White mainline Protestants	53.2	58.3	54.4	52.0
Other faiths	51.9	58.7	74.3	55.6
African American Protestants	53.3	45.4	38.2	36.4
Unaffiliated	43.6	36.2	56.5	46.1
ALL	**53.7**	**50.6**	**51.8**	**48.7**

Source: Author's compilation based on General Social Survey 2004 (N = 2,812).

A similar but weaker pattern held for income. The most affluent traditionalist groups were Catholics and mainline Protestants, and the least
affluent were black Protestants. Here, traditionalist evangelicals, other
Christians, and mainline Protestants were more affluent than their less
traditional counterparts. Meanwhile, among Catholics, other faiths, and
African American Protestants, the traditionalists were less affluent. The
potential allies in the traditionalist alliance, then, were divided in part
by social class.

Thus some key demographic attributes, such as gender and age,
could help foster the traditionalist alliance, whereas other factors, such
as education and income, could hinder it. Traditionalist evangelicals
were generally found toward the center of the potential allies in these regards. Overall, though, demography does not appear to strongly reinforce social insularity among the traditionalists.

Civic Engagement and the
Traditionalist Alliance

In sum, the potential traditionalist allies display some religious particularism and social insularity. These factors, however, do not appear to

have inhibited a high level of civic engagement by the traditionalist groups. For example, although traditionalists' friends and confidants were concentrated within their own religious traditions, most traditionalists also had friends outside of their traditions as well. The 2000 Social Capital Benchmark Survey found that nearly 80 percent of the most traditional evangelicals had a friend with a different religious orientation. The most traditional Catholics and mainline Protestants scored only slightly higher in this regard, and the lowest score, a little under 65 percent, was found among African American Protestants. In this regard, the more traditional adherents differed little from their less traditional coreligionists.[17]

The friendship networks of the most traditional groups were quite diverse in other ways as well, including occupation, social class, and race-ethnicity—patterns that fit well with the demography patterns in table 4.5. Indeed, the most traditional groups appear to have just about the same scores on an index of friendship diversity, scoring modestly higher than their less traditional coreligionists. Other evidence finds that the most traditional groups were all about as likely to report knowing a wealthy person, a corporate CEO, an elected official, or a scientist in a 2000 survey. On these measures, the traditionalists differed little from their nontraditionalist counterparts.[18]

A similar pattern held true for an index of civic participation (activities such as voting, attending meetings, and demonstrating) and an index of formal group involvement (membership in nineteen kinds of groups excluding congregational membership) in the 2000 Social Capital Benchmark Survey. On these two indices of civic engagement, the most traditional groups had relatively high scores, with mainline Protestants leading the way and evangelicals trailing slightly behind. In this regard, the more traditional groups had significantly higher scores than their less traditional coreligionists. As one might expect, if congregational membership is added to the index of formal group involvement, the civic engagement gap between traditionalists and nontraditionalists widens substantially. Finally, the more traditional groups were also more likely to volunteer and make charitable contributions than the less traditional, with mainline Protestants the most active on both counts.

These patterns of civic engagement extend to measures of social distance. Table 4.6 presents the percentage of each religious group who reported being favorable toward a variety of religious communities.[19] Favorability is a more general and public measure of group affect than proximity—after all, one might well have a favorable view of a group to which one does not feel close. It may be that having a favorable attitude is more important to joint action than proximity (Koch 1995).

One point of similarity between the proximity data in table 4.4 and

Table 4.6   Exploring the Traditionalist Alliance: Favorability Toward Religious Groups

Percent Favorable, Very Favorable	Evangelical Protestants	Mainline Protestants	Catholics	Jews	Mormons*	Muslims	Buddhists	Atheists
Traditionalist								
White Evangelical Protestants	80.5	68.4	59.4	75.2	34.8	27.2	17.1	14.9
White Catholics	59.4	67.1	90.9	77.8	60.3	49.0	37.4	20.5
Other Christians	63.4	65.3	70.6	71.8	54.2	55.0	40.6	20.3
White mainline Protestants	59.5	79.0	80.0	76.1	52.9	44.1	39.7	23.2
Other faiths	46.2	67.0	74.5	83.0	42.0	59.0	60.0	40.0
African American Protestants	58.6	61.0	66.2	76.2	47.5	43.3	24.3	7.1
Less traditional								
White Evangelical Protestants	67.6	71.9	73.2	73.7	53.2	40.1	30.7	19.4
White Catholics	44.2	64.8	91.0	74.5	59.2	48.7	41.5	31.5
Other Christians	52.8	53.3	75.9	65.4	54.9	53.3	39.4	30.1
White mainline Protestants	50.2	67.2	75.9	68.3	64.0	39.0	37.6	32.2
Other faiths	34.1	53.5	68.7	66.2	44.0	46.5	46.5	47.5
African American Protestants	56.9	63.8	68.1	63.3	37.8	51.9	34.8	19.0
Unaffiliated	34.3	49.4	60.6	64.9	52.2	50.6	49.2	57.0
ALL	**54.6**	**64.2**	**74.1**	**71.5**	**52.7**	**44.6**	**37.0**	**28.7**

Sources: Author's compilation based on Religion and Public Life Survey 2001 (N = 2,041) and Religion and Public Life Survey 2007 (N = 3,000).
Note: *2007 Pew Research Center Survey.

the favorability data in table 4.6 is that the traditionalist groups tend to also have favorable views of their own religious tradition. For example, 80.5 percent of traditionalist evangelicals have a favorable view of evangelical Christians, and 90.9 percent of traditionalist Catholics view Catholics favorably. A major difference is the relatively high levels of favorability toward the other large traditions, traditionalist evangelicals toward mainline Protestants (68.4 percent) and Catholics (59.4 percent). This level was much larger than that of those who felt close to these traditions (45.5 and 14.4 percent, respectively). In fact, with one exception, the view of evangelicals by traditionalists in the other faiths, a majority of each traditionalist group held a favorable view of the four largest Christians traditions and Jews. Here, the less traditional groups showed a more complex pattern, with Jews and Catholics enjoying the highest favorability ratings, and evangelical Protestants scoring the lowest (Bolce and De Maio 1999).

The traditionalist groups were not, however, uniformly favorable toward all religious groups. Mormons, Muslims, and Buddhists each received low scores, as did atheists. Traditionalist evangelicals had the least favorable views of these groups, ranging from 34.8 percent favorable toward Mormons to 14.9 percent toward atheists. Most other traditionalists showed a similar pattern across the groups, but at a somewhat higher level. For instance, traditionalist Catholics were about as favorable toward Mormons as they were toward evangelicals. However, all the traditionalist groups had unfavorable views of atheists. The less traditional groups showed a similar pattern, but often with modestly higher favorability toward the religious minorities and markedly higher evaluations of atheists. These patterns suggest that traditionalists may be able to identify relatively easily with believers from within the confines of the Judeo-Christian tradition, but may not as readily identify with those perceived to be outside this context.

This evidence suggests that despite some religious particularism and social insularity in religious life, the elements of the traditionalist alliance are engaged in public life. In fact, opportunity for traditionalists to interact with each other—and other people—in civic venues appears to be ample. Evidence from surveys of political activists and the parish clergy supports this high level of civic engagement by religious traditionalists (see Green 2007, chap. 7), as do interviews with evangelical Protestants among political, media, and governmental elites (Lindsay 2007). Michael Lindsay found that during the period in which the traditionalist alliance appeared at the ballot box, evangelicals gained greater access to the political power—presumably joining members of other religious traditions, such as mainline Protestants, that already had such access (Lindsay 2007; Davidson 1994).

The Christian Right and the Traditionalist Alliance

One important form of civic engagement associated with the traditionalist alliance is involvement with the Christian Right, a social movement dedicated to restoring traditional morality to public policy (Wilcox and Larson 2006). This movement was present at the origins of the traditionalist alliance, including key special purpose organizations central to the restructuring of American religion (Wuthnow 1988, chap. 6) and prominent in waging the culture wars (Hunter 1991, 89–97). Table 4.7 indicates the percentages of the religious groups reporting active membership in Christian conservative and pro-family groups as well as their affect toward the Christian Right in 2000.[20]

In these data, 6.5 percent of the adult population claimed to be active members of Christian conservative organizations, which by way of comparison, is a little larger than the 5.8 percent who reported active membership in environmental groups in the same survey. Almost 14 percent of traditionalist evangelicals and Catholics reported participating in a Christian Right organization, but the largest membership was reported by traditionalist African American Protestants, nearly 20 percent, followed by traditionalist other Christians, about 16 percent (for African American Protestant support for the Christian Right, see Wilcox 1990). Traditionalist mainline Protestants were much less likely to report active membership, and the traditionalist other faiths were the least likely. As one might expect, the traditionalist groups were far more likely to report active membership in such organizations than their less traditional coreligionists. Among the less traditional groups, however, evangelicals, African American Protestants, and other Christians reported somewhat higher membership.

Proximity toward the Christian Right shows a somewhat different pattern. Overall, a little more than 30 percent of the adult population reported feeling close to the movement. By way of comparison, about half said they felt close to environmental organizations in the same survey. Traditionalist evangelicals reported feeling the closest, more than 75 percent, followed by traditionalist African American Protestants and traditionalist other Christians, each at a little less than 65 percent. Traditionalist mainline Protestants lagged behind, with a little more than 50 percent reporting feeling close to the Christian Right. Traditionalist Catholics were even further back, at less than 50 percent. The smallest positive affect came from traditionalist other faiths, at about 30 percent. Here, too, the traditionalists had more positive evaluations of the Christian Right than their less traditional counterparts, but African American Protestants and evangelicals showed higher affect than the other less traditional groups.

Table 4.7   Exploring the Traditionalist Alliance: The Christian Right

	Percent Active Member in Organization	Percent Close to Christian Right
Traditionalists		
White Evangelical Protestants	13.8	77.2
White Catholics	13.6	48.3
Other Christians	16.1	64.4
White mainline Protestants	7.6	54.2
Other faiths	5.7	34.4
African American Protestants	19.2	65.0
Less traditional		
White Evangelical Protestants	5.5	40.2
White Catholics	2.4	17.7
Other Christians	5.6	30.2
White mainline Protestants	3.9	20.0
Other faiths	0.5	3.0
African American Protestants	5.9	48.0
Unaffiliated	1.2	8.9
ALL	**6.5**	**36.0**

Source: Author's compilation based on National Survey of Religion and Politics 2000 (N = 6,000).

Taken together, these patterns reflect two features of the movement that have implications for the traditionalist alliance. First, the movement has always been made up of numerous organizations (Wilcox and Larson 2006, chap. 3). Some groups were national in scope, and others either state or local. Different organizations specialized in different kinds of activities, ranging from voter mobilization to litigating in the courts. For some groups, the pro-family agenda was broad and for others it focused on a single issue. Most such groups operated for a relatively short time and were replaced by new organizations. Thus the reported membership and affect in table 4.7 may well reflect the numerous and varied movement organizations.

Second, religious particularism was an important factor in the creation of these multiple organizations. The best known of the movement groups drew most of their support from particular kinds of evangelical Protestants: the Moral Majority from fundamentalist Baptists, the Christian Coalition from Pentecostals and charismatics, and Focus on the Family from nondenominational evangelicals (Green et al. 1996; Smith 2000). Some of these organizations eventually gained a wider following among traditionalists, but mostly by uniting various kinds of traditionalist evangelicals rather than by uniting all kinds of traditionalists. By the mid-1990s, Ralph Reed of the Christian Coalition recognized these limitations, and founded the Catholic Alliance to mobilize Catholics and a special outreach effort to African Americans (Watson 1999). Although these initiatives were short-lived, they point to the fact that traditionalists were best mobilized within their own religious context. This pattern fits with the evidence of religious particularism and social insularity noted earlier.

A good example is the development of special movement organizations among Catholic traditionalists. Deal Hudson, former editor of *Crisis* and former chairman of Catholic Outreach for the Republican National Committee, described these organizations this way: "Is there a Catholic Religious Right? Yes. For the past thirty years, Catholics have been integral to its strategic, political, and grassroots leadership. . . . And after several misfires, socially conservative Catholics created their own identity in the Republican Party through Catholic outreach efforts in 2000 and 2004. Most importantly, Catholic leaders have arisen that are no longer dependent on the U.S. Conference of Catholic Bishops, evangelical organizations, or the Republican Party for their influence" (2008, 149).

Such Catholic groups include Priests for Life, Catholic Vote.org, and Catholic League for Religion and Civil Rights. Similar efforts have arisen in other religious traditions, such as the Institute for Religion and Democracy (mainline Protestants), High Impact Leadership Coalition (African American Protestant clergy), and Toward Tradition (Jews). Whether these efforts follow the path of their evangelical and Catholic counterparts remains to be seen.

Such tradition specific organizations can increase the strength and scope of the traditionalist alliance, but require a high degree of coordination. To fill this need, various interfaith coordinating groups have developed. A good example is the National Policy Council, created in 1981 as a networking organization for social conservatives (Bruce 1988, 57). A more recent example is the Arlington Group, a committee established in 2002 to coordinate opposition to same-sex marriage (Scott Helman, "Coalition seeks to Reframe GOP Race." *Boston Globe*, March 25, 2007). Its official membership included more than fifty organizations, most of which are headed by evangelicals, including James Dobson (Focus on the Family), Gary Bauer (American Values), Charles Colson (Prison Fellowship), Tony Perkins (Family Research Council), Franklin Graham (Samaritan's Purse), Richard Land (Southern Baptist Convention); Lou Shelton (the Traditional Values Association), and a representative from the National Association of Evangelicals. But the list also includes some mainline Protestants (Donald Wildmon of the American Family Association) and African American Protestants (William Owens of the Coalition of African American Pastors) as well as Catholics, such as William Bennett (Empower America), Raymond Flynn (Catholic Vote.org), and Richard Viguerie (ConservativeHQ.com). The late Paul Weyrich (Free Congress Foundation), a Melkite Greek Catholic, was also a member.

These coordinating efforts notwithstanding, religious particularism has regularly created difficulties for the traditionalist alliance. For example, Bob Jones III, a fundamentalist Protestant leader, had this to say in 1980: "The aim of the Moral Majority is to join Catholics, Jews, Protestants of every stripe, Mormons, etc., into a common religious cause. Christians can fight on the battlefield alongside these people, can vote with them for a common candidate, but they cannot be unequally yoked with them in a religious army or organization. . . . A close, analytical look at the Moral Majority . . . reveals a movement that holds more potential for hastening the church of the Antichrist and building the ecumenical church than anything that has come down the pike in a long time" (quoted in Bruce 1988, 173).

Such tensions were also important in the early 1990s when some movement organizers attempted to build a successor organization to the Moral Majority with financing from Reverend Sung Yung Moon of the Unification Church (Moen 1992, 45–52). They appeared again when Governor Mitt Romney, a Mormon, sought the support of the movement in his quest for the 2008 Republican presidential nomination (Noah Feldman, "What Is It About Mormons?" *New York Times*, January 6, 2008).

The impact of religious particularism changed somewhat, however, as the traditionalist alliance grew stronger at the ballot box. For example, Mitt Romney was endorsed by Bob Jones III for the 2008 Republican presidential nomination. Jones, however, following his own advice from the 1980s, took pains to "vote for a common candidate" but not become "unequally yoked." "As a Christian," he said, "I am completely opposed to the doctrines of Mormonism. . . . But I'm not voting for a preacher. I'm voting for a president. It boils down to who [*sic*] can best represent conservative American beliefs, not religious beliefs" (Rob Barnett, "Bob Jones III Endorses Romney for President," *Greenville News*, November 16, 2007).

This argument parallels Romney's 2007 speech on religion and politics, with its stress on political issues over religious doctrine. In fact, one of the best examples of the traditionalist alliance in action occurred in 2008 when Mormons, evangelicals, Catholics, and the Orthodox churches— along with African American Protestants and Latino Catholics—came together to pass Proposition 8, a constitutional amendment that overturned the California Supreme Court's ruling that legalized same-sex marriage (Jesse McKinley and Laurie Goodstein, "Bans in 3 States on Gay Marriage," *New York Times*, November 6, 2008). Mormons played a critical role in the Proposition 8 campaign, drawing special ire from supporters of same-sex marriage after the elections—and a strong defense from traditionalists leaders, including prominent evangelicals (see, for example, www.nomobveto.org).

Another good example of the changed circumstances occurred when Senator John McCain, the 2008 Republican presidential nominee, sought and received the endorsement from Reverend John Hagee, a televangelist best known for his support for Israel. Shortly thereafter, one of Hagee's previous sermons came to light that was interpreted as anti-Catholic, provoking a critical reaction from William Donohue of the Catholics League for Religion and Civil Rights. This episode had all the hallmarks of past evangelical-Catholic tensions. But in a new twist, Catholic activist Deal Hudson arranged a meeting between Hagee and a group of Catholic conservatives. After the meeting, Hagee issued an apology in a letter to Donohue, who promptly accepted it.

All this negotiating took place among activists associated with the traditionalist alliance, and the episode appeared to resolve a potential disruption in the alliance—until another of Hagee's previous sermons was interpreted as anti-Semitic. At that point McCain rejected, and Hagee withdrew, the endorsement (Jim Kuhnhenn, "Pastor Hagee Apologizes for Anti-Catholic Remarks," *Realclearpolitics*, May 13, 2008).[21] McCain experienced a similar problem with an endorsement from Reverend Rod Parsley from Ohio, but in this case the controversial sermon was viewed as anti-Muslim (Adelle Banks, "McCain Rejects Second Minister's Endorsement," *Religion News Service*, May 23, 2008). Compared with Catholics, Jews and Muslims have been at the margins of traditionalist alliance.

Thus movement organizations have been an important place for traditionalist activists to engage with each another for political purposes (Green, Conger, and Guth 2006). Surveys of presidential campaign contributors and national convention delegates reveal that religious traditionalists often belong to such organizations. Among traditionalist evangelicals, 60 percent or more claim to belong, and among other traditionalists, more than 25 percent do so. Surveys of parish clergy show much lower rates of membership in such organizations, but with traditionalist evangelicals, mainliners, and Catholics participating in roughly the same numbers. Indeed, the impact of religious particularism has typically been lower among activists than among the public at large.[22]

Issues and the Traditionalist Alliance

By all accounts, the development of the traditionalist alliance was associated with the appearance of cultural issues (or moral values) on the national political agenda. For example, speaking of the political rapprochement between evangelicals and Catholics, William Shea concluded, "Circumstances and conditions impel evangelical and Catholic conversation: the brute, experiential facts of another century of war, the Holocaust, policies legitimizing abortion and threatening to legalize mercy killing and suicide, and American cultural and religious pluralism. . . . Even were the two sides not Christian, these circumstances would drive them into each other's arms. The same circumstances have forced a change in Catholic ways of speaking about Jews, and brought the pope to pray with an unusual assortment of religious leaders from round the world's religions" (2004, 285).

An even more direct description of the role of cultural issues is found in a pamphlet by an evangelical activist. After recounting the long-standing conflict between evangelicals and Catholics, the author remarked: "So what has changed? Why do Protestant Christians respect Catholic Christians now? Perhaps, the answer can be found in the key social policies Catholics push in the American social and political scenes. Namely, they are prohibitions in the following areas: abortion, pre-martial sex, and homosexuality" (Fields 2005, 21).

Table 4.8 reports the issue positions and other political attitudes of these religious categories in 2004. The first column looks at abortion, perhaps the central controversy in the culture wars. Here a majority of the traditionalist groups held a pro-life position.[23] Traditionalist evangelicals, other Christians and Catholics were the most pro-life, and traditionalist mainline Protestants and other faiths were the least so. Without exception, the traditionalists were more pro-life than their less traditional counterparts, though a large majority of less traditional evangelicals were pro-life as well. Similar patterns held for other cultural issues not included in the table, such as opposition to same-sex marriage.

The second column shows a foreign policy attitude, that is, support for international engagement by the United States.[24] Here the views of the traditionalists were mixed. Traditionalist evangelicals were the most likely to be internationalists, and traditionalists from among the other faiths, African American Protestants, and mainline Protestants were the least likely. Interestingly, the second most internationalist group was that of less traditional other faiths, largely on the strength of its Jewish members. Overall, the traditionalist groups were slightly more internationalist than their less traditional coreligionists, but considerable variation existed among them.

The third and fourth columns in table 4.8 report attitudes on other domestic issues. The first is environmental protection, which also shows a mixed pattern. Traditionalist mainline Protestants scored highest on this issue, but traditionalist evangelicals, Catholics, and other Christians were not far behind. The traditionalists most opposed were African American Protestants and other faiths, perhaps because of the economic

Table 4.8   Exploring the Traditionalist Alliance: Issues and Political Attitudes, 2004

	Percent Pro-Life	Percent for International Engagement	Percent for Environmental Protection	Percent Disadvantaged Need Help	Percent Conservative	Percent Republican
Traditionalists						
White Evangelical Protestants	88.3	64.9	55.4	50.4	74.8	77.1
White Catholics	79.2	57.4	53.9	51.3	64.9	58.4
Other Christians	82.2	54.2	51.1	59.8	47.0	41.3
White mainline Protestants	56.5	44.6	58.3	54.3	57.7	60.7
Other faiths	53.4	34.2	41.0	52.2	27.4	25.6
African American Protestants	64.6	43.7	41.9	62.6	33.9	10.9
Less traditional						
White Evangelical Protestants	58.2	44.9	50.9	59.8	49.0	46.0
White Catholics	35.7	49.3	62.7	55.9	32.8	35.5
Other Christians	49.0	44.6	50.7	63.7	30.7	24.4
White mainline Protestants	26.5	49.3	61.7	53.2	35.1	38.6
Other faiths	7.4	63.7	69.3	77.8	13.2	11.7
African American Protestants	40.7	31.7	37.4	61.5	28.0	11.5
Unaffiliated	23.7	44.4	57.5	62.7	25.1	26.3
ALL	**48.2**	**48.3**	**54.7**	**58.5**	**40.0**	**37.8**

Source: Author's compilation based on National Survey of Religion and Politics 2004 (N = 4,000).

implications of the question.[25] A similar mixed pattern held true for the less traditional groups. For example, less traditional evangelicals scored lower than their traditionalist coreligionists, but less traditional mainline Protestants and Catholics scored higher. Overall, the less traditional groups were more supportive of environmental protection, with other faiths scoring the highest.

The next issue is a social welfare policy: the percentage of the religious groups who agreed that disadvantaged persons need special assistance from the government.[26] Here the most supportive traditionalists were African American Protestants and the composite category of other Christians, which contains many nonwhites. The least supportive groups were traditionalist evangelicals and Catholics, but in both categories a majority agreed with government help for the disadvantaged. In most cases, the less traditional groups were more likely to agree with this issue than their traditionalist counterparts.

The final two columns in table 4.8 report general political attitudes across the religious groups, the percentages of self-identified conservatives and Republicans. Here the traditionalists were more conservative and Republican than their less traditional counterparts, with just two exceptions—other faiths on ideology and African American Protestants on partisanship. Differences among the traditionalists were also significant. Traditionalist evangelicals were the most Republican and conservative, followed by mainline Protestants and Catholics. In contrast, traditionalist African American Protestants, other faiths, and other Christians scored much lower in both conservative ideology and Republican partisanship. Evangelicals were the most conservative and Republican among the less traditional groups, but dramatically less conservative and Republican than the traditionalist counterparts.

A comparison of these broader political attitudes and the issue positions in table 4.8 strongly suggests that cultural issues have been a powerful source of ideology and partisanship within the traditionalist alliance, and that the priority traditionalists assigned to cultural issues was central to this connection (Layman and Green 2005). By the same token, noncultural issues contributed to less conservative and less Republican views—and might have had an even greater impact had traditionalists given priority to economic and foreign policy matters rather than cultural issues. In any event, political variation among the potential allies is considerable, and if cultural issues were to become less salient, the traditionalist alliance would likely be weaker (Leege et al. 2002).

Political Activists and Leaders and the Traditionalist Alliance

Does the traditionalist alliance extend beyond voters to political activists and leaders? This question is important because of the critical role activists and leaders play in the conduct of presidential politics. After all, it is these key actors who develop coalitions in the public and mobilize the coalition to vote (Layman 2001; Leege et al. 2002). Four surveys taken during the 2000 presidential election of key political actors—voters, presidential campaign donors, national convention delegates, and parish clergy—are useful for addressing this question. Table 4.9 compares the support for the Republicans among the religious groups in all four sets of political actors (see the appendix for a description of these surveys). The 2000 presidential election, one of the closest in American history, is a good case for such an assessment (see table 4.9).

Voters   The first pair of columns report on voters in 2000, and the pattern is familiar, resembling table 4.1, but with the more precise measure of the religious groups. In 2000, Republican George W. Bush received nearly 90 percent of the votes from traditionalist evangelical Protestants, 75 percent from traditionalist mainline Protestants, and 60 percent from traditionalist Catholics and the composite category of other Christians. He lost the traditionalist vote in the composite category of other faiths and among African American Protestants, however. He also did poorly among the less traditional groups, winning majorities only among less traditional evangelicals and mainline Protestants. A quick glance back to table 4.1 suggests some shifts within the traditionalist alliance between 2000 and 2004, with Bush improving among traditionalist Catholics but losing ground among traditionalist mainline Protestants (see Green et al. 2007).

Donors   The second pair of columns in table 4.9 reports on individual donors to the major presidential campaigns in 2000. These data are drawn from a stratified random sample of campaign contributors to presidential primary campaigns, including large (more than $200) and small (less than $200) donors (for more detail, see the appendix; see also Wilcox et al. 2003). Donors to the Bush and Gore campaigns accounted for most of these donors, but the sample also includes donors to their rivals, including candidates strongly backed by the Christian Right—Gary Bauer and Alan Keyes. Besides helping to pay for presidential campaigns, donors are quite active in other ways: they help conduct voter registration and grassroots voter contract, and participate in campaign, interest group, and party organizations (Brown, Powell, and Wilcox 1995). These donors are thus political activists directly relevant to the presidential campaigns.

In 2000, nearly 90 percent of traditionalist evangelicals donors gave to Republican presidential candidates. Traditionalist mainline Protestants, Catholics, and other Christians also strongly supported GOP campaigns, but at a lower level of about 65 percent. Unlike voters, these

Table 4.9   Exploring the Traditionalist Alliance: Republican Support from Voters, Activists, and Leaders, 2000

	Voters		Donors		Delegates		Clergy	
	Bush	Gore	Republican	Democrat	Republican	Democrat	Bush	Gore
Traditionalists								
White Evangelical Protestants	87.3	12.7	91.4	8.6	86.5	13.5	97.6	2.4
White Catholics	60.7	39.3	65.5	34.5	77.0	23.0	86.3	13.7
Other Christians	60.7	39.3	66.7	33.3	69.4	30.6	*	*
White mainline Protestants	75.9	24.1	65.9	34.1	84.6	15.4	90.3	9.7
Other faiths	20.4	79.6	38.9	61.1	48.1	51.9	6.8	93.2
African American Protestants	4.3	95.7	*	*	14.1	85.9	11.2	88.8
Less traditional								
White Evangelical Protestants	56.6	43.4	59.6	40.4	34.7	65.3	79.8	20.2
White Catholics	45.1	54.9	44.0	56.0	23.6	76.4	53.5	46.5
Other Christians	21.8	78.2	58.8	41.2	31.7	68.3	*	*
White mainline Protestants	52.7	47.3	44.3	55.7	50.1	49.9	41.9	58.1
Other faiths	25.0	75.0	15.0	85.0	11.6	88.4	2.3	97.7
African American Protestants	2.7	97.3	*	*	9.9	90.1	7.3	92.7
Unaffiliated	38.2	61.8	44.7	55.3	26.9	73.1	*	*
ALL	**49.5**	**50.5**	**50.0**	**50.0**	**50.0**	**50.0**	**60.0**	**40.0**

Sources: Author's compilation based on National Survey of Religion and Politics 2000 (N = 3,000); Presidential Campaign Finance Survey 2001 (N = 2,327); Cooperative Clergy Survey 2001 (N = 8,805); Convention Delegate Survey 2001 (N = 2,870).

three groups had very similar partisan preferences. However, the traditionalists among other faiths and African American Protestants strongly backed the Democratic Party (because there were too few African American Protestant traditionalists to report results from the donor survey). Among donors, the less traditional evangelicals and mainliners were also strongly Republican, but all other groups were more supportive of Democratic presidential candidates.

Delegates   The third pair of columns in table 4.9 reports on national convention delegates, drawn from the 2000 Convention Delegate Study (2001), a sample of the universe of all delegates to the Republican and Democratic national conventions (for more detail, see the appendix; see also Carsey et al. 2006). These delegates formally nominated George Bush and Al Gore as candidates. Most major party elites were chosen to be part of the primary campaigns because they were among the active in party politics (Green and Jackson 2007). Delegates are thus the major party elites most directly concerned with presidential nominations.

In 2000, nearly all of the traditionalist evangelical Protestant delegates attended the Republican national convention and nearly as many traditionalist mainline Protestants were there as well. Traditionalist Catholics were also strongly Republican, but slightly less so, followed by the composite category of other Christians. However traditionalist other faiths, on balance, attended the Democratic convention. Black Protestants did so in huge numbers. As with voters and donors, the difference between the traditionalists and their less traditional counterparts in each pair of religious groups was sharp—with the traditionalists always more common at the GOP convention. The Republicans did best with less traditional mainline Protestants.

Clergy   The final pair of columns in table 4.9 turns to the parish clergy, using the results of the Cooperative Clergy Survey, a national survey of a stratified random sample of the parish clergy of twenty-three major denominations (for more detail, see the appendix; see also Smidt 2004). Although this survey does not cover all of the denominations in the United States by any means, it does provide a sense of the presidential preferences of religious leaders thought to be critical to faith-based politics in general. Clergy can be effective grassroots activists as individuals, but are also important opinion and institutional leaders in local congregations (Guth et al. 1997).

In 2000, traditionalist evangelical Protestant pastors voted almost unanimously for Bush over Gore. Traditionalist mainline Protestant ministers were only a little less Republican and traditionalist Catholic priests also strongly backed Bush, though at a slightly lower level. Traditionalist other Christians also appeared to support Bush but were too

few to isolate in these surveys. Here the composite category of traditionalists in other faiths voted strongly for Gore, as did the African American Protestant clergy. The differences between the pairs of traditionalist
and nontraditionalist categories were also large, with the traditionalists
always more Republican. Even so, majorities of the less traditional evangelical pastors and Catholic priests voted for Bush as well.

Relative Size of the Traditionalist Alliance   Table 4.10 shows the portion of
Republican and Democratic supporters from the traditionalist alliance
among voters, donors, delegates, and clergy. These figures provide a
sense of the relative size of the traditionalist alliance among these key
political actors.

Traditionalist voters made up a large portion, almost 50 percent, of
the Bush vote in 2000. (This more precise measure of traditionalists produces a smaller estimate of the relative size of the traditionalist alliance
than the estimate in table 4.1, based only on worship attendance.) All
traditionalist groups combined also made up about 20 percent of the Republican donors as well as a majority of the GOP delegates and Bush
backers among the parish clergy. Traditionalist evangelical Protestants
were the largest single group of voters, accounting for roughly 25 percent of Bush ballots, and also the single largest source of Republican delegates (about 20 percent) and Bush's clergy backers (almost 50 percent).
Traditionalist evangelicals were the second largest source of GOP
donors (about 16 percent), close behind less traditional mainline Protestants. If less traditional evangelicals are added to measures of the traditionalist alliance, the figures increase to solid majorities of voters,
donors, delegates, and clergy. Although the focus of this discussion has
been on the traditionalist alliance, the importance of less traditional voters, donors, delegates, and clergy among supporters of Gore and the Democrats is significant.

Willingness to Compromise   Taken together, the patterns in tables 4.9 and
4.10 suggest that the traditionalist alliance was well represented among
the political activists and leaders who play a critical role in presidential
elections. Even among activists and leaders, however, the alliance does
not extend much beyond the white Christian traditions. Variation in the
level of support for the GOP among the allies is still considerable—and
support appears to vary somewhat from one election to the next, with
some clear differences, for example, between 2000 and 2004. Assembling
and managing these coalitions is no easy task. This last point raises another question, to what extent is the traditionalist alliance a product of
cooperative efforts?

These surveys contain questions directly relevant to such cooperation, specifically, about the willingness or unwillingness to compromise

Table 4.10 Exploring the Traditionalist Alliance: Coalitions among Voters, Activists, and Leaders, 2000

	Voters		Donors		Delegates		Clergy	
	Bush	Gore	Republican	Democrat	Republican	Democrat	Bush	Gore
Traditionalists								
White Evangelical Protestants	24.9	3.5	17.0	1.6	20.7	3.2	45.6	1.7
White Catholics	8.4	5.3	15.3	8.0	13.7	4.1	2.2	0.5
Other Christians	4.4	2.8	2.1	1.0	7.7	3.4	*	*
White mainline Protestants	8.5	2.7	10.6	5.5	19.1	3.4	5.6	0.9
Other faiths	1.3	4.9	0.5	0.8	1.8	2.0	0.6	12.3
African American Protestants	0.4	8.5	*	*	0.7	4.3	1.0	12.1
Less traditional								
White Evangelical Protestants	12.8	9.6	10.6	7.2	2.5	4.6	22.8	8.7
White Catholics	12.4	14.8	7.5	9.5	5.3	17.1	2.7	3.5
Other Christians	1.5	5.4	0.7	0.5	3.1	6.7	*	*
White mainline Protestants	13.7	12.0	20.2	25.4	17.9	17.8	18.7	38.9
Other faiths	2.2	6.4	4.8	27.3	2.0	15.6	0.2	10.7
African American Protestants	0.3	9.1	*	*	0.5	4.5	0.6	10.7
Unaffiliated	9.2	15.0	10.7	13.2	5.0	13.5	*	*
ALL	**100.0**	**100.0**	**100.0**	**100.0**	**100.0**	**100.0**	**100.0**	**100.0**

Sources: Author's compilation based on National Survey of Religion and Politics 2000 (N = 3,000); Presidential Campaign Finance Survey 2001 (N = 2,327); Convention Delegate Survey 2001 (N = 2,870); Cooperative Clergy Survey 2001 (N = 8,805).

Table 4.11   Exploring the Traditionalist Alliance: Views of Compromise, 2000

Percent Unwilling to Compromise Principles	Voters	Donors	Delegates	Clergy
Traditionalists				
White Evangelical Protestants	71.2	65.0	48.9	58.1
White Catholics	52.7	41.8	37.6	43.6
Other Christians	64.1	56.8	36.2	*
White mainline Protestants	56.4	35.6	26.3	56.2
Other faiths	52.8	28.6	47.2	20.2
African American Protestants	70.3	*	27.5	70.3
Less traditional				
White Evangelical Protestants	61.7	42.2	35.0	40.1
White Catholics	49.2	31.9	28.1	24.3
Other Christians	54.0	37.5	36.2	*
White mainline Protestants	44.0	28.3	25.8	30.2
Other faiths	33.0	27.4	39.0	16.5
African American Protestants	51.4	*	42.6	60.8
Unaffiliated	44.7	26.5	38.9	44.1
ALL	**53.9**	**35.4**	**34.6**	**44.1**

Sources: Author's compilation based on National Survey of Religion and Politics 2000 (N = 3,000); Presidential Campaign Finance Study 2001 (N = 2,870); Convention Delegate Survey 2001 (N = 2,327); Cooperative Clergy Survey 2001 (N = 8,805).

one's principles in order to achieve desirable results. Table 4.11 reports the percentages of the religious groups holding such views among voters, donors, delegates, and clergy. Attitudes like this have been studied extensively because building successful electoral coalitions in the United States is inherently difficult. On the one hand, such coalitions benefit from the intense commitments of their constituencies. On the other, they require regular pragmatic adjustments among their component parts (see Wilson 1966).

One pattern is immediately apparent in table 4.11. Large numbers of traditionalists of all sorts reported an unwillingness to compromise their principles in politics. With just a few modest exceptions, traditionalists were less willing to compromise than their counterparts. Traditionalist evangelicals were the most uncompromising group among voters and donors (by a large margin) and among delegates and clergy (by smaller margins). Less traditional evangelicals were also unwilling to compromise among voters and donors, but among delegates and clergy African American Protestants were more unwilling. As one might imagine, unwillingness to compromise tended to be more common among voters than clergy, donors, or delegates. After all, such activists and leaders are the most involved in the mechanics of coalition building.

One must view these results with special caution because of the common stereotype of religious traditionalists, especially evangelical Protestants, as being dogmatic and intolerant. After all, these responses might well represent a strong commitment to principle, a quality generally seen as admirable in politics. In addition, these questions ask about compromise in the abstract, not in real situations with tangible goals at stake. Furthermore, these questions do not ask about compromise among the traditionalists but rather compromise in general—an unwillingness to compromise with less traditional groups is less relevant to the effectiveness of the traditionalist alliance. All this said, these figures suggest that barriers to cooperation may exist based on commitment to principles among the potential traditionalist allies (for a similar conclusion, see Evans 2006).

The Future of the Traditionalist Alliance

What have we learned from this exploration of the traditionalist alliance? First, the claims of journalists and pundits about the religious elements of the 2004 Republican presidential vote have considerable merit. These patterns developed over the last thirty years and now extend beyond voters to political activists and party leaders. The alliance is most evident among white Christian communities, led by traditionalist evangelicals. The allies have several things in common: traditional religiosity (fostered by ecumenical orthodoxy), a high level of civic engagement (aided by the Christian Right), and a focus on cultural issues (such as abortion and same-sex marriage). Thus the traditionalist alliance displayed considerable strength and breadth in the early twenty-first century.

At the same time, it faced some significant limitations that are likely to continue. It is hampered by some religious particularism and social insularity, and by diverse opinions on noncultural issues. These differences lie at the center of ecumenical orthodoxy, are woven into the organizations of the Christian Right, and pose challenges to coalition building. In addition, the alliance does not typically extend much beyond white Christian communities, and the potential allies are characterized by an unwillingness to compromise on principle, which threatens cooperation.

What do these conclusions suggest about the future of the traditionalist alliance?

The traditionalist alliance is fundamentally a political alliance, and as such is a continual work in progress. Its effectiveness in any particular election depends on the skill of its activists and leaders, but also on the broader political environment, including the choice of presidential candidates and the nature of the issue agenda. In this regard, the political conditions may have been quite favorable for the alliance in the 2000 and 2004 elections, and may be far less favorable in the other elections. One key variable is the relative importance of cultural issues: greater prominence of issues such as same-sex marriage may unite the traditionalist groups, but the prominence of economic or foreign policy issues may weaken the alliance. Here the ethnic and social diversity of the evangelical community may be a factor, with the growing Latino and suburban evangelicals likely to increase the diversity of evangelical opinion on noncultural issues. A number of writers forecast trouble for the traditionalist alliance for just these kinds of reasons (see, for example, Dionne 2008).

In addition, the influence of the traditionalist alliance is likely to depend as much on the Republican Party as what the allies do. The alliance and its component parts are minorities within the Republican coalition, albeit often large minorities. To win presidential elections, the Republican coalition must be broad and diverse, including the corporate and entrepreneurial business community, affluent professionals, members of the military, those concerned with national security, gun owners, opponents of government social welfare programs, antitax and property rights activists, critics of immigration—and many other constituency groups. Members of the traditionalist alliance are an important part of this mix, but just one element among many. It is surely not entirely an accident that the traditionalist alliance came to the attention of many observers during the sophisticated coalition building of the George W. Bush campaigns. Some writers from within the alliance are keenly aware of this and have made a case for broader alliance building and more effective interaction with the GOP (Carlson 2007; Olasky 2007).

There is little doubt that evangelical Protestants will be critical to the success of the alliance in the longer term, with traditionalist evangelicals remaining the most important element of the alliance among voters, activists, and leaders for the foreseeable future. Developments and debates among evangelicals will thus have a significant impact on the alliance. For instance, continued growth and vitality among evangelicals may well aid the alliance. Sectarian disunity, however, may be damaging (Green and Dionne 2008). The direction of less traditional evangelicals will matter as well: this group has been an important adjunct to the traditionalist alliance in recent elections. But if American religion continues to follow the restructuring process, sharper divisions may appear between the traditionalist and less traditional evangelicals, leading to more Democratic votes among the latter. Indeed, the appearance of vocal centrist and progressive evangelical leaders in the wake of the 2004 campaign may be a harbinger of such developments in the longer term (see Sullivan 2008).

Initial evidence from the 2008 presidential election provides some confirmation of these points. On the one hand, the traditionalist alliance was apparent in voting returns and benefited Republican John McCain. On the other hand, the alliance was weaker than in 2004, with Democratic Barack Obama making modest gains among the allies. The weakness of the alliance among minority Christians was strongly evident as well, with these groups backing Obama at an extraordinary rate. Obama also improved among both less traditionally religious and unaffiliated voters, sharply reducing the GOP support in these quarters. Key to these patterns may have been a sharp shift in the issue agenda to economic issues. Indeed, the 2008 election results may offer a counterpoint to the 2000 and 2004 results, revealing the traditionalist alliance's strengths and weaknesses under sharply different political circumstances.

Appendix: Religious Categories and Surveys

The religious categories used throughout this chapter are based an analysis on the National Surveys of Religion and Politics from 1992 to 2004 (for a full description, see Green et al. 2007). These surveys were a national random sample of adult Americans (eighteen or older), conducted in the spring of the election years and reinterviewed after the election. In 2000, the preelection sample was 6,000 cases and the post-election sample 3,000 (National Survey of Religion and Politics 2000). In 2004, it was 4,000 cases and 2,730 cases, respectively.

The basic religion categories were calculated as follows. First, the major religious traditions were created by recoding detailed measures of denominational affiliation, race, and ethnicity (following Green 2007 and Steensland et al. 2000), and then combined into the six affiliation categories in table 4.2, with nonwhite Protestants and Catholics placed in the other Christians category. Second, a factor-based index of traditional beliefs and practices was calculated using five beliefs (in God, in life after death, view of Scripture, the devil, and evolution as the best explanation for life on earth) and five practices (frequency of worship attendance, prayer, Scripture reading and small group participation, and financial contribution to a congregation). Third, for each affiliation category, the factor score was then partitioned into the most traditional respondents using the mean score for the highest level of religious salience; the analogous category among the unaffiliated respondents was combined with the other faiths category.

These procedures produced the categories for the public in table 4.2 for 2004 and in tables 4.9, 4.10, and 4.11 for 2000 for voters. The other surveys of the public used in the chapter did not always have exactly the same religion measures, but in all cases it was possible to calculate the six affiliations categories from the measure of denominational affiliation and a factor-based index of religious beliefs and behavior. When religious salience was not available, the traditionalist categories were created by partitioning the factor-based index to match the size of the traditionalist categories in National Surveys of Religion and Politics.

In tables 4.9, 4.10, and 4.11, three other surveys were also used. The first was the Presidential Campaign Finance Survey, a stratified random sample of large ($200 or more) and small (less than $200) donors to all of the Democratic and Republicans presidential primary campaigns drawn from the records of the Federal Elections Commission and conducted by mail in 2001 at Duke University (N = 2870) (Presidential Campaign Finance Survey 2001). Sample strata were weighted to reflect the overall distribution of the initial sample of donors. For more detail, see Wilcox et al. (2003).

The second study was the 2000 Conventional Delegate Survey, a survey of the universe of delegates to the Democratic and Republican national conventions drawn from the official lists of party delegates and conducted by mail in 2001 at Arizona State University (N = 2327) (Conventional Delegates Survey 2001). For more detail, see Carsey et al. (2006).

Third was the Cooperative Clergy Survey, a stratified random samples of the clergy in twenty-three denominations drawn from the official denomination records and conducted by mail at participating universities in 2001, coordinated at Calvin College (N = 8805) (Cooperative Clergy Survey 2001). The denominational samples were weighted to reflect the relative size of the clergy in the universe of denominations included. The denominations surveyed were the American Baptist Convention; Disciples of Christ; Evangelicals Lutheran Church in America; Presbyterian Church (USA); Reformed Church in America; United Methodist Church; Southern Baptist Convention; Churches of Christ; Lutheran Church-Missouri Synod; Presbyterian Church in America; Christian Reformed Church; Church of the Nazarene; Assemblies of God; Evangelical Free Church of America; Mennonite Church USA; Reform, Conservative, Orthodox, and Reconstructionist Judaism; Roman Catholic Church; African Methodist Episcopal Church; Church of God in Christ; and the Unitarian-Universalist Association. For more detail, see Smidt (2004).

Notes

1. These data come from the 2004 National Election Pool and are based on analysis by the author (for the basic coding of these categories, see Green 2007, 186, note 21).
2. At the same time, there was a modernist-secular alliance or a religious left in the Democratic presidential vote (see Kellstedt, Smidt et al. 2007a).

3. For the full text of Romney's speech, see http://www.thebostonchannel
.com/politics/14789305/detail.html.

4. James Hunter and his students are the chief proponents of the culture wars perspective on these matters (1991, 1994; see also Himmelfarb 1991). Among the skeptics are Steven Brint (1992), Rhys Williams (1997), Alan Wolfe (1998), and Morris Fiorina and his colleagues (2005). For a good overview of this debate, see James Hunter's and Alan Wolfe's comments in "Is there a Culture War?" Pew Forum on Religion & Public Life, available at: http://pewforum.org/events/?EventID=112; see also Geoffrey Layman and John Green (2005).

5. These data come from the 2007 U.S. Religious Landscape Survey (U.S. Religious Landscape Survey 2007) and are based on analysis by the author (available at: http://religions.pewforum.org). Previous surveys have shown similar patterns.

6. These data come from the 2002–2003 Religious and Diversity Study (Religion and Diversity Survey 2002–2003) and are based on analysis by the author.

7. A good example is the recent *Evangelical Manifesto*, which states: "As an open declaration, *An Evangelical Manifesto* addresses not only Evangelicals and other Christians but other American citizens and people of all other faiths in America, including those who say they have no faith. It therefore stands as an example of how different faith communities may address each other in public life, without any compromise of their own faith but with a clear commitment to the common good of the societies in which we all live together." Although opposed to uncritical support of the Republicans by evangelicals, the political message of the Manifesto is on balance conservative politically (available at: http://www.evangelicalmanifesto.com).

8. In fact, the survey used in table 4.2 shows significant differences between evangelicals, mainline Protestants, and Catholics on views of Scripture, the role of good behavior in obtaining life after death, and the existence of the devil, items left out of the table in view of space considerations.

9. The internal diversity of American Judaism and Islam can be seen in the 2007 U.S. Religious Landscape Survey (available at: http://religions.pew forum.org).

10. The survey was the 1996 Second National Survey of Religion and Politics, conducted at the University of Akron and based on analysis by the author.

11. These data come from the 1998 National Congregation Study and based on analysis by the author (available at: http://www.thearda.com/Archive/Files/Descriptions/NCS.asp).

12. The survey was undertaken by Public Agenda (Farkas, Johnson, and Foleno 2001).

13. These data come from the 2004 General Social Survey and are based on analysis by the author.

14. These conclusions are based on analysis of data in the 2004 General Social Survey.

15. These data come from the Third National Survey of Religion and Politics, conducted at the University of Akron, and based on analysis by the author (National Survey of Religion and Politics 2000).

16. These data come from the 2004 General Social Survey.

17. The findings reported in this section come from the 2000 Social Capital Benchmark Survey and based on analysis by the author (available at: http://www.thearda.com/Archive/Files/Descriptions/SCCBS.asp)

18. These findings are based on the 2000 Religion and Politics Survey and based on analysis by the author (available at: http://www.thearda.com/Archive/Files/Descriptions/Relpol2000.asp).

19. The data for all groups except Mormons came from a 2001 survey by the Pew Forum on Religion & Public Life and the Pew Research Center (Religion and Public Life Survey 2001), and the data for Mormons came from a 2007 survey (available at: http://people-press.org/dataarchive) (Religion and Public Life Survey 2007a). The results are based on analysis by the author.

20. These data come from the Third National Survey of Religion and Politics, conducted at the University of Akron, and are based on analysis by the author (Green 2000).

21. Realclearpolitics, available at: http://www.realclearpolitics.com/news/ap/politics/2008/May/13/pastor_hagee_apologizes_for_anti_catholic_remarks.html.

22. These findings come from the surveys of presidential campaign contributors, national convention delegates, and parish clergy discussed here (see Appendix).

23. The question was a four-point item ranging from "It should be legal and solely up to a woman to decide" to "It should not be legal at all." The two most restrictive responses were coded as pro-life.

24. The question was a five-point Likert-scale item: "The U.S. should mind its own business internationally and let other countries get along as best they can on their own." Disagree and strongly disagree options were coded as internationalist on foreign policy.

25. The question was a five-point Likert-scale item: "Strict rules to protect the environment are necessary even if they cost jobs or result in higher prices." Agree and strongly agree options were coded as supportive environmental protection.

26. The question was a five-point Likert-scale item: "The economically disadvantaged need government assistance to obtain their rightful place in America." Agree and strongly agree options were coded as favoring aid to the disadvantaged.

References

Bishop, Bill. 2008. *The Big Sort: Why the Clustering of Like-Minded America is Tearing Us Apart*. Boston, Mass.: Houghton Miffin.

Bloomberg, Craig L., and Stephen E. Robinson. 1997. *How Wide the Divide? A Mormon and An Evangelical Conversation*. Downers Grove, Ill.: InterVarsity Press.

Bolce, Louis, and Gerald De Maio. 1999. "The Anti-Christian Fundamentalist Factor in Contemporary Politics." *Public Opinion Quarterly* 63(4): 508–42.

Bolin, Bob, Edward J. Hackett, Sharon L. Harlan, Andrew Kirby, Larissa Larsen, Amy Nelson, Tom R. Rex, and Shaphard Wolf. 2004. "Bonding and Bridging: Understanding the Relationship between Social Capital and Civic Action." *Journal of Planning Education and Research* 24(1): 64–77.

Brint, Steven. 1992. "What If They Gave a War . . . ?" *Contemporary Sociology* 21(4): 438–40.

Brown, Clifford W., Lynda W. Powell, and Clyde Wilcox. 1995. *Serious Money: Fundraising and Contributing in Presidential Nomination Campaigns.* New York: Cambridge University Press.

Bruce, Steve. 1988. *The Rise and Fall of the New Christian Right.* Oxford: Clarendon Press.

Carsey, Thomas M., John C. Green, Richard Herrera, and Geoffrey C. Layman. 2006. "State Party Context and Norms Among Delegates to the 2000 National Conventions." *State Politics & Policy Quarterly* 6(3): 247–71.

Colson, Charles, and Richard John Neuhaus, eds. 1995. *Evangelicals and Catholics Together: Toward a Common Mission.* Dallas, Tex.: Word Publishing.

Colson, Charles, and Richard John Neuhaus. 2002. *Your Word Is Truth: A Project of Evangelicals and Catholics Together.* Grand Rapids, Mich.: William B. Eerdmans.

Convention Delegate Study. 2001. [machine-readable data file]. Principal investigator: Richard Herrera. Tempe: Arizona State University.

Cooperative Clergy Survey. 2001. [machine-readable data file]. Principal investigator: Corwin Smidt. Grand Rapics, Mich.: Calvin College.

Davidson, James D. 1994. "Religion Among America's Elite: Persistence and Change in the Protestant Establishment." *Sociology of Religion* 55(4)(Winter): 419–31.

Davidson, James D., Andrea S Williams, Richard A. Lamanna, Jan Stenftenagel, Kathleen Weigert, William Whalen, and Patricia Wittberg. 1997. *The Search for Common Ground: What Unites and Divides Catholic Americans.* Huntington, Ind.: Our Sunday Visitor.

Dionne, E. J. 2008. *Souled Out: Reclaiming Faith & Politics After the Religious Right.* Princeton, N.J.: Princeton University Press.

Evans, John H. 2006. "Cooperative Coalitions on the Religious Right and Left: Considering the Resilience of Sectarianism." *Journal for the Scientific Study of Religion* 45(2): 195–215.

Farkas, Steve, Jean Johnson, and Tony Foleno, with Ann Duffett and Patrick Foley. 2001. *For Goodness' Sake: Why So Many Want Religion to Play a Greater Role in American Life.* Washington, D.C.: Public Agenda.

Fields, Peter. 2005. *How Catholics Won Protestant Respect: A Candid Look at America.* Cheltenham, Pa.: The Hermit Kingdom Press.

Fiorina, Morris P., with Samuel J. Abrams and Jeremy C. Pope. 2005. *Culture War? The Myth of a Polarized America.* New York: Pearson Longman.

Freedman, Samuel G. 2000. *Jew vs. Jews: The Struggle for the Soul of American Jewry.* New York: Simon & Schuster.

General Social Survey. 2004. [machine-readable data file]. Principal Investigators: James A. Davis and Tom W. Smith. Chicago: National Opinion Research

Center (producer); Storrs, Conn.: The Roper Center for Public Opinion Research, University of Connecticut (distributor).

Green, John C. 2005. "Seeking a Place: Evangelical Protestants and Public Engagement in the 20th Century." In *Toward an Evangelical Public Policy*, edited by Ronald Sider and Diane Knipper. Grand Rapids, Mich.: Baker Press.

———. 2007. *The Faith Factor: How Religion Influences the Vote*. Westport, Conn.: Praeger Press.

———. 2009. "The Faith-Based Politics in American Presidential Elections: Trends and Possibilities." In *The Future of Religion in American Politics*, edited by Charles W. Dunn. Lexington: University of Kentucky Press.

Green, John C., Kimberly H. Conger, and James L. Guth. 2006. "Agents of Value: Christian Right Activists in 2004." In *The Values Campaign?* edited by John C. Green, Mark J. Rozell, and Clyde Wilcox. Washington, D.C.: Georgetown University Press.

Green, John C., and E. J. Dionne, Jr. 2008. "Religion and American Politics in the Post-War Period: More Secular, More Evangelical—or Both." In *The Future of Red, Blue and Purple America: The Future of Election Demographics*, edited by Ruy Teixeira. Washington, D.C.: Brookings Institution Press.

Green, John C., James L. Guth, Corwin E. Smidt, and Lyman A. Kellstedt. 1996. *Religion and the Culture Wars: Dispatches from the Front*. Lanham, Md.: Rowman & Littlefield.

Green, John C., and John S. Jackson. 2007. "Party Profiles: 2004 National Convention Delegates." In *Rewiring Politics: Presidential Nominating Conventions in the Media Age*, edited by Costas Panagopoulos. Baton Rouge: Louisiana State University Press.

Green, John C., Lyman A. Kellstedt, Corwin E. Smidt, and James L. Guth. 2007. "How the Faithful Voted: Religious Communities and the Presidential Vote." In *A Matter of Faith: Religion in the 2004 Presidential Election*, edited by David E. Campbell. Washington, D.C.: Brookings Institution Press.

Guth, James L., John C. Green, Corwin E. Smidt, Lyman A. Kellstedt, and Margaret Poloma. 1997. *The Bully Pulpit: The Politics of Protestant Clergy*. Lawrence: University Press of Kansas.

Himmelfarb, Gertrude. 1991. *One Nation, Two Cultures*. New York: Vintage Books.

Hudson, Deal W. 2008. *Onward Christian Solders: The Growing Political Power of Catholics and Evangelicals in the United States*. New York: Threshold Editions.

Hunter, James Davison. 1991. *Culture Wars: The Struggle to Define America*. New York: Basic Books.

———. 1994. *Before the Shooting Beings: Searching for Democracy in America's Culture War*. New York: Macmillan.

Kellstedt, Lyman A., John C. Green, James L. Guth, and Corwin E. Smidt. 2007. "Faith Transformed: Religion and American Politics from FDR to George W. Bush." In *Religion and American Politics: From the Colonial Period to the Present*, 2nd ed., edited by Mark A. Noll and Luke E. Harlow. Oxford: Oxford University Press.

Kellstedt, Lyman A., Corwin E. Smidt, John C. Green, and James L. Guth. 2007. "A Gentle Stream or a 'River Glorious'? The Religious Left in the 2004 Election." In *A Matter of Faith: Religion in the 2004 Presidential Election*, edited by David E. Campbell. Washington, D.C.: Brookings Institution Press.

Koch, Jeffery W. 1995. *Social Reference Groups and Political Life*. Lanham, Md.: University Press of America.

Kohut, Andrew, John C. Green, Scott Keeter, and Robert Toth. 2000. *The Diminishing Divide: Religion's Changing Role in American Politics*. Washington, D.C.: Brookings Institution Press.

Layman, Geoffrey C. 2001. *The Great Divide: Religious and Cultural Conflict in American Party Politics*. New York: Columbia University Press.

Layman, Geoffrey C., and John C. Green. 2005. "Wars and Rumors of Wars: The Contexts of Cultural Conflict in American Political Behavior." *British Journal of Political Science* 36(1): 61–89.

Leege, David C., Kenneth D. Wald, Paul D. Mueller, and Brian S. Krueger. 2002. *The Politics of Cultural Differences: Social Change and Voter Mobilization Strategies in the Post-New Deal Period*. Princeton, N.J.: Princeton University Press.

Lindsay, D. Michael. 2007. *Faith and the Halls of Power: How Evangelicals Joined the American Elite*. New York: Oxford University Press.

McCormick, Richard L. 1974. "Ethno-Cultural Interpretations of Nineteenth-Century American Voting Behavior." *Political Science Quarterly* 89(June): 351–77.

Moen, Matthew C. 1992. *The Transformation of the Christian Right*. Tuscaloosa: University Press of Alabama.

National Election Pool. 2004. [machine-readable data file]. Sommerville, N.J.: Edison Media (producer); Storrs, Conn.: Roper Center of Public Opinion Research, University of Connecticut (distributor).

National Survey of Religion and Politics. 2000. [machine-readable data file]. Principal investigator: John C. Green. Akron, Ohio: Bliss Institute, University of Akron.

———. 2004. [machine-readable data file]. Principal investigator: John C. Green. Akron, Ohio: Bliss Institute, University of Akron.

Neuhaus, Richard John, and Michael Cromartie, eds. 1987. *Piety and Politics*. Lanham, Md.: Ethics and Public Policy Center and University Press of America.

Oden, Thomas C. 2003. *The Rebirth of Orthodoxy: Signs of New Life in Christianity*. Sam Francisco: HarperOne.

Olasky, Marvin. 2007. "Add, Don't Subtract: How Conservative Christians should Engage American Culture." In *The Future of Conservatism: Conflict and Consensus in the Post-Reagan Era*. Wilmington, Del.: ISI Books.

Olson, Laura R., and John C. Green. 2008. "The Worship Attendance Gap." In *Beyond Red, Blue State*, edited by Laura R. Olson and John C. Green. Upper Saddle River, N.J.: Prentice Hall.

Pew Forum on Religion and Public Life. 2008. "How the Faithful Voted." Washington, D.C.: The Pew Forum on Religion and Public Life. Available at: http://pewforum.org/docs/?DocID=367.

Presidential Campaign Finance Study. 2001. [machine-readable data file]. Principal investigator: Alexandra Cooper. Durham, N.C.: Duke University.

Putnam, Robert D. 2000. *Bowling Alone*. New York: Simon & Schuster.

Religion and Diversity Survey. 2002–2003. [machine-readable data file]. Principal investigator: Robert Wuthnow. Princeton, N.J.: Princeton Survey Center (producer); State College, Penn.: Association of Religion Data Archives, The Pennsylvania State University (distributor).

Religion and Public Life Survey. 2001. [machine-readable data file]. Pew Forum on Religion and Public Life. Washington, D.C.: Pew Research Center.

———. 2007. [machine-readable data file]. Pew Forum on Religion and Public Life. Washington, D.C.: Pew Research Center.

Rozell, Mark J., and Debasree Das Gupta. 2006. "The 'Values Vote?' Moral Issues and the 2004 Election." In *The Values Campaign?* edited by John C. Green, Mark J. Rozell, and Clyde Wilcox. Washington, D.C.: Georgetown University Press.

Shea, William M. 2004. *The Lion and the Lamb.* New York: Oxford University Press.

Smidt, Corwin E. 2004. *Pulpit and Politics: Clergy in American Politics at the Advent of the Millennium.* Waco, Tex.: Baylor University Press.

Smith, Christian, with Michael Emerson, Sally Gallagher, Paul Kennedy, and David Sikkink. 1998. *American Evangelicalism: Embattled and Thriving.* Chicago: University of Chicago Press.

Smith, Christian. 2000. *Christian America? What Evangelicals Really Want.* Berkeley: University of California Press.

Steensland, Brian, Jerry Z. Park, Mark D. Regnerus, Lynn D. Robinson, W. Bradford Wilcox, and Robert D. Woodberry. 2000. "The Measure of American Religion: Toward Improving the State of the Art." *Social Forces* 79(1): 291–318.

Sullivan, Amy. 2008. *The Party Faithful: How and Why Democrats Are Closing the God Gap.* New York: Scribner & Sons.

U.S. Religious Landscape Study. 2007. [machine-readable data file]. Pew Forum on Religion and Public Life. Washington, D.C.: Pew Research Center.

Watson, Justin. 1999. *The Christian Coalition.* New York: St. Martin's.

Wilcox, Clyde. 1990. "Blacks and the New Christian Right: Support for the Moral Majority and Pat Robertson among Washington D.C. Blacks." *Review of Religious Research* 32(1): 43–56.

———. 1992. *God's Warriors: The Christian Right in Twentieth-Century America.* Baltimore, Md.: Johns Hopkins University Press.

Wilcox Clyde, and Carin Larson. 2006. *Onward Christian Soldiers? The Religious Right in American Politics.* Boulder, Colo.: Westview Press.

Wilcox, Clyde, Alexandra Cooper, Peter Francia, John C. Green, Paul Herrnson, Lynda Powell, Jason Reifler, and Benjamin Webster. 2003. "With Limits Raised, Who Will Give More? The Impact of BCRA on Individual Donors." In *Life After Reform,* edited by Michael Malbin. Lanham, Md.: Rowman & Littlefield.

Williams, Rhys H., ed. 1997. *Cultural Wars in American Politics: Critical Reviews of a Popular Myth.* New York: Aldine de Gruyter.

Wilson, James Q. 1966. *The Amateur Democrat.* Chicago: University of Chicago Press.

Wolfe, Alan. 1998. *One Nation, After All: What Middle-Class Americans Really Think About: God, Country, Family, Racism, Welfare, Immigration, Homosexuality, Work, the Right, the Left, and Each Other.* New York: Viking.

Wuthnow, Robert. 1988. *The Restructuring of American Religion.* Princeton, N.J.: Princeton University Press.

———. 1996. "Restructuring of American Religion: Further Evidence." *Sociological Inquiry* 66(3): 303–29.

———. 2005. *America and the Challenges of Religious Diversity.* Princeton, N.J.: Princeton University Press.

Wuthnow, Robert, and John H. Evans. 2002. *The Quiet Hand of God: Faith-Based Activism and the Public Role of Mainline Protestants.* Berkeley: University of California Press.

Chapter 5

Evangelical Strength and the Political Representation of Women and Gays

JENNIFER MEROLLA, JEAN REITH SCHROEDEL,
AND SCOTT WALLER

MOST PEOPLE have normative beliefs about what constitutes masculine and feminine, even if they have not given much conscious thought to the question (Duerst-Lahti and Kelly 1995, 16–17). These beliefs generally fall into two camps: those, often religious traditionalists, who believe in sharp divisions between male and female roles, and those who believe that both men and women can take on many different roles. Gender ideology not only shapes beliefs about what it means to be biologically male and female, but also can be used to determine positions on a whole host of contentious social issues (for example, abortion, birth control, gay rights, same-sex marriage, home schooling, family values, pornography, sex education, HPV vaccinations, employment discrimination, welfare reform, and tax policy, to mention just a few). Elizabeth Oldmixon went so far as to argue that the predominant political division in the United States is between "those who embrace religious traditionalism and those who embrace progressive sexual norms" (2005, 2).[1]

Beginning in the 1970s, well-known evangelicals such as James Dobson (1975), Beverly LaHaye (1976), and Tim LaHaye (1977) began devoting substantial attention to defending what they considered to be biblically ordained gender essentialism and male headship from feminist challenges.[2] According to Dobson, "God apparently expects *man* to be the ultimate decision maker in the family" (1980, 64). Although some evangelicals, such as those associated with Sojourners, Christians for Biblical Equality, and Call to Renewal, have espoused gender egalitarian beliefs, they are a minority. Evangelical Protestants are substantially more likely than other Protestants and Catholics to agree that the "husband should be the head of the family" (reprinted in Gallagher 2003, 69).

But exactly what male headship means is under dispute. Although a few evangelical elites argue that God's divine order mandates a complete separation of roles with women limited to child care and homemaking (Christenson 1970), most have developed a more nuanced understanding of male headship—one that also emphasizes that marriage is a partnership. Even the leading gender essentialist evangelical parachurch group, the Council on Biblical Manhood and Womanhood, stresses that men and women "were created in God's image, equal before God as persons" before going on to state that they are "distinct in their manhood and womanhood" (1998).

According to Sally Gallagher, evangelicals increasingly use the language of complementarity, partnership and equality, as well as male headship, to describe male-female relationships. "What is distinctive is the idea that headship—centered on men's responsibility for spiritual leadership—reflects a nonnegotiable, God given spiritual hierarchy established in creation. . . . Yet even among those who affirm headship, the idea of men's leadership and accountability is held in tension with ideas about partnership and equality" (2003, 84; for further discussion of conservative Protestant views of family and family policy, see chapter 8, this volume.)

Those who reject gender essentialism are likely to concur with Georgia Duerst-Lahti and Rita Kelly that "gender is the socially constructed meaning given to biological sex, especially sex differences. Gender is how we come to understand, and often magnify, the minor differences that exist between biological males and females" (1995, 13). They tend to be much more accepting of a range of differing lifestyles, including homosexuality. Familial and work place roles and responsibilities are socially determined rather than innate. The extent to which those work-family arrangements are the product of private decisions or influenced by activist state policies designed to support a particular gender ideology differs across societies (Morgan 2006, 53).

Although a comprehensive test of the impact of religious traditionalism on gender roles is beyond the scope of this study, it is possible to determine whether a relationship exists between evangelicals and the range of acceptable gender roles within the political sphere. We explore here whether a statistically significant relationship exists between the strength of politically engaged evangelicals—those from denominations that encourage involvement in the political world—and the election to political office of women and gays, two groups whose involvement in politics strongly violates gender essentialist norms. Willingness to vote women and gays into political office is a good, if indirect, indicator of the erosion of traditionalist gender ideology, because these decisions reflect the extent to which conservative Christians are willing to entrust high levels of political authority to groups not sanctioned by the Bible as social or political authorities. If differences in gender ideology are as stark as critics of the Christian Right argue,[3] we would expect areas where traditionalism is strong to elect far fewer women and gays to political office than areas where it is weak.[4] On the other hand, if gender essentialist views are not that pronounced, we would not expect as sharp a difference.

Evangelical opposition to the election of gays should be stronger than their opposition to the election of women. Several studies examining General Social Survey data indicate a consensus among conservative Protestants that homosexual relations are always wrong, but much less agreement about women's roles (Gay, Ellison, and Powers 1996, 11; Hoffman and Miller 1997, 65). Moreover, although social attitudes toward gays have gradually become more favorable across the American public generally (Bolzendahl and Brooks 2005; Loftus 2001), strong opposition both to homosexuality as a lifestyle and to gay marriage remain particularly strong mobilizing elements in evangelical Protestant rhetoric.[5] Social distance theory therefore leads us to postulate that the evangelical electorate will be more open to women serving in political office than it is to homosexuals (Williams 1964, 29).

Although we expect to find an inverse relationship between the strength of politically engaged evangelical Protestants and the representation of women and gays in elected office, determining exactly how this relationship occurs is beyond the scope of this chapter. Several reasons might account for it. On the supply side, women and gays may choose not to run for office because they think they cannot win in these areas. Also, women holding religious traditionalist beliefs may be less likely to put themselves forward as candidates because they believe it is not appropriate, thereby decreasing the potential pool of female candidates. Party leaders may discourage female and gay candidates as well as erect institutional barriers to entry. On the demand side, voters may be unwilling to vote for candidates who do not conform to religiously based gender norms.

We focus on politically engaged evangelical Protestants rather than the entire traditionalist alliance—which would also include Mormons, traditionalist Catholics, conservative Jews, and conservative members of mainline Protestant denominations. We do so for two principal reasons. First, there has been a tremendous upsurge over the past thirty-five years in the political involvement of evangelicals.[6] Moreover, as George Marsden noted, "the issues of family and sexuality proved the key to unlocking evangelical potential to become overtly political" (2006, 5). Second, we were able to develop a good empirical measure of the strength of politically engaged evangelical Protestants, but do not have a comparable measure for distinguishing among other religious traditionalists. For example, how does one identify the strength in the electorate of traditionalistic Catholics over more moderate and liberal Catholics? However, we do consider the effect of Catholicism in our models.

The United States in Comparative Context

Cross-national researchers have found that religious beliefs are very important in determining the types of work and family roles suitable to men and women (Inglehart and Norris 2003; Norris and Inglehart 2005). Because religions have traditionally assigned a separate and subordinate role to women, countries in which more citizens are secular typically have provided more opportunities for women than highly religious countries have (Swatos and Christiano 2001). For historical reasons, predominantly Protestant countries have generally also been more open to a range of gender roles for men and women (Inglehart and Norris 2003).[7] Although evangelicals in the United States were at the forefront of struggles for women's rights in the nineteenth and early twentieth centuries (Bendroth 1993), that is no longer the case. Comparative politics scholars have found that predominantly Protestant and predominantly secular countries have the highest levels of women serving in elected office, but the United States is an outlier in that it has a very low proportion of women in elective office (Inglehart 1979; Inglehart and Norris 2003; Norris and Inglehart 2005). We posit that an important reason for the discrepancy lies in the nature of Protestantism in this country.

Over the past thirty years, social scientists have documented a dramatic decline in the proportion of the U.S. population associated with more liberal Protestant denominations and a commensurate increase in the proportion associated with socially conservative ones (Masci 2004, 7). The 1998 National Congregational Study showed that 59 percent of congregations self-identified as theologically "more on the conservative side" and only 11 percent as "more on the liberal side" (Chaves 2004, 28). The breakdown was similar when regular attendance at religious services was studied, with 53 percent of regular attenders belonging to theologically conservative congregations and only 10 percent to theologically liberal ones (Chaves 2004, 28; for further discussion, see chapter 7, this volume).

These fast-growing evangelical churches espouse a conservative gender ideology. The Southern Baptists, which has one of the highest growth rates, in 1998 revised their Baptist Faith and Message to read: "A wife is to submit graciously to the servant leadership of her husband even as the church willingly submits to the headship of Christ" and then went on to state that the wife "has the God given responsibility to respect her husband and to serve as his helper in managing her household and nurturing the next generation" (Larry Stammer, "A Wife's Role is 'to Submit,' Baptists Declare," *Los Angeles Times*: June 10, 1998, A1, A28). Two years later at their convention, the Southern Baptists voted to limit church leadership positions to men (Mead and Hill 2001, 66).

Although a liberalizing trend is evident in views about the morality of homosexuality over time, with a slight dip in the 1980s, this pattern does not hold among socially conservative Protestants (Loftus 2001). Researchers have consistently found that members of socially conservative Protestant churches exhibit far less social tolerance toward gays than members of other Protestant churches and Catholics do (Britton 1990; Button, Rienzo, and Wald 1997; Haider-Markel and Meier 1996; Nice 1988; Wald, Button, and Rienzo 1996). A recent survey of more than 35,000 Americans found that only 28 percent of respondents belonging to traditionally white evangelical churches believed that homosexuality should be accepted by society versus 56 percent and 58 percent, respectively, of those belonging to mainline Protestant churches and the Catholic Church (Pew Forum on Religion & Public Life 2008, 92).

Again, the Southern Baptists provide a good example of church teachings. The 1987 Southern Baptist Convention condemned homosexuality as a "manifestation of a depraved nature and a perversion of divine standards," but its current website offers a more muted condemnation: "Homosexuality is not a 'valid alternative lifestyle.' The Bible condemns it as sin. It is not, however, unforgivable sin. The same redemption available to all sinners is available to homosexuals."[8]

This promulgation of a religiously based gender ideology also occurs in para-church organizations that cut across denominational divisions. Since its founding in 1990, Promise Keepers has drawn more than 5 million men to its more than 170 stadium and arena events, and held numerous special conferences that have brought together 39,000 ministers to hear its message about what it means to be "real men" (Gutterman 2005, 95). According to David Gutterman, Promise Keepers believe that the nation's social problems are a direct result of the "breakdown of the traditional family" due to a "crisis in masculinity" brought about by "the confusing of 'divinely ordained' categories of sex, sexuality and gender" (2005, 102). Bill McCartney, the founder of Promise Keepers, was one of the main proponents of Colorado's Amendment 2, the 1992 ballot initiative that prohibited any governmental entity in the state from extending protected status to homosexuals,[9] and referred to homosexuality as an "abomination against almighty God" (Abraham 1997, 25).

Politics and Gender Ideology in the United States

According to the sociologist Joan Acker, institutional life is gendered in that stereotypical expectations about men and women's attributes and behavior, the appropriate distribution of power, and organizational processes are all designed in a way that privileges one biological sex over another (1992). Institutions become gendered over time as one biological sex becomes associated with the activities of the organization. The preferences of the founders become the norm and establish ongoing power relations (Duerst-Lahti 2005, 231). Although these power relations may erode over time, many are remarkably "sticky" and resistant to change. Some, such as the Southern Baptists, react to the erosion of traditional relations by replacing informal norms with statutory restrictions on who may serve in power positions.

Political institutions also reflect ongoing gender power relations, and may be more resistant to change than most other social institutions (Duerst-Lahti 2005; Jillson and Wilson 1994). After centuries of heterosexual white men (at least nominally heterosexual men) virtually monopolizing political office holding, it is not surprising that women and men who do not conform to the expected gender norms are outsiders.[10] Although nontraditional candidates have made inroads into political office, the political system, in both subtle and blatant ways, is skewed against their participation.[11] Moreover, social psychology studies have found that the desire for a prototypical male leader is strongest during times of uncertainty and stress, such as since 9/11 in the United States (Hogg 2005a, 2005b).[12]

Many religious conservatives use jeremiad language to claim that the United States is currently in a crisis, which necessitates a return to "traditional family values"—a term which is, among other things, a shorthand for traditional gender roles (Gutterman 2005; Morone 2003). Yet even very socially conservative religious leaders recognize that gender relations in contemporary America are radically different than they were a generation ago. Marvin Olasky, an early advisor to President George W. Bush, admitted to instances when he might vote for a woman running for political office, but went on to state that "there's a certain shame attached to it" and that these occurrences are likely to be the result of men abdicating their rightful position as leaders (Wegner 1998, 5). Pat Robertson also acknowledged that women are capable of doing virtually every task, including governing, as well as men, but went on to argue that the very survival of the nation requires women to return to being "a wife, a mother and a homemaker" (1995, 163, 166). Another indicator of reduced orthodoxy is that many conservative evangelicals were enthusiastic about the pick of Sarah Palin for the Republican vice presidential spot in John McCain's run for the presidency in 2008.

Gender, Religion, and Electoral Office; Past Work

Much of the sizable literature on women's representation in elected office indicates that a candidate's biological sex impacts vote choice. Some experimental studies have found that gender stereotypes influence decisions in hypothetical elections (Eckstrand and Eckert 1981; Huddy and Terkildsen 1993; Rosenwasser and Dean 1989; Sanbonmatsu 2002), and others that voters use the biological sex of candidates as an information shortcut, assigning to candidates attributes typically identified as male or female (McDermott 1997, 1998; King and Matland 2003). Analyses of individual-level data from congressional races have shown that being a woman, a Democrat, a liberal, and supporting liberal women's issues are associated with support for female candidates (Cook 1994; Dolan 1998; Huddy 1994; Huddy and Terkildsen 1993; McDermott 1997, 1998; Paolino 1995; Schroedel and Snyder 1994). Studies using aggregate state level data have identified sociodemographic measures, the state's history of electing women to political office, institutional variables, the type of office, the pool of potential candidates, and aggregate partisanship as important indicators (Arceneux 2001; Fox and Oxley 2003; Nechemias 1987; Norrander and Wilcox 1998; Rule 1981, 1990; Wilcox and Norrander 2005).

With respect to the impact of religion on the representation of women in political office, the research is mixed. Although experimental studies found that gender stereotypes influenced choices, they did not find that religiosity had an independent effect on an individual's propensity to vote for the female candidate (Ekstrand and Eckert 1981; Sanbonmatsu 2002). Other research, however, showed that those with higher levels of religiosity were less likely to vote for female congressional candidates (Dolan 1998). One state-level study found that the proportion of Catholics had no effect, but that the proportion of fundamentalists and Pentecostals had a positive effect on the proportion of women in state legislatures. The authors attributed this finding to aggressive Republican efforts to recruit women candidates during the particular year they examined (Norrander and Wilcox 1998).

Since the late 1990s, the Republican Party has been much less willing to recruit and support female candidates for political office. For example, a record number of women ran for state legislative office, generally a prerequisite for higher levels of office, in 2006. Of those 2,429, 64 percent were Democrats, and they comprised 68 percent of the 1,731 women elected. This is a much larger partisan disparity than that among male state legislators, where the split is 53 percent Democratic and 45 percent Republican. Furthermore, the positive effect that Barbara Norrander and Clyde Wilcox found does not hold up when other years are examined (1998). Sue Vandenbosch examined a different year and found that the percentage Christian had a negative effect on the proportion of women serving in state legislatures, and that the effect was strongest among states with high membership in nonegalitarian Christian denominations (1996). More recent studies have found that states with large numbers of evangelicals are less likely to elect women (Schroedel, Merolla, and Foerstel 2005; Merolla, Schroedel, and Holman 2007).

Until very recently, the empirical research on gay political candidates has been quite limited, including the determinants of voting for gay and lesbian candidates (Cook 1999, 679). Some of the most interesting studies have involved experiments, in which respondents were asked to evaluate hypothetical candidates running for political office. Researchers found that evaluations of hypothetical gay and lesbian candidates are influenced by group stereotypes and the political context (Golebiowska and Thomsen 1999; Herrick and Thomas 1999). When participants were asked whether they were likely to vote for hypothetical candidates for city council seats, researchers found that political conservatives and members of conservative Protestant churches were significantly less likely to support hypothetical candidates perceived to be gay (Herrick and Thomas 1999, 2001).

The most significant empirical analysis of community receptivity to gay candidates was conducted by James Button, Kenneth Wald, and Barbara Rienzo as an extension of their much larger study of gay rights politics in 126 cities and counties (1999, 1997).[13] Among this atypical sample of communities, the authors found that population size, the percentage of nonfamily households (a proxy measure for gay density), electoral rules, and social movement organization were significant predictors of gay electoral activity, and to some extent gay electoral success. Somewhat surprisingly, they did not find that political opposition from socially conservative Christian groups was a factor in gay electoral activity (Button, Wald, and Rienzo 1999, 203). Their sample, however, was comprised of the most gay-friendly communities in the country.

As is evident from this survey of the literature, no consensus exists concerning whether religion exerts a significant impact on the representation of women or gays in elected office. We believe the contradictory findings in the literature are due to limitations in the studies' research design. The one important empirical study of gay and lesbian candidates was limited in that its sample consisted of the most pro-gay communities in country. The more extensive literature on voting for female candidates also has limitations. First, of the few studies that have looked at the relationship between religion and the representation of women in political office, many use a rough proxy for socially conservative Protestants or one that breaks denominations into egalitarian and nonegalitarian denominations. Second, the few aggregate-level studies have yielded contradictory results, possibly because they have examined a single atypical election or only looked at state legislative offices. In this chapter we try to overcome some of these limitations by developing a more theoretically grounded measure of the presence of engaged evangelical Protestants, testing this measure at the aggregate level for more recent data and using a composite indicator at the state level that incorporates different levels of office.

Studying Political Representation

In designing a study to examine the electoral prospects of women and gays in states with large evangelical populations, we faced several methodological issues. These included construction of dependent variables to measure accurately the electoral prospects of women and gays, construction of the key independent variables to measure the influence of politically engaged evangelicals, and the choice of appropriate control variables. We discuss each of these issues briefly.

Dependent Variables

To measure a state's propensity to elect women to political office, we use a composite variable constructed for 2004 by the Institute for Women's Policy Research (IWPR) and derived by determining the proportion of women in five types of elective office in each state for the given year: state representatives, state senators, elected state executive officers, members of the U.S. House of Representatives, and U.S. senators. For each type of office, a state's observed value was then divided by the highest value for all the states. The scores for each office in each state were then adjusted to take into account the differences in the degree of political influence wielded by individuals in each office: 1.0 for state representatives, 1.25 for state senators, 1.5 for statewide executive officers other than governors, 1.5 for U.S. representatives, and 1.75 for U.S. senators and state governors. The weighted scores for each office were added together to reach a composite score for the state (Werschkul and Williams 2004, 61). The resulting scores range from a low of 0.78 in Mississippi to a high of 4.38 in Washington. The mean score was 1.93, with a standard deviation of .837.

It was somewhat more difficult to construct a measure for gay elected officials. For one, it is only possible to obtain data on openly gay elected officials. Second, there are not many gay elected officials at the state and national level. For example, there are only three openly gay U.S. House members and no openly gay U.S. senators or governors. We therefore decided to extend the analysis of gay elected officials to the local level. We were able to obtain current data on gay elected officials at the local, state, and national level from the Gay and Lesbian Victory Fund and Leadership Institute. We then constructed a score similar to the way in which the IWPR developed the composite measure for women in elected office. For each type of office, a state's observed value was then divided by the highest value for all of the states. The scores for each office in each state were then adjusted to take into account the differences in the degree of political influence wielded by individuals in each office: 1.0 for all local offices, 1.25 for state house, 1.5 for state senate, and 1.75 for U.S. House of Representatives. The weighted scores were then summed to reach a composite score for the state. The mean value on the composite measure was only .633, and the standard deviation .918. Resulting score ranges from a low of 0 in Alaska, Alabama, Arkansas, Louisiana, North Dakota, South Carolina, South Dakota, Tennessee, and West Virginia, to a high of 3.44 in California.

Independent Variables

According to Frank Mead and Samuel Hill, there are more than 250 different Protestant sects within the United States and trying to ascertain the social views and degree of politicization of these entities would be an enormous undertaking (2001). Moreover, not all socially conservative Protestant denominations encourage their members to become involved in the affairs of the world. For example, Jehovah's Witnesses espouse very conservative gender views, but their members rarely engage in political activities. In fact, the vast majority of Jehovah's Witnesses do not even register to vote (Pew Forum on Religion & Public Life 2008, 81).

To study the effects of conservative religion on the electoral chances of women and gays, we wanted a more nuanced measure than the broad categories often used in this research. We also wanted a measure that incorporated a political dimension, such as one based on the identification of evangelical Protestant denominations. As noted earlier, religion and politics scholars have identified the political engagement of evangelicals as a key factor in the rise of the Republican Party since the 1980s. Recent survey data indicate strong support for the political engagement of evangelicals. More than 75 percent of evangelical respondents to a large 2007 survey were registered to vote and nearly 65 percent believed that churches should express political views from the pulpit (Pew Forum on Religion & Public Life 2008, 81, 98). To measure

the impact of evangelical Protestant denominations that support political engagement, we created a composite measure that includes denominations associated with the National Association of Evangelicals (NAE)
and Baptists. The NAE encourages political engagement by its members, is comprised of forty-nine socially conservative churches, and is an
activist organization that lobbies government on a wide range of social
and political issues (Schultz, West, and Maclean 1999, 322). We also included Baptists in our measure because they comprise a very large portion of the evangelical community but do not belong to the NAE. In the
contemporary period, they also encourage political activism. The Southern Baptists, who make up more than 75 percent of all Baptists, have
provided many of the most important leaders of the religious right.
Their Ethics & Religious Liberty Commission is very active on Capitol
Hill and has worked hard to politically mobilize Southern Baptists
throughout the country.

To create our politically engaged evangelical variable, we used
church membership data obtained by the 2001 American Religion Identification Survey of 50,281 residential households in the continental
United States (Kosmin, Mayer, and Keysar 2001, 6). The uneven distribution of evangelicals across the country permits the use of state level
data to test our hypotheses. The percentage of a state's population identifying as belonging to Baptist and NAE churches ranges from 3 percent
in Utah to 61 percent in Mississippi, with a mean of 20.08 and a standard
deviation of 14.22.

We believe this measure has advantages over the alternatives. Unlike
measures that focus on individual behavior, ours takes into account the
importance of church community in shaping social behavior and avoids
problems of bias in self-reported measures of behavior. It is nuanced
and, more important, allows us to distinguish between denominations
that support political involvement from those that favor withdrawal
from the world.

We also included the proportions of Catholics, nonengaged evangelicals, and nonevangelical Protestants as independent variables. This data
comes from the same source as the NAE-Baptist measure. Although Andrew Reynolds found predominantly Catholic countries to be as open to
women in elected office as predominantly Protestant and predominantly secular countries, other comparative scholars have not (1999).
Comparative politics scholars have not taken up the question of a possible relationship between religion and the propensity to elect gays to political office. However, as we indicated earlier, ties between traditionalist
Catholics and conservative Protestants in the United States have been
increasing. Therefore, we would expect a negative effect for Catholics on
women, but not necessarily with respect to gays. The remaining mea-

sures for nonevangelical Protestants and nonengaged evangelicals could have null, positive, or negative effects relative to the baseline.[14]

Control Variables

We controlled for the general socioeconomic context of a state. From the U.S. census, we collected data on the percentage living in urban areas, the percentage with a college degree, the unemployment rate, the percentage of owner-occupied housing, and the Gini coefficient, which is a standard measure of economic inequality.[15] Because of the high correlation between many of these variables, we use the method of principal component factor analysis. Two factors emerged with eigenvalues greater than 1. The state's percentage urban, percentage with a college degree, and percentage of owner-occupied housing loaded highly on the first factor, which we label *Economy 1*.[16] Based on previous research, we expected a positive coefficient for this variable on women's electoral prospects (Rule 1981; Nechemias 1987). We expected a similar effect for gay elected officials. The state's percentage with a college degree, percentage unemployed, and the Gini coefficient loaded highly on the second factor, which we label *Economy 2*.[17] This latter factor is a measure of state-level income inequality, and we expected it to have a negative coefficient on the electoral prospects of women and gays, given that higher values indicate more inequality (Paglin 1975).

We included several political control variables used in previous studies. First, we control for baseline partisanship and ideology, using the variables Robert Erikson, Gerald Wright, and John McIver created (1993).[18] Using national polls conducted by CBS and the *New York Times*, Erikson and his colleagues created a measure of mean party identification by state, which is coded so that higher values are more Republican. They also created a measure of mean ideology by state, which is coded so that higher values are more liberal. We used the latest year available, 1999.[19] We were uncertain about the direction of the effect for mean party identification because studies have found mixed results for women in elected office (Arceneaux 2001; Nechemias 1987; Rule 1990). However, we expected a positive coefficient on the mean ideology variable because studies have shown that more liberal states have a significant positive effect on the proportion of women in elected office (Norrander and Wilcox 1998). We expected a similar effect with respect to gay elected officials because studies show that conservative individuals are less supportive of gay elected officials in hypothetical races (Herrick and Thomas 1999, 2001).

Finally, we included control variables more specific to women and gays running for office. We controlled for the pool of potential female candidates (Arceneaux 2001; Norrander and Wilcox 1998; Rule 1993;

Wilcox and Norrander 2005). Based on previous research, we included measures of women's economic status in each state and performed a factor analysis on the measures (Norrander and Wilcox 1998; Wilcox and Norrander 2005). Two factors with eigenvalues greater than 1 emerged. We labeled the first Women's Status 1. Four of the variables loaded highly on this factor: the percentage of women in the labor force, with health insurance, with a college degree, and living above the poverty line.[20] This first factor taps into women's overall socioeconomic status in a state. We labeled the second factor Women's Status 2. Again, four of the variables loaded highly on this factor: the earnings ratio, the percentage of women in managerial or professional occupations, the percentage of women with a college degree, and the percentage of women-owned business.[21] The Women's Status 2 factor is associated with the potential pool of female candidates in that it is an indicator of women's success in professional roles. We expected a positive sign on both factors. Finally, following Richard Fox and Zoe Oxley, we developed a measure, which we labeled Average, of the state's history of electing women to statewide legislative office (2003). The measure is the average percentage of women holding office in the state legislature over the past twenty years. We expected this control variable to have a strong positive coefficient, because it indicates which states are more likely to elect women to office (Rule 1990).[22]

U.S. government agencies do not yet collect detailed data on gay-owned businesses or the percentage of gays in the labor force because individuals are not asked about their sexuality. Scholars have, however, been able to approximate the proportion of same-sex households from census forms by matching whether respondents indicate that they have an unmarried partner and whether that person's sex matches the respondent's sex. Of course, such a measure is imperfect in that it underestimates the proportion of homosexuals in the population by counting only those who live together and indicate that they are partners. Although imperfect, such a measure can at least give us a sense of the proportion of gays in a given state. The specific measure we used is the Gay and Lesbian Index, which indicates how concentrated same-sex couples are in a given area. The measure is a ratio of the proportion of same-sex couples living in a region to the proportion of households in the region. More simply, it provides a sense of whether same-sex couples are over- or underrepresented in an area relative to the population. A value of 1.0 means that a same-sex couple is just as likely as a randomly picked household to live in a certain area, and a value of 2.0 indicates that same-sex couples are twice as likely to live in a certain area relative to a randomly picked household (Gates and Ost 2004). As this ratio increases, we expect it to have a positive effect on the gay elected official composite measure. In the dataset, it ranges from .48 to 1.43.

Evangelicals and the Representation of Women and Gays

Before turning to the results of our multivariate analyses, we plot the data to see whether there is initial support for an inverse relationship between the NAE-Baptist measure and the women in elected office and gay in elected office composite scores. Figure 5.1 presents the scatter plot for the women in elected office composite score, and figure 5.2 presents the scatter plot for the gay in elected office composite score.

In figure 5.1, we see an inverse relationship between membership in politically engaged evangelical Protestant churches and women's representation in electoral office, providing some initial support for our hypothesis. In figure 5.2, we also see an inverse relationship between the NAE-Baptist measure and gay elected officials across states.[23] Although religious factors may indeed be a strong predictor, we also find that some states, such as New Jersey and Pennsylvania, are low on the NAE-Baptist measure and on composite measures of women and gays elected to office. Furthermore, from both figures it appears that many of the states that are high on both dimensions are in the South. This suggests that factors other than evangelical strength may also be important for predicting the electoral prospects of women and gays. For example, some states may impose institutional barriers that work against female and gay candidates. Alternatively, the strength of the Catholic Church in New Jersey and Pennsylvania may affect the number of women and gays in elected office.

Although Catholics were a key part of the Democratic Party's New Deal coalition, and might therefore be expected to support the party that has more females and gays running for office, they have become a swing constituency in the electorate. Traditionalist Catholics have formed antiabortion alliances with socially conservative Protestants. In the 2004 election, President Bush used agreement on moral issues to aggressively court the Catholic vote, which he carried by a narrow margin (Oldmixon 2005, 109–12). Moreover, the Catholic Church has an exclusively male hierarchy, which suggests that Catholics may be less socially comfortable with women in positions of leadership. Conversely, the previously cited Pew survey indicated that Catholics were more accepting of homosexuality than members of any other Christian denomination (for further discussion, see chapter 4, this volume). Although we are able in the next section to account for some of these factors that may also influence the proportion of women and gays in elected office, we chose not to control for the South, given its high correlation with the NAE-Baptist measure (0.82).[24] The NAE-Baptist measure more closely approximates our theoretical construct compared to a simple regional measure.

Figure 5.1   NAE and Women in Elected Office

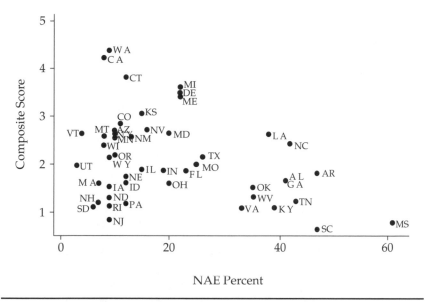

Source: Author's compilation based on the 2001 American Religion Identification Survey (Kosim, Mayer, and Keysar 2001) and Werschkul and Williams 2004.

Figure 5.2   NAE and Gay Elected Officials

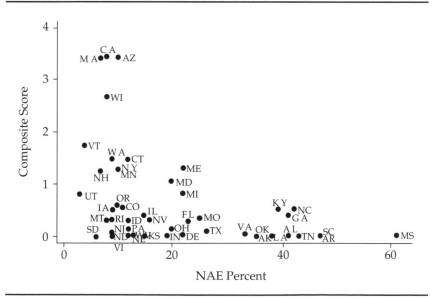

Source: Author's compilation based on the 2001 American Religion Identification Survey (Kosim, Mayer, and Keysar 2001) and the Gay and Lesbian Victory Fund and Leadership Institite 2006.

Religion and the Electoral Prospects of Women

Because our dependent variables are continuous, we used ordinary least squares (OLS) regression in our multivariate analyses. The OLS regression results for women in elected office are presented in model 1 of table 5.1. Turning to the first column of results, we find that our key variable, the NAE-Baptist percentage, is significant and negative, as expected. Thus, as the NAE-Baptist percentage increases in a state, the composite women in elected office variable decreases. Although –.037 may not look like a large substantive effect, it is sizable when compared to the scale of the dependent variable, which ranges only from .78 to 4.38. For example, a state at the mean NAE-Baptist percentage (20 percent) would drop .74 points on the scale, which is substantial. The comparable effect with the maximum NAE-Baptist percentage (61 percent in Mississippi) is a drop of more than 2 points on the scale (2.26), clearly a large drop. Thus we receive strong support for our hypothesis. These results are also in line with other findings (Vandenbosch 1996).

Our key hypothesis is also supported if we look at the results for the other religion measures. The nonevangelical Protestant measure has a negative sign but is not statistically significant, whereas the nonengaged evangelical measure is positively signed but also statistically insignificant. Thus, statistically reliable effects in line with expectations occur only among evangelicals from politically mobilized denominations. With respect to the controls, the Catholic variable is significant and negative. The substantive effect of the Catholic variable is a bit weaker than the NAE-Baptist measure at –.033.

The first economic factor is insignificant, but the second one, which is an indicator of inequality, is positive and comes close to meeting conventional levels of statistical significance ($p = .12$). This suggests that states with higher levels of income inequality are more likely to elect women to office. Although the coefficient seems larger than the NAE-Baptist measure, the range of the independent variable is smaller. For example, a state at the maximum value on the second economy factor would increase only 1.126 units on the women in elected office composite score. This effect is more than a unit smaller than the effect at the maximum value on the NAE-Baptist measure.

The two women's status factors are in the expected positive direction, though only the second measure comes close to reaching statistical significance ($p = .12$). This finding is consistent with those of Barbara Norrander and Clyde Wilcox (1998), who also found that increases in women's status led to higher levels of women in state legislative office. The maximum value on this measure leads to a shift of about 1.103 units on the dependent variable. The state's history of electing women to office, party identification, and the ideology measures are all positive,

Table 5.1   Regression on Women and Gay in Elected Office Composite Measures

Variable	Model 1 Women Coefficient (Standard Error)	Model 2 Gay Coefficient (Standard Error)
NAE-Baptist	−0.037** (0.019)	−0.024* (0.017)
Catholic	−0.033** (0.019)	0.000 (0.017)
Nonevangelical Protestants	−0.006 (0.022)	0.006 (0.019)
Nonengaged Evangelical Protestants	0.095 (0.081)	0.024 (0.075)
Economy 1	−0.090 (0.285)	0.028 (0.181)
Economy 2	0.532 (0.333)	−0.075 (0.158)
Mean party identification	1.470 (1.472)	−1.563 (1.394)
Mean ideology	0.287 (2.053)	−0.577 (1.987)
Women's status 1	0.172 (0.341)	——
Women's status 2	0.409* (0.254)	——
Average	1.569 (1.487)	——
Gay and lesbian index	——	1.977*** (0.865)
Constant	3.284*** (1.014)	−1.065 (1.385)
N	48	48
R^2	0.342	0.415

Source: Author's compilation based on Werschkul and Williams 2004; the Gay and Lesbian Victory Fund and Leadership Institute 2006; the 2001 American Religion Identification Survey (Kosmin, Mayer and Keysar 2001); U.S. Bureau of the Census 2000, 2004a; Erikson, Wright, and McIver 1993; and Gates and Ost 2004.
*** $p < .05$ (two-tailed); ** $p < .10$ (two -tailed); * $p < .10$ (one-tailed)

though none are significant. Finally, the overall model performs fairly well, with an R-square of .34.[25]

Religion and the Electoral Prospects of Gays

The results for the gay elected official composite measure are presented in the column labeled model 2 in table 5.1. Again, we see that the NAE-Baptist measure is significant and negative, with a coefficient of –.024. This appears small, but recall that the gay elected official composite measure ranges only from 0 to 3.44. For example, a state at the mean NAE-Baptist percentage (20 percent) would drop .48 points on the scale. The comparable effect with the maximum NAE-Baptist percent (61 percent in Mississippi) is a drop of 1.6 points on the scale, which is a very large drop. Thus we receive strong support for our hypothesis with respect to gay elected officials.[26] As in the previous model, the other Protestant measures are not statistically significant. However, in this case, the Catholic variable is also not significant. The only other significant variable in the model is the gay and lesbian index.[27] The substantive effect of this measure is very large: a 1 unit change in the index leads to a 1.977 increase in the composite score. The mean value on the measure is .912, thus the average increase would be about 1.80.[28]

Overall, our findings are supportive of our hypotheses. In this well-controlled study, as the percentage of evangelical Protestants from politically engaged denominations increases in a given state, the proportion of female and gay elected officials tends to decline.

Conclusion: Will Gender Traditionalist Norms Continue?

At the beginning of this chapter, we noted that religiously based normative beliefs about the meaning of masculinity and femininity figure prominently in disputes over many social policy issues. Although some conservative evangelicals espouse rigid gender essentialist views, many now use much more egalitarian language along with references to male headship. But exactly what this mix of complementarity, egalitarianism, and male headship means is less clear. Does it provide some opportunities for women to step out of their traditional roles? What about men who do not conform to the masculine norms? In this chapter, we examined just one aspect of this multifaceted phenomenon. Does the presence of large numbers of socially conservative evangelicals in a population act as a check on the representation of women and gays in political office?

As expected, the impact of the NAE-Baptist measure on women in elected office was statistically significant and negative. That the relationship held up after the introduction of a powerful battery of controls is confirmation of our basic contention that the political engagement of evangelicals does appear to have a strong impact on the political empowerment of women. This relationship also held only for politically engaged evangelicals. The proportion of nonengaged evangelicals and nonevangelical Protestants had no effect on the proportion of women and gays in elected office. We also found evidence of a dampening effect of Catholicism on women's political empowerment, perhaps an indication of the success of Republicans in using moral issues to mobilize traditionalist Catholics. Somewhat surprisingly, the impact of the NAE-Baptist variable on the representative of gays, although statistically significant and negative, did not have as strong an effect as it did on women's representation. More research will be needed to tease out the reasons for this unexpected result. One possibility is that antigay feelings are widespread and not limited to politically engaged evangelicals. However, Catholicism did not have a significant effect on the proportion of gay elected officials.

Although our research indicates that states with a strong NAE-Baptist presence have been more resistant than other states to women's political representation, they are not immune to the forces of change, which have led to enormous increases in women's representation in political office over the past three decades. For example, in 1977, eleven states had less than 5 percent female representation in their state legislatures and only four had more than 15 percent.[29] By 1997, only South Carolina's state legislature was comprised of less than 10 percent women, and 30 state legislatures were composed of more than 20 percent women (Center for American Women and Politics 2007). Although eight of the ten states with the lowest current representation of women in state legislatures are among the top ten states with respect to the proportion of their population belonging to conservative evangelical churches, their average percent female is 13.5 percent, which is higher than all but six states in 1977. Furthermore, the high degree of support for Sarah Palin among evangelical conservatives in the 2008 presidential election suggests that many evangelicals are willing to put aside traditionalist gender ideology in the service of partisan causes or revise it so that it does not apply to the secular political sphere (Teresa Watanabe, "Evangelicals Differ on whether Palin's Career Fits Biblical Model," *Los Angeles Times*, October 1, 2008, B1).

The situation is more mixed with respect to gays. Nine states—eight of which are high NAE-Baptist score states—have no openly gay elected officials, but only a few states have relatively high rates of gay representation. Without exception, these states have very small evangelical populations. What cannot be ascertained at this juncture is whether the increase in gays being elected to office will spread beyond this handful of progressive states, perhaps augmented by the occasional election of gays in atypically cosmopolitan urban centers in what are otherwise socially and religiously conservative states. Although it is possible that acceptance of gays serving in elected office will grow, just as it has of women, it is equally plausible that evangelicals near universal condemnation of homosexuality will prevent it.

Given that representation in one form or another is a defining feature of modern democracies, the question of whether all members of our polity have a meaningful seat at the table is not a trivial one. If we interpret our results through this lens, then politically engaged evangelicals play some role in limiting the presence of certain groups at the table. However, one could also interpret the results as a signal that democracy is working as it should, in that conservative evangelicals are realizing their preferences at the ballot box. Even though the proportional representation of women and gays in electoral office is far from their presence in the population, we would argue that an examination of the trends across time are clearly moving in the direction of greater representation—one might even go so far as to posit that the glass is half full rather than half empty. Although many evangelicals are resistant, they have not stopped these changes, even in the states where their numbers are large. Furthermore, the enthusiasm for Sarah Palin suggests that evangelicals may be revising gender traditionalist norms in the secular political sphere.

Notes

1. The authors thank the participants at the Christian Conservative Movement and American Democracy Conference for their comments. We especially thank our discussants, Rogers Smith and Mitchell L. Stevens, for their helpful and constructive feedback. Finally, we thank Pamela Foerstal and Mirya Holman, who assisted with some of the data collection.
2. At the elite level, conservative evangelical groups continue to devote a great deal of attention to issues that run counter to their gender ideology. For example, Steven Brint and Seth Abrutyn in their analysis of issues covered on conservative Christian websites found that gender-related issues, such as denunciations of homosexuality and abortion, were covered far more than other issues (see volume 2, chapter 4).
3. Numerous websites and Internet blogs draw comparisons between the Taliban and the religious right in the United States (see, for example, Tamara Turner 2005 *Online Journal* commentary, "Onward, Christian Theocrats: The Yankee Taliban on the Attack," http://www.onlinejournal.com/TheocracyAlert/html/061105turner.html).
4. Not all offices will necessarily conflict with evangelical gender ideology. For example, if we were to look at offices separately, we might find that a woman serving on a school board would not conflict because it is a part-time position that would not necessarily interfere with a woman's role in the home. If we look across the scope of offices, however, we should find a general negative relationship.
5. See, for example, SBC Positions Statements, "Sexuality," http://www.sbc.net/aboutus/pssexuality.asp.
6. The Supreme Court's decision in Roe v. Wade, 410 U.S. 113 (1973), served

as a catalyst, convincing many socially conservative Protestants that the nation was heading in the wrong direction and that protecting traditional morality and family values required political mobilization (Wilcox 1988, 668). Ronald Reagan's victory in the 1980 presidential election was a direct outgrowth of this mobilization (Masci 2004, 14). In the 2004 presidential election, evangelical voters comprised more than 30 percent of all Bush voters (Pew Research Center 2004).

7. The Protestant Reformation in the sixteenth century undercut the Catholic Church's claim to hegemony in Biblical interpretation. Over time, the many different branches of Protestantism developed their own distinct interpretations of biblical text (Strong 1999, 207–08). Although Reformation theologians continued to uphold the "ideal of the family unit as represented by a male head of household," Protestant churches provided many more opportunities for women to receive divine revelation (Yust 1999, 266). This history of greater religious opportunity for women helps explain why Protestant countries have generally had less rigid gender roles than Catholic countries, as well as those where Islam is predominant.

8. See, for example, SBC Positions Statements, "Sexuality," http://www.sbc .net/aboutus/pssexuality.asp.

9. Amendment 2 was overturned by the Supreme Court in Romer v. Evans, 517 U.S. 620 (1996), on the grounds that it violated the Equal Protection Clause of the Fourteenth Amendment.

10. There are no records of women serving in elected political office during the first hundred years of the country's existence. In 1895, three women were elected to the Colorado statehouse and in 1917 Jeanette Rankin of Montana became the first woman elected to the U.S. House of Representatives. Since the founding era, more than 11,000 men have served in Congress, but only a couple hundred women (Schroedel and Mazumdar 1998, 204). The 1974 election of Kathy Kozachenko to the Ann Arbor city council was path-breaking, in that it was the first time that an openly gay or lesbian was elected to political office in the United States (Singer and Deschamps 1994, 16). According to the Gay and Lesbian Victory Fund (2006), only about 350 of the country's 511,000 state and local elected officials are openly gay.

11. A number of electoral practices, which appear neutral on the surface, in fact advantage traditional candidates. According to Robert Darcy, Susan Welch, and Janet Clark, women are much more likely to be elected if a state or locality uses a multimember electoral system rather than a single-member system (1994, 169–71). At the national level, the biggest barrier to women's electoral success is the power of incumbency (176–77).

12. In a poll conducted one year after the 9/11 attacks, 61 percent of respondents indicated they believed that men were better suited than women at handling military crises. On specific questions related to fighting terrorism and the Middle East conflict, support for male political leaders was 30 to 40 percent higher than it was for female political leaders (Lawless 2004, 484).

13. The authors chose cities and counties, which had adopted antidiscrimination legislation providing legal protection to gays, so their sample is likely to be the most favorable climate for gay candidates (Button, Rienzo and Wald 1997). These communities constitute only 1 percent of all local governments in the United States.

14. Research has shown that evangelicals and Mormons have similar attitudes on gender roles and homosexuality, so we might expect a similar pattern for Mormons here as well (Campbell and Monson 2007). We did run models, including a control, for the proportion of Mormons in the state and it was not statistically significant in the analysis for women or gay elected officials. Furthermore, the results for our key NAE measure remain consistent.

15. The most recent state level data on the Gini coefficient is from 1999 (U.S. Bureau of the Census 2004b). The Gini coefficient is a measure that plots the cumulative share of total income earned by households ranked from the top ten percent to the bottom ten percent of the population. It is based on the Lorenz curve and scores typically range from 0 to 1.0 with a score of 0 indicating perfect equality and a score of 1.0 indicating perfect inequality (Kawachi 2000). We rescaled the Gini coefficient to run from 0 to 100.

16. The loadings for the rotated factors are as follows: percentage urban, .852; percentage of owner occupied housing, −.861; and percentage with a college degree, .587.

17. The loadings for the rotated factors are as follows: unemployment rate, .819; Gini ratio, .688; and percentage with a college degree, −.681.

18. Several papers on women in elected office use some form of Daniel Elazar's political culture measure as a control variable (Elazar 1996; Fox and Oxley 2003; Nechemias 1987; Norrander and Wilcox 1998). This measure, as well as Ira Sharkansky's index (1969), was highly correlated with our NAE-Baptist measure, so we could not include them in the analysis. This is not surprising in that these measures are partially created from religious indicators; our data is more up to date with respect to religious identification.

19. The data were obtained from McIver's website, http://socsci.colorado.edu/~mciverj/wip.html on October 28, 2005.

20. The loadings for the rotated factors are as follows: percentage of women in the labor force, .873; percentage of women with health insurance, .824; percentage of women with a college degree, .529; and percentage of women above the poverty line, .872.

21. The loadings for the rotated factors are as follows: earnings ratio, .613; percentage of women in managerial or professional occupations, .795; percentage of women with a college degree, .725; and percentage of women owned business, .772.

22. We also estimated models to control for some cultural indicators related to incentives for women to hold office. In particular, we ran models with controls for the percentage of married individuals in a state, of unmarried households, and of families with children. We found a significant effect only for unmarried households, which had a positive effect on the proportion of women in elected office. Because the results for our other measures remain consistent, we do not include this measure in the final models. We should also note that if the model is estimated separately for the proportion of women in state and national offices, the NAE measure remains negative and significant (see Merolla, Schroedel, and Holman 2007).

23. The relationship seems to look more like a negative log rather than purely linear.

24. Including two variables that are so highly correlated inflates the standard

errors on each one.

25. If we remove the highly insignificant variables, the p-value gets much smaller on the NAE-Baptist measure ($p = .018$, two-tailed). We do not include a control for the South because it is highly correlated with the NAE-Baptist measure, .82. Furthermore, if the South is included as a dummy variable, it is not significant ($p = .518$), though the p-value for NAE-Baptist does increase as we would expect given the high correlation.

26. Given that the relationship in figure 5.2 looked like a log, we also estimated the model taking the log of the NAE-Baptist measure. This measure was also statistically significant and the p-value was lower ($p = .042$).

27. One may argue that because the data on the proportion of gay elected officials appears left censored, a tobit model may be appropriate, rather than OLS. We also ran our model using tobit and found that the results were consistent. Thus, for ease of presentation, we retain the OLS results.

28. As with the women in elected office model, the p-value on the NAE-Baptist measure gets much smaller ($p = .003$, two-tailed) if we remove highly insignificant variables. We again do not include a dummy variable for the South because it is highly collinear with the NAE-Baptist measure. However, if we include a dummy for the South in the condensed model, the South dummy is highly insignificant ($p = 874$), though the p-value on the NAE-Baptist measure increases. We also estimated models separately for the number of gay elected officials at the local level and state level. The NAE measure was significant and negative in both analyses.

29. In 1977, Mississippi, Louisiana, Alabama, Tennessee, Arkansas, Nebraska, Pennsylvania, New York, New Mexico, Georgia, and Oklahoma had less than 5 percent female representation in their state legislatures. The four with more than 15 percent were Arizona, Connecticut, New Hampshire, and Washington.

References

Abraham, Ken. 1997. *Who Are the Promise Keepers? Understanding the Christian Men's Movement*. New York: Doubleday.

Acker, Joan. 1992. "Gendered Institutions: From Sex Roles to Gendered Institutions." *Contemporary Sociology* 21(5): 565–69.

Arceneaux, Kevin. 2001. "The 'Gender Gap' in State Legislative Representation: New Data to Tackle an Old Question." *Political Research Quarterly* 54(3): 143–60.

Bendroth, Margaret Lamberts. 1993. *Fundamentalism and Gender, 1875 to the Present*. New Haven, Conn.: Yale University Press.

Bolzendahl, Catherine, and Clem Brooks. 2005. "Polarization, Secularization, or Differences as Usual? The Denominational Cleavage in U.S. Social Attitudes Since the 1970s." *Sociological Quarterly* 46(1): 47–78.

Britton, Dana M. 1990. "Homophobia and Homosociality: An Analysis of Boundary Maintenance." *Sociological Quarterly* 31(3): 423–39.

Button, James W., Barbara A. Rienzo, and Kenneth D. Wald. 1997. *Private Lives,*

Public Conflicts: Battles Over Gay Rights in American Communities. Washington, D.C.: Congressional Quarterly Press.

Button, James W., Kenneth D. Wald, and Barbara A. Rienzo. 1999. "The Election of Openly Gay Elected Officials in American Communities." *Urban Affairs Review* 35(2): 188–209.

Campbell, David E., and J. Quin Monson. 2007. "Dry Kindling: A Political Profile of American Mormons." In *From Pews to Polling Places: Faith and Politics in the American Religious Mosaic,* edited by J. Matthew Wilson. Washington, D.C.: Georgetown University Press.

Center for American Women and Politics. 2007. "State by State Information." http://www.cawp.rutgers.edu/fast_facts/resources/state_fact_sheet.php.

Chaves, Mark. 2004. *Congregations in America.* Cambridge, Mass.: Harvard University Press.

Christenson, Larry. 1970. *The Christian Family.* Minneapolis: Bethany.

Cook, Elizabeth Adell. 1994. "Voter Responses to Women Candidates." In *The Year of the Woman: Myths and Realities,* edited by Elizabeth Adell Cook, Sue Thomas, and Clyde Wilcox. Bolder, Colo.: Westview.

Cook, Timothy E. 1999. "The Empirical Study of Lesbian, Gay and Bisexual Politics: Assessing the First Wave of Research." *American Political Science Review* 93(3): 679–92.

Council on Biblical Manhood and Womanhood. 1998. "The Danvers Statement." http://cbmw.org/about/danvers.php.

Darcy, Robert, Susan Welch, and Janet Clark. 1994. *Women, Elections, and Representation,* 2nd ed. Lincoln: University of Nebraska Press.

Dobson, James. 1975. *What Wives Wish Their Husbands Knew About Women.* Wheaton, Ill.: Tyndale.

———. 1980. *Straight Talk to Men and Their Wives.* Waco, Tex.: Word.

Dolan, Kathleen. 1998. "Voting for Women in the 'Year of the Women'." *American Journal of Political Science* 42(1): 272–93.

Duerst-Lahti, Georgia. 2005. "Institutional Gendering: Theoretical Insights into the Environment of women Officeholders." In *Women and Elective Office: Past, Present and Future,* 2nd ed., edited by Sue Thomas and Clyde Wilcox. Oxford: Oxford University Press.

Duerst-Lahti, Georgia, and Rita Mae Kelly. 1995. *Gender Power, Leadership and Governance.* Ann Arbor: University of Michigan Press.

Elazar, Daniel J. 1966. *American Federalism: A View from the States.* New York: Crowell.

Ekstrand, Laurie, and William Eckert. 1981. "The Impact of Candidate Sex on Voter Choice." *The Western Political Science Quarterly* 34(1): 78–87.

Erikson, Robert S., Gerald C. Wright, and John P. McIver. 1993. *Statehouse Democracy: Public Opinion and Policy in the American States.* New York: Cambridge University Press.

Fox, Richard L., and Zoe M. Oxley. 2003. "Gender Stereotyping State Executive Elections: Candidate Selection and Success." *Journal of Politics* 65(3): 833–50.

Gallagher, Sally K. 2003. *Evangelical Identity & Gendered Family Life.* New Brunswick, N.J.: Rutgers University Press.

Gates, Gary J. and Jason Ost. 2004. *The Gay & Lesbian Atlas.* Washington, D.C.: The Urban Institute Press.

Gay and Lesbian Victory Fund and Leadership Institute. 2006. "Gay Candidates Win in Record Numbers Across U.S." Available at: www.victoryfund.org/index.php?src=news&prid=183&category=News%20Releases&PHPSESSI daho=9213a655247fc0dbb8.

Gay, David A., Christopher G. Ellison, and Daniel A. Powers. 1996. "In Search of Denominational Subcultures: Religious Affiliation and 'Pro-Family' Issues Revisited." *Review of Religious Research* 38(1): 3–17.

Golebiowska, Ewa A., and Cynthia J. Thomsen. 1999. "Group Stereotypes and Evaluations of Individuals: The Case of Gay and Lesbian Political Candidates." In *Gays and Lesbians in the Democratic Process*, edited by Ellen D. B. Riggle and Barry L. Tadlock. New York: Columbia University Press.

Gutterman, David S. 2005. *Prophetic Politics: Christian Social Movements and American Democracy*. Ithaca, N.Y.: Cornell University Press.

Haider-Markel, Donald P., and Kenneth J. Meier. 1996. "The Politics of Gay and Lesbian Rights: Expanding the Scope of Conflict." *Journal of Politics* 58(2): 332–49.

Herrick, Rebekah, and Sue Thomas. 1999. "The Effects of Sexual Orientation on Citizen Perceptions of Candidate Viability." In *Gays and Lesbians in the Democratic Process*, edited by Ellen D. B. Riggle and Barry L. Tadlock. New York: Columbia University Press.

———. 2001. "Gays and Lesbians in Local Races: A Study of Electoral Viability." *Journal of Homosexuality*. 42(1): 103–21.

Hoffman, John P., and Alan S. Miller. 1997. "Social and Political Attitudes among Religious Groups: Convergence and Divergence Over Time." *Journal for the Scientific Study of Religion* 36(1): 52–70.

Hogg, Michael A. 2005a. "Organizational Orthodoxy and Corporate Autocrats: Some Nasty Consequences of Organizational Identification in Uncertain Times." In *Identity and the Modern Organization*, edited by Caroline A. Bartel, Steven Blader, and Amy Wrzesniewski. Mahwah, N.J.: Lawrence Erlbaum.

———. 2005b. "Uncertainty, Social identity and Ideology." In *Advances in Group Processes*. Vol. 22. San Diego, Calif.: Elsevier.

Huddy, Leonie. 1994. "The Political Significance of Voters' Gender Stereotypes." *Research in Micropolitics* 4:169–93.

Huddy, Leonie, and Nayda Terkildsen. 1993. "The Consequences of Gender Stereotypes for Women Candidates at Different Levels and Types of Office." *Political Research Quarterly* 46(3): 503–25.

Inglehart, Ronald. 1979. *Modernization and Post modernization: Cutrual, Economic and Political Change in 43 Countries*. Princeton, N.J.: Princeton University Press.

Inglehart, Ronald, and Pippa Norris. 2003. *Rising Tide: Gender Equality and Cultural Change Around the World*. New York: Cambridge University Press.

Jillson, Calvin, and Rick K. Wilson. 1994. *Congressional Dynamics*. Stanford, Calif.: Stanford University Press.

Kawachi, Ichiro. 2000. "Income Inequality." July 20, 2000—last update. *MacArthur Research Network on SES and Health*. San Francisco: University of California. Available at: http://www.macses.ucsf.edu/Research/Social%20Environment/notebook/inequality.html.

King, David C., and Richard E. Matland. 2003. "Sex and the Grand Old Party:

An Experimental Investigation of the Effect of Candidate Sex on Support for a Republican Candidate." *American Politics Research* 31(6): 595–612.

Kosmin, Barry, Egon Mayer, and Ariela Keysar. 2001. *American Religious Identification Survey 2001*. New York: The Graduate Center of the City University of New York. Available at: http://www.gc.cuny.edu/faculty/research_briefs/aris.pdf.

LaHaye, Beverly. 1976. *The Spirit Controlled Woman*. Irvine, Calif.: Harvest House.

LaHaye, Tim. 1977. *Understanding the Male Temperment*. Old Tappan, N.J.: Fleming Revell.

Lawless, Jennifer L. 2004. "Women, War, and Winning Elections: Gender Stereotyping in the Post-September 11th Era." *Political Research Quarterly* 57(3): 479–90.

Loftus, Jeni. 2001. "America's Liberalization In Attitudes toward Homosexuality, 1973–1998." *American Sociological Review* 66(5): 762–82.

Marsden, George. 2006. "The Sword of the Lord: How 'Otherworldly' Fundamentalism Became a Political Power." *Christianity Today: Books & Culture* 12(2) (Mar/April). Available at: http://www.christianitytoday.com/bc/2006/002/3.10.html.

Masci, David. 2004. *CQ Researcher: Religion and Politics*. Washington, D.C: Congressional Quarterly Press.

McDermott, Monika. 1997. "Voting Cues in Low Information Elections: Candidate Gender as a Social Information Variable in Contemporary United States Elections." *American Journal of Political Science* 41(1): 270–83.

———. 1998. "Race and Gender Cues in Low-Information Elections." *Political Research Quarterly* 51(4): 895–918.

Mead, Frank S., and Samuel S. Hill. 2001. *Handbook of Denominations in the United States*, 11th ed. Nashville, Tenn.: Abingdon Press.

Merolla, Jennifer, Jean Reith Schroedel, and Mirya Holman. 2007. "The Paradox of Protestantism and Women in Elected Office in the United States." *Women, Politics & Policy* 29(1): 77–100.

Morgan, Kimberly J. 2006. *Working Mothers and the Welfare State: Religion and the Politics of Work-Family Politics in Western Europe and the United States*. Stanford, Calif.: Stanford University Press.

Morone, James A. 2003. *Hellfire Nation: The Politics of Sin in American History*. New Haven, Conn.: Yale University Press.

Nechemias, Carol. 1987. "Changes in the Election of Women to U.S. State Legislative Seats." *Legislative Studies Quarterly* 12(1): 125–42.

Nice, David C. 1988. "State Deregulation of Intimate Behavior." *Social Science Quarterly* 69(1): 203–11.

Norrander, Barbara, and Clyde Wilcox. 1998. "The Geography of Gender Power: Women in State Legislatures." In *Women and Elective Office: Past, Present and Future*, edited by Sue Thomas and Clyde Wilcox. New York: Oxford University Press.

Norris, Pippa, and Ronald Inglehart. 2005. "Women as Political Leaders Worldwide: Cultural Barriers and Opportunities." In *Women and Elective Office*, 2nd ed., edited by Sue Thomas and Clyde Wilcox. New York: Oxford University Press.

Oldmixon, Elizabeth Anne. 2005. *Uncompromising Positions: God, Sex and the U.S. House of Representatives*. Washington D.C.: Georgetown University Press.

Paglin, Morton. 1975. "The Measurement and Trend of Inequality: A Basic Revision." *The American Economic Review* 65(4): 598–609.

Paolino, Phillip. 1995. "Group-Salient Issues and Group Representation: Support for Women Candidates in the 1992 Senate Elections." *American Journal of Political Science* 39(2): 294–313.

Pew Forum on Religion & Public Life. 2008. *U.S. Religious Landscape*. Washington, D.C.: Pew Research Center. Available at: http://religions.pewforum.org/pdf/report2religious-landscape-study.pdf.

Pew Research Center. 2004. *Religion and the Presidential Vote: Bush's Gains Broad-Based*. Washington, D.C.: Pew Research Center. Available at: http://people-press.org/commentary/display.php3?Analysisid-103.

Reynolds, Andrew. 1999. "Women in the Legislatures and Executives of the World: Knocking at the Highest Glass Ceiling." *World Politics* 51(4): 547–72.

Robertson, Pat. 1995. *The Turning Tide*. Dallas, Tex.: Word.

Rosenwasser, Shirley M., and Norma Dean. 1989. "Gender Role and Political Office: Effects of Perceived Masculinity/Femininity of Candidate and Political Office." *Psychology of Women Quarterly* 13(1): 77–85.

Rule, Wilma. 1981. "Why Women Don't Run: The Critical Contextual Actors in Women's Legislative Recruitment." *The Western Political Quarterly* 34:60–77.

———. 1990. "Why More Women Are State Legislators: A Research Note." *The Western Political Quarterly* 43(2): 437–48.

———. 1993. "Why Are More Women State Legislators?" In *Women in Politics: Outsiders or Insiders?*, edited by Lois Lovelace Duke. Englewood Cliffs, N.J.: Prentice Hall.

Sanbonmatsu, Kira. 2002. "Gender Stereotypes and Vote Choice." *American Journal of Political Science* 46(1): 20–34.

Schroedel, Jean Reith, and Nicole Mazumdar. 1998. "Into the Twenty-First Century: Will Women Break the Political Glass Ceiling?" In *Women and Elective Office: Past, Present and Future*, edited by Sue Thomas and Clyde Wilcox. Oxford: Oxford University Press.

Schroedel, Jean Reith, and Bruce Snyder. 1994. "Patty Murray: The Mom in Tennis Shoes Goes to the Senate." In *The Year of the Woman: Myths and Realities*, edited by Elizabeth Adell Cook, Sue Thomas, and Clyde Wilcox. Bolder, Colo.: Westview Press.

Schroedel, Jean Reith, Jennifer Merolla, and Pamela Foerstel. 2005. "Women's Relative Lack of Electoral Success in the United States." *Human Rights Global Focus* 2(3): 5–13.

Schultz, Jeffrey D., John G. West, and Iain Maclean. 1999. *Encyclopedia of Religion in American Politics*. Phoenix, Ariz.: Oryx Press.

Sharkansky, Ira. 1969. "The Utility of Elazar's Political Culture." *Polity* 2(1): 66–83.

Singer, Bennett L., and David Deschamps. 1994. *Gay and Lesbian Stats*. New York: The New Press.

Strong, Gregory S. 1999. "Reformation." In *Encyclopedia of Religion in American Politics*, edited by Jeffrey D. Schultz, John G. West, and Iain Maclean. Phoenix, Ariz.: Oryx Press.

Swatos, William H., and Kevin J. Christiano. 2001. "Secularization Theory: The Course of a Concept." *Sociology of Religion* 60(3): 209–28.

U.S. Bureau of the Census. 2000. "Census of Population and Housing, 2000: Summary Population and Housing Characteristics: U.S. States." Washington: Government Printing Office, 2001.

———. 2004a. "American Community Survey: General Demographic Characteristics: 2004." Washington: Government Printing Office, 2005.

———. 2004b. "Gini Ratios by State: 1969, 1979, 1989, 1999." Washington, D.C.: U.S. Department of Commerce. Available at: http://www.census.gov/hhes/www/income/histinc/state/state4.html.

Vandenbosch, Sue. 1996. "A Negative Relationship between Religion and the Percentage of Women State Legislators in the United States." *The Journal of Legislative Studies* 2(4): 322–38.

Wald, Kenneth D., James W. Button, and Barbara A. Rienzo. 1996. "The Politics of Gay Rights in American Communities: Explaining Antidiscrimination Ordinances and Policies." *American Journal of Political Science* 40(4): 1152–78.

Wegner, David. 1998. "The Impact of Feminists: An Interview with World Magazine Editor, Marvin Olasky." *Journal for Biblical Manhood and Womanhood* 3(4): 1–5.

Werschkul, Misha, and Erica Williams. 2004. "The Status of Women in the States." Washington, D.C.: The Institute for Women's Policy Research. Available at: http://www.iwpr.org/States2004/PDFs/National.pdf (accessed May 20, 2009).

Wilcox, Clyde. 1988. "The Christian Right in Twentieth Century America: Continuity and Change." *The Review of Politics* 50(4): 659–81.

Wilcox, Clyde, and Barbara Norrander. 2005. "Change in Continuity in the Geography of Women Legislators." In *Women in Elective Office*, 2nd ed., edited by Sue Thomas and Clyde Wilcox. New York: Oxford University Press.

Williams, Robin. 1964. *Strangers Next Door: Ethnic Relations in American Communities*. Englewood Cliffs, N.J.: Prentice Hall.

Yust, Karen Marie. 1999. "Women in Religion and Politics." In *Encyclopedia of Religion in American Politics*, edited by Jeffrey D. Schultz, John G. West, and Iain Maclean. Phoenix, Ariz.: Oryx Press.

Chapter 6

Race-Bridging for Christ? Conservative Christians and Black-White Relations in Community Life

PAUL LICHTERMAN, PRUDENCE L. CARTER, AND MICHÈLE LAMONT

M ANY PEOPLE have heard the phrase, sometimes attributed to Martin Luther King Jr., that from eleven to twelve on a Sunday morning is the most segregated hour in America. Fewer may know that at least since the 1960s, some evangelical Protestant leaders and publicists have promoted racial reconciliation. Nurtured at first by three African American religious figures who were willing to identify with the primarily white-associated term *evangelical*, the promotion of racial reconciliation remained a relative exception within evangelical Protestantism until the late 1980s. Since then, a stream of books, magazine articles, study guides, inspirational speeches, and denominational public statements has earned attention for a discourse of racial healing within and beyond evangelical church circles (Wadsworth 1997; Emerson and Smith 2000; Rehwaldt-Alexander 2004).

This cultural movement has made brief appearances in the political arena. In 1997, 400 evangelical African Americans gathered in Baltimore with leaders of the Christian Coalition, including Ralph Reed and Pat Robertson, to kick off the Samaritan Project—an initiative to bring black[1] and white evangelicals under the fold of the politically conservative Christian Coalition so influential in Republican Party politics. Black and white evangelicals would work together in communities on issues such as school choice and tax breaks for minority-owned businesses and collaborate on antiabortion and antigay rights campaigns. Republican political alliances between conservative Christian whites and blacks developed little in the decade following the Baltimore conference, however, and the Samaritan Project floundered. Although African American and white conservative Christians take similar stands on several red-button moral issues, such as homosexuality, only 7 percent of conservative Christian blacks identify themselves as Republicans, and white evangelicals are more than ten times as likely to vote Republican as their black counterparts (see Fowler et al. 2004).

The discourse of racial healing has not been only promoted by conservative political operatives in search of new constituencies. Witness the June 1995 statement on racial reconciliation issued by the Southern Baptist Convention, the largest theologically conservative Protestant denomination in the United States: "Be it further resolved, that we apologize to all African-Americans for condoning and/or perpetuating individual and systematic racism in our lifetime; and we genuinely repent of racism of which we have been guilty, whether consciously (Psalm 19:13) or unconsciously (Leviticus 4:27); and be it further resolved, that we ask forgiveness from our African-American brothers and sisters, acknowledging that our own healing is at stake."[2] Southern Baptists evidently found legitimate and pressing motives for confronting racism, individual and systematic, in biblical teachings—the sine qua non of truth in evangelical Protestantism.

This chapter explores ordinary conservative Christians' attitudes about race and looks closely at their attempts to create or improve interracial relationships in church and community life outside the electoral political arena. These efforts, which we conceive as race-bridging practices, are noteworthy, even historic, because they take place in the context of long-established racial discrimination in conservative Christian theology and practice. Using several kinds of evidence, we place these endeavors in the context of American black-white relations. Survey data analyses from the General Social Survey and the Social Capital Community Benchmark Survey reveal large differences in a variety of current attitudes on race between theologically conservative white and African American Christians and between white conservative Christians and other whites. The qualitative case studies we draw on include churches and community service organizations that identify explicitly with the racial reconciliation initiatives of evangelical leaders, and that promote interracial relationships without referring to the racial reconciliation movement. These studies do not speak to the extent of these efforts in local church and community life nationwide, or whether they are successful. Yet they are significant because the number of multiracial congregations is growing (Emerson and Woo 2006). It is imperative that we gain a better understanding of the transformation in interracial dynamics that such growth suggests.

Race-bridging efforts speak directly to the conditions of and the prospects for democracy in the United States. Indeed, following de Tocqueville, many scholars assess the health of a democracy by its citizens' abilities to work together to solve public problems, relate to those who are different from themselves, and trust one another. From this point of view, democracy is not only a form of governance but a way of life (Dewey 1927), and a vibrant democracy depends partly on the character of civic relationships inside and between religious groups (Lichterman and Potts 2009), the kinds of relationships that Sikkink's essay in this volume also explores (see chapter 9). We have reasons to worry. Membership in a great variety of civic associations has been declining over the past four decades (Putnam 2000), while social distance between racial groups in the United States is growing (McPherson, Smith-Lovin, and Brashears 2006).

A variety of authors propose that given U.S. cultural history and the prevalence of religious groups in American community life, religion may be one important way to reweave the fraying fabric of social and associational life (Skocpol 2000; Smidt 2003; Bellah et al. 2007; Putnam 2000). That is one more reason to focus our attention on race-bridging strategies. Because conservative Protestantism is the dominant theological strain of the dominant faith in the United States today (Smith 1998), we need to understand what Americans do as conservative Protestants when they try to redefine interracial relationships. Our approach, similar to many other recent studies, focuses on the active, classifying work that people do either to expand or to narrow the circle of insiders, instead of assuming that people's ideas about insiders and outsiders directly and unambiguously reflect professionally written position statements, governmental policies or theological dicta (see Lamont 2006; Lamont and Fleming 2005; Lichterman 2005, 2008; Bail 2008; Brubaker 2004).

Although survey data reveal important differences between white and black conservative Christians on issues such as national civil rights—with whites less supportive of the policies than blacks, the case studies show that at least some white conservative Christians want to engage in race-bridging efforts. These efforts sometimes produce informal friendships, and this counts as successful race-bridging to white conservative Christians. Such efforts, however, often downplay racial identities and socioeconomic differences between groups, and evidence suggests that this downplay in turn limits the ability of whites to build bridges across racial groups. Moreover, white Christians often do not realize the extent to which they use racial differences in styles of worship and other cultural practices to draw moral boundaries between themselves and blacks (Lamont 2000).

White and black conservatives share some understandings of moral issues and uphold the singular moral authority of the Bible, yet the boundary work we infer from survey and ethnographic evidence would reinforce rather than blur racial boundaries within congregations or between whites and blacks. This boundary work would inhibit the type of egalitarian, horizontal relations that scholars of civic engagement think of as empowering and democratic (Putnam 2000; Skocpol 2000), and that some conservative Christian leaders seem to have been calling for in the past fifteen years. Our findings suggest, then, that the relation between evangelical Protestantism and democratic social life is complex. To understand it, we need to distinguish between Christian theologies of racial reconciliation or egalitarianism on the one hand and the more un-self-conscious, enduring, everyday practices that may run counter to antiracist statements on paper. Toward that end, our discussion introduces a contextual approach to religion, one that sensitizes us to the social relations and cultural styles through which people put religious beliefs, including well-intended antiracist beliefs, into practice.

This chapter focuses only on black-white relations. There are good reasons, of course, to ask how evangelical Protestants may try to create bridges toward other racial groups or religious organizations. In the United States, evangelical and more broadly conservative Christianity is growing among Latinos (Greeley 1998; Hernández 1999) and Korean Americans (Ecklund 2006) and other East Asians. But there are better reasons to limit our inquiry here. The great bulk of founders and leading popularizers of modern evangelical Protestantism in the 1940s and after were, unremarkably, white and directed their ministries to whites as a matter of course (Smith 1998). Modern evangelical racial reconciliation discourse began with a focus on relations between African Americans and whites, and the focus has remained there as racial reconciliation has become represented increasingly by white spokespersons trying to reach out to blacks (Emerson and Smith 2000, 63).

Context: Black-White Social Inequality

Although the United States is increasingly multiracial, the black-white divide has had a foundational and highly significant role in American history. Scholars have repeatedly buttressed the view that black-white relations are unique because of the enduring racial discrimination that is the legacy of slavery. Despite perceiving itself as the world guardian of democracy and freedom, the United States has been exceptionally slow to grant its main minority group, blacks, full privileges of social citizenship, especially in relation other advanced industrial societies. Rates of racial intermarriage remain lower for blacks than for any other group (Qian 1997) and rates of residential segregation remain higher (Logan, Alba, and Leung 1996). In 2000, whites in metropolitan areas lived in neighborhoods that were 80 percent white and only 7 percent black. Their black counterparts, meanwhile, lived in neighborhoods where more than 50 percent of the residents were black and only 30 percent were white (Lewis Mumford Center 2001). The persistence of residential segregation has led one scholar to conclude that "either in absolute terms or in comparison to other groups, blacks remain a very residentially segregated and spatially isolated people" (Massey 2001, 132). The sociologist Herbert Gans even argued that American society is moving toward a racial divide opposing all nonblacks to blacks (1999). Without doubt, the black-white divide continues to hew the American social fabric deeply, if unevenly, across regions.

Of course, socioeconomic inequalities between whites and blacks also persist. By 2001 nearly 65 percent of whites age twenty-five to twenty-nine had completed some college, compared to just 50 percent of blacks of the same age.[3] The 2001 national median family income for whites was $54,067 and $33,598 for blacks.[4] At the same time, more than half of all African American children under the age of six live in poverty, three times more than the proportion in the white community (Conley 1999, 10). Even those blacks who are integrated in the middle class face a comparative disadvantage. The net worth of black professionals is $12,303, versus $66,800 for whites. At income levels above $75,000, whites have a median net worth of $308,000 but blacks only $114,000. To reach middle-class status, a larger proportion of black middle-class couples both work than their white middle-class counterparts, 78 to 62 percent, respectively (Oliver and Shapiro, 1995, 96–97).

These figures suggest a clear and persistent racial gap in life chances. However, as Orlando Patterson argued, important gains have been made over the past forty years, due in large part to the civil rights movement (1997). School enrollment among blacks has grown rapidly. The gap in high school completion has decreased from 12 percent for blacks and 41 percent for whites in 1940 to 86 percent for blacks and 87 percent for whites respectively in 1995 (19–20). The median income of black families headed by a married couple was $44,307 in 1995, some 87 percent of the amount a similar white family earned, up from 68 percent in 1967 (27). Thus, social (structural) boundaries between blacks and whites remain strong, even if they do show signs of weakening (see also Oliver and Shapiro 1995; Conley 1999).

Context: Shared Theology, Segregated Practice

Conservative Protestant blacks and whites, from as early as the seventeenth century until today, have shared many religious convictions. For conservative Protestants, and especially for evangelical Protestants, the central accomplishment for any Christian believer is a personal relation-

ship with Jesus Christ. Certainty of faith and certainty in the Bible's exclusive and inerrant authority are widely shared among conservative
Protestants (Smith 1998).

Yet from the start, African Americans were inducted into Christian religion in the context of institutionalized subordination. Archival records
show that vigorous preaching and converting occurred among slaves
and freed blacks in the antebellum period, and that white evangelical
Christians attracted large numbers of blacks to the church. Traveling
itinerant preachers would minister to interracial—and spatially segregated—crowds of hundreds. Whites crowded inside the churches and
blacks observed from windows, or in some instances, from balconies—
the places to which they were consigned. Protestant U.S. denominations
developed along sharply segregated lines, such that scholars continue to
speak of a black church separate from American Christian church life in
general (for instance, Lincoln and Mamiya 1990), even if the formal theologies of black churches resemble those of some de facto white, conservative Protestant churches and denominations.

White evangelical Baptists and Methodists did debate the morality of
slavery, the relationships between masters and slaves, and the induction
of black ministers into church leadership. The ambivalence of many
evangelicals over these issues became very evident in the varying positions that both Baptist and Methodist conferences began to take and im-
plement. Many mid-nineteenth-century abolitionists were evangelical
Protestants. Yet even by the turn into the nineteenth century, most evangelical churches and preachers avoided the troublesome question of
slavery and made their mission instead to secure the souls of as many
whites and blacks as they could (Haller 2003). Theologically conservative Christian leaders and congregations frequently condoned and
sometimes actively supported segregation and subordination of African
Americans up through the civil rights movement of the 1950s and 1960s
(Emerson and Smith 2000; Haynes 2002).

What has emerged from the interplay between evangelism and race
relations is a dialectical tension: evangelical blacks and whites, from as
early as the seventeenth century until today, have shared many religious
convictions and a deep faith in God; yet those shared convictions alone
have not been enough to bridge the divides between the races. Then and
now, theologically conservative whites have differed from their theological black counterparts in their attitudes on many contemporary social
issues, especially as these issues pertain to the economic and political
mobility and social well-being of African Americans.

Racial Attitudes: The Color of Religion

The General Social Survey (GSS) and the Social Capital Benchmark Survey (SCBS) together offer an overview of individual attitudes, prefer-

ences, and practices that seem to reflect the historical and social-structural realities reviewed in the previous section (National Opinion Research Center 2002; Saguaro Seminar 2000; see also tables 6.1–6.5). The evidence provided in these two data sets is illuminating but must be interpreted carefully, given that each required a different strategy for identifying conservative Christians in the sample.[5] The SCBS included questions on the respondent's religious denomination, which enabled us to identify respondents in more specific terms than the GSS's predefined response categories of fundamentalist, moderate, and liberal. In the GSS dataset, we compare those Christians who identified explicitly as fundamentalist to other nonfundamentalist Christians. We used restrictive criteria to identify conservative Christians in the GSS and SCBS to lessen the likelihood of having captured nonconservative Christians in our subsamples. Our resulting categories likely miss some conservative Christians in each original survey.

Multivariate logistic and ordinary least squares regression analyses of certain racial attitudes show both differences and similarities between conservative and nonconservative Christians. In the GSS, respondents were asked a host of yes-no questions about the reasons for African Americans' having worse jobs, housing, and income than white people, on average. They were also asked whether they favored laws against interracial marriage. Findings from the GSS indicate that theologically conservative white Christians have more racially exclusive attitudes than other white Christians when it comes to interracial marriage, even once we control for education, gender, income, and marital status and their exposure to other racial and ethnic groups in their respective community (see table 6.1). In the GSS, although only 10 percent of those surveyed responded that they were likely to favor laws against interracial marriage, white fundamentalists were four times more likely to favor these laws than all blacks and white nonfundamentalists. Data from the SCBS point toward similar conclusions. Conservative Christian whites are significantly more likely to oppose marriage between blacks and whites, even after controlling for education, age, and income (see table 6.2). Also, compared to white women, white men are more likely to oppose interracial marriage. Among blacks, no significant difference in their views on interracial marriage exists either before or after the controls.

At the same time, GSS data reveal that both conservative and nonconservative Christian whites appear to adhere to a similar racial logic in U.S. society in terms of their connection to African Americans. Blacks and whites were asked to respond to a nine-point scale, ranging from very cool to very warm, about their feelings toward their own and the other racial group. Both fundamentalist and nonfundamentalist Christian whites expressed significantly more social and emotional distance from blacks than their black counterparts expressed about them (see table 6.3). Notably, fundamentalist Christians feel slightly less connected

Table 6.1   Racial Attitudes among Fundamentalist and Nonfundamentalist Black and White Christians

Independent Variables	Favor Laws Against Inter-racial Marriage		Blacks Shouldn't Push for Rights		Racial Differences Due to Discrimination		Racial Differences Due to Inborn Disability		Racial Differences are Due to Lack of Education		Racial Differences are Due to Lack of Will	
	Logit	Odds Ratio	Logit	Odds Ratio	Logit	Odds Ratio	Logit	Odds Ratio	Logit	Odds Ratio	Logit	Odds Ratio
Fundamentalist Christian	1.06*** (.32)	2.90	.34* (.21)	1.41	-.18 (.20)	.83	-.17 (.30)	.84	-.49** (.19)	.61	.34* (.19)	1.40
White	1.84*** (.64)	6.27	.60** (.30)	1.81	-.80*** (.26)	.45	-.34 (.36)	.71	-.56** (.25)	.57	-.05 (.25)	.95
Politically conservative	-.09 (.45)	.91	.58** (.27)	1.79	-.16 (.21)	.85	.33 (.39)	1.39	.10 (.23)	1.10	.76*** (.23)	2.15
Politically moderate	-.27 (.45)	.76	.43 (.27)	1.54	-.01 (.24)	.99	.55 (.38)	1.73	.18 (.23)	1.19	.75*** (.23)	2.13
Constant	-.95		.11		-.68		-.69		-1.23**		.89	
Chi-square, df	88.04, 11		67.43, 11		18.37, 11		32.89, 11		32.53, 11		31.64, 11	
Number of observations	595		552		584		583		582		565	

Source: Authors' compilation.
Notes: Numbers in parentheses are standard errors. All analyses control for education, income, gender, and marital status. Blacks, nonfundamentalists, and political liberals are the reference categories.
*** $p = 0.00$; ** $p <= .05$; * $p <= .10$

Table 6.2   Views on Interracial Marriage[a] on Key Social Traits

	Blacks			Whites		
Independent Variables	Model 1	Model 2	Model 3	Model 1	Model 2	Model 3
Conservative Christian (=1)	.06	.06	.05	−.25***	−.22***	−.15***
	(.09)	(.09)	(.09)	(.05)	(.05)	(.05)
Married		.00	−.00		−.01	.03
		(.10)	(.11)		(.06)	(.06)
Divorced		−.09	−.10		17**	.20***
		(.12)	(.13)		(.07)	(.07)
Separated		−.23	−.23		.10	.14
		(.17)	(.17)		(.14)	(.14)
Widowed		−.28	−.26		−.02	.07
		(.18)	(.18)		(.09)	(.09)
Age			−.01*		−.02***	−.02***
			(.00)		(.00)	(.00)
Male (=1)			.11		−.12***	−.14***
			(.08)		(.04)	(.04)
Education			−.02			.08***
			(.02)			(.01)
Income			.02			−.01
			(.02)			(.01)
Percentage black in community			.47			−3.57**
			(3.85)			(1.4)
Percentage white in community			.75			−2.72**
			(3.83)			(1.4)
Percentage Asian in community			2.26			−.98
			(4.09)			(1.44)
Percentage Latino in community			.24			−2.69*
			(4.06)			(1.53)
Constant	2.7	2.94	2.31	2.20	3.27	5.65
R^2	.00	.02	.02	.01	.09	.12
Sample size	958	958	958	4063	4063	4063

Source: Authors' compilation.
Notes: [a]Dependent variable's values range from 1 strongly oppose to 5 strongly favor. Numbers in parentheses are standard errors.
*** $p = 0.00$; ** $p <= .05$; * $p <= .10$.

Table 6.3   Feelings of Connectedness on Key Social Traits

Independent Variables	Blacks[a] Model 1	Whites[a] Model 2
Fundamentalist Christian (=1)	−.12	−.44*
	(.25)	(.25)
White (=1)	−1.60***	.25
	(.22)	(.22)
White Fundamentalist	.02	.38
(Interaction Term)	(.27)	(.27)
Married	−.27*	−.26**
	(.13)	(.13)
Divorced	−.04	−.20
	(.16)	(.15)
Separated	−.31	−1.06***
	(.27)	(.26)
Widowed	−.02	.20
	(.21)	(.21)
Age	−.01*	−.01**
	(.00)	(.00)
Male (=1)	−.47***	−.29***
	(.09)	(.09)
Education	.08***	.01
	(.02)	(.02)
Income	.05**	.05**
	(.02)	(.02)
Constant		
	7.04	6.89
R^2	.12	.04
Sample size (N=)	1834	1835

Source: Authors' compilation.
Notes: [a]Closeness scale: 1 (not close at all) to 9 (very close) [5 = neither one nor the other]. Numbers in parentheses are standard errors.
*** $p = 0.00$; ** $p <= .05$; * $p <= .10$

to whites than nonfundamentalist Christians; the significance of this difference is only marginal, however.

The GSS reveals other racial and theological differences in intergroup attitudes. With an odds ratio of 1.40 and .61, respectively, logistic regression results show that fundamentalist Christians are more likely to disagree that racial differences between blacks and whites owe to lack of education and to agree that these differences are attributable to lack of will. These findings suggest that either a traditional Protestant or traditional American (or both) regard for individual effort is shared widely among conservative Christians across racial lines (see table 6.1).

To investigate whether political orientations might be the hidden cause of differences between whites and blacks, or white religious conservatives and other whites, we examined GSS data for the probability that political orientation matters. Respondents self-identified as either liberal, moderate, or conservative. Table 6.1 also shows that political conservatives are more than one and a half times more likely as political liberals to believe that blacks should not push for civil rights (odds ratio = 1.79). Similarly, fundamentalist Christians believe that blacks should not push for rights, although the difference is marginally significant between them and nonfundamentalist Christians (odds ratio = 1.41). Furthermore, both political conservatives and moderates are more than twice as likely as political liberals to believe that racial differences are due to lack of will on the part of blacks (odds ratios = 2.15 and 2.13, respectively).

The color of religion matters, too. Black and white fundamentalists diverge in their social attitudes and practices, which indicate that racial dynamics penetrate church walls. Whites across the theological spectrum are significantly more likely than blacks (both conservative and nonconservative Christians) to disagree that the lack of education is the cause of the mobility gap between blacks and whites (odds ratio = .57), less likely to believe that discrimination has anything to do with these differences (odds ratio = .45), and more likely to believe that blacks should not push for civil rights (odds ratio = 1.81). In 2002, conservative Christian whites, on average, visited a friend of a different race or had the friend visit their home less often (8.04 times) than conservative Christian blacks (12.06 times) and other whites (10.17 times); the difference is statistically significant (see table 6.4). In general, whites engage in these interracial visits less often than blacks; the differences are significant, as were the differences between all blacks and all whites on opposition to marrying interracially. Still, though conservative Protestant Christian whites reported spending less time with a friend of an opposite race in either their home or the friend's, they had more diverse friendship networks than nonconservative Protestant Christian whites, even after statistical controls for education, income, marital status, and age were entered into the OLS regression (see table 6.5). The SCBS friendship diversity scale includes eleven traits, including four categories of race and ethnicity, welfare status, business ownership, religious and sexual orientation, and status as a community leader, manual worker, and vacation home owner; it is therefore possible that a social trait other than race characterizes conservative white Christians networks. Nonetheless, it is worth noting that significantly more conservative Protestant white Christians in the SCBS reported having black

Table 6.4   **Friendship Practices**

	Black Conservative Christians	Other Blacks	White Conservative Christians	Other Whites
Percent has a personal friend who is black	94.6% N = 533	93.4% N = 2,958	63.6% N = 1,658	59.7%*** bc N = 19,146
Percent has a personal friend who is white	76.7% N = 532	73.5% N = 2,959	97.8% N = 2,959	97.8%***b N = 19,165
Percent has a personal friend who is Asian	24.9% N = 531	27.7% N = 2,953	30.5% N = 1,653	37.6%***c N = 19,108
Percent has a personal friend who is Latino-Hispanic	40.5% N = 533	44% N = 2,949	40.1% N = 1,652	44.4%*** c N = 19,104
Mean diversity of friendship[i]	5.95***b N = 536	6.04 N = 2,966	6.26**c N = 1,660	6.42 N = 19,217
Mean number of times R has had a friend of a different race at home or visited theirs	12.06 N = 532	13.01 N = 2,952	8.04 N = 1,651	10.17*** bc N = 19,111

Source: Authors' compilation.
Notes: [i] The friendship diversity scale includes eleven traits, including race and ethnicity, welfare status, business ownership, and sexual orientation. [a] significant difference between conservative and nonconservative Christians; [b] significant difference between the races; [c] significant within-race difference
*** $p = 0.00$; ** $p <= .05$; * $p <= .10$

friends than nonconservative Protestant whites. This combination of findings on friendship networks bids us look more closely at the meanings of relationships represented by the statistics.

Overall, these indicators show that U.S. blacks as a whole have less exclusive racial attitudes and privilege their own racial category less than whites as a whole do. Within these broad outlines, conservative Christian whites maintain stronger boundaries than other whites on a variety of indicators. In all, the survey data on attitudes, along with an historical legacy of institutionalized racism in American Protestantism, support the view that American conservative Protestantism remains racialized. In this context, white evangelicals' current race-bridging efforts take on special significance for American religious history as well as American civic life.

Theoretical Framework: Religion in Civic Action

Survey analysis can take us only so far. The remainder of our analysis takes a contextual approach to religion (Lichterman 2007), one that we

Table 6.5   Diversity of Friendship Networks, Key Social Traits

	Blacks			Whites		
Independent Variables	Model 1	Model 2	Model 3	Model 1	Model 2	Model 3
Conservative Christian (=1)	−.24*	−.27*	−.13	−.04	−.04	.12*
	(.14)	(.14)	(.14)	(.07)	(.07)	(.07)
Married		.77***	.32**		.32***	.15*
		(.16)	(.16)		(.08)	(.08)
Divorced		.60***	.43**		.26**	.35***
		(.20)	(.19)		(.11)	(.10)
Separated		.12	.12		−.02	.18
		(.27)	(.26)		(.20)	(.19)
Widowed		−.00	.18		−.67***	−.30**
		(.29)	(.27)		(.13)	(.13)
Age		−.00	.00		−.01***	−.01***
		(.00)	(.00)		(.00)	(.00)
Male (=1)		.26**	.24**		.07	−.06
		(.13)	(.13)		(.06)	(.05)
Education			.35***			.22***
			(.04)			(.02)
Income			.20***			.21***
			(.04)			(.02)
Percentage black in community			−.24			−1.94
			(5.94)			(1.96)
Percentage white in community			.63			−2.40
			(5.90)			(2.0)
Percentage Asian in community			7.86			−1.51
			(6.29)			(2.07)
Percentage Latino in community			−1.02			−.89
			(6.25)			(2.19)
Constant	6.16	5.86	3.70	6.32	6.81	7.33
R²	.00	.02	.12	.00	.03	.10
Sample size	1909	1909	1909	8366	8366	8366

Source: Authors' compilation.
Notes: [i] The friendship diversity scale includes eleven traits, including four categories of race and ethnicity; religious orientation; sexual orientation; welfare status; is a community leader, manual worker, business ownership, and vacation home owner. Numbers in parentheses are standard errors.
*** $p = 0.00$; ** $p <= .05$; * $p <= .10$

believe is well suited to telling us how religious people get involved in civic life and how religion informs their efforts. First, ours focuses on cultural frameworks that are mobilized in and around action, not on abstract belief systems embedded in theological texts (Swidler 1986; Wimmer and Lamont 2006). We aim to see what people say and do in church and community life as conservative Christians, rather than taking sacred texts or belief systems as direct causes of what people do. For this study's purposes, conservative Protestantism is a loose cultural repertoire of images, vocabularies, and skills that we can see and hear people using in everyday life, rather than a set of silent beliefs or private motives inferred from survey data (Lichterman 2008). We investigate how conservative Christians do things with this cultural repertoire, including drawing boundaries between people "like us" and "not like us" (Lamont 1992; Lamont and Molnar 2001). Second, a contextual approach holds that when people act as religious people, they draw on secular as well as religious culture. Even if their religion is conservative, people do not live out religious dictates in a cultural vacuum. Religion is embedded in other cultural understandings that accompany action (Hall 1997; Ammerman 2007). Finally, and also crucial to a contextual perspective, social and institutional resources condition the ways people use religious idioms or styles of action as much as those of any other cultural repertoire (Sewell 1992; Lamont 1999; Lincoln and Mamiya 1990). People of different races or classes bring different cultural and social resources to the same religious texts, so that acting in a Christian, moral, or even conservative way can vary for different groups.

Previous scholarship has tended to treat religion differently, as an independent variable that has effects on social attitudes or behaviors. In a prominent statement on conservative Protestantism and race, for instance, the sociologists Michael Emerson and Christian Smith explained that white evangelicals favor interpersonal, individualistic responses to racism because their theology conditions them to do so (2000). In this view, theological beliefs such as accountable freewill individualism are cognitive building blocks that make it difficult for evangelicals to construct racial issues in social-structural terms, and also doom concrete attempts at race-bridging to failure.

Why does this difference in approach matter for understanding conservative Christian race relations? Theological or denominational teachings may offer some of the cognitive building blocks people use to answer survey questions on beliefs about the causes of and solutions to racial inequality. Yet, in everyday life, people use those building blocks to build different kinds of relationships. Theologies, formal or fragmentary, are not the only resources on which people—especially lay people—rely when trying to engage in interracial relationships. Our contextual approach helps us understand how black and white conservative

Christians may share theological beliefs yet relate to their beliefs differently, with different consequences for both attitudes and actions. If African Americans understand themselves as inextricably members of a collectivity—sharing a linked fate with other African Americans based on historical experience (Dawson 1994)—then they will interpret theological beliefs in ways that most white conservative Protestants do not. The contextual approach also helps us understand why the attempts of white political conservatives to ally with African American religious conservatives have borne relatively little fruit to date (Robinson 2006). For our purposes here, the approach illuminates why even the best-intentioned efforts of white religious conservatives to foster interracial relationships can produce tensions and miscommunication across racial groups.

It may seem like common sense that, at least for conservative Protestants, biblical dictates by themselves have strong effects on what people say and do. We do not dispute correlations drawn in other studies between religious preferences and voting behavior. Rather, we think that in addition to asking what conservative Christian survey respondents say about God, society, and politics, we also should ask what conservative Christians say and do in everyday life, and discover how religion enters into the process. The contextual perspective bids us ask what conservative Christians do with biblical dictates as well as other elements of their cultural environment and how they interpret sacred texts; the texts do not speak and produce action by themselves (Eliasoph and Lichterman 2003). The biblical scholar Stephen Haynes has shown, for instance, that even biblical dictates long used as rationales for racial subordination have been interpreted differently and also have been reinvoked to justify a succession of racial regimes, from slavery to post–Civil War segregation (2002). Properly speaking, southern conservative Christians were not driven by the Bible to support slavery and then racial segregation. Rather, as Haynes observed, they used biblical passages that were especially convenient for, but not naturally tied to, racist purposes. That is why we ask how conservative Christians attempt to build interracial relationships when they are acting as conservative Christians, rather than assume that we can explain their action directly from values or beliefs, or infer their action from sacred texts.

Race-Bridging

We call the action we are studying *race-bridging*. This term encompasses a variety of efforts at creating relationships across racial groups. When we say *bridging*, we refer to actions in process. Bridging for us does not necessarily mean successful outcomes of efforts to reduce social inequality between groups. It means efforts at creating enduring relationships across what the actors perceive to be social or cultural distance. The bridging term has become popular especially through the work of Robert Putnam, whose *bridging social capital* refers to efforts at creating relationships across social distance, successful outcomes of those efforts, and the social resources for those efforts (2000; for critiques of the social capital concept, see Lichterman 2006, 2005; Somers 2005).

Unlike Putnam, we are particularly concerned with the actors' social and cultural assumptions on which these bridges are built. Some may promote color blindness, others may recognize social-structural asymmetries, and others still may celebrate diversity. These strategies rely on different ways of conceiving differences between groups, relations between groups, different notions of intergroup power, and therefore different understandings of how to create successful interracial collaboration (Besecke 1999; Lamont 2000).

Exploring Conservative Christians' Race-Bridging Strategies

Others have surveyed the evangelical literature on racial reconciliation. Our goal here is to discern patterns of race-bridging from the point of view of the actors. Again, a contextual analysis holds that ordinary citizens and church leaders alike do not simply put religious teachings or how-to manuals into practice in a single, obvious way or in randomly varying ways. Rather, they create interracial relationships in a relatively few, patterned ways (Eliasoph and Lichterman 2003).

We draw on a small collection of available case studies that reveal some of the folk categories that white conservative Christians work from when they try to create relationships and collectivities with African Americans. Close-up case studies exist for two kinds of local sites in which white conservative Christians attempt race-bridging. In some of these sites, race-bridging was an explicit goal. In others it was implicit as whites attempted to develop friendships with blacks while downplaying racial differences, with a goal of creating Christ-like relationships. These sites include multiracial congregations and religiously based community service organizations, both important locations of civic life in the United States (Lichterman and Potts 2009).

The Multiracial Congregation   The multiracial church cases we discuss are evangelical Protestant, and all have significant white and African American participation (at least 20 percent each) and, in some cases, other racial-ethnic groups. They are located in different parts of the American South or Midwest. Multiracial congregations are defined in the research literature as congregations in which no single racial group constitutes more than 80 percent of the whole. There are few in the

United States—only 7 percent of all congregations, by the best estimate (Emerson and Woo 2006). It is worth taking these seriously though as sites for race-bridging, not only because they may be growing in number but also because they may foster more open racial attitudes: George Yancey found that compared with other church attenders, whites who attend interracial churches—churches in which African Americans are present—felt less social distance toward African Americans and were less likely to stereotype African Americans (1999).

The Religiously Based Community Service Organization   Cases include several community service organizations sponsored either by evangelical churches or individuals affiliated with evangelical churches or associations (see table 6.6). The first is Adopt-a-Family, an organization headed by a nonprofit group with a largely evangelical board of directors. It was a loose network of eight evangelical congregations, each of which organized volunteer groups to adopt a family whose breadwinner was leaving the welfare rolls and attempting to enter the paid workforce (in accordance with the welfare policy reforms of 1996). Adopting meant supporting family members informally, by driving a mother to appointments with doctors or potential employers, helping a son get a driver's license, or babysitting children while a parent looked for work, for example. The second is the Religious Antiracism Coalition, which brought together a pastor group of roughly twelve core members, five evangelical, the others mostly mainline Protestant. The group publicized opposition to racism by holding a multicultural celebration timed to coincide with a KKK march. They also held a monthly speaker series on topics related to race issues. Third is the Two Moms project. This organization cooked and served free dinners twice monthly at the neighborhood center of a low-income minority neighborhood. The fourth case is the Main Street Southern Baptists, a social outreach group attached to a Southern Baptist church in Mississippi that participated in the state's charitable choice program for faith-based groups that received government money for offering social services.

The case studies are not a statistical sample of bridging attempts, for which no sampling frame is available. Close-up research on race-bridging by religious groups remains relatively rare; rather than sample from available cases, we analyzed all the studies identified through an extensive literature review.[6]

The Dominant Strategy

Evidence points toward a dominant, white, conservative Christian race-bridging strategy and at least one variant seemingly preferred by black conservative Christians. We identify these patterns by drawing on par-

Table 6.6   Qualitative Case Studies of Conservative Christian Race-Bridging

Case Name	Type of Case	Study
Wilcrest Church	Multiracial congregation	Emerson and Woo 2006; Christerson, Edwards, and Emerson 2005
Crosstown Community Church	Multiracial congregation	Christerson, Edwards, and Emerson 2005
International Church of Christ	Multiracial congregation	Jenkins 2003
Grace Fellowship Church	Multiracial congregation	Rehwaldt-Alexander 2004
Faith Community Church	Multiracial congregation	Rehwaldt-Alexander 2004
Joy Bible Church	Multiracial congregation	Rehwaldt-Alexander 2004
Main Street Southern Baptist	Community service outreach	Bartkowski and Regis 2003
Adopt–a-Family	Community service organization	Lichterman 2005
Religious Anti-Racism Coalition (RARC)	Community service organization	Lichterman 2005
"Two Moms" project	Community service project	Lichterman 2005

Source: Authors' compilation.

ticipant descriptions and contrast them where appropriate with African American understandings. We then focus on several kinds of tension observed when whites and blacks tried to worship or work together. We characterize these tensions sociologically as indicative of a color-blind strategy.

From the point of view of conservative white Christians, race-bridging had to be a Christ-centered strategy, and so we name it that. In this mode, participants tried hard to privilege Christian identity over other identities when engaging with others. As one member of a multiracial church in the Northeast put it, only Jesus Christ could bring the races together, because only Jesus Christ doesn't discriminate. Any other basis for interracial relationships would be biased (Emerson and Woo 2006). Thus, Christ culture was a kind of racial zero-point, as an assistant pastor in Atlanta who described racial reconciliation explained: "There's a Christ-controlled culture that somehow we need to embrace" (Rehwaldt-Alexander 2004, 128). Within the Christ-centered strategy, race-bridging was not a civic, political, or moral end in itself but rather a means to becoming a better emulator of Christ. In this context, racism was defined as a sin that any good Christian must address like other sins, to be "right with God."

The relatively little available literature on this Christ-centered approach implies that it is more the product of cultural and theological themes in evangelical Protestantism than a self-conscious political strategy to trump race with religion (Emerson and Smith 2000). The Christ-centered style of creating relationships in local community life may have important political affinities and consequences, but sociologically speaking it is risky to assume that most local churchgoers or participants in community service efforts are political operatives consciously promoting a Christian Right ideology. Scholars frequently have observed a gap between the politics or ideology of national religious leaders or interest groups, whether liberal or conservative, and the less systematically organized, less ideological views expressed by local congregants (for instance, Wuthnow and Evans 2002; Hunter 1994). This is not so surprising considering that only a minority of churchgoers of any denomination get involved in politics through their congregations (Chaves 2004).[7]

Simplifying the Social Map

Churchgoers tried to achieve Christ-centeredness by downplaying the importance of racial differences and racial lenses—similar to the way they saw Christ ignoring differences between rich and poor. Successful race-bridging in this strategy was evident when one no longer saw race or felt a racial identity. This strategy was particularly common at multiracial congregations such as Faith Community and Grace Fellowship churches. Some white congregants spoke of achieving a Christ culture and losing other cultural attributes attached to racial or ethnic identity. Others said with pride that when they walk into a room, they simply didn't "see color" (Rehwaldt-Alexander 2004, 135). This facilitated the creation of personal relationships across racial groups, as illustrated by an African American congregant who said that his congregation "helped me to develop relationships with people outside my race. . . . I've gotten to know other people on that more personal level where I've said, 'wow, you know, it's not that much of a difference'" (Christerson, Edwards, and Emerson 2005). Multiracial congregations aimed to foster such relationships. For example, the demanding International Church of Christ structured discipleship within the church to encourage interracial relationships. Members had daily contact with what the church called discipling partners, and these discipling groups rotated members regularly. This heightened the likelihood of close, cross-racial contacts that would help crystallize the church's multiracial identity over time, at least ideally in the eyes of church leaders (Jenkins 2003).

Community service projects adopted the same strategy of downplaying race and encouraging a focus on commonalities among churchgoers and outsiders. At the orientation meeting for Adopt-a-Family volunteers, for instance, the trainer, an African American Christian day-care teacher, told volunteers that though she knew about "cultural differences," these differences were barriers to "seeing people with God's eyes" (Lichterman 2005, 133). For their part, volunteers monitored their own social biases. For instance, two volunteers in one group reminded each other not to push breast-feeding on a mother who had already decided on bottles for her newborn because doing so would be judgmental and risk highlighting social differences. They tried hard not to see race, as the following scenarios describe, which only underscores that they did indeed imagine themselves bridging racial differences in some way, even though they called their efforts not racial reconciliation but Christlike care. In this view, Christ, not race, was what mattered most for one to develop a successful relationship with a member of another racial group.

The Two Moms project started with a similarly simple social map. Inspired by prayerful reflection, two mothers decided to serve meals in a neighborhood because, they explained, they knew how to cook, and needed to find someplace where there were needy people to serve. They emphasized needs over differences—racial or other. The neighborhood they chose had a large minority population. That was not supposed to matter, though, and they did not mention it in their story of how prayer led them to the neighborhood (Lichterman 2005).

In both church and community service settings, downplaying racial (and class) difference was motivated by a well-intended effort to avoid discriminating unfairly by race. If Christ is all that really matters then one would do well to try ignoring or minimizing other markers of personhood. Doing otherwise might risk failing the Christ-centered strategy and reproduce discriminatory racial boundary-drawing.

This latter possibility is exemplified by the pastor of Main Street Southern Baptist. His congregation participated in the state-sponsored Faith and Families of Mississippi program that gave money to churches to assist former welfare recipients. Presuming that these helping relationships would be interracial, the pastor said that participants in this program would realize that "if they are going to get involved in having a church and a mentorship, they. . . are going to have to face some responsibilities they don't want to face." In an interview he offered, unprompted, that "southerners have always seen themselves as having to help, say, the black community. . . . Even when you had the active Ku Klux Klan and the marchers and everything, there's always been a desire to help. And I don't think that's ever been on a racial basis" (Bartkowski and Regis 2003, 116). This quote implies that the helper quite clearly is white and those helped are black. The pastor did not think southerners helped on a racial basis, yet in this account the black community is uniformly in need of help by a southern community assumed to be white (Bartkowski and Regis 2003). The pastor could not help but symbolize race aloud while discussing religiously based benevolence.

Emphasis on Informal Interpersonal Relations

In multiracial churches, many blacks as well as the great majority of whites defined racial reconciliation as working successfully when people are socializing informally and keeping up interpersonal relations across racial lines. One African American congregant characterized it as "doing everyday normal things with them just like I would with somebody who was black. Going out to dinner with them, our kids playing together." A white man put it similarly: "When church lets out . . . it's not pockets of people, it's not, oh the Asians are over here, the white people are running out the door . . . the black people are pocketed and hugging and loving on each other over here. It's everybody, all intertwined, intermixed" (Rehwaldt-Alexander 2004, 126). Leaders of one congregation contacted local restaurants, asking them to offer two-for-one dinner coupons so that congregants could invite a family of another race to dinner.

Community service efforts similarly relied heavily on socializing as a race-bridging strategy. Adopt-a-Family church volunteer groups arranged picnics, parties, and in one case a baby shower, with their "adopted" families so that the volunteers and the families could get to know one another. When volunteers complained that an adopted mother was often uncommunicative, or that the baby shower was an awkward gathering, it became all the more clear that they considered easy interpersonal socializing the sign of a successful bridge.

African American members of congregations and community service projects quite often appeared to have shared whites' valuation, and sheer enjoyment, of interpersonal socializing across race. However, they also emphasized other elements of a race-bridging strategy more than whites did. In the churches Jeremy Rehwaldt-Alexander studied, some black respondents stated that friendly socializing by itself was not enough, and that congregants needed to discuss public policy issues. Black and white members of the Joy Bible Church, discussed later, agreed that discussion of political issues were a critical part of the racial reconciliation process. Survey data corroborate this greater concern of blacks with exchanging about society and politics. Conservative Christian blacks were significantly more likely to interpret racial differences in terms of different educational opportunities and discrimination than conservative Christian whites were. They were significantly less likely than conservative Christian whites to oppose black collective action to secure rights, or to risk airing some divisive differences over worship or leadership style in their own churches.

Points of Tension in the Dominant Christ-Centered Strategy

In the Adopt-a-Family community service group, church volunteers sometimes tried to suppress the salience of socioeconomic differences between racial groups in order to sustain the Christ-centered strategy. Volunteers trained in social work would systematically downplay their knowledge of inequality within the community. When early in Adopt-a-Family's history these members suggested that the program should consider the families' social networks and neighborhoods when planning activities, the suggestions fell flat and were not picked up. Picnics and parties were held in parks or in church social halls, but not in the homes of volunteers or families, so that social class differences would not be so obvious. It became clear that this was a point of potential tension when a church volunteer told the researcher that her adopted family's apartment that was too "small and dark" for group events like the afternoon barbecue currently in progress, but that such an event could not take place at her house either because the adopted family's mother "would see that our social backgrounds are different. I wouldn't want that to become a factor in the relationship" (Lichterman 2005, 159). In a similar vein, this church group invited adopted family members to social events in their small church basement hall because the group considered it less socially threatening than inviting mother and kids to "go off with old white guys" to a private home (Lichterman 2005, 156).

Despite these efforts to downplay socioeconomic differences across racial groups, race-bridging was difficult. In their relation with service recipients, the volunteers of Adopt-a-Family were often put into awkward situations of sharing pleasantries and trying to build relationships without exchanging significant information about who they were. At one event for the families of all of the church volunteer groups, a painfully quiet dinner was followed by brief comments from the director of Adopt-a-Family and an invitation to stay around and play board games. At the baby shower, church volunteers had a difficult time getting the mother being celebrated at this event to say anything about her new baby—result of a pregnancy she had originally wanted to abort—and ended up putting a great deal of conversational energy into jokes about the new stroller they bought as a shower gift.

Styles of Worship and Timing

Frustrations over differing worship styles were present in several of the multiracial congregations in our sample. Wilcrest Church, for instance, made ongoing efforts to diversify its music at worship—in one instance, by adding an immigrant percussionist from Cameroon to its all-white worship band. At least one white member was not happy about the addition, and said in an interview that "if our worship changes much more, I will be embarrassed to invite others to come. The pace of some of the music, the loudness, it is just not right" (Christerson, Edwards, and Emerson 2005, 50). Most of Wilcrest's nonwhite congregants interviewed said that they wanted a wider variety of music than the typically white hymns and praise music that dominated their worship. Similar sensibilities and divisions were apparent at Grace Fellowship and Faith Community churches.

In several of the congregations studied, researchers observed or heard interviewees say that different timekeeping habits were a barrier to interracial worship. One Sunday school teacher was annoyed that black members of his adult class came up to a half-hour late to his one-hour Sunday course (Christerson, Edwards, and Emerson 2005). In examples like these, whites see not arriving to worship or meetings at the stated starting time as not taking things seriously. This was the case in the three multiracial congregations Rehwaldt-Alexander studied.

Similar sentiments characterized Adopt-a-Family volunteers. Members of one church volunteer group aired their frustrations one afternoon when their adopted family had not shown up an hour after the picnic starting time. Frustrations and mistrust mounted when they telephoned the family's home and heard an account of an accident and a hospital visit that they found hard to believe. The group's informal leader said that these were the difficulties one encounters when the "church community interacts with the non–church community" and that when one "adds races in" it gets more difficult still. Another member observed in a perplexed, somewhat dismayed voice that black church services might start late and last for hours. And, as we have already seen, although they tried to be Christ-centered and color-blind, white volunteers remained aware of racial differences, and felt awkward about being painfully different from adopted family members.

Differences in music and timing of activities can become grounds for evaluating people's worthiness or desirability, that is, for engaging in moral boundary work toward blacks by associating their behavior with lower moral worthiness (Lamont 1992). But does this boundary work matter in the bigger picture? Social research strongly suggests that it does: Tastes in music are not minor matters of leisure but integral to core personal identities (DeNora 2000) and social identities—racial and class identities, among others—that are anything but trivial (Bryson 1996; see also Lamont and Molnar 2001).

Networks and Friendships at Church

The case of Crosstown Church suggests that taken-for-granted differences in relationship style might combine with racial intolerance to strain relationships among members of multiracial churches (Christerson, Edwards, and Emerson 2005). Two white families explained to the researchers that they were going to leave the multiracial church because their son and daughter were the only white members of their church youth group. They were uncomfortable and had a hard time making friends with kids who were "loud," acted differently, had "different lifestyles." Perhaps the simple perception of being a white minority in a majority-black group might impel white members to depart, no matter how consonant the group's religious practices were with them. Other studies have commented little on this aspect of interracial relationship-building, emphasizing simply that interpersonal sociability matters to congregants. It makes sense to think that different styles of relationship-building and different styles of selfhood would affect the fortunes of a multiracial congregation that defines its mission strongly in terms of interpersonal relationship goals. In the ICOC congregation that discipled intensively, for instance, leaders sometimes assigned members to discipling groups on the basis of race or ethnicity, counter to the larger principle of interpersonal, interracial solidarity, because they assumed people of like backgrounds would understand each other's personal lives better (Jenkins 2003).

Encountering the Unsaved

For evangelical Christians, those who are not Christian, no matter what race, may appear morally inferior. This may even extend to Christians who are not congregational members. This is of course a matter of drawing sharp group boundaries, as was the case in Grace Fellowship and Faith Community churches. Pastors said that the real dividing lines were not between races but between Christian believers and those outside the church. Because the blacks to whom congregants reached out were not in their churches, congregants assumed them probably not saved, not truly Christian (Rehwaldt-Alexander 2004, 204–5). At Crosstown Church, one white family that had sought out a multiracial congregation also left the church because the teenage son found it hard to form friendships in the church youth group, which was reaching out to inner-city youth in an adjacent, largely working-class, and African American town. In the words of his mother, the organizers "were really reaching out to the [black working class] kids. And so, it was geared for sort of non-Christian kids." Implying that lower-income black youth probably are not Christian, she characterized her son as a "white suburban kid" in need of a different church in which they could "keep him growing spiritually." The Christ-centered intention here came cloaked in a set of preferences and assumptions regarding race and class as well as religion—assumptions that would be hard to articulate from within the dominant Christ-centered strategy (Christerson, Edwards, and Emerson 2005, 74). That social differences were muted and not openly discussed was likely to reinforce the homophilic character of the life of these congregations.

Discussions of church leadership suggested a similar issue in Grace Fellowship and Faith community churches. African American members complained that they could not take on leadership positions because the positions paid too little to live on. Because these evangelical churches defined freedom from financial debt as part of the essence of being a good Christian, systematic differences in the likelihood of having debts to pay off translated into lower chances of becoming church leaders (Rehwaldt-Alexander 2004).

White evangelical members of the Religious Antiracism Coalition (RARC) similarly emphasized Christian identity without reflecting fully on the consequences of this emphasis for race relations. When evangelicals joined discussions on how to publicize antiracism in their city of Lakeburg, they said repeatedly that they wanted to focus primarily on the racial divisions within the church—here meaning within the "circle of Christianity," as one pastor put it. The church was racist, they acknowledged, and needed to work on its own sins. Yet their approach strengthened the boundary between Christian and non-Christians. The RARC spent much more time discussing the possibility that non-Christians would participate in an anti-KKK event than they did discussing ways to boost attendance at the event by minorities, Christian or not. The maintenance of religious boundaries took precedence over publicizing antiracist efforts (Lichterman 2005).

Christ-Centeredness as Color Blindness

Many scholars argue that the ideology of color blindness is a neoliberal response to the establishment of equal opportunity legislation and policy (see, for example, Frankenberg 1993; Doane 1999). It lends support to the false notion that race no longer matters because of the accomplishments of the civil rights agenda in the 1960s and 1970s. Not acknowledging the importance of racial inequality often reinforces an unequal distribution of educational, economic, and social resources between minorities and whites. Color-blind positions also frequently discourage whites in more privileged social positions to question why their social location and life opportunities are different from those of the less fortunate. In this way color blindness sustains continual residential segregation and attendant disparities in local schools where minorities are the majority (Massey and Denton 1993). It maintains exclusive social networks among professionals (Collins 1989) and a sense of entitlement to placement in selective academic courses and schools (Wells and Serna 1996).

A further consequence of the race-blind approach is that it limits people's understandings of the different contexts in which whites and minorities live. Although conservative Christians often implied or said explicitly that race did not matter in their own relationships, racial and social differences were often salient, belying the raceless, dominant Christ-centered approach. Despite their good intentions, the individuals described in these case studies kept themselves from pondering or criticizing the social realities in which African Americans are embedded.

An Alternative: Christ-Centered and Socially Reflexive

One multiracial church in the sample of qualitative cases, Joy Bible Church, presented a somewhat different race-bridging strategy (Rehwaldt-Alexander 2004). Congregants discussed racial reconciliation in terms similar to those used at other churches, that is, by emphasizing the importance of interpersonal relations. They used a vocabulary of social justice rarely present in the other congregations, however, and spoke little if any about color blindness. Joy Bible Church interviewees valued pleasant interpersonal socializing as a means to creating interracial relationships, but also learned to value interracial teaching about group differences. The pastor, an African American, advocated that white congregants learn about racism from blacks, implicitly challenging the status equality that conventional socializing presumes, and in some ways reversing the surrounding society's social hierarchy. In contrast with the other conservative Christian groups, Joy Bible Church's practice was closer to that of race-bridging discussion programs that a variety of churches and secular organizations have used (Study Circles Resource Center 1997).

The congregation also became interested in race issues beyond the congregation itself. On one occasion, 100 church members attended a hearing on affordable housing. A member interpreted the event in terms of racial reconciliation: "People look out and see Joy Bible Church, they see all these different races and all these different people . . . that's how you are going to fight racism" (Rehwaldt-Alexander 2004, 238) In the same spirit, the church sponsored a low-cost medical clinic and a multiracial summer camp. The church's own staff included many African Americans and whites; the pastor reported that the church needed to work more on finding Latino personnel. It is possible of course that congregants shared left-liberal politics as much as faith in Christ, making it possible for them to openly discuss racial inequality. Although people in the other cases might interpret Joy Bible Church's race-bridging as un-Christ-like, Joy Bible Church congregants may have embedded their religious faith in an activist sensibility widely shared at this church but not in others.

In this case, instead of distinguishing Christ-like from non-Christ-like approaches, white and African American congregants learned to have what the pastor called a difficult conversation about race. The pastor instituted ongoing and sometimes tense churchwide dialogues about race relations in which many congregants participated. They learned to see themselves on a more complicated social map, so as to gain a better understanding of differences in experience and conditions across racial and class group divides. Congregants tried to relate to other congregants as people with racial identities, as well as Christians. United by a specifically Christian commitment against racism, they aimed to weaken racial boundaries. They thus tried to make racial identity itself an object of critical reflection, rather than to focus on racially blind Christ-centeredness. They had a socially reflexive understanding of their racial identities in relation to those of others (Lichterman 2005).

Something similar happened to the Two Moms organization. Having come into a low-income neighborhood as servants of Christ, the project leaders discovered that residents perceived them in more prosaic and social terms, as outsiders with paternalistic if well-intended ideas. The mothers engaged in difficult conversation, that is, held a public forum with neighborhood residents about their free-meals effort. Afterward they began organizing the meals alongside neighborhood residents rather than doing it for them. Only after this public meeting did they come to feel trusted and appreciated.

Conclusion

White and black conservative Christians have identities other than religious ones. These identities and the social preferences that accompany them inform their use of religious teachings—the dictate to make Jesus Christ central in their lives, for instance—and influence their race-bridging efforts. Our contextual perspective thus helps us understand the mother who believed that that the spirituality of her white suburban son was hindered if the church surrounded him with a group of black inner-city youth. To her, moral, racial, and religious identities had to coincide for spiritual growth to occur. Our analysis also helps make sense of the fact that for some, the boundaries of the Christian community include only individuals who have similar views on worship or timekeeping habits. When individuals assume that being a good Christian means being respectably suburban, or singing hymns that happen to derive from white-associated musical traditions, they are bringing nonreligious, social categories into their understanding of their religious practices and their definition of their religious community, even as they believe they are doing what Jesus would do.

When white gestures of friendliness, like a hand on the shoulder, were interpreted as condescending by blacks, the director of Adopt-a-Family explained it this way: "Race is—the dominant—way of talking, and it's not just race. It's not just racial. It's how to be with each other. If I put my hand—an innocent gesture—it gets so complicated!" (Lichterman 2005, 156). For this man, the core problem of social life is the challenge individuals face regarding how to be with each other. In this context, governmentally enforced policies based on race could seem of secondary importance at most. Conservative Christians might perceive them as a cold-hearted distraction from the work of "upping our compassion levels," to quote a favorite expression among Adopt-a-Family volunteers.

A focus on the race-bridging strategies of conservative Christians shows us how their preferred styles of everyday, local relationships may influence their political imaginations. It helps us understand the context through which some white, conservative Christians may interpret national policies and programs, including their lesser support for equal rights, compared to other whites. Committed to interpersonal closeness (Smith 1998) and hesitant to see people in terms of social structure, they may see civil rights or affirmative action policies as wrongheaded or irrelevant.

The combination of survey data and case studies support Emerson and Smith's pessimistic prognosis for the continued dominance of color-blindness within Christian conservatism in the United States (2000). Our analysis suggests that the Christ-centered strategy most popular among white conservative Christians more generally downplays racial differences and often devalues religious and cultural practices associated with African Americans. This strategy cultivates unequal relationships that are at odds with the civic ideal that motivates much current writing on the health of American civic life (Skocpol and Fiorina 1999; Putnam 2000). The decline in the civic engagement of Americans over the past thirty years reflects in large measure the diminishing participation of socially subordinate—low-income, nonwhite—citizens (Wuthnow 2002). Whatever its virtues, the dominant Christ-centered strategy seems unlikely to contribute to reversing this trend. Indeed, it steers people away from publicly acknowledging racial categories and racial inequality, which may be necessary to change attitudes and sensibilities tapped in the survey data. The Christ-centered strategy also does little to weaken the strong sense of distance that many white conservative Christians have in relation to African Americans—a sense of distance reinforced by a commitment to the view that racial differences are less important to believers than sharing Christian beliefs. An alternative approach is to cultivate difficult conversations about race. Yet given survey evidence on social distance between white conservative Christians and African Americans, it is unlikely that these difficult conversations will soon become widespread in conservative churches.

White conservative Christians surveyed appear to draw stronger racial boundaries than the individuals pictured in the case studies, who may not be visible in aggregated survey responses concerning race relations. It would be useful to survey systematically the racial attitudes in race-bridging groups and compare those with attitudes found among the broader samples. Moreover, studies reviewed here do not offer comparable criteria for successful race-bridging in multiracial churches or community service organizations. Although people in some of our ethnographic cases clearly were frustrated with their race-bridging efforts, we are unable to assess whether these efforts as a whole succeed by the members' own standards. We resist specifying standards, preferring instead to document the repertoire of approaches used in the United States.

Further work should investigate race-bridging approaches historically and across institutions. More studies should investigate our hunch that conservative Christians' race-bridging strategies inform their political orientations. Important survey research on religion and voting behavior teaches us much about recent political change in the United States but less about how exactly religion informs ordinary people's politics or civic engagement (Wuthnow 1999), or how public involvement informs people's religious commitments. We need more research that asks how people use religion in everyday settings—churches, civic associations, rallies and protests, for instance—to make political candidates and policies meaningful to them. Common sense dictates that religious people use religious teachings as rationales or ideological frames for their politics. Although people certainly do use religion this way, research shows that they also use religion in other ways to get their bearings on the public world (see Lichterman 2008).

Finally, we need research that can locate religiously based race-bridging strategies within a broader context, so that we can assess their relative importance in relation to race-bridging strategies that emphasize shared citizenship, consumption, or work. This broader agenda may illuminate aspects of racialized culture that have yet to be considered systematically and are likely to have enormous implications for how Americans define democracy and community in the future.

Notes

1. Our paper uses black and African American interchangeably. Following widespread usage, we do not capitalize color terms for race.
2. SBC.net, available at: http://www.sbc.net/resolutions/amResolution.asp ?ID=899.
3. National Center for Education Statistics, available at: http://nces.ed.gov/programs/coe/2002/section3/indicator25.asp.
4. U.S. Bureau of the Census, available at: http://landview.census.gov/hhes/income/histinc/f05.html.
5. In the GSS, respondents who identified as fundamentalist were counted as conservative Christians (the other categories were moderate and liberal.) Of course, not all conservative Christians would count as fundamentalists in the proper sense of the term (see Smith 1998); important differences between evangelicals and fundamentalists often fly under the radar of survey research, not to mention popular discourse. The Social Capital Benchmark Survey allowed respondents to identify with particular denominations, and using Smith as our initial guide, we chose and coded conservative Christian denominations that had a sufficient number of respondents for reliable analyses (1998, 2000). We intentionally used a restrictive coding strategy, so as to select only those denominations very safely considered very largely conservative theologically. They included Southern Baptist, Independent Fundamentalist Churches, Lutheran-Missouri or Wisconsin Synods, Pentecostal-Assembly of God or Pentecostal, and Church of God.
6. Proceeding inductively, we read through the cases, searching for patterns of interaction within them, in the same way that ethnographers analyze patterns of interaction in their field notes. Existing overviews of evangelical Christian social relations informed but did not exclusively determine our search for these patterns (Smith 1998; Emerson and Smith 2000; Warner 1988). We focused closely on styles of relationship, stated and implicit goals of relationship-building, and actors' own assessments of those relationships. Following the constant-comparative method, we developed classifications for the emerging patterns, and coded those classifications when we found them in the case studies, checking continuously see if codes used in one case could apply to others (Glaser and Strauss 1967; Strauss 1987). Coding in this way revealed a dominant strategy that held across congregations and community service organizations, and two strong components of that strategy that most of the cases displayed.
7. It may be easy to assume that local congregations' race-effacing, Christ-centered style of building relationships must have been designed intentionally to serve the interests of people hoping to diminish African American political power or opportunities. Yet we learn more about local churchgoers' race-bridging, and its relation to national politics, if we resist that assumption and

focus at least initially on what conservative Christians say and do, where.

References

Ammerman, Nancy. 2007. *Everyday Religion: Observing Modern Religious Lives.* New York: Oxford University Press.

Bail, Christopher. 2008. "The Configuration of Symbolic Boundaries against Immigrants in Europe." *American Sociological Review* 73(1): 37–59.

Bartkowski, John P., and Helen A. Regis. 2003. *Charitable Choices: Religion, Race, and Poverty in the Post-Welfare Era.* New York: New York University.

Bellah, Robert N., Richard Madsen, William M. Sullivan, and Ann Swidler. 2007. *Habits of the Heart: Individualism and Commitment in American Life.* Berkeley: University of California Press.

Besecke, Kelly. 1999. "Culture, Power and Politics in Multiculturalist and Anti-Racist Activism." Paper presented at the annual meeting of the American Sociological Association. Chicago (August 14, 1999).

Brubaker, Rogers. 2004. *Ethnicity Without Groups.* Cambridge, Mass.: Harvard University Press.

Bryson, Bethany. 1996. "'Anything but Heavy Metal': Symbolic Exclusion and Musical Dislikes." *American Sociological Review* 61(5): 884–99.

Chaves, Mark. 2004. *Congregations in America.* Cambridge, Mass.: Harvard University Press.

Christerson, Brad, Korie L. Edwards, and Michael O. Emerson. 2005. *Against All Odds: The Struggle for Racial Integration in Religious Organizations.* New York: New York University Press.

Collins, Sharon M. 1989. "The Marginalization of Black Executives." *Social Problems* 36(4): 317–31.

Conley, Dalton. 1999. *Being Black, Living in the Red: Race, Wealth, and Social Policy in America.* Berkeley: University of California Press.

Dawson, Michael 1994. *Behind the Mule: Race and Class in African American Politics.* Princeton, N.J.: Princeton University Press.

DeNora, Tia. 2000. *Music in Everyday Life.* New York: Cambridge University Press.

Dewey, John. 1927. *The Public and Its Problems.* Denver, Colo.: Allan Swallow.

Doane, Ashley W. 1999. "Dominant Group Ethnic Identity in the United States: The Role of 'Hidden' Ethnicity in Intergroup Relations." In *Majority and Minority: The Dynamics of Race and Ethnicity in American Life,* edited by Norman R. Yetman. Boston, Mass.: Allyn & Bacon.

Ecklund, Elaine Howard. 2006. *Korean American Evangelicals: New Models for Civic Life.* New York: Oxford University Press.

Eliasoph, Nina, and Paul Lichterman. 2003. "Culture in Interaction." *American Journal of Sociology* 108(4): 735–94.

Emerson, Michael O., and Christian Smith. 2000. *Divided by Faith: Evangelical Religion and the Problem of Race in America.* New York: Oxford University Press.

Emerson, Michael O., and Rodney M. Woo. 2006. *People of the Dream: Multiracial Congregations in the United States.* Princeton, N.J.: Princeton University Press.

Fowler, Robert Booth, Allen D. Hertzke, Laura R. Olson, and Devin R. Den Dulk.

2004. *Religion and Politics in America: Faith, Culture, and Strategic Choices*. New York: Westview Press.

Frankenberg, Ruth. 1993. *White Women, Race Matters: The Social Construction of Whiteness*. Minneapolis: University of Minnesota Press.

Gans, Herbert J. 1999. "Twenty-First Century United States." In *The Cultural Territories of Race: Black and White Boundaries*, edited by Michèle Lamont. Chicago and London: University of Chicago Press and The Russell Sage Foundation.

Glaser, Barney G., and Anselm Leonard Strauss. 1967. *The Discovery of Grounded Theory: Strategies for Qualitative Research*. Chicago: Aldine Transaction.

Greeley, Andrew. 1998. "Defections Among Hispanics." *America* 177(8): 12–15.

Hall, David D. 1997. *Lived Religion in America: Toward a History of Practice*. Princeton, N.J.: Princeton University Press.

Haller, Charlotte. 2003. "'And Made Us to be a Kingdom': Race, Antislavery, and Black Evangelicals in North Carolina's Early Republic." *The North Carolina Historical Review* 80(2): 125–55.

Haynes, Stephen. 2002. *Noah's Curse: The Biblical Justification of American Slavery*. New York: Oxford University Press.

Hernaìndez, Edwin I. 1999. "Moving from the Cathedral to Storefront Churches: Understanding Religious Growth and Decline among Latino Protestants." In *Protestantes/Protestants: Hispanic Christianity within Mainline Traditions*, edited by David Maldonado Jr. Nashville, Tenn.: Abingdon Press.

Jenkins, Kathleen E. 2003. "Intimate Diversity: The Presentation of Multiculturalism and Multiracialism in a High-Boundary Religious Movement." *Journal for the Scientific Study of Religion* 42(3): 393–409.

Lamont, Michèle. 1992. *Money, Morals, and Manners: The Culture of the French and American Upper-Middle Class*. Chicago: University of Chicago Press.

———. 1999. *The Cultural Territories of Race: Black and White Boundaries*. Chicago, New York: University of Chicago Press; Russell Sage Foundation.

———. 2000. *The Dignity of Working Men*. Cambridge, Mass. and New York: Harvard University Press and The Russell Sage Foundation.

———. 2006. "Destigmatization Strategies and Inclusion as Dimensions of Successful Societies." In *Successful Societies: The Impact of Culture and Institutions on Capabilities and Health*, edited by Peter A. Hall and Michèle Lamont. Cambridge, Mass.: Radcliffe Institute for Advanced Study.

Lamont, Michèle, and Crystal Fleming. 2005. "Everyday Anti-Racism: Competence and Religion in the Cultural Repertoire of the African American Elite." *Du Bois Review* 2(1): 29–43.

Lamont, Michèle, and Virag Molnar. 2001. "How Blacks Use Consumption to Shape their Collective Identity." *Journal of Consumer Culture* 1(1): 31–45.

Lewis Mumford Center. 2001. "Ethnic Diversity Grows, Neighborhood Integration Lags Behind." Albany: State University of New York.

Lichterman, Paul. 2005. *Elusive Togetherness: Church Groups Trying to Bridge America's Divisions*. Princeton, N.J.: Princeton University Press.

———. 2006. "Social Capital or Group Style? Rescuing Tocqueville's Insights on Civic Engagement." *Theory and Society* 35(5/6): 529–63.

———. 2007. "Beyond Dogmas: Religion, Social Service and Social Life in the United States: A Review Essay." *American Journal of Sociology* 113(1): 243–57.

———. 2008. "Religion and the Construction of Civic Identity." *American Sociological Review* 73(1): 83–104.

Lichterman, Paul, and C. Brady Potts. 2009. *The Civic Life of American Religion.* Stanford, Calif.: Stanford University Press.

Lincoln, C. Eric, and Lawrence H. Mamiya. 1990. *The Black Church in the African American Experience.* Durham, N.C.: Duke University Press.

Logan, John R., Richard D. Alba, and Shu-Yin Leung. 1996. "Minority Access to White Suburbs: A Multiregional Comparison." *Social Forces* 74(3): 851–81.

Massey, Douglas. 2001. "Residential Segregation and Neighborhood Conditions in U.S. Metropolitan Areas." In *America Becoming: Racial Trends and their Consequences,* edited by William Julius Wilson, Neil Smelser, and Faith Mitchell. Washington, D.C.: National Research Council.

Massey, Douglas, and Nancy Denton. 1993. *American Apartheid.* Cambridge, Mass.: Harvard University Press.

McPherson, J. Miller, Lynn Smith-Lovin, and Matthew E. Brashears. 2006. "Social Isolation in America: Changes in Core Discussion Networks over Two Decades." *American Sociological Review* 71(3): 353–75.

National Opinion Research Center. 2002. *General Social Survey.* Chicago: University of Chicago.

Oliver, Melvin L., and Thomas M. Shapiro. 1995. *Black Wealth/White Wealth: A New Perspective on Racial Inequality.* New York: Routledge.

Patterson, Orlando. 1997. *The Ordeal of Integration: Progress and Resentment in America's "Racial" Crisis.* Washington, D.C.: Counterpoint/Civitas.

Putnam, Robert. 2000. *Bowling Alone: The Collapse and Revival of American Community.* New York: Simon & Schuster.

Qian, Zhenchao. 1997. "Breaking the Racial Barriers: Variations in Interracial Marriage Between 1980 and 1990." *Demography* 34(2): 263–76.

Rehwaldt-Alexander, Jeremy. 2004. "Racial Reconciliation Among Evangelicals: The Limits and Possibilities of Congregational Efforts." Ph.D. diss., Vanderbilt University.

Robinson, Carin. 2006. "From *Every* Tribe and Nation? Blacks and the Christian Right." *Social Science Quarterly* 87(3): 591–601.

Saguaro Seminar. 2000. "Social Capital Community Benchmark Survey." Storrs: University of Connecticut, Roper Center for Public Opinion Research. available at: http://www.ropercenter.uconn.edu/data_access/data/datasets/social _capital_community_survey.html.

Sewell, William H. Jr. 1992. "A Theory of Structure: Duality, Agency, and Transformation." *The American Journal of Sociology* 98(1): 1–29.

Skocpol, Theda. 2000. "Religion, Civil Society, and Social Provision in the U.S." In *Who Will Provide? The Changing Role of Religion in American Social Welfare,* edited by Mary Jo Bane, Brent Coffin, and Ronald Thiemann. Boulder, Colo.: Westview Press.

Skocpol, Theda, and Morris P. Fiorina, eds. 1999. *Civic Engagement in American Democracy.* Washington, D.C.: Brookings Institution Press; New York : Russell Sage Foundation.

Smidt, Corwin, ed. 2003. *Religion as Social Capital: Producing the Common Good.* Waco, Tex.: Baylor University Press.

Smith, Christian. 1998. *American Evangelicalism: Embattled and Thriving*. Chicago: University of Chicago Press.

———. 2000. *Christian America?: What Evangelicals Really Want*. Berkeley: University of California Press.

Somers, Margaret. 2005. "Beware Trojan Horses Bearing Social Capital: How Privatization turned Solidarity into a Bowling Team." In *The Politics of Method in the Human Sciences*, edited by George Steinmetz. Durham, N.C.: Duke University Press.

Strauss, Anselm 1987. *Qualitative Analysis for Social Scientists*. New York: Cambridge University Press.

Study Circles Resource Center. 1997. *The Busy Citizen's Discussion Guide: Facing the Challenge of Racism and Race Relations*, 3rd ed. Pomfret, Conn.: Topsfield Foundation.

Swidler, Ann. 1986. "Culture in Action: Symbols and Strategies." *American Sociological Review* 51(2): 273–86.

Wadsworth, Nancy. 1997. "Reconciliation Politics: Conservative Evangelicals and the New Race Discourse." *Politics & Society* 25(3): 341–76.

Warner, R. Stephen. 1988. *New Wine in Old Wineskins*. Berkeley: University of California Press.

Wells, Amy Stuart, and Irene Serna. 1996. "The Politics of Culture: Understanding Local Political Resistance to Detracking in Racially Mixed Schools." *Harvard Educational Review* 66(1): 93–118.

Wimmer, Andreas, and Michele Lamont. 2006. "Boundary-Making: A Framework and a Research Agenda." Paper presented at the annual meeting of the American Sociological Association. Montréal (August 2006).

Wuthnow, Robert D. 1999. "Mobilizing Civic Engagement: The Changing Impact of Religious Involvement." In *Civic Engagement in American Democracy*, edited by Theda Skocpol and Morris Fiorina. Washington, D.C.: Brookings Institution Press; New York: Russell Sage Foundation.

———. 2002. "The United States: Bridging the Privileged and the Marginalized?" In *Democracies in Flux: The Evolution of Social Capital in Contemporary Society*, edited by Robert Putnam. New York: Oxford University Press.

Wuthnow, Robert D., and John Evans. 2002. *The Quiet Hand of God: Faith-Based Activism and the Public Role of Mainline Protestantism*. Berkeley: University of California Press.

Yancey, George. 1999. "An Examination of the Effects of Residential and Church Integration on Racial Attitudes of Whites." *Sociological Perspectives* 42(2): 279–304.

Chapter 7

Where Is the Counterweight? Explorations of the Decline in Mainline Protestant Participation in Public Debates over Values

JOHN H. EVANS

C HARLES TAYLOR defines the public sphere as "a common space in which the members of society are deemed to meet through a variety of media: print, electronic, and also face-to-face encounters; to discuss matters of common interest; and thus to be able to form a common mind about these" (1995, 185–86). The public sphere in liberal democratic societies exists to promulgate the values of the public, which can be communicated to the elites who lead us. That is, we have public debates about our values, and about the policies that might flow from such values. For example, a fairly vigorous public debate has continued in recent years about the Iraq war. This debate is partly about policies, such as whether having more soldiers in Iraq would lessen sectarian violence. The debate is also, and often implicitly, about values that support or lead to various strategies or policies. For example, the pottery barn rule, famously articulated by Colin Powell, is essentially a values statement: people who break something are obligated to fix it. Certain policies probabilistically flow from this value.

In America, religion has been a major influence on public debate about values and policies, both through the pronouncements of religious institutions, and through individual religious citizens who express through

their political participation religiously derived values and policy pro-
posals. The consensus view of scholars is that one religious tradition—
mainline Protestantism—dominated the debate in the public sphere
from the colonial era until the 1960s at the expense of evangelical Protestants, Catholics, and Jews (Thuesen 2002; Demerath 1995). The sociologist Jay Demerath, describing the "de facto establishment of the major
liberal Protestant groups for another 150 years after the First Amendment's passage," wrote that the mainline championed "a set of liberal
values central to American culture more generally . . . such as individualism, freedom, pluralism, tolerance, democracy, and intellectual inquiry" (1995, 460). One pair of scholars went so far as to say, speaking of
the 1950s, that "so wedded were the liberal, mainline churches to the
dominant culture that their beliefs, values, and behavior were virtually
indistinguishable from the culture" (Roof and McKinney 1987, 22). Exemplary of the peak of mainline Protestant dominance was the theologian Reinhold Niebuhr, a central figure in the public sphere, whose
ideas had influence on domestic and international policy. Niebuhr's influence was such that *Time* magazine featured him on its cover in 1948.
Niebuhr died in 1971, and no similarly influential mainline figure has
arisen to take his place.

Indeed, nobody would say that mainline Protestants dominate the
public sphere in the current era. This perception of conservative Protestant dominance is not new; by the mid-1980s, only a few years after the
rise of the new Christian Right, scholars had concluded that mainline
dominance was collapsing.[1] In this chapter I examine the relative decline
in the number of explicitly mainline voices discussing values in the public sphere. It is important to note what this chapter does not do. I cannot
examine the relative success of the mainline in supporting its policies or
whether the mainline voices in the public sphere have changed anyone's
values. Like trying to measure the success of social movements (Earl
2004), this may be beyond the capacity of social science; too many influences are typically at work to isolate the unique influence of one set of
voices or actions. Instead, I focus on what appears to be a differential decline in the amount of of mainline compared to fundamentalist and evangelical Protestant values discourse in the public sphere. Put simply, nobody talks about the moral values of mainline Protestants, even though
they represent 25 percent of the population, but everyone talks about the
moral values of fundamentalist and evangelical Protestants, even though
they represent a similar percentage. How did this happen?

What Is Mainline Protestantism?

Mainline Protestantism is both an institutional and a cultural phenomenon. Unlike evangelical Protestants, mainline Protestants have a fairly

bounded institutional form. Although fundamentalists eschew centrally controlled denominations, and evangelicals are divided among many dozens of smaller denominations—often with weak centralized control—the mainline is generally thought to be synonymous with a small handful of strongly bureaucratized denominations whose origins largely lie in the colonial era.

Although people with a mainline cultural orientation can be found in many Protestant denominations, most cluster within a small number of denominations affiliated with the National Council of Churches. The six largest mainline denominations today are the United Methodist Church, the Episcopal Church, the Presbyterian Church (USA), the United Church of Christ, the Evangelical Lutheran Church in America, and the American Baptist Churches (Wuthnow and Evans 2002, 4). There are other, smaller denominations that most scholars would consider institutionally part of the mainline, such as the Christian Church (Disciples of Christ), the Church of the Brethren, the Reformed Church in America, and the tiny 157-congregation Moravian Church, which, despite its size, has the motto that I consider to be the best concise summary of the mainline theological orientation: "In essentials, unity; in nonessentials, liberty; in all things, love" (http://www.moravian.org).

Culturally, the mainline refers to theological and social beliefs which, compared to fundamentalist and evangelical Protestants, are generally more liberal. For example, whereas mainliners adhere to basic Christian beliefs—with 92 percent believing that the Bible is the inspired word of God and 88 percent believing that God has been fully revealed to humans in Jesus Christ—only 28 percent think the Bible should be read literally. Despite believing in their own religion, 81 percent of mainliners think that all religions contain some truth about God (Wuthnow and Evans 2002). As has been shown in dozens and perhaps hundreds of studies, mainliners are more liberal than fundamentalist and evangelical Protestants on social issues, such as abortion and homosexuality. Demographically, mainliners are older, wealthier, whiter, and more educated than other Christians. They predominate in socially elite circles.

What Would Be an Equitable Distribution of Voices?

My goal here is to explain what scholars perceive to be the relative underrepresentation of the mainline voices in the debate over values. I take proper representation to be an amount that matches mainline Protestantism's numerical representation among Americans. By this standard, I am obliged to note that mainliners did not deserve their historical disproportionate influence given that they have not been in the majority since at least the mid-nineteenth century, or even earlier, depending on how we categorize groups from earlier centuries (Finke and Stark 1992).

There are many ways to try to calculate the relative numbers of different religious traditions in contemporary America, each of which produces a slightly different result. One way is to conduct a survey and ask people whether they identify with a particular tradition. A 2000 survey found that 26 percent of the population identified with a denomination classified as evangelical Protestant, 26 percent with Roman Catholicism, five percent with a black Protestant denomination, 14 percent with a denomination classified as mainline Protestant, 13 percent with a heterogeneous Other category, and 15 percent not affiliated (Steensland et al. 2000).[2] Using a slightly different method, the sociologists Andrew Greeley and Michael Hout calculated that 26 percent of people had a religious preference for a conservative Protestant denomination, 25 percent for Roman Catholicism, 23 percent for a mainline Protestant denomination, and 6 percent for an African American Protestant denomination (Greeley and Hout 2006). Another approach is to focus on the proportion of the population who actually attend religious services. The sociologist Mark Chaves found that 41 percent of those who attend were fundamentalist and evangelical Protestants, 29 percent were Catholics, and 24 percent were mainline Protestants (Chaves 2004).[3] Obviously, these figures exclude the nonreligious.

No definitive criteria exist to adjudicate between these approaches, but it is safe to say that conservative Protestants should be expected, based on sheer numbers, to have a slightly greater representation in the public sphere than mainline Protestants.

Is the Question Only What Is Labeled as Values?

If we were to keep this analysis on a simple level and focus only on the topics that dominate public understandings about the values debate, we would quickly come to the conclusion that mainliners are almost totally absent from the public sphere because they are not involved in values debates. This conclusion would flow from the observation that on issues that the media have determined to be values issues, such as abortion and same-sex marriage, the mainline is not present.

The confusion lies in whether public discourse has to be either self-labeled—or labeled by the media gatekeepers in the public sphere—as being about values for the discourse to be about values. This question builds from an obvious observation: evangelicals tend to say publicly that their positions on abortion, homosexuality and other social issues derive from their values, but mainliners do not. This does not mean that mainliners have no values, nor does it mean that mainliners are not advocating values in the public sphere. They simply do not use the term. The most obvious example of this labeling phenomenon is the evangelical discourse about family values, which encompasses positions on abortion, homosexuality, gender roles, pornography, and other issues related to sexuality and reproduction. If we look at the home page of the mainline-dominated National Council of Churches website as an example, we see that the Reducing Poverty link under Resources for Ministry and Mission includes several links below it, without the term *values* mentioned even once, even though it is apparent that mainline values must figure into the desire of the National Council of Churches to reduce poverty (http://www.ncccusa.org).

This avoidance of the word is probably a reflection of what Robert Wuthnow called the quiet influence of the mainline (2002). Mainliners are famously pluralistic, not wanting to push their moral values on others. In a conversation with me, a pastor of a liberal Protestant American Baptist congregation said that during the early 1980s, when Jerry Falwell was the public personification of *Baptist*, he wanted to put "not the kind of Baptist you are thinking of" on the sign in front of the church building. He wanted to say, "We are not the type of intolerant Baptists who push our values on you." Twenty-five years later this congregation offers the following self-description:

> First Baptist is a warm and welcoming community that strives to live the Christian faith with an open heart, an open mind, and an open spirit. We are a family of faith who is not afraid to ask tough questions as we seek to be wise and intelligent Christians in the modern world. We are a family who seeks to freely embrace people of diverse backgrounds and experiences, welcoming them into our lives. We are a people who strive to faithfully engage the great issues of our day by reaching out into our world with God's love, justice, and mercy. We are a people who would love to have you share with us in our life together as we join in following Jesus Christ into our future. (www.firstbaptistmadison.org)

The one conclusion you can reach from this statement is that this congregation is not going to explicitly push their values onto you, but rather you explore your own values yourself. This reticence is also evident in the interviews with mainliners I conducted for a book on religious discourses about reproductive genetic technologies. In these interviews, I asked respondents about scenarios, such as "how about if you had friends, Mark and Mary, both of whom carried the gene for cystic fibrosis. They were trying to decide whether they should use preimplantation genetic diagnosis to avoiding having a baby with this disease. What should they do?" In response such questions, the conservative Protestants would usually just say what they should do. The mainline respondents tended to start by saying that they of course would never tell Mark and Mary what to do, but that they would have certain concerns.

But, this linguistic issue is not what the reader is interested in. The reader does not want to know whether the term *values* is more used by fundamentalist and evangelical Protestants than mainline Protestants. I suspect upon reflection, it is noncontroversial that this is the case. Therefore, a contribution to a debate about values in the public sphere is made whenever someone gives a reason for their support or opposition to some policy. To further hone in on the question before us, I am then interested in the cause of the decline in the amount of mainline discourse about values, as defined above, compared to fundamentalist and evangelical Protestants.

Possible Causes of Decline in Mainline Values Discourse

Social science often aspires to find the most important cause of a phenomenon. In my view, the decline in the voice of the mainline in public debates about values does not have a singular cause, but rather many interwoven partial causes that sum to an explanation. I discuss each of these, but in the end cannot say that one is more important than another. Given that these causes are in many cases connected to one another— and that there are intractable empirical measurement issues involved in untangling effect sizes—we need to be satisfied with deciding whether the entire package is persuasive.

Declining Size of Mainline Relative to Fundamentalist and Evangelical Protestants

What is undoubtedly a primary cause of the decline of the mainline Protestant voice is the declining size of the mainline itself. The mainline denominations reached their peak in terms of raw numbers of members in the 1960s, plummeted in the 1970s, and have continued a slower but continued decline since that time (Wuthnow and Evans 2002, 6). Between 1965 and 1990, three of the dominant mainline denominations lost 25 percent of their members, though the rest lost less (Wuthnow and Evans 2002, 7). Contrary to the polemical diagnosis of mainline numerical decline favored by some evangelicals—that it is due to liberal theology—it appears that the primary cause is not theological, but demographic. Mainline women do not have nearly as many children as fundamentalist and evangelical Protestant women do. This in turn reflects differences in the educational and professional status of women in the two groups (Hout, Greeley, and Wilde 2001).

The consequence of the decline in members is real, however. There are not only fewer mainliners, there are also fewer mainline seminaries that produce public discourse, fewer seminary professors, fewer publishing houses, smaller budgets for the national church and society ministries, fewer campus ministries, and on and on. It is probably impossible to quantify the effect of these developments on the public representation of mainline Protestant values, but there is no question that it could be sizable. If it matched membership decline, we could roughly estimate it at 25 percent since the 1950s.

During this time, the number of evangelical Protestants has grown. One study of fifteen evangelical denominations found a 47 percent increase in members between 1968 and 2003. In terms of representative percentage of the population, this translates into an increase of 2 percent of the U.S. population. The study also found that in these denominations the membership rate as a proportion of the number of people in the country peaked in the mid-1980s and began to decline slowly through 2003.[5]

More members only matter insofar as members and their leaders are comfortable entering the public sphere. This has also changed for fundamentalist and evangelical Protestants. In the standard historical narrative, these Protestants withdrew from the public arena after the embarrassment of the Scopes Monkey Trial in 1925 and turned toward saving individual souls (Reichley 1985, 311–27). Robert Wuthnow reported that between 1953 and 1974 more than a dozen studies were conducted on the relationship between conservative theology and political activity and that "without exception, these studies indicated that evangelicals were less inclined toward political participation than were their less evangelical counterparts" (1983, 167–68). Rejecting their isolationist orientation, evangelical Protestants decided by the late 1970s to reenter the public sphere, with the emergence of what we now call the Christian Right. It is hard to say how many millions of dollars have been spent by the Christian Right on values discourse in the public sphere, but we know that the figure is at least many millions. Thus, together with the relative decline in numbers of mainline Protestants, we also find a relative increase in the propensity of another large religious group to join the debate in the public sphere. This, in itself, would by definition lower the relative mainline representation in public discourse, even if mainline numbers had remained stable.

Of course, a subtle qualifier is whether each conservative Protestant has the same access to the public sphere as each mainline Protestant. One of the themes in the Wuthnow and Evans 2002 study of mainline Protestants in the public sphere is that mainliners are more powerful people than fundamentalist and evangelical Protestants, and therefore have larger soapboxes. They are more often white in a society that values whiteness. They have more education in a society that values education, and nearly half are professionals, managers, or owners of businesses in an occupational structure in which 26 percent of jobs are found in these categories (2002, 11). When asked whether they had "close personal friends who were public officials, corporation executives, scientists, or wealthy individuals, two-thirds of mainline members (66 percent) said they did, compared with only 42 percent in the general population" (2002, 13). Mainline Protestants also enjoy the advantage of belonging to institutions that began in the colonial era; many mainline institutions have a lot of money, despite having fewer members to spend their money on. To take but one example, Trinity Episcopal Church in Manhattan was once the owner of much of what is today lower Manhattan, having received a land grant from Queen Anne in 1705. It currently owns twenty-seven commercial buildings in Manhattan, making it one of the largest commercial landlords in New York City (2002, 14).

On balance, it is likely that the decline in the numbers of mainline Protestants relative to other groups, and notably fundamentalist and evangelical Protestants, has contributed to lesser representation of the mainline voice in public debate. However, it is not the only cause. A useful thought experiment is this: if the mainline suddenly retrieved all of its lost members, would it also regain the voice it lost? Or, more important, would we perceive that mainline Protestants had become, once again, as influential in the public sphere as fundamentalist and evangelical Protestants have become? The answer to both questions is no, because other factors are working against the mainline voice in contemporary values debates.

Lack of Mainline Interest in Contemporary Religious Debates

It is possible that mainline Protestants are not interested in the contemporary debates in the public sphere that conservative Protestants have constructed as religious, and therefore do not participate. Insofar as this is true, the question of why the mainline voice has declined could be restated as, "why are mainliners not countering the values of the evangelicals on the issues raised by the evangelicals?" It follows that to the extent these issues dominate public debates related to religion, mainliners would be inherently less interested in participating.

For example, one of the sources of recent interest in values voters grew out of the 2004 presidential election; exit polls showed that nearly 25 percent of the voters described what mattered most in their vote was moral values, and that these same people tended to vote for George W. Bush (Langer and Cohen 2005). Supposedly, it was social issues like gay marriage with strong resonance in fundamentalist and evangelical

Protestant communities that brought value voters out to the polls, thus tipping the election to Bush. Although the institutions of fundamentalist and evangelical Protestantism (such as allied social movement organizations, magazines, and denominational agencies) have spent many resources on their value preferences for banning gay marriage, I think it is safe to say that the institutions of the mainline have spent virtually nothing on one side or the other of this issue.

This is not because they lack the ability, which is the implication of the numerical declension explanation. Rather, I think that they do not want to spend money on this issue simply because it is not their issue. We could, as amateur theologians, say that it should be, that it is more consistent with mainline notions of justice and so on to support gay marriage. We can also identify prominent mainliners who think so. But I do not think that most mainliners see it that way. They do not adhere to one of the extremes in the debate, but rather inhabit the "mushy middle." Insofar as the media is more interested in the clash of perspectives of those at opposite ends of the debate, the mushy middle will be ignored.

The same could be said about abortion. The conservatives have spent many hundreds of millions of dollars on this debate, and though the mainline Protestant denominations are generally officially in favor of defending the Roe decision (Evans 1997), and mainliners are more supportive of legal abortion than their religious counterparts are (Evans 2002), institutionally the mainline spends essentially nothing on the defense of abortion rights. There is one social movement organization, named the Religious Coalition for Reproductive Choice, that, despite having mainline denominational agencies as members, has traditionally received essentially no money from mainline institutions and survives like many other Washington interest groups—through direct mail fundraising. In sum, it is difficult to construe abortion rights as a mainline priority. The mainline is somewhere in the mushy middle on that issue as well.

To determine what the institutional priorities of the mainline in the public sphere actually are, I looked at one way these denominations try to speak of their values in the public sphere—through their press releases,[6] examining those of the six largest mainline denominations. The releases of the United Methodist Church (UMC) are an example. Its website features the top news stories the church is trying to promote as public issues. The day I wrote this passage, five stories were being promoted.

The first, titled "United Methodists lead dialogue at global health summit," discussed how bishops and other leaders in the UMC were advocating for health care for poor people in the third world. "'This is a conversation among leaders about a potential major initiative to invite the people of the United Methodist Church to help end the diseases of poverty,' said the Rev. Larry Hollon, chief executive of United Methodist Communications." Although the story did not explicitly mention values, probably because people do not need to be convinced that saving poor people from dying is a good thing, the release did end with a values statement of a bishop who said: "It's about justice and equality and hearing the call of Jesus to that."

The second press release, titled "'Last Minute Toy Store blesses families," covered a congregation that gives out Christmas toys to poor families before Christmas. The third, titled "Movie spotlights church's role in saga of homeless man," discussed a new movie starring actor Will Smith, based on a real story that took place partly in Glide Memorial UMC in San Francisco. The movie featured the story of a man who briefly stayed in Glide's homeless shelter with his baby son and went on to a successful career in the finance industry. "The work that Methodists do makes so much of a difference in someone making it or breaking it," said the man on whose life the film was based. The fourth was about a change in the UMC website and communications strategy. The fifth, "Senator gives little hope to interfaith coalition on Darfur," reported on a senator's discussion with Methodists and other religious groups on their efforts to end the genocide in Darfur.

Similarly, former general secretary of the mainline dominated National Council of Churches, Bob Edgar described in an interview about his new book titled *Middle Church* that he wants to "espouse the values of 'mainstream people of all faiths' that are misrepresented by the religious right" ("Edgar urges move to key 'middle' values," *Christian Century*, September 5, 2006, 15–16). Although the author of the story wrote that Edgar has "conventionally liberal views on abortion rights, homosexuality and stem cell research," it is all a "matter of priorities" when he picks the issues to focus on: "Abortion, homosexuality and stem cell research are 'the holy trinity of the religious right,' but [Edgar] figured that if Moses and the Gospel writers did not make those issues central, he wouldn't either. The three issues would not even be mentioned in an 'executive summary' of scripture, [Edgar] wrote, whereas 'poverty and peace . . . come up in the Bible more than 2000 times.'"

The point is that the mainline is promoting issues and their associated values in the public sphere, and policies that flow from these values, but they are generally not the issues and policies that fundamentalist and evangelical Protestants are discussing. More accurately, they are not the ones that fundamentalist and evangelical Protestants have received attention for promoting (that is, the central issues of the culture wars), given that the these Protestants are also interested in issues such as Darfur and international poverty.

This institutional effort at promoting particular values in the public sphere is generally matched by the efforts of individual mainliners. The sociology literature and public opinion data gathering is geared toward the debates that concern fundamentalist and evangelical Protestants insofar as these are the issues that have been most controversial in recent years. But what if we asked about debates that more match what the mainline Protestant institutions are trying to promote in the public sphere? In a 2000 survey, respondents were asked their level of interest in "social issues facing our country today," with each issue phrased in a liberal direction.[7] For example, they were asked about legislation to protect the environment, not about their interest in failing to protect the environment.

Table 7.1 contains a column of the percentage of mainline Protestant respondents who were either "quite" or "fairly" interested in the issues listed in the left column.[8] Note that helping the poor, protecting the environment, and promoting international peace were supported by 90 percent or more of mainline respondents. This corresponds to stories featured on the UMC website: the story about the homeless man at Glide Memorial is a story about helping the poor, and the story about Darfur is a story about international peace. Barely below this level of support is the issue of overcoming discrimination against women. This could be construed as a culture wars issue, except that there is almost no one in the public square is officially in favor of discrimination against women. The one clear culture war issue on this list, reducing intolerance toward homosexuals, has the least support from mainline Protestants.

This analysis suggests that it is plausible that the mainline is trying to make its voice heard in the public sphere, but that people do not notice it because they are looking to other debates over culture war issues. This cause is intertwined with the next I discuss, possible media bias in favor of culture war issues.

Possible Media Bias

Another possible and related cause is that there actually is no difference in the amount of mainline Protestant discourse about values that enters the public sphere, but that the media as gatekeeper tends to amplify and repeat only or primarily the discourse on issues of primary interest to fundamentalist and evangelical Protestants. "The calling card for entering the news is conflict, and any group that is able to create such situations typically gains access to media through the reports of hungry journalists," wrote Quentin Schultze (cited in Dart and Allen 1993, 15). The media do not report on the everyday activity of religious groups, such as feeding the hungry, holding worship services, or ordaining clergy. Rather, they only report when there is conflict, particularly between or within religious groups (Dart and Allen 1993, 15). Moreover, as Rhys

Table 7.1   Respondents "Quite" or "Fairly" Interested in Selected Issues

	Mainline Protestant	Fundamentalist or Evangelical Protestant
Social policies that would help the poor	92%	91%
Legislation to protect the environment	91	86***
Government policies to promote international peace	90	86*
Overcoming discrimination against women in our society	89	84**
Achieving greater equality for racial and ethnic minorities in our society	86	87
International human rights issues	82	81
The social responsibilities of corporations	78	79
Maintaining strict separation between church and state	69	67
Relief and development programs for people in third world countries	68	72*
Campaign finance reform	61	61
Reducing intolerance toward homosexuals	57	43***

Source: Author's compilation.
Note: Asterisks indicate statistical significance of difference between mainline and fundamentalist or evangelical Protestants using a chi-squared test.
*** $p < .001$, ** $p < .01$, * $p < .05$

Williams notes, evangelical discourse is based in an inherent conflict in that it posits a secular enemy (see volume 2, chapter 5). Mainline Protestants do not have this built-in conflict, because they do not, at least publicly, posit an enemy.

As one religion writer put it in a meeting I attended, "mainline Protestants are boring." In recent decades, most conflict has surrounded issues promoted by fundamentalist and evangelical Protestants, issues that mainline Protestants have been silent on. Studies show that mainline churches provide more social services than other Protestant churches do (Chaves 2004, 53), but this is the sort of values-based act that does not interest the media. Moreover, to the extent that reporters are more liberal or secular than the rest of the population, conservatives may be more interesting because they are more "foreign."

Although no formal content analysis of the coverage of religious groups in the media has been conducted, an examination of the annual Religion Newswriters Association poll of the top ten religion stories of the year is instructive. The stories the media gravitate to are the culture war issues now synonymous with fundamentalist and evangelical Protestant discourse in the public sphere. If we look at the stories on the 2002 list, some are not about American religious groups, such as the ninth top story, that Palestinian gunmen took refuge in Bethlehem's Church of the Nativity. The first, second, fourth, and fifth top stories, however, were aspects of the sexual abuse scandal in the Catholic church, the third was the remarks of the evangelical Franklin Graham about Islam, the sixth concerned school vouchers for religious schools, the seventh concerned the phrase "under God" in the pledge of allegiance, and the eighth was about the opposition of American religious goups to the Iraq War ("What Led the News," *Houston Chronicle*, December 28, 2002, Religion, 4.). The eighth topic here might give mainline Protestants a chance to exercise their voice, but not the others.

The 2001 poll was dominated by stories focused not on American religious groups per se, but primarily on the aftermath of the September 11 terrorist attacks. Results from the 2000 poll are more illuminating. The top story was about the Pope's extensive travels, and the third was on the Israeli-Palestinian conflict, an issue that the mainline has sometimes focused on. The second was about vice-presidential candidate Joseph Lieberman's orthodox Jewish observance. Other stories were close to the fundamentalist and evangelical Protestant public agenda. The fourth story was about debates within mainline denominations over homosexuality; the fifth was about the Southern Baptist Convention's ban on women pastors and requirement that women to submit to their husbands; the sixth was about the Catholic Church's teaching that "only Jesus Christ saves souls"; the seventh was about struggles within the Southern Baptist Convention on gender issues, which resulted in former President Carter's renouncing his ties to the convention; the eighth was about the Pope's apology for the sins Catholics committed against "Jews, women, indigenous peoples, immigrants, the poor and the unborn." The ninth—on the near merger of the Episcopalians and the Lutherans—had no obvious message for public debates. Finally, the tenth was about gender roles—the story of the first woman bishop in the African Methodist Episcopal Church (Tara Dooley, "Lieberman, Pope John Paul Head Top 10 Stories," *The Houston Chronicle*, December 30, 2000, Religion, 1).

The overwhelming conclusion about media coverage of American religious groups is that when a story can be thought of as expressing information about the culture wars, it is reported on. Even the mainline story about mainline debates about homosexuality is a culture wars issue. It appears that the only mainline debates that easily enter the public debate are the ones that fit neatly within the culture wars narrative. It is possible, of course, that the media does not have a bias against mainline Protestants and their issues, but that mainline Protestants are simply not media savvy and have not been able to convince the media to give their issues a fair share of the spotlight.

Mainline and Consensual Values

The values that the media do like to talk about—the culture wars issues—have no public consensus. Because they are controversial, they are of interest. Moreover, for reasons beyond the scope of this chapter, American culture is obsessed with sex. Sex sells, as the saying goes, and the fundamentalist and evangelical issues are disproportionately related to sex: abortion, homosexuality, pornography, sex education, gender roles, and so on. This may lead to additional media interest in fundamentalist and evangelical issues. The issues that mainline Protestants promote in the public sphere are less interesting because they are less about sex. They are also less controversial; in most cases there is a higher societal consensus about the values that drive them. Nearly everyone wants to keep people from starving to death; the only debate is over how to do it.

To see whether mainline issues are consensual, I compare mainline Protestants to fundamentalist and evangelical Protestants. The third column in table 7.1 shows the percentage of fundamentalist and evangelical Protestants who are quite or fairly interested in these issues. A few differences are statistically significant, but by and large they are not substantively significant. Ninety-two percent of mainliners are interested in polices that would help the poor, and 91 percent of fundamentalist and evangelical Protestants are. Ninety-one percent of mainliners are interested in legislation to help the environment, and 86 percent of fundamentalist and evangelical Protestants are. We go down the list and see general agreement, except on one issue. The substantive difference between mainliners and other Protestants is on reducing intolerance toward homosexuals. Here there is a difference, a conflict that the media can write about. But it is on an issue that the mainline does not promote, at least partly because within the mainline there is no consensus.

There is a more subtle issue. To the extent that debate in the public square arises on issues that implicate more consensual values, the values beneath policies might not be discussed. That is, even on the issues that the mainline seems to focus on, like Darfur, universal health care, and reducing poverty, perhaps mainliners talk only about their policy preferences, not their values. In Weberian language, they may talk only about their means and not their ends.

The explanation is straightforward: if people agree with you on values issues, the only debate is how to achieve those values. If you took the policy statements of all mainline denominations on social issues, those on issues that implicated less consensual values would be longer than those that implicated more consensual values. For example, the statement on abortion rights would be longer than that on avoiding genocide in Darfur. Again, the explanation is logical: on issues addressing controversial values, advocates often feel the need to first defend their values. So, if mainline Protestant issues in the public sphere are more consensual, it is likely that there will be less discussion about mainline values. Of course, this is not necessarily bad for mainline Protestants, in that if everyone already agrees with your values, you are not required to convince others of their merit. Or, to use the language from Charles Taylor's definition of the public sphere, the "common mind" is already formed about these values, so explicit debate about values is not necessary.

Internal Polarization

A related issue is why the mainline seems to be interested in high consensus issues. For example, there are probably no mainliners who question the values behind the effort to save Darfuris from genocide. On other issues, however, the mainline has a problem with internal consensus, and an even bigger problem with it than other religious traditions do.

One of the theological features of the mainline is that it is liberal in a Lockean sense, not just in a political one. That is, it is open to many competing views of theology. This is evident in the survey data. Eighty-one percent of mainliners agreed that "all religions contain some truth about God" and 70 percent agreed that "all religions are equally good ways of knowing about God" (Wuthnow and Evans 2002, 10). Such an orientation is not likely to lead to members to try to suppress each other for divergent theological views and values.

Therefore, one reason that the mainline may focus on more consensual issues, and thus have less visibility, is that mainliners who control the institutions that communicate with the public are not willing to promote issues that are internally polarizing. By contrast, it appears from the available evidence that fundamentalist and evangelical Protestant leaders are willing to do so. Evidence for this can be found in the literature on the clergy-laity gap. Scholars of the mainline have often heard the claim that it is the mainline elite who are out of touch with their masses, not the fundamentalists and evangelicals. It is said that it is the mainline leadership that promotes their agenda despite the beliefs of the people in the pews (Hadden 1969). Although this might once have been true, I see little evidence for a large gap in the current era.

Part of the confusion comes from looking at the denominational position statements passed at annual meetings to examine how liberal the elites are, compared to the masses. But, what are these statements? Do they mean that the institution is then instructed to spread the view to the public sphere? Perhaps, in theory, but the reality is different. Audrey Chapman, a former employee of mainline social action agencies, wrote that these policy statements "assign the denominations a comprehensive role responsible for virtually every facet of society, for which they have neither membership commitment nor staff resources. . . . [that] there is little basis within the statement[s] on which to set priorities or develop a focus. Often written serially, they reflect the American penchant for discovering issues with an evangelical zeal but retaining only short-term interest. Each new problem, each new issue clamors for denominational commitment, with the result that few can be pursued effectively" (1991, 86–87).

Given the number of these statements that are made, if the mainline elites are really picking the most liberal ones to focus on—being prophetic, in mainline parlance—then we should see the denominational agencies focusing on these prophetic issues. There is no doubt that what the institutions promote is somewhat more liberal than what the laity would want. But evidence suggests that the agencies and other elites lean toward promoting the more consensual issues. Laura Olson quoted the director of the Washington office of the Episcopal Church, who said, "I've tried to take into account the [church's] diversity . . . when taking positions on issues and setting priorities. . . . Those issues that have passed 51 to 49 percent are probably not the ones we're going to be on the bleeding edge of at this point. We're trying to find those issues that [have] a little wider support in the church" (2002, 65).

So, if the mainline institutions are promoting issues and values with higher consensus within the denomination, what about fundamentalist and evangelical Protestants? Here I would argue, contrary to commonly held opinion, that they have a larger clergy-laity gap than the mainliners, and fundamentalist and evangelical Protestant leaders are willing to take controversial positions in the public sphere despite these issues generating at least equal levels of internal dissensus as the mainline. This willingness to promote controversial issues allows them, as explained, more visibility in the public sphere.

First, studies of public opinion show that fundamentalist and evangelical Protestants and mainliners have similar levels of internal polarization. For example, using General Social Survey data from 1993 and 1994, John Hoffmann and Alan Miller found that the variance in opinions within what they call conservative Protestantism on abortion was .206. The variance within moderate and liberal Protestantism was .249 and .245, respectively (1997, 65). In the terminology adopted in this chapter, their moderate and liberal Protestants would be classified as mainline. On the abortion issue, conservative Protestants did seem to have slightly more consensus. Examination of the constant in the models in other research suggests something similar, albeit with a different method (Evans 2002, 412). However, on views of women's roles, Hoffmann and Miller found that conservatives, moderates, and liberals had variance scores of .168, .124, and .106, respectively. Here, conservatives had the least consensus. The data on attitudes toward premarital sex were similar, where the scores were .246, .236, and .218. On the other issues they examined, school prayer and marijuana use, mainliners had more variance (Hoffmann and Miller 1997, 65).[9]

Using the 1982–1991 General Social Survey, David Gay and his colleagues examined the variance in attitudes within religious groups. They showed that on the issues of homosexuality and extramarital sex, denominations they called other conservative and the Southern Baptists had more consensus than the mainline Protestant denominations. However, on the issues of gender roles, abortion, and premarital sex, the situation was reversed (Gay, Ellison, and Powers 1996, 11).

Yet the leaders within fundamentalist and evangelical Protestantism ignore the dissenting views in the tradition and promote their favored positions. The gap between what the elites say and do and what the masses believe is, then, very large within the fundamentalist and evangelical Protestant churches. How can we know this? We can look at some of the recent books on what evangelicals "really" think, which share the theme that evangelicals are not as conservative as you would think from their leaders.

In the conclusion to their book titled *The Truth about Conservative Christians* (by which they mean conservative Protestants), Andrew Greeley and Michael Hout established the general theme that conservative Protestants are not as conservative as you would think from the positions taken by their leaders. For example, the authors found that conservative Protestants were "somewhat different from the rest of Americans, but even on issues like abortion and homosexuality and voting behavior not all that different from [mainline] Protestants. There is a whiff of fact behind some stereotypes but no basis for the venomous denunciations that one hears so often" (2006, 180). They conclude by saying that

a sensible observer will always wonder how well those one observes on the television screen actually represent the various ascending minorities [conservative Protestants]. It is part of the American political game for the person in the spotlight to claim the largest possible constituency. However, the aforementioned sensible observer will resist the impulse to attribute to a large group of fellow Americans the claims being made by the self-anointed spokesperson. . . . So, those zealous Conservative Christians who try to use their smoke and mirrors to enforce their convictions on the media, school districts, courts, and local governments have every right to create whatever illusions they find useful. If others, such as many American liberals, buy into these illusions, it's their own fault. (181–82)

Also in this genre is Christian Smith's *Christian America? What Evangelicals Really Want*. The answer is that they do not want what the elites say they want. Smith wrote that "most ordinary American evangelicals are not very fairly represented by many of the single-minded and often self-appointed conservative Christian leaders who claim to speak for them" (2000, 194). This willingness to ignore diversity within one's own ranks allows for more exposure in the public sphere than the mainliners—more attuned to diversity of opinion—can achieve.

Why do fundamentalist and evangelical Protestant elites tend to ignore the people in the pews who disagree with them? First, remember that, unlike the mainline, fundamentalist and evangelical Protestant elites are not liberal in a Lockean sense. They are not inclined to think that everyone could be right in their interpretations, but rather that there is a single right position. Biblical interpretation is a good example. Fundamentalist and evangelical Protestant elite versions of biblical interpretation tend toward a claim of one true plain surface reading of the text, whereas mainline interpretation is much more diffuse. This belief in one true value or position results in a more authoritarian style of leadership than the mainline's.

Mainline Values Are Not Supposed to Be Distinct from Secular Values

Another component of the explanation for why mainline values do not appear in the public sphere is that the mainliners who are speaking in the public sphere are less likely to use explicitly religious values, and thus the connection to the mainline is not made. In the mainline, religion is not supposed to have a specific answer for everything. Fundamentalist and evangelical Protestants, more than their mainline counterparts, believe that one's religion is relevant to many more contemporary decisions. This takes its extreme position with the fundamentalists who believe that the answer to any question can be found in the Bible. It is unlikely one could find a mainliner who believes that the Bible has an answer for everything.

Another way of putting this in the terms of an existing literature is that mainliners are more privatized than members of other religions are (Regnerus and Smith 1998). The idea of privatization is related to a type of secularization—institutional differentiation. In the institutional differentiation explanation for secularization, religion—at one time the legitimator of an entire host of institutions, such as the family, education, and the state—becomes a separate institution alongside the others. Religion stops legitimating other forms of action. In colloquial terms, religion becomes something you definitely practice only in your private life, and probably something you practice only during worship services. Religions differ in the extent to which they accept this privatization, but recent studies suggest that, among Protestants, mainliners are more privatized and that fundamentalist and evangelical Protestants are less so (Regnerus and Smith 1998). So, although mainline values about war, for example, may ultimately derive in some deep sense from the pacifist teachings of Jesus, mainliners are unlikely to think there is an explicit religious commandment about war that they bring in so many words to the public sphere.

Contributing to this tendency toward privatization of religion is that mainliners are involved with more civic organizations than evangelicals or Catholics are (Smidt 1999, 185). Religion does not, then, have as central a place in the lives of mainliners as it does among fundamentalist and evangelical Protestants. Mainliners are exposed to the arguments of more organizations and institutions—not all of them religious. Therefore, even though they may have a religious reason for their pro-choice policy stance, a mainliner may well articulate the reasoning given instead by Planned Parenthood.

As an example, I analyzed a 2001 survey on Religion and Public Life conducted by the Pew Research Center for the People and the Press. I created variables for fundamentalist and evangelical Protestants as well as mainline Protestants.[10] Respondents were asked their positions on a number of social issues. More critically for our purposes, after being asked about each social issue they were also asked "which one of the following has had the biggest influence on your thinking on this issue?" The possible answers were "a personal experience," "the views of your friends and family," "what you have seen or read in the media," "your education," "something else," and "your religious beliefs." Table 7.2 presents the issues asked about, with the first column being the percentage of fundamentalist and evangelical Protestants who selected "your religious beliefs" as the biggest influence on their thinking on the issue, and the second column the percentage of mainline Protestants who did so. The general point here is that fundamentalist and evangelical Protestants see every issue as more connected to religion than mainline Protestants do and are both less privatized and less exposed to other influences.

Mainliners may be in the public sphere, but they may not be identifiable as mainliners per se, because they do not think of their values as deriving from their religion. This raises the unanswerable question of whether a mainliner's values are in fact derived from their religion even

Table 7.2   Religious Reasons Were Biggest Influence on Thinking about Social Issues

	Fundamentalist or Evangelical Protestant	Mainline Protestant
Death penalty for those convicted of murder	36.5	25.4**
People should do more to help the needy, even if costs them time and money	33.0	17.7***
Favor allowing gays and lesbians to marry legally	65.5	36.6***
In future, the U.S./Western powers have obligation to use force to prevent genocide	19.6	13.8*
Providing more generous government assistance to the poor	22.4	14.7*
Unrestricted scientific research related to human cloning	56.9	32.3***
Letting doctors give terminally ill patients means to end their life	46.5	26.3***

Source: Author's compilation.
Note: Asterisks indicate statistical significance of difference between mainline and fundamentalist or evangelical Protestants using a chi-squared test.
*** $p < .001$, ** $p < .01$, * $p < .05$

if they do not claim that they are. Are they opposed to war because they heard the beatitudes in church their whole life or because they get e-mails from Moveon.org? We will never know. I would argue that at least in the limited instance of debates in the public sphere which are based upon people's utterances, what someone in fact believes is not important. If mainliners do not use religious values in their arguments, then there is less mainline discourse in the public sphere, even if people are in fact motivated by religious beliefs (for more on this issue, see Klemp and Macedo, volume 2, chapter 7).

Self-Immolation After the Emergence of Christian Right

I finish on a more speculative note, with a partial cause of mainline decline in the public sphere for which no specific research has been conducted but which is consistent with what we otherwise know about mainline Protestants. Jay Demerath, in an underappreciated essay, explained the organizational decline of the mainline denominations as being the result of their cultural triumph. If we go back to the Reformation, we see that Protestantism itself brought with it what Demarath referred to as a new religious relativism. "To the extent that pluralism became increasingly valued in its own right," Demarath wrote, "no single doctrine or polity could be taken absolutely" (1995, 460). Moreover, he continued, in the United States, the mainline came to advocate "liberal values central to American culture" such as "individualism, freedom, pluralism, tolerance, democracy, and intellectual inquiry," though "liberal values may represent a dagger aimed at the institutional jugular" (460–61). For example, individualism and freedom in an institutional context are "basically centrifugal organizational forces, leading away from obedience and commitment" that are needed to sustain any institution (461).

Demarath was concerned with explaining the decline in the number of mainliners. I tweak his thesis to posit another interwoven cause of the decline of the mainline voice in the public sphere. I argue that the mainline retreated to consensual issues in the public sphere paradoxically to fulfill its own values—and thus triggered the other causes of decline I have discussed.

One of the common explanations for the rise of the Christian Right is that religious conservatives thought that America shared their values, and then a series of events in the 1960s and 1970s showed that this was wrong. They then entered the public sphere to change the values of America back to their liking. This is, for example, Luker's explanation for the rise of the antiabortion movement. The conservatives thought that America agreed with them that abortion was always wrong, and then the 1973 Roe decision shocked them into realizing that a good portion of the country in fact disagreed with them (Luker 1984). Wuthnow explained the rise of the Christian Right in similar terms. Shocked by the events of Watergate and other events that brought to light a deep corruption in public culture, and the nation's turn to concern with public morality, conservative Protestants began to fight back in the public sphere (Wuthnow 1983).

I propose an analog for what happened to the mainline voice in the public sphere. The mainliners also thought that people in America generally agreed with them. Then, in the early 1980s, the emergence of the Christian Right taught them that mainline Protestant values were not the U.S. default. Here was a group of citizens—the fundamentalist and evangelical Protestants—who clearly wanted to challenge for power in the public sphere that the mainliners had created and had dominated to that point. Mainliners discovered that they did not like being preached to by the likes of Jerry Falwell, and chafed at the idea of people like Falwell forcing their religious values on them through public law. Unlike the conservative response, which was to fight back, the mainline response was to retreat, or at least retreat to what they perceived to be consensual issues, so that they were not forcing their values on others. Why?

The mainline cultural form, which first and foremost believed in individualism, freedom, pluralism, tolerance, and democracy—to use most of Demerath's list, could not justify trying to make its other values normative for everyone else in the public sphere once they knew they were not consensual. If there was indeed a time when mainliners would explicitly claim religious justification for their publicly stated values, they would do so less because they did not want to sound like the illiberal Jerry Falwell. They then slowly pulled back to consensual issues, where they could not be accused of forcing their religion on anyone.

Conclusion

In the past few years there has been talk in the media about developments in religion and politics that would destabilize some of the categories I have been using. Much has been made, for example, of the supposed broadening of the issue agenda among evangelicals beyond issues involving sexuality. Of course, there has long been an evangelical Left, including Jim Wallis's Sojourners organization and Ron Sider's Evangelicals for Social Action. It appears that after the Democratic Party began to talk about God on the campaign trail, reporters finally noticed this faction of fundamentalist and evangelical Protestants who endorse liberal positions on social issues. It is notable, given the thesis of this chapter, that attention was put not on mainline Protestants, but instead on the seemingly incongruent and thus interesting evangelical Left.

Moreover, it appears that a new generation of evangelical Protestant leaders are emerging who, though perhaps holding the same views on sexuality issues as their predecessors, also want to emphasize a broader range of issues, such as environmental activism. This became most evident in a dispute between Christian Right social movement organizations and the National Association of Evangelicals (NAE), a coalition of evangelical denominations whose members hold a broader range of views. Christian Right leaders complained that an employee of the NAE was "moving the emphasis of evangelicals away from the 'great moral issues of our time: notably the sanctity of human life, the integrity of marriage and the teaching of sexual abstinence and morality to our children.'"[11] The NAE rebuked the Christian Right leaders and reaffirmed its position supporting environmental activism and opposition to torture. The earlier generation of Falwell, Pat Robertson, and James Dobson is seemingly being replaced by people like megachurch pastor Richard Warren, who, though clearly an evangelical, has a more expansive view of social issues.

As of this writing, it remains unclear how much influence this new generation of conservative Protestant leaders, as well as the rising attention given to the traditional evangelical Left, will have on the machinery of conservative Protestant activism. However, to the extent that they are successful and focus on values that are more consensual, such as maintaining the environment, the media will likely focus on them less, relegating them more to the status of the mainline.

There are also continued efforts to encourage mainline Protestant political activism outside the aegis of denominational structures. If the collective structures, such as the social action agencies of the denominations, are limited to consensual issues, a small subset of mainliners will continue to try to act on less consensual issues in independent or quasi-independent social movement organizations. For example, the Religious Coalition for Reproductive Choice is nominally controlled by its member denominations, but calls on selected individuals from within those denominations who agree with its stances for support. In the mid-1990s, activists formed the Interfaith Alliance, a group of religious liberals devoted to combating the religious conservatives in the public square. These groups remain fairly small, and even when you add even smaller groups like the Tikkun Network of Spiritual Progressives, they may not amount to much. They do have some advantages though, in that they avoid many of the structural impediments to influence in the public sphere I identified earlier. For example, denominational consensus is not an issue if the organizations are individual membership organizations, such as the Christian Right groups. Second, as individual membership organizations, they can include as members mainliners who are the least mainline in the sense of being reticent to push their values in the public sphere. How many mainliners are there who want to engage in this type of political activism? It is an open question for future examination.

I have provided seven interconnected causes for a decline in the mainline voice in the public sphere. First is that numerical decline in the mainline and growth in conservative Protestantism has simply resulted in fewer mainline voices than fundamentalist and evangelical Protestant voices. Second is that the issues defined as religious by fundamentalist and evangelical Protestants—and the press—are not of strong interest to the mainline, so the mainline has become less involved. Third is that even if the mainline speaks on issues, the press amplifies the culture war issues of the fundamentalist and evangelical Protestants only because they are more controversial and therefore interesting. Fourth, because the values of the mainline are more consensual, underlying values are not used in public debates, only competing policy prescriptions. Fifth, although all are internally polarized on culture war issues, the fundamentalist and evangelical elites are more likely to take positions at odds with their membership. This allows them to take more controversial stands and consequently triggers more media attention. Sixth, the mainline does not express its underlying values because it has a more privatized tradition. Seventh, and finally, the mainline willingly pulled back from participation in the public sphere to fulfill its own cultural orientation of tolerance, democracy, and pluralism.

As noted, it is not possible to weigh these different causes in an overall explanation, not only because to do so would imply a false precision, but also because they are interlinked. But considering them all in concert creates a more nuanced picture of mainline involvement in the public sphere and, therefore, perceptions of fundamentalist and evangelical Protestant dominance.

Would it be possible that the mainline would return to dominance in the public sphere? Of course it is possible. We are talking about relative dominance, so if other religious groups decline in their representation, the mainline rises. An implosion of the Christian Right, which draws largely from fundamentalist and evangelical Protestantism, would lead to an increase in the mainline voice. Although some pundits claim that the Christian Right will decline in the wake of Bush's leaving office, reports of imminent decline seem premature. Moreover, different religious traditions have different foci when it comes to public issues, for particularistic historical and theological reasons. As mentioned, fundamentalist and evangelical Protestantism, as well as traditional Catholicism, is often concerned with issues that have to do with sex. The mainline is much less concerned with such issues. If the Christian Right were to decisively lose debates about sexuality—say, if the public changed decisively to consider homosexuality completely normal, then fundamentalist and evangelical Protestants might retreat to focusing on their own communities and saving souls, as their predecessors did after the Scopes trial. It is also possible that the world might change in such a way that mainline values become the central debating point in the public sphere, though this does not seem to be on the immediate horizon.

It is also possible, to revisit Demerath's observation, that an indicator of the power of the mainline in the public sphere is its disappearance. It advocated a public sphere open to all, where ideas do not necessarily need to be expressed in religious languages out of respect for others' views. Whereas in an earlier era the mainline might have tried to keep fundamentalists and evangelicals from having a seat at the table, as they did with Catholics, now the presence of diverse religious voices in the public sphere can be seen as a celebration of mainline liberal values. In the end, their destruction may be, paradoxically, evidence of the victory of their basic values.

Notes

1. Most scholars would also place conservative Catholics beside these fundamentalist any evangelical Protestants in the contemporary public sphere. When I want to refer to all of these together in the public sphere, I will call them the religious right.

2. Religion and Politics Survey, January 2000, Robert Wuthnow, principal investigator.

3. Mark Chaves broke these data down by denomination and denominational family, and I aggregated them into these three broader traditions (2004). Thus these numbers are ultimately my interpretation of Chaves's data.

4. Of course, this is a bit of a liberal myth, in that all communities have values that they are pushing on each other. Some just like to pretend that they are not. One value that is sacrosanct in this congregation is, for example, that you shall not push values on others.

5. Empty Tomb study, http://www.emptytomb.org/Chap5hlites03.html.

6. On January 4, 2007, I downloaded the lists of news releases from the news services of the six primary mainline denominations. These varied in number, depending on how often the denomination made press releases and how far back their online archives went. As one would expect, many of these releases are on internal housekeeping matters pertinent to the denomination, such as the appointment of a new director an agency. Also, as those who study the mainline denominations and political involvement would expect, some of these denominations are more internally focused than others, most notably the Lutherans and the American Baptists.

7. I use the nationally representative religion and politics survey, available at http://www.arda.tm. The survey was conducted between January 6 and March 31, 2000. It contains 5,603 cases.

8. This analysis was conducted by using the self-identification method of assigning respondents to a particular religious tradition (for more details, see Evans 2006). I combined the mainline and liberal Protestant self-identifiers into a mainline Protestant category.

9. Note that their statistical test was not designed to determine statistical significance between groups.

10. Fundamentalist and evangelical Protestants were those who claimed to be Protestant and either a born again–evangelical Christian, a fundamentalist Christian, or a Pentecostal or charismatic Christian. Mainliners were the remainder of the Protestants. I analyzed only those who claimed to attend services once or twice a month or more because I wanted to be a comparison among people who actually participate in the religions instead of just identifying with it.

11. "NAE Rebuffs Critics, Affirming Cizik and a Wider Agenda." *Christian Century*, April 3, 2007; see also "Evangelical Angers Peers with Call for Action on Global Warming," *Washington Post*, March 3, 2007, A04.

References

Chapman, Audrey R. 1991. *Faith, Power, and Politics: Political Ministry in Mainline Churches*. New York: Pilgrim Press.

Chaves, Mark. 2004. *Congregations in America*. Cambridge, Mass.: Harvard University Press.

Dart, John, and Jimmy Allen. 1993. *Bridging the Gap: Religion and the News Media*. Nashville, Tenn.: Freedom Forum First Amendment Center.

Demerath, N. Jay. 1995. "Cultural Victory and Organizational Defeat in the Para-doxical Decline of Liberal Protestantism." *Journal for the Scientific Study of Religion* 34(4): 458–69.

Earl, Jennifer. 2004. "The Cultural Consequences of Social Movements." In *The Blackwell Companion to Social Movements*, edited by David A. Snow, Sarah A. Soule, and Hanspeter Kriesi. Malden, Mass.: Blackwell Publishing.

Evans, John H. 1997. "Multi-Organizational Fields and Social Movement Organization Frame Content: The Religious Pro-Choice Movement." *Sociological Inquiry* 67(4): 451–69.

———. 2002. "Polarization in Abortion Attitudes in U.S. Religious Traditions 1972–1998." *Sociological Forum* 17(3): 397–422.

———. 2006. "Cooperative Coalitions on the Religious Right and Left: Considering the Resilience of Sectarianism." *Journal for the Scientific Study of Religion* 45(2): 195–215.

Finke, Roger, and Rodney Stark. 1992. *The Churching of America, 1776–1990: Winners and Losers in Our Religious Economy*. New Brunswick, N.J.: Rutgers University Press.

Gay, David A., Christopher G. Ellison, and Daniel A. Powers. 1996. "In Search of Denominational Subcultures: Religious Affiliation and 'Pro-Family' Issues Revisited." *Review of Religious Research* 38(1): 3–17.

Greeley, Andrew, and Michael Hout. 2006. *The Truth About Conservative Christians: What They Think and What They Believe*. Chicago: University of Chicago Press.

Hadden, Jeffrey K. 1969. *The Gathering Storm in the Churches*. Garden City, N.Y.: Doubleday.

Hoffmann, John P., and Alan S. Miller. 1997. "Social and Political Attitudes Among Religious Groups: Convergence and Divergence Over Time." *Journal for the Scientific Study of Religion* 36(1): 52–70.

Hout, Michael, Andrew Greeley, and Melissa J. Wilde. 2001. "The Demographic Imperative in Religious Change in the United States." *American Journal of Sociology* 107(2): 468–500.

Langer, Gary, and Jon Cohen. 2005. "Voters and Values in the 2004 Election." *Public Opinion Quarterly* 69(5): 744–59.

Luker, Kristin. 1984. *Abortion and the Politics of Motherhood*. Berkeley: University of California Press.

Olson, Laura R. 2002. "Mainline Protestant Washington Offices and the Political Lives of Clergy." In *The Quiet Hand of God: Faith-Based Activism and the Public Role of Mainline Protestantism*, edited by Robert Wuthnow and John H. Evans. Berkeley: University of California Press.

Regnerus, Mark D., and Christian Smith. 1998. "Selective Deprivatization Among American Religious Traditions: The Reversal of the Great Reversal." *Social Forces* 76(4): 1347–72.

Reichley, A. James. 1985. *Religion in American Public Life*. Washington, D.C.: The Brookings Institution Press.

Roof, Wade Clark, and William McKinney. 1987. *American Mainline Religion*. New Brunswick, N.J.: Rutgers University Press.

Smidt, Corwin. 1999. "Religion and Civic Engagement: A Comparative Analysis." *Annals of the American Academy of Political and Social Science* 565(1999): 176–92.

Smith, Christian. 2000. *Christian America? What Evangelicals Really Want*. Berkeley: University of California Press.

Steensland, Brian, Jerry Z. Park, Mark D. Regnerus, Lynn D. Robinson, W. Bradford Wilcox, and Robert D. Woodberry. 2000. "The Measure of American Religion: Toward Improving the State of the Art." *Social Forces* 79(1): 291–318.

Taylor, Charles. 1995. "Liberal Politics and the Public Sphere." In *The New Communitarian Thinking*, edited by Amitai Etzioni. Charlottesville: University Press of Virginia.

Thuesen, Peter J. 2002. "The Logic of Mainline Churchliness: Historical Background Since the Reformation." In *The Quiet Hand of God: Faith-Based Activism and the Public Role of Mainline Protestantism*, edited by Robert Wuthnow and John H. Evans. Berkeley: University of California Press.

Wuthnow, Robert. 1983. "The Political Rebirth of American Evangelicals." In *The New Christian Right*, edited by Robert C. Liebman and Robert Wuthnow. New York: Aldine.

———. 2002. "Beyond Quiet Influence? Possibilities for the Protestant Mainline." In *The Quiet Hand of God: Faith-Based Activism and the Public Role of Mainline Protestantism*, edited by Robert Wuthnow and John H. Evans. Berkeley: University of California Press.

Wuthnow, Robert, and John H. Evans. 2002. *The Quiet Hand of God: Faith-Based Activism and the Public Role of Mainline Protestantism*. Berkeley: University of California Press.

PART III

RELIGIOUS CONSERVATIVES AND AMERICA'S SOCIAL INSTITUTIONS

Chapter 8

How Focused on the Family? Evangelical Protestants, the Family, and Sexuality

W. Bradford Wilcox

Social scientists refer to the first demographic transition as the decline in fertility associated with the shift from agricultural to industrial production. In this chapter, I discuss a second demographic transition, unfolding over the last half century in the United States (as in most other advanced industrial countries), which is characterized by a decline in the social power, functions, and moral authority of the nuclear family. I argue that this second transition (or revolution) has not, in the main, been a salutary development for American society or for American democracy.[1] This demographic revolution should be distinguished from the gender revolution of the same period, which had, by contrast, many positive consequences for both children and adults, including increasing women's economic opportunities and women's participation in public life (Spain and Bianchi 1996).

Since the 1960s, this second demographic revolution—marked by the declining role of marriage as the publicly recognized vehicle for lifelong, heterosexual love, and by dramatic increases in childrearing outside of marriage—has contributed to jeopardizing the emotional and social welfare of millions of children, and to fueling increases in economic inequality and child poverty (Amato 2005; McLanahan 2004; Thomas and Sawhill 2002). Increases in out-of-wedlock births, divorce, and single parenthood account for a substantial portion of the rise in crime, child poverty, economic inequality, and substance abuse that the United States has witnessed since the 1960s (Akerlof, Yellen, and Katz 1996;

Sawhill 1999; Amato 2005). One Brookings Institution study, for instance, found that recent increases in female-headed families explain most of the increase in child poverty in the nation from 1970 to 1998 (Thomas and Sawhill 2002). Another study found that changes in family structure accounted for 41 percent of the increase in income inequality in the United States between 1976 and 2000 (Martin 2006). Moreover, because family breakdown has been concentrated in poor, working-class, and minority communities, the sociologist Sara McLanahan concluded that this revolution in American family life has had particularly negative consequences for children in those communities, and has played an important role in fueling "widening social-class disparities in children's resources" (2004, 608; see also Ellwood and Jencks 2004). In these ways, then, American citizens—especially America's most vulnerable citizens, namely, children, the poor, the working class, and minorities—have paid a high price for the second demographic transition of the last half century.

An argument can be made that the family breakdown associated with this second demographic transition has also threatened values linked to the health of American democracy, such as the diffusion of knowledge, respect for persons, and the capacity for self-governance. Even after controlling for socioeconomic status, studies find that children who grow up outside of an intact, married household are two to three times more likely to drop out of high school and to engage in delinquent or criminal behavior (Amato 2005), and that unmarried adults are significantly less likely to vote (Wolfinger and Wolfinger 2006). At the national level, the aggregate consequences of family breakdown are particularly striking. For instance, looking at educational outcomes alone, the sociologist Paul Amato estimated that increasing the current percentage of adolescents who live in an intact, married family to the 1960 level of family stability would reduce the annual number of children repeating a grade by nearly three-quarters of a million and the number of school suspensions by more than 1 million every year (2005).

Evangelical Protestants are notable among the groups contesting this second demographic transition. In this chapter, I attempt to answer the question, what contribution have evangelical Protestants made to the renewal of marriage and family life in the United States? In answering, I summarize evangelical Protestant family ideology, explain its cultural and social sources, and reflect on the impact it has had on American family policy, as well as the family-related beliefs and behaviors of ordinary evangelical Protestants.[2] The evangelical Protestant record in renewing family life is important, of course, because this subculture's successes and failures in focusing on the family have a lot to do with the state of the family in the American nation—and, by extension, also with the strength of the American social fabric. Although I focus on evangeli-

cal Protestants, it is clear that other members of the traditionalist alliance—which includes conservative Catholics, Mormons, and conservative and orthodox Jews—share similar ideas about marriage and family and support similar public policies in support of marriage (see
chapter 4, this volume).

Resisting Family Change

Although most culture-producing institutions in the United States—
from higher education to Hollywood to mainline Protestantism—accommodated or advanced the demographic revolution of the late 1960s
and 1970s, evangelical Protestantism resisted key elements. It did so in
part by articulating a familistic ideology that endowed the family with
transcendent significance as the primary locus of social, emotional, and
moral life; in particular, this outlook sought to preserve marriage's social status as the institutional anchor for sexual activity, childbearing,
and childrearing. Partly as a consequence, evangelical Protestant leaders
targeted nonmarital sex, homosexuality, abortion, parenting, and divorce as topics of central concern (Wilcox 2004).

One indication of the distinctive evangelical Protestant response to
the consequences of the second demographic revolution comes from my
survey of *Christianity Today*, the flagship journal for evangelical Protestantism, and the *Christian Century*, the leading journal of mainline
Protestantism. I found that *Christianity Today* devoted nearly four times
as many articles and editorials to family-related topics than did the
Christian Century from 1970 to 1990—19 percent versus 5 percent
(Wilcox 2004, 52). This is one indication of the distinctive family focus in
evangelical Protestant circles. I also found that 58 percent of *Christianity
Today*'s family-related articles from 1970 to 1990 focused on matters related to sex—including nonmarital sex, homosexuality, and abortion
(46). In 1970, for instance, *Christianity Today* ran an editorial asking if the
nation needed a "new Gibbon to write *Decline and Fall of the United States
of America*" in light of "signs of decay" such as pornography, the sexual
revolution, and abortion (44). Likewise, a 1980 resolution passed by the
Southern Baptist Convention deplored the "homosexual lifestyle" and
any efforts to make "it equally acceptable to the biblical heterosexual
family life style" (47). And though abortion did not initially garner
much attention among evangelical Protestant institutions and leaders,
they began to turn against the practice once they connected it to the sexual revolution and to what they saw as a feminist assault on motherhood. In 1980, for instance, Jerry Falwell, then head of the Moral Majority, wrote that "for six long years Americans have been forced to stand
by helplessly while 3 to 6 million babies were legally murdered through
abortion on demand. . . . When a country becomes morally sick, it be-

comes sick in every other way" (47). In these ways, then, the family culture produced by evangelical Protestant institutions sought to reinforce traditional normative links between sex, childbearing, and marriage by critiquing departures from traditional norms about sex and reproduction.

Evangelical Protestant familism is also apparent in elite discourse on parenting and divorce. Because they see the home as a bulwark of faith and morality for God and country, evangelical Protestant leaders place a high priority on fostering an ethic of intensive, affectionate, but strict parenting. One such leader explained: "If we are to rebuild our nation we must first strengthen our homes and make sure that they are Christ-centered. Husbands and wives must assume the full responsibilities of Christian parents so that children may walk in the ways of the Lord" (Wilcox 2004, 49). Among other things, this means that parents are to conduct themselves as God does to his children—that is, they are supposed to be attentive, loving, and just in their interactions with their children. James Dobson, the founder of Focus on the Family, put it this way: "Healthy parenthood can be boiled down to those two essential ingredients, love and control, operating in a system of checks and balances ... the objective for the toddler years is to strike a balance between mercy and justice, affection and authority, love and control" (1978, 52).

By and large, evangelical Protestant elites have also expressed considerable concern with the divorce revolution of the last thirty years. For instance, Dobson had this to say about the dramatic increase in divorce in the 1970s: "Come on, America. Enough is enough! We've had our dance with divorce, and we have a million broken homes to show for it. We've tried the me-philosophy and the new morality and unbridled hedonism. They didn't work. Now it's time to get back to some old-fashioned values, like commitment and sacrifice and responsibility and purity and love and the straight life. Not only will our children benefit from our self-discipline and perseverance, but we adults will live in a less neurotic world, too!" (quoted in Wilcox 2004, 45).

Here, however, it is important to note that evangelical Protestant discourse on divorce has been more equivocal than evangelical Protestant discourse has been on, say, homosexuality. A large number of evangelical Protestant leaders do not follow a strictly biblical approach to divorce—which would only allow divorce and remarriage in cases of adultery (Matt 19:9) or the desertion of a nonbelieving spouse (1 Cor. 7:15)—and instead argue that remarriage should be available to any believer who repents of previous marital sins; from this perspective, biblical themes of compassion, second chances, and forgiveness are deployed against more legalistic responses to divorce (Wilcox 2004, 48). For instance, 36 percent of Southern Baptist pastors took this more permissive view of divorce and remarriage, according to a 1980 poll (49). In general, then, evangelical Protestantism has been a force for familism, though it has been less consistent when it comes to the issue of divorce.

Understanding Evangelical Protestant Family Culture

The evangelical Protestant concern with the state of the family is largely rooted in three cultural and four social sources. First, evangelical Protestantism subscribes to a traditional form of the Christian faith that sees the Bible as a literal and authoritative guide to moral truth. Many of evangelical Protestantism's positions—especially on topics such as premarital sex and homosexuality, to which behaviors numerous biblical passages speak directly—are derived from this traditional outlook (Wilcox 2004, 47). A lead editorial in a 1980 issue of *Christianity Today* is suggestive in this regard: "What does Scripture teach? *Heterosexuality is the biblical norm*. . . . Throughout the whole of Scripture, heterosexuality is both assumed and affirmed as God's order of creation" (cited in Wilcox 2004, 47).

Second, evangelical Protestant familism is rooted not only in its distinctive religious ideology, but also in its commitment to a traditional form of Americanism that links the health of the nation to the health of the family. This is why, for instance, James Dobson can be found issuing an antidivorce appeal to Americans ("Come on, America"), rather than to Christians, or why a evangelical Protestant family expert would link Christian parenting to efforts to renew the nation ("If we are to rebuild our nation"). The demographic revolution of the late 1960s and 1970s struck these evangelical Protestants as an attack not only on their faith but also on the American way of life, one they sought to resist at nearly every turn (Wilcox 2004; for the role of Christian reconstructionism in contemporary theological and social thought, see the Ingersoll, volume 2, chapter 6).

Third, many evangelical Protestant leaders are deeply concerned about the manifestations of the demographic revolution in their own lives, the lives of friends and family, and their congregations and communities. Having witnessed divorce on the rise in their churches, seen a family friend have a child outside of wedlock, or watched neighborhood children grow up without a father, evangelical Protestant leaders are quick to connect these family developments to human suffering and social decline (Wilcox 2004, 49; Smith 2000, 138–41). Hence they are motivated—as was Dobson, a professor of pediatrics and a child psychologist at the University of Southern California until he started Focus on the Family in 1977—to try to do something to reverse the family revolution.

But the sources of evangelical Protestant familism are rooted not only in cultural factors but also in four important social factors and processes. First, when the cultural shifts of the late 1960s and 1970s surfaced, evangelical Protestants were markedly more southern and working class than the nation as whole. In the 1970s, 58 percent of evangelical Protestants were southern and 46 percent were high school dropouts, that is, markedly more southern and less educated than the nation as whole in the 1970s (Wilcox 2004, 32). Because of their regional identity and class location, evangelical Protestants—and their institutions—were not inclined to identify with the ethic of liberation then emanating from elite East Coast and West Coast centers of cultural production. Instead, they were more likely to identify with an ethic of moral order that fit their experience of economic limitation and suited a southern culture that relied, in part, on its religious faith to distinguish itself from the North (32–33).

Indeed, issues of religious identity also figure prominently in evangelical Protestantism's embrace of a familistic outlook. The sociologist Christian Smith has argued that religious subcultures thrive on "distinction, engagement, tension, conflict, and threat" and the vitality of evangelicalism is "not a product of its protected isolation from, but of its vigorous engagement with pluralistic modernity" (1998, 89). The distinctive ideology produced by evangelical Protestantism on family-related matters has allowed this religious subculture to signal to the world and to its members that it is distinctive; the adversarial stance it takes to the broader society also helps it generate a sense of internal solidarity.

For instance, Al Mohler, president of Southern Baptist Theological Seminary, wrote a guest editorial for the *New York Times* explaining his denomination's family focus: "Southern Baptists are engaged in a battle against modernity, earnestly contending for the truth and authority of an ancient faith. To the cultured critics of religion, we are the cantankerous holdouts against the inevitable. But so far as the Southern Baptist Convention is concerned, the future is in God's hands. If faithfulness requires the slings and arrows of outraged opponents, so be it" (cited in Wilcox 2004, 63). Martial language like this on family matters helps build a strong sense of collective identity among evangelical Protestants. The success that evangelical Protestant elites have in connecting their faith to familism also explains in part why evangelical Protestants have retained traditional family values even as they have experienced marked social mobility in the last four decades (Wilcox 2004, 62–63). That is, even though evangelical Protestants have in some respects become more integrated into mainstream society, they still hold on to their unusual family-related ideology because it helps them build and sustain a distinctive collective identity (Gallagher 2003; for a discussion of the importance of "moral others" in the discourse of evangelical Protestantism, see Rhys Williams, volume 2, chapter 5).

Third, evangelical Protestantism has been able to articulate and defend its familistic ideology, even when elements of this ideology are unpopular, because of the large collection of institutional resources it controls. Evangelical Protestantism has a multi-billion-dollar publishing industry, more than 400 colleges and seminaries, more than 100,000 congregations, and hundreds of special purpose organizations, such as Focus on the Family. For instance, Focus on the Family has an annual budget exceeding $100 million dollars, employs more than 1,000 people, broadcasts a radio show on more than 2,900 stations in North America, and boasts 2.3 million members who draw regularly on its audio, video, web, and literary offerings (Wilcox 1998, 2004). These institutional resources provide this tradition with the means to resist, at least to a degree, many of the broader cultural trends in the United States.

Fourth, evangelical Protestants—partly because of their socioeconomic status—have been particularly vulnerable to the practical manifestations of the demographic revolution of the last half century. Evangelical Protestants, especially nominal evangelical Protestants (those who do not attend church frequently), and the communities they live in have been especially affected by the revolution in American family life; for instance, divorce is more common among nominal evangelical Protestants and southerners than it is in the nation as a whole (on evangelical Protestant divorce, see Wilcox and Williamson 2006; on divorce in the South, see Lesthaeghe and Neidert 2006). These changes—coupled with their distinctive theological and moral commitments—have also contributed to evangelical Protestants' concern about the state of the American family, their own families, and the families in their communities. As described by pollsters Stanley and Anna Greenberg, "they . . . are alarmed about pervasive moral laxity and threats to the traditional family" (2004). The irony, here, of course, is that one reason that evangelical Protestants are talking about family matters is that they do not like the fact that they have sometimes followed an expedient approach to family relationships or that their friends, family members, or neighbors have done so.

Indeed, their own failures in family domains such as divorce helps explain why—at least at the pastoral level—conservative rhetoric around homosexuality has been more strident than evangelical Protestant rhetoric around divorce. Homosexual desires and behaviors affect relatively few evangelical Protestants; divorce, by contrast, affects a large minority (Greeley and Hout 2006, 132–33, 146). For this reason, among others, pastors and evangelical Protestant leaders probably feel more comfortable signaling their familistic commitments by attacking homosexuality rather than divorce. And, as we have seen, they also appear somewhat more willing to look for the spirit of the gospel rather than the letter of the biblical law when it comes to divorce, as opposed to homosexuality.

Nevertheless, even though it has softened its position on divorce to some degree, evangelical Protestantism has been a major voice for familism in the United States in the last three decades. This support is particularly striking because most major culture-producing institutions in the United States and in Europe have not articulated a strong familistic ideology or resisted the family revolution in sharp terms. Of course, there are nonreligious exceptions to this trend; for instance, a growing number of academics and policymakers have underlined the public purposes served by marriage in recent years (see McLanahan, Donahue, and Haskins 2005; Wilcox et al. 2005). Undoubtedly, evangelical Protestantism's distinctive religious ideology and its substantial command of institutional resources—among other factors—has enabled it to chart a different course than most culture-producing institutions when it comes to the family.

Evangelical Protestant Discourse and Influence on Family Policy

Conservative and family organizations founded and supported by evangelical Protestants have emerged as major players in family-related policy in the last two decades. At the national level, since the late 1970s, evangelical Protestants and others in the traditionalist alliance have founded groups like the Christian Coalition (1989), Concerned Women for America (1979), Focus on the Family (1977), and the Family Research Council (1983) to promote their pro-family agenda (Wilcox 2002, 2004). At the state level, thirty-five groups have been formed since 1988—many at the behest of Focus on the Family—to promote a range of family-related policies.[3] Pro-life organizations, such the American Life League and the National Right to Life Committee, also rely on evangelical Protestant support, though these organizations also draw substantial practical and financial support from Catholics. Collectively, these groups attract regular support from more than 3 million Americans and annually raise more than $200 million to advance their agendas; these institutional resources help them play an important role in contemporary debates about abortion, divorce, same-sex marriage, and stem cell research.[4]

These family-oriented organizations have pursued a mix of policies. In the last three years, for instance, the Georgia Family Council has focused on divorce reform, marriage education, and school choice (Randy Hicks, personal interview, March 22, 2007). Over the same period, the Family Research Council has focused on abortion, pornography, religious freedom, and same-sex marriage.[5] Even though the diverse policy agendas of these institutions and their leaders are shaped by religious commitments and theological ideas, their public discourse tends to be secular. Specifically, they rely on utilitarian, scientific, and therapeutic arguments they think have a greater chance of resonating with the public and especially with the policy and media elites who tend to set the terms of public discourse (Wilcox 2002).

Evangelical Protestant leaders report that their own experience with legislators, journalists, and the public has led them to believe that overtly religious appeals are not as effective as appeals that conform to the largely utilitarian, scientific, or therapeutic canons of discourse in the public square. For instance, Tony Perkins, who became president of the Family Research Council in 2003, was one of the primary sponsors of Louisiana's 1997 covenant marriage law when he was a state representative. Perkins reported that his initial bill on covenant marriage was shaped by his own reading of biblical teachings on divorce and marriage, and by input he received from pastors in his district (Wilcox 2002, 9). Perkins said, however, that he did not refer to the Bible in arguing for covenant marriage because the society is moving in a post-Christian direction and because most people don't understand how the Bible would be applied in a legislative context (13). Instead, he relied on social scientific evidence about the effects of divorce to make his public case for covenant marriage, which allows heterosexual couples to enter into marriages that provide more restrictive grounds for divorce (abuse, adultery, a felony conviction, or abandonment) than conventional marriage in Louisiana does (Nock 2005).

On the other hand, some evangelical Protestant politicians also report that they do not wish to impose positions shaped only by religious beliefs on the public. Thus, they argue that they only pursue policies that have some reasonable connection to the common good (Wilcox 2002, 13). For instance, former Arkansas Governor Mike Huckabee, who has also pushed through covenant marriage and a range of other marriage-related policies in Arkansas, argues that his policy agenda is not directed by his faith, even though he is a former Baptist minister: "[I] have tried not to assume that my position as Governor gave me the right to impose my faith on others" (cited in Wilcox 2002, 13).

Similarly, Wade Horn, former assistant secretary for Children and Families in the U.S. Department of Health and Human Services, and the Bush administration's point man on marriage policy, has said that his marriage agenda is directed to the common good, not his Presbyterian faith. He said that there is a "line as a government official between being motivated [by faith] and then taking it and imposing it as the only proper view on a particular question [like marriage]." Horn added that his agenda is driven by "what empirical literature tells us, not just what our personal faith tells us" (cited in Wilcox 2002, 13). Although Huckabee's and Horn's support for marriage policy is undoubtedly shaped by their theological and ideological commitments, their understanding of their own approach to family policy, as well as their secular tactics, indicate the increasing sophistication and maturation of evangelical Protestant efforts to influence American debates about life issues, sexuality, and marriage. More and more, evangelical Protestant groups are trying to influence public discussions and policies related to the family by approaching the contemporary public square in a secular spirit—that is, with a desire to pursue the common good or at least to rely on secular reason and arguments in their pursuit of a religiously grounded good (for further discussion of evangelical Protestantism's adoption of secular norms of public discourse, see Klemp and Macedo, volume 2, chapter 7).

On the other hand, one striking and implicitly religious feature of the legislative agenda advanced by evangelical Protestant family groups is that they rarely pay attention to the economic or material challenges facing American families. Rarely do state and particularly national pro-family organizations directed by evangelical Protestants make a full court press for policies such as expanded child tax credits, universal health-care vouchers, or the elimination of the substantial marriage penalties facing poor and working-class Americans.[6] For instance, not only did Tony Perkins of the Family Research Council oppose passage of an expanded State Children's Health Insurance Program (SCHIP) that would have provided health insurance to children in many working-class families, but he has also not been a prominent voice for any kind of health-care reform that would help ordinary American families.[7] Instead, evangelical Protestant family leaders remain preoccupied with values issues (Smith 2000, 28). Their preoccupation with public policies that focus explicitly on moral matters rather than economic matters is largely an outgrowth of an evangelical Protestant theological emphasis on personal moral and spiritual renewal as the key to societal renewal. Many ordinary and elite evangelical Protestants seem to think that family renewal in the United States is achievable simply through widespread religious conversion or cultural change. Partly because they do not have a tradition of sustained reflection on social ethics, which Roman Catholicism and mainline Protestantism *do* have, evangelical Protestants and their pro-family organizations do not believe or are unaware of the possibility that social structural changes may also be required for the renewal of family life.

When it comes to advancing their public policy agenda, evangelical Protestant leaders and organizations have had varying degrees of success. In general, their record is closely connected to the level of popular support their legislative objectives engender at the federal or state level. This mixed record is reflected on life issues such as abortion and stem cell research. For instance, in the 1990s, pro-family and pro-life organizations succeeded in getting legislation mandating parental consent in cases involving abortion for minors passed in twenty-seven states (New 2007, 2). Most of these states are culturally conservative, and pro-life groups have been able to take advantage of the political climate in these states, as well as the fact that most Americans believe that parents should have a role in deciding whether or not their teenage daughters get an abortion (New 2007, 15; Pew Research Center, 2005). By contrast, pro-family groups have been less successful in stopping public initiatives to fund or allow stem cell research in states with large numbers of liberal or moderate-minded citizens, in part because of the state political climate and in part because stem cell research enjoys the support of a majority of Americans (Gary Langer, "Public Backs Stem Cell Research," *ABCNews*, June 26, 2001). In the last five years, for instance, pro stem cell legislation or policies have passed or been implemented by executive order in nine states—from California to Missouri to New Jersey; in most of these states, a coalition of scientists, medical professionals, and patient advocacy organizations (the National Parkinson Foundation, for example) spearheaded efforts to pass pro stem cell legislation or propositions.[8]

Evangelical Protestant groups have also had mixed success on marriage policy. After the Supreme Judicial Court of Massachusetts ruled that same-sex marriage was required by the Massachusetts constitution in 2004, conservative Christian groups launched efforts to amend both state constitutions and the U.S. constitution to prohibit same-sex marriage. The latter effort has failed so far, but these groups have succeeded in passing constitutional amendments against same-sex marriage in twenty-seven states (losing so far only in Arizona).[9] At the federal level, they also helped the Bush administration pass a $500 million Healthy Marriage Initiative in 2006 designed primarily to provide relationship skills and social services to low-income couples interested in getting marrying or staying married (Nock 2005).[10] Legislative successes in these domains can be attributed to widespread popular opposition to gay marriage, to more modest support for government programs to promote marriage between men and women, and to the fact that most legislators are not strongly opposed—at a personal level—to these policies.[11]

On the other hand, conservative Christian groups have had little success in their efforts to reform divorce laws at the state level. Recent efforts on the part of pro-family organizations in Georgia, Michigan, and Virginia to make modest changes to state divorce laws have not succeeded. In Georgia, for instance, the Georgia Family Council tried to extend the waiting period for married couples with children who are seeking a divorce from 30 days to 120 days. Their effort failed. Randy Hicks, the president of the Georgia Family Policy Council, attributes their failure to two factors: first, many legislators are divorce attorneys and have a vested interest in current divorce law and, second, many legislators and ordinary citizens in Georgia have been divorced. As a consequence,

in Hicks' experience, legislators and citizens both bridle at any suggestion that they have done anything wrong and are also "concerned about
government becoming more involved in people's lives by extending the
waiting period on divorce" (Hicks, personal interview, March 22, 2007).
Family advocates working in other states report similar challenges in reforming divorce (Wilcox 2002, 13). Their difficulties are not surprising,
given that only 37 percent of the American public thinks that divorce
laws should be tightened, according to a 1999 TIME/CNN poll, and that
a large minority—29 percent—of American adults are divorced, according to 2000–2002 General Social Survey (GSS) data.[12]

In sum, then, efforts by pro-family organizations have met with
mixed success, in part because some of their objectives do not enjoy
widespread popular support. On the other hand, these organizations
have been influential precisely because they have been willing to spear-
head causes that are popular among ordinary Americans but not always
among policy, media, and academic elites—such as the drive against
same-sex marriage. When they highlight these issues and pressure
politicians to vote in conformity with majority opinion, they are exercising a unique role in American public life and family policy. In other
words, on a number of family-related issues, they represent the only
organized institutional force advancing a more traditional perspective
that has popular but not elite support, and their leadership can crystallize popular support for traditional family causes that would otherwise
be ignored or rejected by elites. Indeed, their efforts on behalf of conservative family-related causes is one reason that American public discourse and public policy remains more conservative, and more ideologi-
cally heterogeneous, than family-related discourse and policy in other
western countries (for a similar point regarding American exceptionalism on sex education, see Luker 2006).

Evangelical Protestant Family-Related Beliefs and Behaviors

Evangelical Protestant institutions and elites responded in a distinctive
fashion to the demographic revolution of the last half century in the
United States. Unlike many culture-forming institutions in the United
States, they sought to resist this family revolution and renew family life
in America by producing and promoting a familistic ideology. At the
pastoral level, how successful have they been in shaping the beliefs and
behaviors of ordinary evangelical Protestants?

To answer this question adequately, I first address the subject of religious effects on human beliefs and behaviors. The social scientific literature indicates that religion influences family-related beliefs and behaviors through—among other things—theological beliefs and religiously

grounded moral norms related to the family, social networks that offer social support and control for a range of family-related beliefs and behaviors, and a religious nomos that endows family life with transcendent meaning and purpose and buffers against the stresses that can hurt family life. In part because they are exposed to these norms, networks, and a religious nomos more frequently, those who attend religious services on a regular basis, that is, several times a month or more, are more likely to have their family-related beliefs and behaviors shaped by the religious tradition to which they are affiliated than those who attend services infrequently are (Wilcox 2004, 99–14; Regnerus 2007, 43–56). Consequently, in discussing the links between evangelical Protestantism and family life, I distinguish between effects for active and nominal members of the evangelical Protestant tradition. Approximately 12 percent of the American population attends conservative and evangelical Protestant churches several times a month or more, and 10 percent of the American population is only nominally affiliated with this tradition, attending church once a month or less, according to GSS data from 1998 to 2002. The vast majority of these evangelical Protestants are white, and the vast majority of the evangelical Protestant respondents in the analyses are also white.

My analysis of GSS data from 1974 to 2002 suggests that evangelical Protestantism has largely been successful in fostering a more familistic outlook among its members. Take premarital sex as an example. From 1974 to 2002, evangelical Protestants remained markedly more traditional than other Americans on this issue. In 1974, 49 percent of evangelical Protestants but only 28 percent of other Americans reported that sex before marriage is always wrong; in 2002, the evangelical Protestant proportion rose to 57 percent and the other American proportion dropped to 24 percent. Among evangelical Protestants attending church several times a month or more, opposition was even stronger. In 1974, 60 percent of active evangelical Protestants always opposed premarital sex, but 64 percent did in 2002. Moreover, my statistical models indicate that the effects of evangelical Protestantism, especially church-going evangelical Protestantism, far outweigh the effects of sociodemographic factors such as education, gender, and age in shaping public opinion about premarital sex.[13]

With respect to divorce, evangelical Protestants have become slightly more familistic, as has the population at large. From 1974 to 2002, opposition to divorce rose. In 1974, 58 percent of evangelical Protestants reported that divorce should be more difficult to obtain, compared to 41 percent of other Americans; in 2002, both proportions had risen, evangelical Protestants to 70 percent, and other Americans to 49 percent. Among frequently attending evangelical Protestants, opposition to divorce rose from 71 percent to 75 percent over the period. My analysis of the GSS data indicated that an evangelical Protestant affiliation, and especially an active evangelical Protestant affiliation, was strongly associated with opposition to divorce and was a better predictor of divorce attitudes than were sociodemographic characteristics such as education, gender, and age (for data on evangelical Protestants and divorce, see Wilcox 2004, 77–78, 217).[14]

These results suggest that evangelical Protestant institutions have been at least somewhat successful in resisting the family revolution at the level of individual attitudes. Evangelical Protestant views on premarital sex and divorce have become somewhat more familistic since the 1970s, and churchgoing evangelical Protestants were significantly more familistic than average Americans. Of course, evangelical Protestant views on family matters are not monolithic; for instance, about 30 percent of churchgoing evangelical Protestants did not think premarital sex was always wrong, even though virtually no evangelical Protestant leader would endorse such a view.

In considering the association between evangelical Protestantism and attitudes, as well as behavior, selection undoubtedly plays some role in accounting for the strong links between evangelical Protestantism and familistic attitudes and the more inconsistent links between evangelical Protestantism and familistic behavior. Specifically, it is possible that socially conservative Americans are drawn to evangelical Protestant churches, which could drive up familism among churchgoing evangelical Protestants (Wilcox 2004). Nevertheless, because a clear majority of evangelical Protestants are lifelong members of this tradition (Smith 1998), it is unlikely that changing religions accounts for much of these associations. At the same time, socially conservative evangelical Protestants are probably more likely to attend church than evangelicals who are not socially conservative. So, selection into active churchgoing is probably a bigger factor for Americans who were raised as and remained evangelical Protestants.

At the same time, my research suggests that no other major religious group or institutional actor in the United States has devoted as much attention to fostering familism among its members. Given the strong association between active evangelical Protestantism and familistic beliefs, it seems safe to conclude that this tradition has been at least partly successful in convincing its members to subscribe to a familistic ideology. Accordingly, at least when it comes to family-related beliefs, it would seem that evangelical Protestant institutions have achieved a measure of success in resisting the revolution in American family life of the last half century.

On the other hand, a close look at the influence of evangelical Protestantism on family-related behaviors such as premarital sex, cohabitation, marriage, divorce, and parenting suggests a more mixed portrait of effectiveness. On some outcomes, evangelical Protestants are indeed more familistic than the population at large; on others, however, they are not markedly different.

In terms of sexuality and cohabitation, the picture is mixed—especially when it comes to nominal evangelical Protestants. My analysis of the 2002 National Survey of Family Growth (NSFG) indicates that evangelical Protestant adolescents typically had sex somewhat earlier than other adolescents—respectively, at 16.38 years old versus 16.52. For churchgoers, the mean age was 16.86, and for nonchurchgoers it was 16.23. Multivariate analyses incorporating controls for a range of socioeconomic factors indicated that the differences between other Americans and nominal evangelical Protestants, as well as evangelical Protestants as a whole, were not statistically significant; by contrast, churchgoing evangelical Protestants were marginally more likely ($p < .10$) to delay first sex.[15] On the whole, then, evangelical Protestant teenage sexual behavior was no different than that among the population at large, even though evangelical Protestant teens were more likely to subscribe in theory to a traditionally restrictive understanding of sex.

On the other hand, NSFG data indicate that evangelical Protestant young adults were less likely to cohabit than other Americans. Only 6 percent of evangelical Protestant young adults aged fifteen to forty-four said they were cohabiting, versus 10 percent of other young adults. Nevertheless, the patterns of cohabitation among evangelical Protestants diverged markedly by church attendance. Among those who attended church weekly, only 1 percent of evangelical Protestant young adults cohabited—the lowest figure for any major religious tradition in the United States; by contrast, among nominal evangelical Protestant young adults, the figure was 10 percent. This means that nominal evangelical Protestants were no different than other young adults in their cohabitation rates. These patterns stood up in a multivariate context; after controlling for socioeconomic characteristics, unmarried young evangelical Protestants, especially churchgoing ones, were less likely to cohabit than their peers, whereas nominal evangelical Protestants were about as likely.[16]

When it comes to childbearing, marriage, and divorce, the picture is, once again, mixed: some behaviors seem congruent with evangelical Protestant familism, others do not. Evangelical Protestant women were less likely to bear a child out of wedlock than other American women. Data taken from the 2002 NSFG indicated that 24 percent of children born to evangelical Protestant mothers were born out of wedlock, versus 33 percent of other American children. Furthermore, churchgoing evangelical Protestants were particularly likely to avoid nonmarital childbearing. Only 12 percent of children born to churchgoing evangelical Protestant women were born out of wedlock. On the other hand, 33 percent of children born to nominal evangelical Protestant women were; this means, once again, that nominal evangelical Protestant women were no different than other women in the United States. Multivariate models that control for socioeconomic characteristics indicated that these bivariate patterns were partly due to socioeconomic differences between evangelical Protestants and other American women. Specifically, only church-going evangelical Protestant women were significantly less likely to bear a child outside of wedlock than other American women; their nominal peers were no different than other American women in their rates of out-of-wedlock childbearing.[17]

Evangelical Protestants have been more likely to be married than other Americans, have married at younger ages, and have been significantly more likely to be married at any given time during their adult lives than other adults (Eggebeen and Dew 2007). My estimates from the 1998–2002 GSS data indicate that 54 percent of evangelical Protestant adults were married, compared to 45 percent of other adults. Frequent churchgoers among evangelical Protestants were especially likely to be married, 59 percent to 47 percent among nominal evangelical Protestants. Once again, nominal evangelical Protestants were no different statistically speaking in the likelihood that they were married than other American adults. No other major religious or secular group in the United States was as likely to be married, with the possible exception of Mormons, for whom there were not enough cases in the GSS to determine their marriage rates with statistical certainty. Note that these bivariate patterns hold up in multivariate models when I controlled for socioeconomic factors such as age, education, race, and region.[18] In sum, evangelical Protestants, especially churchgoers, seem particularly likely to marry.

On the other hand, evangelical Protestants have not been any more likely to stay married than the population at large. My analyses of the National Survey of Families and Households (NSFH) indicate that married evangelical Protestants were slightly more likely to divorce than other Americans between 1988 and 1993, though the differences were not statistically significant. Specifically, between the two waves of the NSFH, about 10 percent of evangelical Protestant couples divorced, versus approximately 9 percent of other couples. But here again, religious attendance mattered. Only 7 percent of churchgoing evangelical Protestant couples divorced in this period, whereas 16 percent of nominal evangelical Protestant couples did. Indeed, after controlling for socioeconomic factors, my statistical analyses of the NSFH indicate that churchgoing evangelical Protestant couples were marginally ($p < .10$) less likely to divorce than other Americans, whereas nominal evangelical Protestants were significantly more likely to do so.[19] When it comes to divorce, religious attendance was a strong marker, dividing divorce-averse churchgoing evangelical Protestants from their divorce-prone nominal peers.

Finally, with regard to parenting, I found—consistent with their commitment to the ideology of familism—that evangelical Protestants were significantly more likely to express attitudes and behaviors consistent with active and affectionate parenting than other Americans (Wilcox 1998). For instance, using data from the 1987–1988 NSFH and controlling for a range of sociodemographic characteristics, such as income, education, and race, I found that evangelical Protestant mothers and fathers were more likely to praise and hug their school-age children than other American parents were (Wilcox 1998, 804). Likewise, after controlling for a range of sociodemographic factors, I found that evangelical Protestant fathers said they spent about 2.0 hours more per week on youth activities such as sports activities, scouting programs, and religious youth groups than unaffiliated fathers (Wilcox 2004, 229). Once again, churchgoing evangelical Protestant fathers stood out: they spent 3.75 more hours per week on such activities than unaffiliated fathers did, but their nominal counterparts were not significantly different (Wilcox 2004).[20] Again, evangelical Protestant fathers who were frequent churchgoers were markedly more family-oriented than their nominal peers.

How do we make sense of evangelical Protestantism's mixed record when it comes to family-related behaviors? Part of the story here regarding sex, cohabitation, and divorce involves social class. Evangelical Protestants tend to be less educated than other Americans and, as a consequence, are more vulnerable to early sex and divorce.[21] This chapter indicates that nominal evangelical Protestants were especially likely to fail to live up to the familistic standards of the subculture; this may be in part because they, particularly those from poor and working-class communities in the South marked by higher levels of family breakdown, were not benefiting from the family-oriented social networks and the religious nomos cultivated by their churches (Lesthaeghe and Neidert 2006). Indeed, as noted, nominal evangelicals' inability to meet familistic standards on many outcomes may help explain why churchgoing evangelicals are so concerned about the family. If churchgoing evangelicals see their friends, family members, and neighbors who are only nominally affiliated with churches engaging in premarital sex, cohabitation, nonmarital childbearing, or divorce, that may heighten their desire to focus personal and pastoral attention on the family (Wilcox 2004).

The sociologist Christian Smith has argued that the distinctive moral beliefs articulated by evangelical Protestants are designed to build collective identity as much or more than they are designed to shape personal behavior (1998). Thus, one reason that some evangelical family-related beliefs are only loosely coupled to family-related behaviors may be that these beliefs' primary purpose is not to guide behavior, but instead to serve as markers of evangelical Protestantism's religious and moral traditionalism (Wilcox 2004, 194–96). For example, the Southern Baptist Convention's vociferous public support for traditional marriage even in the face of high rates of divorce among Baptists may have as much to do with the church's effort to signal its symbolic position in relation to secular liberalism (recall Al Mohler's desire to "battle against modernity") as it does with any effort to influence the marital behavior of Southern Baptists (Wilcox 2004, 194).

Still, despite the fact that evangelical Protestants do not live in complete conformity with their familistic beliefs, the more devout—that is, those who attend church several times a month or more—tend to live more familistic lives than most Americans. Churchgoing evangelicals are less likely to cohabit, have fewer children out of wedlock, marry at higher rates, divorce at lower rates, and express higher rates of parental affection than the national average. Of course, as noted, it is possible that Americans who are attracted to a family-centered way of life find their way to evangelical Protestant congregations, or that Americans who are raised in this tradition are more likely to be active churchgoers if they also live family-centered lives. But it also appears that the family-oriented norms, networks, and nomos that evangelical Protestants encounter in their congregations and in para-church institutions like Focus on the Family often, if not always, foster a more family-centered way of life.

Conclusion

The experience of the United States with the demographic revolution of the last fifty years would seem to vindicate the views of Founders, such as John Witherspoon and John Adams, who saw marriage as a seedbed of social virtue (Cott 2000). Indeed, even contemporary liberal political theorists, such as William Galston, and social scientists, such as Linda Waite, have come to see the ways in which this demographic revolution threatens important social and political values (Galston 1991; Waite and Gallagher 2000; see also Macedo 1990).

In the last two decades, a growing consensus has emerged among social scientists that marriage serves the common good and especially the welfare of children. As Ron Haskins, Sara McLanahan, and Elisabeth Donahue recently observed in a Princeton University–Brookings Institution policy brief, "Marriage provides benefits both to children and society. Although it was once possible to believe that the nation's high rates of divorce, cohabitation, and non-marital childrearing represented little more than lifestyle alternatives brought about by the freedom to pursue individual self-fulfillment, many analysts now believe that these individual choices can be damaging to the children who have no say in them and to the society that enables them" (2005, 1). This chapter has sought to determine how much evangelical Protestantism has contributed to strengthening the social fabric and the possibilities of democracy by renewing marriage as the primary institutional anchor for sexual activity, childbearing, and child rearing—and the vehicle for lifelong love.

In the public sphere, evangelical Protestant institutions and elites have had a record of mixed success in shaping public policy and public opinion related to family matters. They have scored successes on issues where public opinion supports them—for example, gay marriage—but have not made headway on issues where public opinion is opposed— for example, reforming divorce law. Furthermore, their theological commitment to individual moral and spiritual renewal has led many pro-family institutions and elites from the world of evangelical Protestantism to overlook the need to advance economic policies to strengthen American families. This is a major blind spot, given the influence that economic forces have on American families. For instance, Sara McLanahan has pointed out that poverty and declining real wages among men without a college degree have played a key role in fueling nonmarital childbearing and divorce among the poor and working classes in the United States over the last forty years (2004); accordingly, if they wish to strengthen families, evangelical Protestant institutions and elites will need to identify economic policies—for example, expanded child tax credits, universal health-care vouchers—that will help poor and working-class Americans and their families.

Nevertheless, in a number of policy domains, the presence and voice of evangelical Protestant institutions and elites in the American public square has pushed federal and state policy in a more pro-marriage direction. For instance, the sociologist Andrew Cherlin has pointed out that marriage policy—including the Bush administration's $500 million Healthy Marriage Initiative—has recently received a great deal of attention in the United States, even though virtually no political actors in Europe are concerned with marriage policies (2007). Undoubtedly, one reason that marriage policy is a going concern in the United States is because of the determined advocacy, the substantial institutional resources, and the political influence of evangelical Protestant family organizations. Thus, marriage in the United States has more institutional power and influence—including higher levels of policy support and a distinctive legislative standing in family law—than it does in northern European countries such as Norway and Sweden. This outcome is due, in part, to the activity of pro-family organizations that have sought both to resist the deinstitutionalization of marriage and to strengthen marriage, and have brought substantial resources to the public sphere to advance these agendas.

In the pastoral sphere, evangelical Protestant institutions and elites have also had mixed success in fostering strong families in their own subculture. On the one hand, drawing largely on their traditional religious belief system and their substantial institutional resources, they have for the most part succeeded in articulating and fostering a distinctively familistic ideology among their members and among conservative Christians in other traditions. On the other hand, the evangelical Protestant record of success when it comes to shaping behavior has been decidedly mixed. Evangelical Protestants engage in premarital sex and divorce at higher rates than members of other religious traditions. Nevertheless, they are more likely to bear children in wedlock, to be married, and to express active and affectionate behaviors in parenting than the population at large. Moreover, churchgoing evangelicals, who are exposed more frequently to religious messages and embedded more often in subcultural social networks, do show a greater commitment, on average, to the norms and practices of familism than Americans of other religious traditions do. This result is particularly impressive, given that many evangelical Protestants face social class obstacles that may make it more difficult for them to abide by familistic beliefs.

In sum, then, in the public and pastoral domains of American life, evangelical Protestants have made modest contributions to resisting the family revolution of the last half century and to renewing marriage in the United States. In my view, if they aim to achieve more substantial success in renewing American family life they will have to broaden their policy agenda (and their rhetoric) beyond values issues to include economic issues that affect the quality and stability of family life in the United States. They will also have to make a more sustained and sophisticated effort to offer secular reasons, arguments, and stories in a wide range of elite and popular venues to push the broader culture, as opposed to just their own subculture, in a more familistic direction. Without such efforts to expand their agenda and to make their public case more attractive, and less sectarian, evangelical Protestant family organizations and elites are not likely to renew marriage in the United States or, more broadly, to strengthen the fabric of American society.

Notes

1. I use the term *second demographic revolution* to encompass the range of behavioral and normative changes in American family life that occurred primarily in the late 1960s and the 1970s in the United States (Lesthaeghe and Neidert 2006; see also Ellwood and Jencks 2004; McLanahan 2004). Here, I am thinking specifically of increases in premarital sex, non-marital childbearing, divorce, and their normative concomitants. Given that these changes occurred at the same time, and reflect in one way or another the

deinstitutionalization of marriage as the social institution designed to govern sex, childbearing, child rearing, and the adult life course (Cherlin 2004), I think it appropriate to refer to these related changes as components of a larger social revolution in American family life.

2. By *evangelical Protestants*, I refer to American men and women who belong to theologically conservative denominations such as the Southern Baptist Convention, Assemblies of God, and the Evangelical Free Church. More broadly, this term captures Protestants who would typically be classified as evangelical Protestants, fundamentalist Protestants, or Pentecostal Protestants (see Steensland et al. 2000).

3. Focus on the Family, "Family Policy Council," Citizenlink.com, http://www.citizenlink.org/fpc (accessed April 1, 2007).

4. My estimates of group membership and budgets for these organizations are derived from information assembled by People for the American Way (available at: http://www.pfaw.org/pfaw/general/default.aspx?oid=158) (accessed April 1, 2007).

5. Family Research Council, available at: http://www.frc.org (accessed April 1, 2007).

6. For a discussion of public polices influencing the economic welfare of families, see Ross Douthat and Reihan Salam, "The Party of Sam's Club," *The Weekly Standard*, November 14, 2005, vol. 11, no. 9, available at: http://www.weeklystandard.com/Content/Public/Articles/000/000/006/312korit.asp (accessed April 1, 2007).

7. See http://www.womenstake.org/2007/08/pro-family-but-.html (accessed March 27, 2009).

8. The states that have passed legislation, propositions, or garnered executive orders funding stem cell research are California, Connecticut, Illinois, Massachusetts, Maryland, New Jersey, Washington, and Wisconsin. Legislatures passed stem cell bills in Connecticut, Massachusetts, Maryland, New Jersey, and Washington. Governors took executive action to fund stem cell research in Illinois and Washington. And, the voters passed the pro stem cell proposition 71 in California providing $3 billion in bonds for research beginning in 2005. For details, see the National Conference of State Legislatures, "Stem Cell Research," updated January 2008, available at: http://www.ncsl.org/programs/health/genetics/embfet.htm (accessed July 6, 2007). In addition, in 2006, Missouri voters approved the Stem Cell Research and Cures Amendment, which allows stem cell research and stem cell derived therapies to be conducted in the state (see the Missouri Coalition for Lifesaving Cures website, available at: http:///www.missouricures.com/site/PageServer?pagename=stemcell_protectingresearch (accessed March 26, 2009).

9. The following states have passed constitutional amendments prohibiting same-sex marriage since gay marriage was legalized in Massachusetts in 2004: Alabama, Alaska, Arkansas, Colorado, Georgia, Hawaii, Idaho, Kansas, Kentucky, Louisiana, Michigan, Mississippi, Missouri, Montana, Nebraska, Nevada, North Dakota, Ohio, Oklahoma, Oregon, South Carolina, South Dakota, Tennessee, Texas, Utah, Virginia, and Wisconsin (see Heritage Foundation, "Family and Religion," available at: http://www.heritage.org/Research/Family/Marriage50) (accessed July 6, 2007).

10. See also U.S. Department of Health and Human Services, Administration for Children and Families, "General Information," available at: http://www .acf.hhs.gov/healthymarriage/about/mission.html#goals (accessed April 1, 2007).

11. For polling data on same-sex marriage, see Joel Roberts, "Poll: Legalize Same-Sex Marriage?" July 30, 2003, available at: http://www.cbsnews.com/ stories/2003/07/30/opinion/polls/main565918.shtml (accessed April 1, 2007). For polling data on the Healthy Marriage Initiative, see Anne Farris, "Most Americans Want to Promote Marriage, Surveys Say, but Aren't Sure How," The Future of Children, November 22, 1005, available at: http://www.futureofchildren.org/newsletter2861/newsletter_show .htm?doc_id=321689 (accessed April 1, 2007).

12. I analyzed data from the 2000 and 2002 waves of the General Social Survey to determine what percentage of American adults aged eighteen and older had ever been divorced. The GSS data indicate that 29 percent of American adults have been divorced (for the Time/CNN poll data, see http://pa triot.net/~crouch/wash/timetable.html (accessed April 1, 2007); on the prevalence of divorce, see Cherlin 2008).

13. These figures are based on my analysis of 1974–2002 GSS data. Here, frequent churchgoing is defined as attending church several times a month or more. Note also that the trend line in evangelical Protestant attitudes toward premarital sex from the 1970s to the 2000s runs in a more familistic direction over this entire period; 2002 is not an outlier (Wilcox 2004, 80). Note also that the standardized beta coefficient for churchgoing evangelical Protestantism when it comes to premarital sex is larger than the standardized beta coefficient for education, gender, race, age, and year.

14. Note that figures for "other Americans" were calculated from 1974–1998 GSS data specifically for this paper. Here, frequent churchgoing is defined as attending church several times a month or more. Note again that the trend line in evangelical Protestant attitudes toward divorce from the 1970s to the 2000s runs in a more familistic direction over this entire period; 2002 is not an outlier (Wilcox 2004, 77). Note also that the standardized beta coefficient for churchgoing evangelical Protestantism when it comes to divorce attitudes is larger than the standardized beta coefficient for education, gender, race, age, and year.

15. These figures are based on analyses of the 2002 National Survey of Family Growth. Here, frequent churchgoing is defined as attending weekly or more. Multivariate models control for age, education, race, ethnicity, gender, family structure at age fifteen, and region.

16. These figures are based on analyses of the 2002 NSFG. Once again, multivariate models control for age, education, race, ethnicity, gender, family structure at age fifteen, and region.

17. These estimates are based on 2002 NSFG data. Once again, multivariate models control for age, education, race, ethnicity, gender, family structure at age fifteen, and region.

18. These estimates are based on analyses of 1998–2002 GSS data. Here, frequent churchgoing is defined as attending several times a month or more.

19. These figures are based on analyses of Wave 1 (1987–1988) and Wave 2

(1992–1994) of the National Survey of Families and Households. For these analyses, frequent church attendance is defined as attending once a week or more. Multivariate models of divorce control for age, region, ethnicity, race, and education. Note that the lower divorce rate for churchgoing evangelical Protestants was significant at the $p < .10$ level.

20. Here, frequent churchgoing is defined as attending church several times a month or more.

21. For instance, after controlling for sociodemographic factors including education, the association between evangelical Protestantism and divorce in the NSFH declines by about 75 percent.

References

Akerlof, George A., Janet L. Yellen, and Michael L. Katz. 1996. "An Analysis of Out-of-Wedlock Childbearing in the United States." *Quarterly Journal of Economics* CXI: 277–317.

Amato, Paul. 2005. "The Impact of Family Formation Change on the Cognitive, Social, and Emotional Well-Being of the Next Generation." *Future of Children* 15(2): 75–96.

Cherlin, Andrew. 2004. "The Desintitutionalization of American Marriage." *Journal of Marriage and Family* 66(4): 848–61.

———. 2007. "Marriage and Public Policy." Paper presented to the Population Association of America, Annual Meeting. New York (March 30, 2007).

———. 2008. *Public and Private Families*. Boston, Mass.: McGraw-Hill.

Cott, Nancy. 2000. *Public Vows: A History of Marriage and Nation*. New Haven, Conn.: Yale University Press.

Dobson, James. 1978. *The Strong-Willed Child: Birth through Adolescence*. Wheaton, Ill.: Living Books/Tyndale House.

Eggebeen, David, and Jeffrey Dew. 2007. "The Role of Religion in the Family Formation Processes of Young Adults." Paper presented to the Population Association of America, Annual Meeting. New York (March 29, 2007).

Ellwood, David T., and Christopher Jencks. 2004. "The Uneven Spread of Single Parent Families: What Do We Know? Where Do We Look for Answers?" In *Social Inequality*, edited by Kathryn Neckerman. New York: Russell Sage Foundation.

Gallagher, Sally. 2003. *Evangelical Identity and Gendered Family Life*. New Brunswick, N.J.: Rutgers University Press.

Galston, William. 1991. *Liberal Purposes: Goods, Virtues, and Diversity in the Liberal State*. Cambridge: Cambridge University Press.

Greeley, Andrew, and Michael Hout. *The Truth About Conservative Christians*. Chicago: University of Chicago Press.

Greenberg, Stanley B., and Anna Greenberg. 2004. "Contesting Values." *The American Prospect* 15(3). March 5, 2004. Available at: http://www.prospect.org/cs/articles?article=contesting_values (accessed March 31, 2007).

Haskins, Ron, Sara McLanahan, and Elisabeth Donahue. 2007. "The Decline in Marriage: What to Do." *The Future of Children/Princeton-Brookings* Policy Brief (Fall). Princeton, N.J.: Princeton University Press.

Lesthaeghe, Ron J., and Lisa Neidert. 2006. "The Second Demographic Transition in the United States: Exception or Textbook Example?" *Population and Development Review* 32(December): 669–98.

Luker, Kristin. 2006. *When Sex Goes to School*. New York: W. W. Norton.

Macedo, Stephen. 1990. *Liberal Virtues: Citizenship, Virtue, and Community in Liberal Constitutionalism*. New York: Oxford University Press.

Martin, Molly A. 2006. "Family Structure and Income Inequality in Families with Children, 1976 to 2000." *Demography* 43(3): 421–45.

McLanahan, Sara. 2004. "Diverging Destinies: How Children Fare Under the Second Demographic Transition." *Demography* 41(4): 607–27.

McLahanan, Sara, Elisabeth Donahue, and Ron Haskins. 2005. "Introducing the Issue: Marriage and Child Wellbeing." *The Future of Children* 15(2): 3–12.

New, Michael J. 2007. "Analyzing the Effect of State Legislation on the Incidence of Abortion Among Minors." *Heritage Center for Data Analysis* Report CDA01–01. Washington, D.C.: Heritage Foundation.

Nock, Steven L. 2005. "Marriage as a Public Issue." *The Future of Children* 15(2): 13–32.

Pew Research Center. 2005. "Abortion and Rights of Terror Suspects Top Court Issues." Survey Report, August 3, 2005. Washington, D.C.: Pew Research Center for the People & the Press. Available at: http://people-press.org/reports/pdf/253.pdf (accessed April 1, 2007).

Regnerus, Mark D. 2007. *Forbidden Fruit: Sex and Religion in the Lives of American Teenagers*. New York: Oxford University Press.

Sawhill, Isabel. 1999. "Families at Risk." In *Setting National Priorities: the 2000 Election and Beyond*, edited by Henry J. Aaron and Robert D. Reischauser. Washington, D.C.: Brookings Institution Press.

Smith, Christian. 1998. *American Evangelicalism: Embattled and Thriving*. Chicago: University of Chicago Press.

———. 2000. *What Do Christians Really Want?* Berkeley: University of California Press.

Spain, Daphne, and Suzanne M. Bianchi. 1996. *Balancing Act: Motherhood, Marriage, and Employment among American Women*. New York: Russell Sage Foundation.

Steensland, Brian, Jerry Park, Mark Regnerus, Lynn Robinson, Bradford Wilcox, and Robert Woodberry. 2000. "Classifying American Religion: A New Method." *Social Forces* 79(1): 291–318.

Thomas, Adam, and Isabel Sawhill. 2002. "For Richer or Poorer: Marriage as an Antipoverty Strategy." *Journal of Policy Analysis and Management* 21(4): 587–99.

Waite, Linda, and Maggie Gallagher. 2000. *The Case for Marriage: Why Married People are Happier, Healthier, and Better Off Financially*. New York: Doubleday.

Wilcox, W. Bradford. 1998. "Conservative Protestant Childrearing: Authoritarian or Authoritative?" *American Sociological Review* 63(4): 796–809.

———. 2002. *Sacred Vows, Public Purposes: Religion, the Marriage Movement, and Marriage Policy*. Washington, D.C.: The Pew Forum of Religion & Public Life.

———. 2004. *Soft Patriarchs, New Men: How Christianity Shapes Fathers and Husbands*. Chicago: University of Chicago Press.

Wilcox, W. Bradford, William J. Doherty, Helen Fisher, William A. Galston, Norval D. Glenn, John Gottman, Robert Lerman, Annette Mahoney, Barbara

Markey, Howard J. Markman, Steven Nock, David Popenoe, Gloria G. Rodriguez, Scott M. Stanley, Linda J. Waite, Judith Wallerstein.. 2005. *Why Marriage Matters, Second Edition: Twenty-Six Conclusions from the Social Sciences.* New York: Institute for American Values.

Wilcox, W. Bradford, and Elizabeth Williamson. 2006. "The Cultural Contradictions of Mainline Protestant Family Ideology and Practice." In *American Religions and the Family: How Faith Traditions Cope with Modernization*, edited by Don S. Browning and David A. Clairmont. New York: Columbia University Press.

Wolfinger, Nicholas, and Raymond Wolfinger. 2006. "Family Structure and Voter Turnout." Department of Family and Consumer Studies Working Paper. Salt Lake City: University of Utah.

Chapter 9

Conservative Protestants, Schooling, and Democracy

David Sikkink

I N THE works of prominent democratic theorists, conservative and evangelical Protestants are sometimes seen as a potential threat to a healthy democracy. One of the more visible and debated aspects of this threat are the curriculum challenges to public schools and the nature of conservative Protestant schools (Binder 2002; McLaren 1987). Democratic theorists are alarmed by the conservative religious parent's view of education and support public education in part out of concern that "Christian fundamentalism rejects the value of racial nondiscrimination" (Gutmann 1987, 120). Others are concerned that religious parents and conservative Protestant schools may not be willing to abide a genuinely liberal democratic education, because they are not likely to ensure that students are made "aware of the ethnic, racial and religious diversity that constitutes our society so that they can think as citizens and so that they will not live in a mental straightjacket at odds with freedom" (Macedo 2000, 240). Although the case of conservative Protestant families and schools plays a large role in the deliberation of democratic theorists, there is little evidence on the schooling attitudes of conservative Protestants and the practices within conservative Protestant schools that influence democratic education.

Are conservative Protestants posed to exit public schools and to build alternative schools that threaten democratic education? Are they content to exercise voice within the public schools, pursuing relatively minor reforms? Or are they on a crusade to challenge the traditional public character of public schools?

This chapter provides an overview of conservative Protestant schooling attitudes and practices, paying particular attention to the implications of conservative Protestants for democratic education and the common good. It investigates the extent that conservative Protestants favor putting sectarian religion and morality back into public schools, and evaluates the relation between conservative Protestant schools and democratic education. It shows the complexity of the conservative Protestant take on schooling in American democracy. As I explain, conservative Protestant attitudes and practices are to some extent contradictory.

The field of conservative Protestantism is far from united on schooling attitudes and practices. Within the Christian Reformed denomination, predominately evangelical and known for its Christian schooling tradition, the cross pressures found among conservative Protestants were on display in the official magazine of the denomination. The stories of two families who took different schooling paths were presented to illustrate the legitimate struggle of parents to choose a school for their children. One family chose a Christian school "out of faith, hope and love," and the other chose public school "to fully intersect our lives with the community of people we were called to reach . . . [since] all our new neighbors . . . spent time and built relationships in the school community" (Hogendoom and Hogendoom 2005). Two evangelical families, two very different choices—or callings, as conservative Protestants would put it.

As this example shows, conservative Protestants reconstruct deeply held traditions to give meaning to both alternative and public schooling strategies. The result is that conservative Protestants of different stripes have exercised all three of the available options regarding public schools: exit, voice, and loyalty (Hirschman 1970). The National Center for Education Statistics estimates that 880,000 students are in conservative Protestant schools (Broughman, Swaim, and Keaton 2008). Other data show that about 8 percent of conservative Protestant families choose to opt out of public schools for at least one of their children, which is higher than mainline Protestants (5 percent), but lower than Catholics (11 percent). Of the approximately 1 million children in home schooling, at least half are conservative Protestants. Yet 92 percent of conservative Protestant families have their children in public schools, which is nearly identical to the national average.[1]

One reason is that a dominant position within conservative Protestantism is the activist, engaged tradition of evangelicalism. This tradition is rooted in evangelicals' perceived need to be active in non-Christian institutions as "salt and light," biblical phrasing for taking one's religious faith into all spheres of life to preserve and lift up one's society and culture. Many conservative Protestants believe that working within the public schools is one way to be faithful to the evangelical tradition of engagement in the public square. Questions remain about what conservative Protestant propose to do in public schools, and how they propose to do it. And for those who choose to leave the public schools, what kind of democratic education do children get at conservative Protestant schools?

This chapter argues that conservative Protestants support public schooling and many of its public intentions, but are not comfortable with a pluralistic and completely secular public school environment. In most cases, conservative Protestants do not stand in the way of an effective democratic education through public schools. For example, though some favor an exclusively Christian prayer within public schools, others are content with schools that allow students to organize prayer groups on campus. The conservative Protestant voice within public schooling is muddled. Divides within conservative Protestantism on schooling issues make it less likely that a political movement to Christianize public schools could gain much traction within conservative Protestantism.

Despite an historical emphasis on supporting public schools, a significant minority of conservative and evangelical Protestants have chosen some form of an exit strategy in favor of religious schools. I argue that there is little reason to be concerned that these schools will have dire consequences for a healthy democracy—at least judging in terms of curriculum, practices, and civic philosophy. In fact, I show that the moral order of the schooling community offers some advantages for democratic education. At the same time, support within conservative Protestant schools for the principle of free speech and for democratic governance is less than in other schools. Although conservative Protestant school students are learning to be involved in their communities, their civic participation is not as strong as that found in Catholic schools. The structural divides between conservative Protestants and local community organizations reduce civic engagement for students in conservative Protestant schools.

Conservative Protestants and Public Schools

Media accounts of the so-called Exodus movement, which called on conservative Protestants to abandon public schools en masse, seemed to provide evidence for a widespread disaffection from public schooling. The situation on the ground was much more ambiguous. There are several reasons for this. First, there are various religious traditions within conservative Protestantism that differ in their orientation to education and public schooling. The histories and practices of these religious movements have led to differing educational views. The 1940s revealed the beginnings of a divide in the religious field between evangelical and fundamentalist Protestants (Marsden 1980). In the first half of the twentieth century, the fundamentalist movement within conservative Protestantism responded to the fundamentalist-modernist controversies and the loss of control of the major denominations, schools, and seminaries with a separatism that focused on establishing an institutional enclave of denominations and educational institutions (Carpenter 1997). This orientation to public life would later contribute to the growth of religious schools within the fundamentalist movement. The neo-evangelicals of the 1940s attempted to counter the separatism of fundamentalism. Out of these beginnings, the evangelical movement came to dominate the conservative Protestant field, advocating a strategy of "engaged orthodoxy" (Smith et al. 1998). In the view of evangelicals, public schools are seen as an important aspect of the public realm, and a faithful evangelical witness requires active engagement in the public school system to preserve this "public" institution and witness to "the world" through their children. A general acceptance of traditional public and private sphere divides coexists with a sense of religious obligation to remain active in the public sphere (Sikkink and Smith 2000).

Conservative Protestant schooling attitudes and practices are further complicated by the rapid expansion of the Pentecostal and charismatic movements. The lower-class, Pietist origins of the Pentecostal movement (Anderson 1979), as well as their emphasis on special spiritual experience, include a strong sense of outsider status in relation to the surrounding society and culture (Wacker 2001). Pentecostal cultural frameworks tend to contrast the emotional, anti-institutional spiritual experience with intellectual pursuits in the educational field (Cox 1995; McDonnell 1976).

Besides these theological and denominational divides, several cultural crosscurrents within conservative Protestantism complicate the conservative Protestant voice on schooling issues. To begin with, conservative Protestantism embeds a tradition of separation of church and state, which creates wariness about efforts to bring religion into public schools. One of the largest constituents of the movement, the Southern Baptists, have a history of seeing public schools as an expression of the community, and religion as the expression of the church and home. From this perspective, there is religious warrant for avoiding entanglement of religion and public education.

Second, a relatively strong cultural theme, which is promoted by the evangelical movement but extends beyond it, calls Christians to see educational decisions in terms of witness to unbelievers and a secular world. The argument is that the faith of children must be tested in a hostile world by engaging rather than separating from mainstream society, and that it is important for Christians to attempt to preserve the society and culture by maintaining a presence in major social institutions, such as public schools.

A third cultural strand within conservative Protestantism is the belief that all aspects of life, including teaching and learning, are inherently religious. From this perspective, there is a religious way of doing education, a religious perspective to guide the teaching of each academic subject. The implication of this may be as broad as the claim that the philosophical foundations of education must be criticized from a religious perspective, or as specific as the claim that a Christian approach to reading instruction calls for an emphasis on phonics. Although disagreement about the pedagogical implications of this cultural theme is considerable (Sikkink 2001), one reasonably clear implication is support for distinctively Christian education in private schools and home education.

Fourth, conservative Protestantism embeds a cultural theme that parents are responsible for the education of their children. But conservative Protestants have not reached a consensus on the implications of this principle. The theme has no doubt encouraged home schooling, but many conservative Protestants would take the principle to mean that they must pay close attention to what the child is learning in school, ensuring that spiritual growth of the child is not hindered or neglected by intellectual growth.

Fifth, the conservative Protestant culture embeds a theme of religious purity that is threatened by an expanding, secular government. Public school issues are often constructed in these terms (Arons 1983). Thus, many conservative Protestants would instinctively favor infusing religion into public schools simply to register their concern about what is perceived to be an expansion of the political sphere at the expense of the purity of the religious field. At times, this may be seen as a secular invasion of the sacred sphere, of the normative spheres of the family and church (Wuthnow 1988; Sikkink 1999).

The result of these cultural crosscurrents and religious movement divides is that there is no consensus within conservative Protestantism on what it means to be a faithful religious believer on schooling issues. Cultural tensions lead to divides across as well as within conservative Protestant organizations. Many conservative Protestants are sympathetic to nearly all of these cultural themes, and have not resolved for themselves the implications of their faith for schooling issues.

It would not be surprising, then, that asking conservative Protestants for their position on schooling issues would not lead to consistent and coherent answers. For some, Christian schools and home education are the only way to be faithful to a religious obligation to bring one's religious faith into all of life, including the practice of education of children. But others would see the public schools as the appropriate place for learning reading, writing, and arithmetic, and the family and the church

for maintaining the purity of religious instruction and the faith formation of children. Many Southern Baptists would find a religious ration-
ale for asking public schools to focus on the basics, and for avoiding any
entanglement of religion with the public school curriculum. In contrast,
an exodus from public schools makes sense within a fundamentalist
framework, in which separating from the world is a dominant theme.
And on many issues we may find that some conservative Protestants
would simply like to tweak the nose of Uncle Sam, registering their
complaint with what is seen as a secular imposition of big government
into the intimate and normative affairs of local communities and families. Because several, often contradictory, themes are available to give
meaning to educational views and practices, there is not likely to be any
conservative Protestant consensus that leaving public schools is the
moral equivalent of the Exodus.

Evidence on Conservative Protestant Views

Some evidence for the distribution of these different cultural themes on
schooling is available from a national telephone survey, the Religious
Identity and Influence Survey, which provides numerous measures on
religion as well as schooling attitudes and practices.[2] This survey includes measures of conservative Protestant orientations to public
schools, preferred strategies for schooling children, favored educational
values, and positions on the proper relation between religion, morality,
and public schooling. The survey offers several measures of conservative Protestantism as well. Most of the analysis that follows relies on the
respondents' (self-reported) religious denomination to make distinctions between conservative Protestants, mainline Protestants, African
American Protestants, Catholics (further divided into those who attend
Mass regularly and those who do not), Jews, and a catch-all category for
other religious affiliations.

The findings indicate that conservative Protestants are split on
whether they feel alienated from public schools, though more conservative Protestants experience tension with public schools than other religious groups. According to the 1996 telephone survey data, a slight
majority of Americans affiliated with conservative Protestant denominations, 52 percent, reported that public schools were, in their view,
hostile to their moral and spiritual values, versus about 29 percent of
mainline Protestants. What is most interesting is that conservative
Protestant's felt-hostility toward public schools follows the divide
within the field between the spirit-filled movements, the Pentecostals
and charismatics, and other evangelicals. Charismatics and Pentecostals were very alienated from public schools, and other evangelicals
significantly less so. About 70 percent of the spirit-filled groups strongly

agreed that public schools were hostile to their moral and spiritual values (Sikkink 1999).

Americans have many different reasons—not all religiously inspired—for viewing public schools as hostile to their moral and spiritual values. Conservative Protestants may respond to that alienation by exercising voice, rather than by abandoning public schools. Is conservative Protestant alienation fostering a strategy of exit, rather than voice? Certainly some cultural themes within conservative Protestantism would support separation from mainstream society, as well as an explicitly religious form of education in a religious school or family.

A measure of conservative Protestant strategies for schooling helps put conservative Protestant alienation in context. The survey asked whether respondents would rather continue working with the public schools, build strong Christian schools, or take up home schooling. Here was an opportunity for conservative Protestants to register their misgivings about the public schools and signal a willingness to withdraw from the public square in favor of sectarian educational institutions. Interestingly, 69 percent of conservative Protestants wanted to work with the public schools.[3] This is not too far from the 76 percent of mainline Protestants, and very similar to the 67 percent of Catholics. At least in terms of stated preferences, conservative Protestants do not seem poised to abandon one of the key institutions of American democracy. It would seem that the missionary themes and evangelical elements within conservative Protestantism—not to mention the financial challenge of private education—lead a solid majority of conservative Protestants to want to work with public schools.

Educational Priorities

Even if conservative Protestants are willing to work with the public school, the question of what they want public schools to look like remains. What kind would they favor? Would they turn public schools into illiberal institutions (Macedo 2000)?

We can look for partial answers by assessing the educational values of conservative Protestants. The survey highlighted key educational values, providing a window on what conservative Protestants see as the highest priorities for a child's schooling. Respondents were asked four questions, whether the highest educational priority is to learn skills for getting a job, to gain a higher sense of self-esteem, to learn to obey authority, or to learn to respect people from other races, religions, and cultures.

Each of these priorities has a connection to democratic education in schools. Many democratic theorists argue that schools must not have an exclusively instrumental and private orientation. One implication is that an exclusive focus on job skills rather than a liberal education impedes an effective democratic education. Some democratic theorists would see an overemphasis on instilling obedience to authority as undermining vital citizenship skills. An antidemocratic school environment could hinder students from efforts to achieve social change through democratic institutions (Apple and Beane 1995). Schools should socialize students to be productive citizens in a democratic society, which requires actively exercising voice, including participation in petition and protest of authorities. An effective democratic education would include instilling a high level of personal efficacy. It would also guide students to respect and to interact with people from a variety of social backgrounds. Respecting other races, religions, and cultures is a central citizenship virtue that has long been seen as one of the most important ways that schools contribute to democratic education (Gutmann 1987).

It is difficult to predict where conservative Protestants would place job skills as an educational priority. Some may prioritize learning job skills as one way that schools can get back to basics, and cut out "superfluous" educational goals, such as celebrating cultural differences. Other strands in conservative Protestant culture, however, discount instrumental goals in favor of an education that does not neglect religious socialization.

These cross pressures are perhaps evident in that conservative Protestants were not distinctive in favoring job skills as a top educational priority. The results show that about 78 percent of conservative Protestants thought that learning skills for getting a job should be the top priority, as did a nearly identical 79 percent of mainline Protestants. In fact, regression analysis shows no significant relationship between various measures of conservative Protestantism and placing job skills as a top school priority.[4] Indeed, controlling for sociodemographic background characteristics, mainline Protestants showed a stronger relation to this goal than their conservative counterparts.[5] Perhaps this reflects the tendency of conservative Protestants to discount expediency in favor of religious socialization goals.

Conservative Protestants may be more consistent when it comes to student self-esteem as an educational goal. Opposing this goal would reflect conservative Protestant concerns that public schools are treading on the obligations of parents to form their children's characters. Opposition would also be consistent with an emphasis on getting back to a basic education and supporting the role of the home and church as key authorities for character development.

The results do reveal less enthusiasm among conservative Protestants for concentrating on self-esteem in education, and a strong minority was not interested in prioritizing this goal. Still, about 59 percent did see it as a top priority, and 60 percent of mainline Protestants agreed. Regression results, using a battery of sociodemographic controls, showed that mainline Protestants were significantly more likely than the nonreligious to support self-esteem building as a priority. Conservative Protestants as a whole, meanwhile, showed no statistically significant likelihood, but the subgroup of evangelicals did, albeit strongly negative.[6] Perhaps the tradition of engaged orthodoxy of evangelicals creates higher levels of cultural conflict with dominant educational strategies, and increases the sense that an emphasis on self-esteem encroaches on parental responsibility to socialize their children.

The evangelical opposition to self-esteem as an educational priority may cause some concern for democratic theorists, given that they would see self-efficacy as important for democratic participation. Still, self-esteem is not quite the same thing as efficacy, and does not strongly correlate with participation in civic life. But it is important that many conservative Protestants are directly opposed to the emphasis of progressive educators on building children's self-esteem. The evangelical position here likely reflects opposition to the dominant public school regime, as well as the sense that a focus on self-esteem tends to discount the importance of structure and absolute standards within the curriculum (Kahne 1996).

One might expect that conservative Protestants would stand out in support of obedience to authority as a high educational priority. The relation between conservative religion and authoritarianism has long been a concern of social scientists (Adorno 1950; Allport 1954; Leak and Randall 1995; Lipset and Raab 1970; Peshkin 1986). The putative association between conservative religion and authoritarian values raises questions about whether the ideal public school in conservative Protestant eyes would hinder building effective democratic citizenship skills and orientations. On the other hand, conservative Protestants favor authoritative rather than authoritarian parenting—meaning parenting that emphasizes the development of autonomy through both support and communication of boundaries (Wilcox 1998). This may extend to their view of school authority as well. Some theorists have linked authoritative schools with more favorable outcomes for democratic education (Damon 1995; Etzioni 1993; Grant 1988).

At first glance, conservative Protestants seem quite concerned that children learn in school to obey authority. About 71 percent agreed that this is a top priority. Other groups favored this goal as well, however, about 76 percent of Catholics and 75 percent of mainline Protestants. Regression results with sociodemographic controls showed that those affiliated with conservative Protestant denominations were more likely to support this goal than nonreligious Americans. By a nearly statistically significant margin, mainline Protestants supported it as well. There is no significant difference between conservative and mainline Protestants on this measure.

Although the importance of respect for authority and building self-esteem is contested, most would agree that an effective democratic education must include fostering respect for people from a variety of social backgrounds. Here there would be concern that conservative Protestantism, which tends to attach moral significance to cultural differences, would fall short (Emerson and Smith 2000; Emerson, Smith, and Sikkink 1999). Again, the various cultural strands within conservative Protestantism lead in different directions. Those who favor a separation of religion and schooling and want public schools to avoid anything but a basic education may not support this goal. Other research, however, has shown that charismatics link themes of authenticity through self-expression to the priority for educating students to respect races, religions, and cultures (Sikkink and Mihut 2001).

According to self-reports, conservative Protestants are not opposed to a school that places respect for other races, religions, and cultures as a top priority. About 87 percent see this principle as an important goal for schools, which compares favorably with the 77 percent of mainline Protestants who concur. Regression results show that Jews, Catholics, and mainline Protestants were also strongly supportive. Net of the control variables, however, neither conservative Protestant denominational affiliation nor conservative Protestant identity was associated with support for multiculturalism in schools. On average, conservative Protestants were not significantly different from the nonreligious in terms of their support for multicultural goals in education. They were not notable either for their support for or opposition to this goal.

Religion, Morality, and Schooling

In terms of educational priorities, conservative Protestants express interest in a school that emphasizes obedience to authority and discounts the importance of building self-esteem. What other directions would they take public schools? One question is whether and how they would bring issues of morality and religion into public schools. Would they do so in a way that respects the role of public schools in fostering a democratic education (Gutmann 1987)?

Again, conservative Protestants tend to be of two minds on this issue. On the one hand, they believe that religion and moral formation should be handled by religious experts and parents, and that schools should be limited to the 3Rs. On the other hand, they may want to register their dissatisfaction with what they see as an imposition of secular government, which tends to enervate the normative and moral dimension of education. Others may simply want to be consistent with the claim that education is inherently a moral and religious enterprise, and therefore would be inclined to favor renewed attention to morality and religion in public schools.

The first bit of evidence on this question is whether issues of morality and religion in schools are particularly salient to conservative Protestants. The survey asked an open-ended question about what respondents see as the biggest problem in public schools. Did conservative Protestants point to problems that evidence a form of sectarianism, which is unlikely to be easily accommodated in public debates about education? About 25 percent reported the biggest problem in religious or moral terms, such as a lack of school prayer or religion, or an overly secular or secular humanistic culture. About 16 percent pointed to family breakdown or lack of supportive parents and 21 percent pointed to issues of discipline and respect for authority. Another 26 percent were concerned about more secular problems, such as a lack of funding, underqualified teachers, low academic standards, drugs, and school safety. Altogether, this seems meager evidence that conservative Protestants have radical and illiberal designs on public schools, though a significant minority were clearly focused on problems that might be construed as sectarian interests.

A related question concerned how conservative Protestants draw the line between school, church, and family. As explained, conservative Protestant culture contains several conflicting positions on this question; everything from erasing the line between family and school to drawing an absolute boundary between school and religion has religious traction within conservative Protestantism.

The first evidence is whether conservative Protestants would favor an education that attempts to bring a Christian perspective to learning. The question does not ask about specific substantive changes that would be necessary. Still, responses may provide some indication of whether conservative Protestants seek to Christianize the public schools or leave them to a secular task that does not impinge on religion.

About 81 percent of conservative Protestants favored the goal of Christian perspectives on learning, as did 66 percent of mainline Protestants and 86 percent of African American Protestants. After accounting for other factors that could influence support for this goal, the regression results showed that conservative Protestants, as measured by evangelical or fundamentalist religious identity, were significantly more likely to agree with this goal than nominal Protestants. Respondents who identified as religiously liberal Protestants were significantly unlikely to agree.

A Christian perspective on learning would seem to conflict with the widespread view that the public square must be neutral in regard to religion. To be fair to conservative Protestant respondents, the survey did not allow them to explain whether a Christian perspective on learning was something akin to character education, abstinence sex education programs, or more radical creation science curriculums. Perhaps many were simply complaining against what they saw as an overbearing or overly relativistic secular government penetrating into the normative life of family and community. The term *Christian perspective* is perhaps too vague to be very meaningful.

The survey also asked how conservative Protestants would like to teach morality in schools. Would this need to be from an explicitly Judeo-Christian perspective, or would a general morality suffice? Or would conservative Protestants argue that morality is something to be taught in the home rather than in school? This question teases out where conservative Protestants fall on an important cultural fissure within the movement. The survey evidence pointed most strongly toward a preference for an exclusively Christian morality within the schools, but there are conflicting findings.

After controlling for having children in private schooling or home schooling, those who claim a fundamentalist and evangelical Protestant identity were significantly in favor of a Christian morality, rather than a general morality, in schools.[7] The other religious groups were divided on this question, though there is weak evidence that self-identified mainline and liberal Protestants tended to favor general morality in public schools over Christian.

Interestingly, the findings were not consistent for conservative Protestants. Affiliation with a conservative Protestant denomination was positive on approving the teaching of Christian morality in schools but not statistically significant. And when asking respondents to choose the religious identity that best described them, rather than allowing them to choose multiple religious identities, the results did not show significant effects for evangelicals and fundamentalists, even through the coefficients showed a positive relation to Christian morality. Again, it is reasonable to conclude that the issue of whether to Christianize schools is somewhat controversial among conservative Protestants who do not choose private schooling options.

The conservative Protestant divides are perhaps evident in the lack of a significant conservative Protestant effect when conservative Protestants choose between general moral teaching in the schools and leaving morality to the family. According to the multinomial regression results, those who attend worship services more often were more likely to support leaving morality at home than to support a general morality at school. High attendance at services among conservative Protestants provides them an indirect way of keeping their particularistic morality away from the control of public school authority.

A separate question asked whether respondents would like to see the major religious traditions taught in schools. Some would expect that conservative Protestants, who believe they are second-class citizens in a professional and bureaucratic public schooling system, favor teaching religion as an antidote to what they see as overly secular schools. On the other hand, as a religious minority believing that most other religious traditions are simply untrue, conservative Protestants may see teaching the major religious traditions as a threat or instruction to theological error.

Regression results showed that conservative Protestants strongly favored teaching the major religious traditions in school, as did mainline Protestants. Catholics who attended services regularly were even more strongly in favor.

Teaching about the major religious traditions seems well within the bounds of providing a liberal education that prepares students for participation in a society in which religion has played and continues to play an important role in individual and public life. The more difficult test is whether conservative Protestants would rather see a curriculum that takes a Christian view of science and history seriously. Admittedly, the survey question does not specify precisely what the respondent considers a "Christian view of science and history." It does, though, capture a general sense of the appropriate relation between religious perspectives and school curriculum.

About 80 percent of conservative Protestants favored Christian views of science and history in public schools, versus 61 percent in the general population. About 87 percent of those who identified as evangelical or fundamentalist were in favor of Christian views, as were 68 percent of mainline Protestants. On this issue, some religious divisions were clearer. For example, Catholics who regularly attended worship services and who did not regularly attend services took opposite sides on this question. Jewish respondents, not surprisingly, joined the nominal Catholics in opposing the mixing of Christianity and subjects like science and history. Whether measured in terms of identity or affiliation with conservative Protestant denominations, conservative Protestants favored teaching Christian views. There was limited evidence that mainline Protestants also favored this position, but not nearly as consistently or as strongly as the conservative Protestants.

The answers to this question could be considered troubling from the perspective of democratic theory, insofar as democratic education depends on some form of public knowledge that is not explicitly tied to a particular religious tradition. But we should keep in mind the limits of general survey questions. It is not clear precisely what respondents had in mind when they answered the question. The ambiguity may explain why a significant minority of the nonreligious respondents (37 percent) also supported Christian views of science and history in public schools. Second, the question does not ask whether only Christian perspectives should be taught. There is also evidence that conservative Protestants for theological reasons bounce back and forth between a language of Christendom, which would impose Christianity on the nation's law and ethos, and a pluralism that borders on libertarianism (Smith 2000). Third, many conservative Protestants probably responded with the issue of evolution in mind. If they did think about history, they may have been thinking about spending time on religious history, rather than teaching historical narratives and interpretations that are explicitly religious.

Still, most democratic education theorists would not extend multicultural goals so far as to include young earth theories alongside evolutionary science (see Nord 1995). It is possible that many conservative Protestants are in their answers to this question revealing their unwillingness to respect norms for public discourse, and their desire to reimpose a Protestant establishment in the public school curriculum. But we should keep in mind the emotional aspects of survey responses. In my view, it is equally likely that many conservative Protestants are telling us that they are generally unhappy with a secular environment in public schools, which seems to be imposed by what are considered outside forces (the academy, scientists, and big government). Whether they would like the public schools to stop teaching about evolution or simply to spend more time on the history and impact of Christianity cannot be determined.

A final survey question asked whether and how respondents would like to incorporate prayer in schools. This issue may offer a more nuanced portrayal of what conservative Protestants would like to see in public schools. One option would be to favor a spoken Christian prayer, which clearly indicates a willingness to ignore religious diversity and impose a particular religion in public schools. But less confrontational options were available to respondents that still incorporate religion into schooling. For example, a moment of silence would provide space for all religious traditions within the classroom, and simply allowing students to participate in prayer and prayer groups that are not directly sponsored by the school offers a compromise between religion and schooling that maintains a clear separation between religion and academic tasks.

The findings on this question support the view that conservative Protestants are divided on whether to pursue a Christian America ideal through the public schools. Regression results showed no significant conservative Protestant effect when choosing between student religious groups outside of class and a spoken Christian prayer in the classroom. Conservative Protestants considered all options preferable to not allowing prayer in the schools. Mainline Protestants took a similar stance. My conclusion is that conservative Protestants are divided about whether they would like to see a more complete melding of Christianity and public schools, and, at least on the issue of school prayer, are just as comfortable with a public school that allows students the freedom to organize prayer groups outside of class or pray privately as they are with one that permits spoken Christian prayer in the classroom.

The Schools That Conservative Protestants Built

An assessment of conservative Protestants, schooling, and democracy would not be complete without a look inside conservative Protestant schools, which educate at least 880,000 students in the United States (Broughman, Swaim, and Keaton 2008).[8] Many democratic theorists would view religiously conservative schools as harmful to democratic education because they are built to uphold insular communities. If true, we would expect conservative Protestant school students to be less tolerant of outside groups and less willing or prepared for participation in a multicultural, democratic public sphere, which requires understanding and compromise across great social distances.

For private school students as a whole, existing research shows little cause for concern. On measures of political tolerance, volunteering, political knowledge and participation, and civic skills, private school students are doing as well as public school students, even after extensive controls for family background (Wolf 2007). Private schools may have civic strengths, including an ordered environment and a strong normative climate that provides a strong civic education (Wolf 2007).

This section extends these studies on effective civic education in schools by focusing on conservative Protestant schools. What opportunities for civic education are available at such schools? Opportunities may include an organizational culture that calls students to sacrifice for the common good, as well as a pedagogy and school structure that builds democratic skills and values through, for example, persuasion and debate in class, civic education classes, and student government experiences. Finally, the extent of volunteering and community service is an important aspect of civic education in schools.

The National Household Education Survey (NHES), conducted through the U.S. Department of Education, provides some insight on several dimensions of civic education in conservative Protestant schools (National Center of Education Statistics 1996).[9] This large national survey of sixth through twelfth graders includes measures of student experiences in school, classroom, and extracurricular activities that may contribute to civic education, including volunteering and community service activities. The survey allows for a distinction between Catholic and non-Catholic religious schools. The latter group is a fairly accurate measure of the conservative Protestant school sector, given that the mainline Protestant and Jewish sectors are very small.

Evidence on Student Experience in School

What do students experience in conservative Protestant schools? Whether students are alienated from the school community, or experience school as functional community (Coleman and Hoffer 1987) has important effects on democratic education (Sikkink 1998). By functional community, I mean a setting marked by a relatively dense network of social ties, mutual respect between students and teachers, a normative communal order, and relational trust (Bryk and Schneider 2002). The 1996 NHES data set includes five questions that capture student perceptions of their school. These perceptions are important to civic socialization because they provide an indication of overall student experience of school climate, whether the school is believed to operate as a functional community, and whether students experience some measure of participatory democracy in school.

Students were asked to agree or disagree with several statements about their school, including whether they enjoy school. The students at non-Catholic religious schools scored highest on this measure; 89 percent agreed or strongly agreed with the statement, compared with about 72 percent in public schools. In terms of providing a social context conducive to positive civic socialization, it appears that non-Catholic religious schools, which consist primarily of conservative Protestant schools, are doing quite well.

The survey included two measures indicative of effective authority within the school community: whether the teacher maintained good discipline in the classroom, and whether the principal maintained good discipline in the school. Perceived competence is a key factor in maintaining institutional trust, and for school personnel is indicated by their ability to maintain an effective order in school (Bryk and Schneider 2002). Further, a school climate without effective authority is likely to alienate many students, and likely to disrupt the building of an effective communal organization (Bryk, Lee, and Holland 1993; Lawrence-Lightfoot 1983; McFarland 2001).

On the question of whether the classroom is a disciplined environment, conservative Protestant school students reported higher levels of agreement than public school students, 36 percent to 20 percent, but were not much different than other school sectors, 32 percent for private nonreligious, and 34 percent for Catholic. Parallel results emerged on the issue of whether the principal maintains discipline. Twenty-nine percent of assigned public school students strongly agreed that the principal maintains good discipline, to 49 percent of the conservative Protestant school students.

The survey questions captured student perceptions of the quality of the school community, including the level of trust among members of the community. One measure asked whether students and teachers respect each other, and another asked whether the opinions of students were listened to. The percentage of students in conservative Protestant schools who reported mutual respect between teachers and students was very similar to Catholic schools, and higher than public schools. About 31 percent of religious school students, both Catholic and non-Catholic, strongly agreed that students and teachers respected one another in their school. The public school percentage was about half that. Relational trust, then, was strongly felt by a significant percentage of students in religious schools.

Whether the school functions as an effective community and a participatory organization may also be indicated by the extent to which students feel they have some say in school affairs. One might expect that the authoritarian organizational culture of conservative Protestant schools would mean a disenfranchised student body. The bivariate results reveal that non-Catholic religious schools had the highest percentage of students strongly agreeing that student opinions were listened to (25 percent). Catholic and nonreligious private schools were similar, but students in public schools were only about half as likely to agree strongly (13 percent). This conservative Protestant distinction remained even after adding controls for such variables as school size, socioeconomic characteristics of the student body, and family and student characteristics.[10] At least in creating a participatory environment, which provides an important civic education in itself, conservative Protestant schools appear to be doing much better than local public schools. These results could alleviate the concerns of democratic theorists that religious schools on the whole are overly authoritarian.

Pedagogy and Civic Education

Besides the direct effects of the school organization on civic socialization, schools represent a key setting for building civic skills that are useful for civic engagement (Campbell 2001; Sikkink 1998). Whether schools are successful in developing student civic skills depends on classroom instructional techniques. In particular, an instructional style that allows ample room for active student participation and debate builds student civic skills. A vital democracy depends on citizens' ability to represent interests and deliberate public policy questions, and civic skills lay the foundation for this democratic deliberation. Simply by making room for student participation, a classroom environment reinforces the value of participatory democracy. Students' experience of a relatively democratic classroom provides a model for participation in other public institutions.

Studies show that private school students score higher than their public school counterparts on some civic skills (Neimi, Hepburn, and Chapman 2000), and other research using the 1996 NHES reveals that non-Catholic religious school students have more confidence that they could write a letter to an elected official or give a speech at a community meeting (Campbell 2001). But we would have reason to expect that religious school pedagogy is weak on instilling civic skills. For example, there is evidence of an emphasis on traditional teaching styles in Catholic schools (Bryk, Lee, and Holland 1993). Teacher-centered learning in religious schools may be rooted in views of authority. In conservative religious schools, notions of truth may be grounded in church tradition or scripture (Peshkin 1986; Rose 1988). This authority-based orientation to truth may have its parallel in authority-based teaching styles—increasing the number of teacher-centered classes and thereby reducing opportunities for practicing civic skills.

The percentage of students who reported that they gave a speech or oral report in class, however, showed only marginal differences across educational sectors[11]—about 84 percent in non-Catholic religious schools and 76 percent in local public schools. A separate question asked whether students had taken part in a debate or discussion in which they had to persuade others about their point of view. This question is a classic measure of civic skill building in a nonpolitical institution that is likely to be transferable to political activity. On this score, the non-Catholic religious schools appeared to score somewhat low given their more advantaged clientele (60 percent), just above public schools (57 percent) and well below private nonreligious schools (67 percent). At first glance, this finding is consistent with the theoretical argument that religious conservatives favor an authority-based teaching style, which may not value student participation. Persuasion and debate within the religious school community may be seen as making absolute truths appear relative and contested. However, the regression results, including a battery of statistical controls, did not reveal strong differences across school sector on this question.[12]

Civic Education Classes

A good civic education would include direct opportunities for building civic knowledge. Through discussion of national affairs and learning the history and workings of democratic institutions, students can gain familiarity with the civic and political public sphere in the United States that removes barriers to participation and may improve the quality of democratic debate.

Non-Catholic religious schools are often thought to be religious enclaves isolated from public life, which may reduce both school and student interest in civic education. The extreme case is that of Amish and conservative Mennonite schools, which are isolationist by design and have religious reasons for separation from political affairs. These schools may place less emphasis on traditional civics courses.

There is an important counterargument to consider, however. Institutional theorists have argued that schools tend to follow dominant cultural models about what it means to be a school (Meyer 1977; Meyer and Rowan 1977). This perspective is consistent with the expectation that in formal structure and curriculum religious schools would follow public school models, including cultural norms for civic education classes. As Melinda Wagner argued, religious schools tend to be a collage of Christian and American cultural strands (1990). Even the most conservative Christian schools absorb much from their surrounding cultural milieu.

The NHES asked students whether they had, in the previous school year, taken any courses that required them to pay attention to government, politics, or national issues. The non-Catholic religious school students were actually slightly higher than students in the other sectors (55 percent), but the local public school students were close behind (53 percent). The evidence supports the view that all schools follow cultural models of what it means to be a school. Conservative Protestants students are participating in courses that discuss government and national affairs at similar rates as public school students.

Democratic Values

What are students learning in civics class? Does this enhance democratic citizenship? The specific concern here is whether students are encouraged to value basic democratic principles, such as free speech. Many might expect that conservative religious schools would reinforce intolerance and authoritarianism, rather than support democratic values. However, research shows that Texas students who were educated exclusively in religious schools show higher tolerance levels that comparable public school students (Wolf et al. 2001). There is also some evidence that evangelical private school students support democratic norms as strongly as their public school counterparts (Godwin, Ausbrooks, and Martinez 2001).

The NHES asked one of the standard tolerance questions, whether the respondent would allow a person to make a speech in their community against churches and religion. A second measure asked whether students would allow a book in the library that says it is acceptable to take illegal drugs. Previous research using these data has shown that there are no differences by school sector on the first question, but that non-Catholic religious schools are significantly less supportive of allowing the book in the library than are public school students (Campbell 2001). This provides some evidence of lower support for free speech principles among non-Catholic religious school students. But it should be kept in mind that on issues of legality, conservative Protestants are particularly sensitive (Albrecht, Chadwick, and Alcorn 1977; Grasmick, Kinsey, and Cochran 1991). The differences across sector may be less an indicator of political tolerance differences than of differences in views about illegal drugs.

Political Interest and Efficacy

A civic education that builds citizenship skills should increase interest in political life. Political interest has been shown to be an important determinant of participation in civic life (Rosenstone and Hansen 1993). In the conservative Protestant religious schools, alienation from a secular state, and suspicion of government, may reduce the political interest of students. It would seem more likely, then, that civics courses in conservative Protestant religious schools could be taught in a way that denigrates government institutions and public service.

The NHES asked students whether they became more interested in politics and national affairs after taking civic education courses. The raw data show only small differences by sector in the percentage of students who said that civics course increased their interest in politics a great deal. The local public schools were highest on this measure, with 88 percent saying that the course increased political interest either some or a great deal. Among non-Catholic religious school students, the figure was 21 percent, and among public school students it was 17 percent. After accounting for differences in student characteristics, the results did not show significant differences between the school sectors.[13] Non-Catholic religious schools did not stand out on this measure.

Schools may foster political efficacy, which plays a key role in generating civic engagement (Niemi and Junn 1998). For example, whether a person participates in politics depends on their political knowledge (li Carpini and Keeter 1996). The traditional civic role of public schools may lead to greater emphasis on learning how government works, and this knowledge may increase an obligation and a willingness to participate in democratic institutions. Conservative Protestant suspicion of a secular state and the fundamentalist attempt to separate from worldly endeavors may make political knowledge a lower priority in conservative Protestant schools. Research shows that private school students score modestly higher on political knowledge than public school students (Niemi, Hepburn, and Chapman 2000). Other research using the NHES data show that Catholic school students do better than assigned public school students, net of an extensive set of controls (Campbell 2001).

The NHES asked students to respond to a five factual questions about politics.[14] The Catholic and nonreligious private school students were the most informed, and the non-Catholic religious students the least informed.[15] The non-Catholic religious school students scored much lower than local public school students on political knowledge.[16] The size of the gap was reduced considerably when the extent that students read newspapers was added to the model. Lower levels of political knowledge among non-Catholic religious school children results in part from their aversion to reading the newspapers. This was the strongest evidence available in the NHES data that some religious schools create or reinforce an enclave that ill-prepares students for democratic participation. These results may reflect disaffection with political compromising or qualms about political pursuits among many religious conservatives.

Student Government

Schools often provide rudimentary experiences in formal democratic processes. For example, participation in student government is associated with democratic participation in later life (Brady, Verba, and Schlozman 1995). By participating in student government, students may learn to express positions on public issues and learn the nuts and bolts of organizing.

The NHES asked students whether their school had a student government. Interestingly, only 57 percent of non-Catholic religious school students responded yes, versus 82 percent of local public school students. This finding may be misleading, because non-Catholic religious school students were more likely to be in smaller schools, which may reduce the likelihood of having a formal student government. However, even after controlling for school size and other school characteristics, the results show that non-Catholic religious schools were much less likely to have a student government.[17]

Community Service

Last, democratic education can be promoted in schools through opportunities for community service and volunteering. Student volunteering may increase civic skills and norms for civic participation (Youniss and Yates 1997). These opportunities are important for democratic citizenship not only for developing civic skills, but also to link students to volunteering role models and recruitment networks. Though learning to care is mostly a family endeavor (Wuthnow 1995), certain types of involvement, especially involvement that includes interaction with recipients of services, may reinforce an empathetic orientation that increases altruism over the life course. Research has shown that private school students are more likely to volunteer than public school students, even net of extensive controls (Greene 1998; Godwin and Kemerer 2002). One study of New York City students found that this private school effect is limited to religious private schools (Wolf 1998; Niemi, Hepburn, and Chapman 2000).

The NHES survey asked students whether they had in the previous year, participated in any community service activity or volunteer work at their school or in their community. As shown in previous research, the religious school students tended to be highest on this measure (Campbell 2001). With controls, Catholic school attendees were nearly three times as likely to volunteer compared to local public school students. Including more stringent controls, however, revealed that the non-Catholic religious school effect did not differ statistically from public schools (Campbell 2001).

A General Assessment

In some respects, conservative Protestants are the loyal opposition within public schools (Sikkink 2003). In spite of an active home schooling movement and moderate participation in conservative Protestant private schools, there is not a uniform pull within the movement for exiting public schools. This loyalty mitigates the extent that conservative Protestants challenge democratic education in public schools.

Yet there is concern about what kind of voice is being exercised by conservative Protestants in public schools. The question is whether the ideal public school for the conservative Protestants would uphold democratic principles prohibiting an establishment of religion and protecting free speech. According to survey responses, significant pockets of conservative Protestants do favor teaching a Christian perspective in schools, including in subjects like science and history, and favor teaching a Christian morality as well. But their voice on the most significant problems in public schools and on the appropriate place of prayer in schools seems to uphold the accepted division between religion and public institutions. Conservative Protestants educational priorities also seem little different from other religious groups, such as Catholics and mainline Protestants.

The conservative Protestant schools raise additional questions about whether an effective democratic education is possible in sectarian institutions. Most of the evidence here alleviates concern that conservative Protestants schools are producing students unfit for democracy. The results support the view that such schools are more likely than public schools to be in communal environments in which students feel they play significant roles in school governance. Similarly, the high reported levels of respect between students and teachers and the disciplined environment of private religious schools appear to create environments supporting student participation in governance. However, it is important to exercise caution in drawing conclusions from the evidence presented in this chapter, because longitudinal data are not available that would show the impact of school organization on the development of student norms for democratic participation across the student career.

Although limited support for free speech and the lack of student government remain concerns, conservative Protestants schools do seem to follow norms for civic education classes. On many of traditional measures of civic education discussed in this chapter, the difference between public and non-Catholic religious schools is minimal. The general conclusion is that conservative Protestant schools follow the public school model of civic education. This is consistent with claims of institutional isomorphism within and across school sectors. Although these schools are more authority-based environments, it is encouraging for democratic education that students feel that their voices are heard in their schools.

All told, then, it appears that conservative Protestants and their institutions are not the strongest and most consistent supporters of a traditional democratic education within schools, but divisions on schooling issues within the movement make it unlikely that conservative Protestants pose a significant threat to democracy. There is not consistent support within the movement for changing schools to encourage them to reflect a more Christian orientation. Stronger threats to democratic education are likely to emerge from broader societal trends toward privatization of education. The threats to democratic education from an overemphasis on testing in math and reading, from an increasingly strong cultural assumption that education is about private advancement, and from an emphasis on individual choice seem much more pressing than the muddled conservative Protestant voice on schooling issues.

Notes

1. These figures are based on my analysis of the General Social Survey, 1996 and 1998, conducted by the National Opinion Research Corporation (NORC) at the University of Chicago, which included questions on the schooling of children in the household. Evangelical Protestants are defined by denomination according to the scheme in Steensland et al. (2000).
2. The survey was conducted in 1996 by FGI, a national survey firm based in Chapel Hill, North Carolina. A random digit dial method was used in an attempt to achieve a nationally representative sample. Churchgoing Protestants (attending more than once a month) and Protestants who said their faith was extremely important to them were oversampled. The response rate was 69 percent.
3. Unless otherwise noted, conservative Protestants are measured by a survey

question that asks Protestants what specific denomination they are affiliated with. All respondents in the survey were coded into categories according to the work of Steensland et al. (2000).

4. A standard set of control variables are used in each regression analysis. These include the respondent's gender, age, race, years of education, income, number of children, marital status, region, urbanicity, and whether the respondent's children ever attended a nonpublic school. In addition, an interaction of married and number of children is included in the models as a control variable.

5. Higher worship service attendance is strongly related to support for job skills, which provides an indirect pathway from conservative Protestantism to support for job skill training for students. There is no clear direct effect of conservative Protestantism on support for job skills.

6. Protestant respondents were asked in separate questions if they considered themselves to be evangelical, fundamentalist, mainline Protestant, or liberal Protestant. If multiple identities were chosen, a follow-up question asked respondents to choose the one identity that best described them. Unless otherwise noted, the one best identity is used in the statistical analysis.

7. Respondents were asked in separate questions if they were fundamentalist, evangelical, mainline Protestant, or liberal Protestant. Dummy variables for each of these questions were entered directly into the regression model. Rather than considering mutually exclusive identities, this analysis considers all information available on the religious identities chosen by the respondent.

8. This estimate is probably low, because the NCES defines conservative Christian schools as those that are affiliated with four national conservative Christian schooling organizations. Unaffiliated conservative Protestant schools, or those with an affiliation in a smaller Christian schooling organization, are not included in this total.

9. The youth file of the NHES is a nationally representative telephone survey of American teenagers from the sixth through twelfth grade. The analysis below uses the 1996 version of the NHES, which includes questions on school climate. The total sample size is 7,940. Missing values are imputed by the NCES according to a hot-deck routine.

10. Compared to assigned public school students, non-Catholic religious schools students are about 1.6 times more likely to strongly agree that their opinions are listened to, according to the logistic regression results. This finding is net of child characteristics (age, gender, race, Spanish-speaking, year in school, grades in school), family characteristics (income, education, home ownership, educational expectations for child, discussion of future plans with child, civic participation, and religious service attendance), and school characteristics (percentage same race in school, percentage same race in school interacted with child race, size of student body, region, urbanicity, poverty). Net of these controls, all other types of private school students have significantly higher odds of agreeing with this statement than assigned public school students.

11. David Campbell provided an analysis of private schools and civic skill building that combines the civic skill measures into an index (2001). This is

less useful for detecting differences between conservative Protestant schools on various dimensions of civic skill building within the classroom. It explains why Campbell did not find evidence for lower levels of persuasion and debate among non-Catholic religious schools, and may also explain why he found a significant difference for Catholic school students on civic skills that I do not find here.

12.   The logistic regression results show a negative coefficient for non-Catholic religious school students (–.218) compared to assigned public school students, but it is not significant at the .05 level. Controls included sex, race, age, number of siblings, year in school, four-year college expectations of the child; education, income, family receives food stamps, family receives WIC, family receives AFDC, home ownership of the parent; and school size, urbanicity and region of residence as well as percent black and percent in poverty in area of residence.

13.   The Catholic school sector appears to do a slightly better job of increasing student interest than the local public schools, but this effect is not statistically significant.

14.   For example, students were asked, "Whose responsibility is it to determine if a law is constitutional or not?" and "How much of a majority is required to override a veto?" After summing the answers to five questions, the average correct for all students is 1.8—not too encouraging, but this averages scores from students from sixth to twelfth grade.

15.   Campbell also analyzed the NHES data on political knowledge (2001). It is not clear why he found that non-Catholic religious school students have the highest average without controls. Differences in control variables may explain why he found a significant Catholic school effect on political knowledge, but does not detect a significant negative effect of non-Catholic religious schools. For example, he controlled for political knowledge of the parent and whether the school has a student government—both of which may be low for conservative Protestant school students and may be related to political knowledge.

16.   The gap is about a half a point, which is fairly substantial for this five-point scale (the standard deviation is .29).

17.   The logistic regression results show that net of controls the odds of reporting a student government is about 2.8 times less for non-Catholic religious school students compared to assigned public school students.

References

Adorno, Theodor W. 1950. *The Authoritarian Personality*. New York: Harper.

Albrecht, Stan L., Bruce A. Chadwick, and David S. Alcorn. 1977. "Religiosity and Deviance: Application of an Attitude-Behavior Contingent Consistency Model." *Journal for the Scientific Study of Religion* 16(3): 263–74.

Allport, Gordon W. 1954. *The Nature of Prejudice*. Cambridge, Mass: Addison-Wesley.

Anderson, Robert Mapes. 1979. *Vision of the Disinherited: The Making of American Pentecostalism*. New York: Oxford University Press.

Apple, Michael W., and James A. Beane. 1995. *Democratic Schools*. Alexandria, Va.: Association for Supervision and Curriculum Development.

Arons, Stephen. 1983. *Compelling Belief: The Culture of American Schooling*. New York: McGraw-Hill.

Binder, Amy J. 2002. *Contentious Curricula: Afrocentrism and Creationism in American Public Schools*. Princeton, N.J: Princeton University Press.

Brady, Henry, Sidney Verba, and Kay Schlozman. 1995. "Beyond SES: A Resource Model of Political Participation." *American Political Science Review* 89(2): 271–95.

Broughman, Stephen P., Nancy L. Swaim, and Patrick W. Keaton. 2008. *Characteristics of Private Schools in the United States: Results from the 2005–2006 Private School Universe Survey*. NCES 2008–315. Washington, D.C.: National Center for Education Statistics.

Bryk, Anthony, and Barbara L. Schneider. 2002. *Trust in Schools: A Core Resource for Improvement*. New York: Russell Sage Foundation.

Bryk, Anthony S., Valerie E. Lee, and Peter Blakeley Holland. 1993. *Catholic Schools and the Common Good*. Cambridge, Mass.: Harvard University Press.

Campbell, David E. 2001. "Making Democratic Education Work." In *Charters, Vouchers, and Public Education*, edited by Paul E. Peterson and David E. Campbell. Washington, D.C.: Brookings Institution Press.

Carpenter, Joel A. 1997. *Revive Us Again: The Reawakening of American Fundamentalism*. New York: Oxford University Press.

Coleman, James Samuel, and Thomas Hoffer. 1987. *Public and Private High schools: The Impact of Communities*. New York: Basic Books.

Cox, Harvey Gallagher. 1995. *Fire from Heaven: The Rise of Pentecostal Spirituality and the Reshaping of Religion in the Twenty-First Century*. Reading, Mass.: Addison-Wesley.

Damon, William. 1995. *Greater Expectations: Overcoming the Culture of Indulgence in America's Homes and Schools*. New York: Free Press.

Emerson, Michael O., and Christian Smith. 2000. *Divided by Faith: Evangelical Religion and the Problem of Race in America*. Oxford: Oxford University Press.

Emerson, Michael O., Christian Smith, and David Sikkink. 1999. "Equal in Christ, but Not in the World: White Conservative Protestants and Explanations of Black-White Inequality." *Social Problems* 46(3): 398–417.

Etzioni, Amitai. 1993. *The Spirit of Community: Rights, Responsibilities, and the Communitarian Agenda*. New York: Crown Publishers.

Godwin, R. Kenneth, and Frank R. Kemerer. 2002. *School Choice Tradeoffs: Liberty, Equity, and Diversity*. Austin: University of Texas Press.

Godwin, R. Kenneth, Carrie Ausbrooks, and Valerie Martinez. 2001. "Teaching Tolerance in Public and Private Schools." *Phi Delta Kappan* (March): 542–46.

Grant, Gerald. 1988. *The World We Created at Hamilton High*. Cambridge, Mass: Harvard University Press.

Grasmick, Harold G., Karyl Kinsey, and John K. Cochran. 1991. "Denomination, Religiosity and Compliance with the Law: A Study of Adults." *Journal for the Scientific Study of Religion* 30(1): 99–107.

Greene, Jay P. 1998. "Civic Values in Public and Private Schools." In *Learning from School Choice*, edited by Paul E. Peterson and Bryan C. Hassel. Washington, D.C.: Brookings Institution Press.

Gutmann, Amy. 1987. *Democratic Education*. Princeton, N.J.: Princeton University Press.

Hirschman, Albert O. 1970. *Exit, Voice, and Loyalty: Responses to Decline in Firms, Organizations, and States*. Cambridge, Mass: Harvard University Press.

Hogendoom, Rob, and Coby Hogendoom. 2005. "Why We Chose a Public School." *The Banner* 2005: 30–32.

Kahne, Joseph. 1996. "The Politics of Self-Esteem." *American Educational Research Journal* 33(1): 3–22.

Lawrence-Lightfoot, Sara. 1983. *The Good High School: Portraits of Character and Culture*. New York: Basic Books.

Leak, Gary K., and Brandy A. Randall. 1995. "Clarification of the Link between Right-Wing Authoritarianism and Religiousness: The Role of Religious Maturity." *Journal for the Scientific Study of Religion* 34(2): 245–52.

li Carpini, Michael X., and Scott Keeter. 1996. *What Americans Know About Politics and Why It Matters*. New Haven, Conn.: Yale University Press.

Lipset, Seymour Martin, and Earl Raab. 1970. *The Politics of Unreason: Right Wing Extremism in America, 1790–1970*. New York: Harper & Row.

Macedo, Stephen. 2000. *Diversity and Distrust: Civic Education in a Multicultural Democracy*. Cambridge, Mass: Harvard University Press.

Marsden, George M. 1980. *Fundamentalism and American Culture: The Shaping of Twentieth Century Evangelicalism, 1870–1925*. New York: Oxford University Press.

McDonnell, Kilian. 1976. *Charismatic Renewal and the Churches*. New York: Seabury Press.

McFarland, Daniel A. 2001. "Student Resistance: How the Formal and Informal Organization of Classrooms Facilitate Everyday Forms of Student Defiance." *American Journal of Sociology* 107(3): 612–78.

McLaren, Peter. 1987. "Schooling for Salvation: Christian Fundamentalism's Ideological Weapons of Death." *Journal of Education* 169(2): 132–39.

Meyer, John W. 1977. "The Effects of Education as an Institution." *American Journal of Sociology* 83(1): 55–77.

Meyer, John W., and Brian Rowan. 1977. "Institutionalized Organizations: Formal Structure as Myth and Ceremony." *American Journal of Sociology* 83(2): 340–63.

National Center for Education Statistics. 1996. *National Household Education Survey,1996*. Washington, D.C.: U.S. Department of Education.

Niemi, Richard G., and Jane Junn. 1998. *Civic Education: What Makes Students Learn*. New Haven, Conn.: Yale University Press.

Niemi, Richard G., Mary A. Hepburn, and Chris Chapman. 2000. "Community Service by High School Students: A Cure for Civic Ills?" *Political Behavior* 23(1): 45–69.

Nord, Warren A. 1995. *Religion & American Education: Rethinking a National Dilemma*. Chapel Hill: University of North Carolina Press.

Peshkin, Alan. 1986. *God's Choice: The Total World of a Fundamentalist Christian School*. Chicago: University of Chicago Press.

Rose, Susan. 1988. *Keeping Them Out of the Hands of Satan*. New York: Routledge.

Rosenstone, Steven J., and John Mark Hansen. 1993. *Mobilization, Participation, and Democracy in America*. New York: Macmillan.

Sikkink, David. 1998. "Public Schooling and Its Discontents: Religious Identities, Schooling Choices for Children, and Civic Participation." Ph.D. diss., University of North Carolina at Chapel Hill.

———. 1999. "The Social Sources of Alienation from Public Schools." *Social Forces* 78(1): 51–86.

———. 2001. "Speaking in Many Tongues: Diversity among Christian Schools." *Education Matters* 1(2): 36–45.

———. 2003. "The Loyal Opposition: Evangelicals, Civic Engagement, and Schooling for Children." In *A Public Faith: Evangelicals and Civic Engagement*, edited by Michael Cromartie. New York: Rowman & Littlefield.

Sikkink, David, and Andrea Mihut. 2001. "Religion and the Politics of Multiculturalism." *Religion and Education* 27(2): 30–46.

Sikkink, David, and Christian Smith. 2000. "Evangelicals on Education." In *Christian America? What Evangelicals Really Want*, edited by Christian Smith. Berkeley: University of California Press.

Smith, Christian. 2000. *Christian America? What Evangelicals Really Want*. Berkeley: University of California Press.

Smith, Christian, Michael Emerson, Sally Gallagher, Paul Kennedy, and David Sikkink. 1998. *American Evangelicalism: Embattled and Thriving*. Chicago: University of Chicago Press.

Steensland, Brian, Jerry Park, Mark Regnerus, Lynn Robinson, W. Bradford Wilcox, and Robert Woodberry. 2000. "The Measure of American Religion: Improving the State of the Art." *Social Forces* 79: 291–318.

Wacker, Grant. 2001. *Heaven Below: Early Pentecostals and American Culture*. Cambridge, Mass: Harvard University Press.

Wagner, Melinda Bollar. 1990. *God's Schools: Choice and Compromise in American Society*. New Brunswick, N.J.: Rutgers University Press.

Wilcox, W. Bradford. 1998. "Conservative Protestant Childrearing: Authoritarian or Authoritative?" *American Sociological Review* 63(6): 796–809.

Wolf, Patrick J. 1998. "Democratic Values in New York City Schools." Report of the Workshop in Applied Policy Analysis, School of International and Public Affairs, Columbia University.

———. 2007. "Civics Exam: Schools of Choice Boost Civic Values." *Education Next* 7(3): 66–72.

Wolf, Patrick J., Jay P. Greene, Brett Kleitz, and Kristin Thalhammer. 2001. "Private Schooling and Political Tolerance." In *Charters, Vouchers, and Public Education*, edited by Paul E. Peterson and David E. Campbell. Washington, D.C.: Brookings Institution Press.

Wuthnow, Robert. 1988. *The Restructuring of American Religion: Society and Faith Since World War II*. Princeton, N.J.: Princeton University Press.

———. 1995. *Learning to Care: Elementary Kindness in an Age of Indifference*. New York: Oxford University Press.

Youniss, James, and Miranda Yates. 1997. *Community Service and Social Responsibility in Youth*. Chicago: University of Chicago Press.

Chapter 10

Hollywood and Jerusalem: Christian Conservatives and the Media

GABRIEL ROSSMAN

T HERE IS much in popular culture for theologically and politically conservative Christians to object to. The primary objection is to sex, violence, and profanity in the entertainment media.[1] Media content objected to on these grounds can range from full-blown pornography to comedy programs like *Monty Python's Flying Circus*. In November 2006 and February 2007 network primetime television, 1 percent of programs were self-rated by their networks as TV-G, 55 percent as TV-PG, and 44 percent as TV-14. A content analysis of programs during the same period found that 80 percent contained at least some profanity, 61 percent at least some violence, 43 percent at least some sex, and 52 percent at least some suggestive dialogue. About half the time, the network did not flag the program with the relevant v-chip content descriptor (Parents Television Council 2007). Between February 1995 and March 1996, of films broadcast on weeknights in prime time broadcast and cable television, more than 20 percent contained nudity and more than 50 percent featured violence, with slightly higher figures on weekends (Hamilton 1998, 152). In 2005 on the commercial broadcast networks, the Public Broadcasting System (PBS), and the top four cable networks, 68 percent of programs discussed sex and 35 percent showed sexual behavior, about 30 percent of which implied or depicted intercourse. Furthermore, 45 percent of shows popular with teenagers featured sexual behavior (Kunkel et al. 2005). The report contrasts its findings with the team's results from 1998 using the same methodology, when they found appreciably lower levels of violent and sexual content.

In other cases, conservative Christians, both Protestant and Catholic, object that they or religious people in general are either belittled or ignored by the media. These complaints are similar to, and sometimes consciously modeled on, those made by activists representing ethnic groups. For instance, the Reverend Donald Wildmon, founder of the American Family Association, argued that Americans are a very religious people but that this is not reflected on television, and, moreover, to the extent that religion is shown, it is denigrated (1997). In a similar vein, the Catholic League for Religious and Civil Rights focuses not on content that is inconsistent with Catholic values, but on media stories it perceives to be insulting to Catholics. A popular example among conservative Christian of the belittling media came from a *Washington Post* article that described fundamentalists as "largely poor, uneducated, and easy to command" (Michael Weisskopf, "Energized by Pulpit or Passion, the Public is Calling: 'Gospel Grapevine' Displays Strength in Controversy over Military Gay Ban," February 1, 1993, A1). Years later, this quote is still invoked as evidence of media bias against conservative Christians.

Another complaint is that popular culture advocates ideologies that are contrary to conservative Christian values. One frequently cited early example concerned two episodes of the television show *Maude* in which the title character had an abortion. These episodes drew objections, because they deliberately dramatized the Population Institute's position that abortion is an appropriate way to handle an unwanted pregnancy (Montgomery 1989). More recently, conservative Christians have opposed a variety of programs with sympathetic gay and lesbian characters. The television show *Will and Grace* was a common object of opposition. Although part of the objection appears to have been to the stream of double entendres in the show, a more important base among conservative Christians was the fact that two of the four main characters were gay, the broader milieu was largely gay, and many episodes explicitly conveyed the idea that homosexuality was innocuous and opposition to it a form of bigotry. This sort of programming seemed a particular insult to conservatives Christians because in this case popular culture was not merely salacious, but, at least in their eyes, also engaged in partisan activism.

Compounding these grievances has been a general lack of trust based on the notion that the people who work in the media don't share "middle American" values. This perception is partly based on anecdotes about the lifestyles and public statements of celebrities, but it is also supported by social science evidence concerning the attitudes of people working at high levels in the entertainment industry (see, for example,

Lichter, Lichter, and Rothman 1983). Furthermore, conservatives Christians are sometimes offended by the business practices of entertainment companies; one of the reasons the Southern Baptist Convention decided to boycott the Disney Corporation in 1997 was that the company, like most of its competitors, had extended benefits to the domestic partners of gay and lesbian employees. Religious conservatives took such actions as evidence that the objectionable aspects of entertainment media are not merely accidental by-products of a profit-seeking industry, but motivated attacks on their values that cannot be justified on demand-side business grounds (Baehr 1988; Medved 1992).[2]

Thus conservative Christians deplore many elements commonly found in the popular culture: sex, violence, profanity, insulting portrayals of religious people, and support for socially liberal positions and causes. The question, then, is how do they react to these grievances?

Theoretical Framework

This chapter analyzes conservative Christian efforts to influence the media. Overall, I argue, protest (through the state and otherwise) has proven a disappointing avenue for reform. I show that lobbying efforts to improve the climate for "decent" content in the media, as interpreted by conservative Christians, have been only marginally effective. Throughout the 1980s and 1990s, protest centered on advertiser and producer boycotts. More recently there has been a renewed interest in demanding state action—especially from regulatory bureaucracies like the Federal Communications Commission (FCC).

Perhaps ironically, the market has proven to provide more leverage. Because the primary interest of media companies is to make a profit, Christians have been able to gain a foothold to the extent that they have been able to demonstrate that a sizable market exists for Christian-themed products. At the same time, they have had to overcome the clear evidence that their market power is limited. The market for conservative Christian media is relatively small—typically less than a 10 percent market share in any mass medium, and often well below that. Although conservative Christians make up at least 30 percent of the American population, they are first typical Americans whose media consumption patterns differ little from those of other Americans, and only secondly a religious taste market. Moreover, with a few notable exceptions, the stronger the Christian message, the weaker the potential for the broad crossover appeal that stimulates warm emotions among media executives.

Within this context, conservative Christians were able to leverage a somewhat greater measure of cultural power in the 1980s and 1990s by combining a strategy of *voice* (contestation over content) and *exit* (consumption of subcultural media). The exit strategy, in particular, essentially created a farm system for nourishing Christian talent that was able to cross over into mainstream media, and impressed media executives with the potential of the conservative Christian market. Some Christian publishing houses and radio networks were, consequently, absorbed by the large media conglomerates, and niche marketing to conservative Christians became a well-established practice not only among traditional religious content providers but also in many of the biggest media conglomerates. Nonetheless, however effective exit may be at convincing major media conglomerates to treat conservative Christians as a niche audience, it cannot convince the media to eliminate or mitigate the content it provides to other audiences that Christians find offensive.

As these last observations suggest, this chapter uses Albert Hirschman's schema of exit, voice, and loyalty to describe and interpret conservative Christians' relationship to the mass entertainment media (1970). This schema categorizes the options open to actors when they are dissatisfied with a relationship. Loyalty is in evidence when the actor simply accepts his or her lot, as when conservative Christians consume mainstream media even when they are unhappy with it. Voice is in evidence when an actor makes an effort to change the nature of the relationship. Examples would include efforts of Christian activists to change media content through boycotts or petitions. Exit is in evidence when a person breaks the relationship, such as when conservative Christians abstain from the mainstream popular culture and patronize subcultural alternative media. In the remainder of this chapter, I describe the extent to which conservative Christians practice each of these strategies and how the strategies influence one another.

Loyalty

The most important thing about conservative Christian grievances against the entertainment media is that more often than not they are without observable consequences. Given the number of people belonging to religions that theoretically find major shortcomings in the mass media, it is remarkable that so few use voice to articulate their complaints or exit to avoid offensive offerings and seek alternatives. At least 25 percent of Americans are affiliated with conservative or evangelical Protestant denominations and another 16 percent or so are theological conservatives whose roots lie in other religious traditions (Greeley and Hout 2006). An even larger proportion of Americans, more than 65 percent, tell pollsters they think there is too much sex and violence on television (Hamilton 1998, 72; Kaiser Family Foundation 2007). Politicians know that few constituencies will mobilize in support of the freedom to show sex and violence in the media. This might lead one to assume that massive numbers of Americans are actively opposing or at least avoiding violent and sexually explicit media fare. Yet this is manifestly not the case.

One of the striking conclusions about organized Christian opposition to the mass media and Christian alternative media is that they are both relatively marginal phenomena. For instance, consider the commitment to voice, or expressions of opposition. For the past few years, the FCC has received several hundred thousand complaints about broadcasting indecency every year. Although this speaks well to the efficacy of the Parents Television Council, the secular group that coordinates the majority of these complaints, it is a relatively small volume considering the number of Americans—well above 100 million—who when asked by pollsters will claim that they object to the media.

The truth is that salacious programming is enormously popular. It is difficult to establish firmly how much of this popularity extends to conservative Christian audiences because no reliable data that combine information on both media consumption and religion are publicly available. However, one suggestive finding is that people with ideological objections to television violence consume less of it, but nevertheless many people report both heavy consumption of television violence and misgivings about its impact on society (Hamilton 1998, 74). Likewise, given the sheer numbers of conservative Christians, it is unlikely that sexually charged programs could be so popular without many conservative Christian viewers, though it is very possible that they on average consume less of this programming than other Americans. Seventy-five million evangelicals are not mobilized against popular culture; relatively speaking, only a small number are so engaged. Most may disapprove at times, but they continue to watch anyway.

Voice

One broad family of conservative Christian reactions to popular culture can be described as voice, or activism to change the media. These efforts can be further divided into attempts to lobby the state into censoring offensive media and attempts to work through the private sector by aiming moral suasion and boycotts at the media themselves and at advertisers. When one considers the idea of a culture war between religious conservatives and secular liberals the mental image is of voice, because this is when people neither quietly ignore their own reservations, nor seek to create an alternative, but actively contest for influence in the public square (Hunter 1991; Tepper 2001).

Building on antecedents, such as the New York Society for the Suppression of Vice in the 1870s and the Catholic League of Decency in the

1930s, the current wave of conservative Christian voice organizations can be dated to the founding of Morality in Media (MIM) by Father Morton Hill in 1968 (Zarkin 2003). The organization began after a mother complained to an associate of Father Hill that hardcore pornography was circulating among the adolescent boys at an Upper East Side Manhattan parish school. MIM was organized to fight both pornography and indecency in the media. Almost immediately, Father Hill was appointed to President Johnson's committee on pornography. When that committee issued a report in 1970 finding that pornography was harmless and ought to be legal, Father Hill wrote a minority report contesting the position. MIM was also involved in assisting local officials to prosecute obscenity and to zone strip clubs out of city neighborhoods. MIM's antipornography agenda bore more fruit in the mid-1980s when Ronald Reagan appointed a commission chaired by then Attorney General Edwin Meese to look into pornography. The Meese Commission issued a report suggesting regulation of the pornography industry, which was widely praised by conservative Christian organizations.

Morality in Media has also devoted attention to mainstream media, especially broadcasting. The most noteworthy case occurred in 1973, when a MIM board member complained to the FCC that he and his son had heard WBAI-FM broadcast George Carlin's comedic ode to profanity, "Filthy Words." The FCC fined the station, which in turn appealed on the grounds that the broadcast fell short of the recently defined Miller obscenity test and was therefore constitutionally protected.[3] MIM and the United States Catholic Conference each filed amica curiae defending the fine (and were opposed by several civil liberties and trade groups). In FCC v. Pacifica (1978), the Supreme Court upheld the fine and effectively held that due to intrusiveness, broadcast media deserved less leeway than other speech. In the decision, the court ruled that broadcasts that were indecent but not obscene could be punished.[4]

This victory for MIM appears to have inspired overconfidence. Soon after the decision, MIM filed with the FCC a petition to deny the broadcasting license renewal application of the television station WGBH on grounds that the station had been airing offensive material. This was overreach in several ways:

- WGBH is a flagship of the Public Broadcasting System and one of the most respected television stations in the country.

- MIM was objecting to fairly tame content such as *Masterpiece Theatre* and *Monty Python's Flying Circus*.

- The FCC majority at the time had been appointed by the more liberal President Jimmy Carter, rather than the more conservative President

Richard Nixon, whose appointees heard the successful complaint against WBAI.

- Traditionally, the FCC has had an extremely strong bias in favor of renewal.

The FCC not only renewed WGBH's broadcasting license but also scaled back its enforcement of broadcasting indecency and would not regain interest in the issue again until 1987, when the FCC began its feud with Howard Stern. At present, Morality in Media primarily concentrates on pornography and has relatively little involvement with the mainstream media.

Another major conservative Christian media activist group is the American Family Association (AFA), led by the Reverend Donald Wildmon (Zarkin 2003). Wildmon's involvement with the media began during Christmas 1976 when he was watching television with his family in Southaven, Mississippi, and found every program to include morally objectionable content. Wildmon first asked his Methodist congregation to have a "turn off TV week" and a few months later resigned from the pulpit to devote himself full-time to media activism as the founder of the National Federation for Decency, which changed its name to the American Family Association in 1988. Unlike MIM, AFA has generally focused on mainstream broadcasting, though in the 1980s it conducted a major campaign to pressure bookstore, gas station, and drugstore chains to stop selling pornography. In 1978, the AFA issued a report on sex in television and boycotted Sears department stores, which advertised with several of the programs discussed in the report. After three months, Sears pulled its ads from two of the offending programs. This early campaign established the tactics that AFA has continued to follow.

The American Family Association has continued to focus on the tactic of treating advertisers as the media's Achilles's heel. Their monthly *AFA Journal* contains feature articles on religious, cultural, and political issues. The core of the magazine, however, consists of brief reviews of television programs, listing objectionable content in each. In a sidebar, the sponsors of these programs, sometimes described as the dirty dozen, are listed, along with their addresses. AFA encourages readers to write these companies explaining their disappointment at seeing the companies advertising on programs that contain offensive content.

In addition to petitioning sponsors, AFA also conducts more concerted campaigns. The most noteworthy of these was the 1996–2005 boycott of the Disney Corporation (Land and York 1998). The boycott began with the Catholic League for Religious and Civil Rights, which was initially offended that in 1995 Disney, through its subsidiary Miramax, had distributed *Priest* (1994), a film about a gay priest who ultimately rejects the Church. The Catholic League was further offended by *Nothing Sacred*, an ABC drama about a priest who has reservations about doctrine and celibacy. AFA joined the boycott of Disney on the basis of a variety of concerns, including the unofficial "gay days" annual gathering at Disney World and the company's provision of gay domestic partnership benefits. In 1997, a Southern Baptist pastor who was also an AFA member brought the boycott to the attention of his denominational body. In part because Ellen DeGeneres and her eponymous ABC sitcom character had both come out as lesbians a few months earlier, the Southern Baptist Convention voted to join the boycott. Despite the size of the convention (Southern Baptists are America's largest denomination after Roman Catholicism), the endorsement of other groups such as Focus on the Family, and extensive press coverage, it was difficult to detect an impact on Disney's sales or any concessions in its behavior. Both AFA and the Southern Baptists ended the boycott in 2005.

AFA and other conservative Christian organizations did not directly object to any of the content Disney was producing, however.[5] For instance, there were no allegations that the cartoon *Duck Tales* contained offensive themes, as AFA had plausibly alleged in 1988 against *Mighty Mouse*. Indeed, conservative Christians could not very well threaten to boycott objectionable Disney products given that presumably they were not consuming them to begin with. However, because Disney is a conglomerate offering a mix of innocuous family-friendly products and more adult fare, conservative Christians could plausibly threaten to stop their consumption of the former as a protest against the latter. In this way the Disney boycott was structurally similar to an advertiser boycott: in both cases, activists threaten to cease consuming something they find intrinsically innocuous, such as Sears department stores or Disneyland vacations, to punish something that offends them, such as *Charlie's Angels* or *Ellen*. Aside from providing tactical leverage to activists, the conglomerate form of the Disney Corporation may have provided motivation. In the 1990s, Disney's product line and business practices were, as a whole, similar to those of its competitors and, if anything, more congruent with socially conservative values. It is possible that Disney was targeted because of its strong brand image as a company catering to children. Through the boycott, conservative Christian organizations could dramatize the incongruity that a company built on children's media could now be making a film like *Pulp Fiction*, released in 1994, which featured a heroin overdose, a deadpan comic monologue about dysentery, and many scenes of graphic violence, including a gang rape.

Recently, a new group, the Parents Television Council (PTC), has come to prominence, founded in 1995 by L. Brent Bozell III, a conservative activist and the nephew of William F. Buckley Jr. Unlike Morality in Media (which is primarily Catholic) and American Family Association (which is evangelical Protestant), PTC is a secular social conservative organization. It is discussed here because it fills a niche similar to that of AFA and MIM and has to some extent displaced them. Unlike the ministry model of the older groups, PTC is modeled on Bozell's other organization, the Media Research Center (MRC), a secular think tank dedicated to exposing liberal bias in journalism. Like MRC, a central function of PTC is to archive, document, and code media output. To this end, it has collected an impressive tape library it summarizes in regular reports and press releases. A typical PTC report describes general trends in media content and gives specific examples of entertainment that it deems either desirable or undesirable. These reports are partly intended for parents to use as a resource in shaping their television consumption and partly as a guide to activism.

In addition to its think-tank style research, PTC also engages in activism. Like MIM, it directs its activism at the government rather than advertisers, but like AFA it also mobilizes massive letter-writing campaigns. In the main navigation of the PTC website, for example, is a prominent link to file an FCC complaint that leads to a form in which one can describe offensive media content, which the PTC will then forward to the FCC. The PTC also occasionally makes a major drive to solicit complaints against specific broadcasts. They are so successful that the FCC estimates that 99 percent of all complaints are tied to PTC and that the group is entirely responsible for the recent increase in the volume of complaints (Shields 2004).

The FCC has stated that it discounts complaints originating from PTC, and that it interprets all complaints not as petitions but as referrals. If true, this would severely limit the impact of the large number of complaints filed through PTC. This is, however, clearly not accurate. In January 2003, Bono, the lead singer of the band U2 expressed his happiness with winning a Golden Globe by declaring, "This is really, really fucking brilliant" (Federal Communications Commission 2004). Viewers complained to the FCC that the prime time NBC telecast of the awards dinner had contained profanity. The FCC enforcement bureau decided to let the incident pass without fine both because Bono used the word in a figurative sense and because it was an isolated incident and could be interpreted as an honest mistake in the context of a live broadcast.[6] PTC and other conservative groups were furious and told their constituents that the FCC was now allowing the word on the public airwaves. This interpretation enraged the PTC's supporters, and the FCC received tens of thousands of letters urging zero-tolerance of the offending word. Faced with this deluge of correspondence, the FCC reversed its decision and voted unanimously to consider the word *fuck* intrinsically indecent, regardless of whether it was intended figuratively or literally, or whether it appeared in a live or scripted context. The only disagreement among the commissioners was whether to hold NBC affiliates responsible for violating standards, or to rule that the articulated standard should not be applied ex post facto. The FCC's reversal is testimony to the power of the activist voice to change the media.

Exit

Whereas loyalty involves accepting flaws and voice advocates that flaws be corrected, exit entails withdrawal and substitution of alternatives. Exit is a strategy of separatism. For most of the period between the Scopes trial and the election of Jimmy Carter, this might be considered the characteristic attitude of conservative Protestants toward mainstream politics and culture. Likewise, after most of the country rejected the Clinton impeachment, some prominent figures in the Christian Right argued that the culture war for influence in the public square had been lost and that the best approach would be to withdraw from an incorrigible mainstream culture and to focus on the well-being of the Christian community (Thomas and Dobson 1999; Weyrich 1999). Such recommendations were short-lived, in part because of the galvanizing effects of the 9/11 terrorist attacks and the Goodridge and Lawrence court decisions.[7]

As a cultural strategy, exit consists of creating parallel industries for the production and distribution of Christian media.[8] These parallel industries encompass Christian publishers, Christian record labels, Christian film and television production, Christian broadcasters, and Christian bookstores, not to mention Christian summer camps, youth centers, private schools, and colleges. Subcultural marketing is not an issue unique to Christians, but instead consistent with a general trend toward the "de-massification" of the media and its partial replacement with a "narrow-casting" model in which media are targeted to specific consumption groups (Anderson 2006; Turow 1997). This trend has been facilitated by technological advances that allow more bandwidth and reduce barriers to entry. For instance, in the 1950s, VHF technology allowed only a handful of television stations to broadcast, whereas today digital DVD, cable, satellite, and Internet technology mean that there is effectively no limit to the number of people who can provide video content. Media aimed at taste minorities can now find an audience for their goods.

It is easy to exaggerate the trend, however. As I have noted, most conservative Christians continue to be attached to the mass media, even if they supplement it with subcultural products. Furthermore, there are strong theoretical reasons for expecting the persistence of a mainstream of popular cultural products, even in the absence of technical barriers to entry (Neuman 1991; Salganik, Dodds, and Watts 2006; Webster 2005).

One reason is that because the mainstream can amortize high fixed costs over a larger audience, it will always have the highest production values, and some members of taste minorities will prefer high-quality mainstream products to low-quality subcultural products (Entman and Rojecki 2001). More important, the mainstream media benefits from preferential attachment dynamics, including network externalities—the more popular something is, the more useful it becomes as a basis of small talk—and information cascades—popularity is a heuristic for quality (Adler 1985; Katz and Shapiro 1985; Banerjee 1992; Salganik, Dodds, and Watts 2006).

Christian Publishing

Of course, the oldest Christian medium is publishing, which is historically closely tied to religious revivals and evangelical churches (Haveman and King 2005). Religious magazines vary in how closely they are tied to denominational bodies and in the extent to which they instruct their readers in religious matters (Board 1990). The tendency over time has been for magazines to aspire to achieve a more commercial orientation. For instance, Billy Graham founded *Christianity Today* as a free periodical in 1956 but a few years later it shifted to paid circulation. Other periodicals were established on a commercial basis from their inception, as with Focus on the Family's line of children and teen magazines (Hendershot 2004). The most prominent evangelical magazine, *Christianity Today*, claims a circulation of 145,000 (Christianity Today International 2007). This makes the magazine approximately the 250th most popular title in America.[9]

Christian book publishing grew rapidly in the 1970s, before leveling off in the 1980s (Ferré 1990). Throughout the 1980s and 1990s, religious publishing represented about seven percent of book sales, but since 1999 has consistently captured between 8 and 9 percent of sales (Dessauer 1982–2007). Because the publishing industry as a whole has tripled in real dollars since 1980, this gradually increasing slice of a rapidly increasing pie represents a healthy industry. Most of these books are Bibles, self-help books (including family and financial advice), or apocalyptic literature. Aside from the last category, relatively little in these genres is explicit theological exegesis. Tyler Stevenson noted that not only is theology a small part of Christian publishing, but Bibles tend to be marketed by occasion and audience (for example, wedding gift Bibles or Bibles for teens) rather than for their substantive features such as particular translations or inclusion of a concordance and footnotes (2007).

As with secular publishing, Christian books are a hit-driven industry, with sales propelled by a few bestsellers like Hal Lindsey's *Late Great Planet Earth* (1972), Tim LaHaye's and Jerry Jenkins' *Left Behind* (1995), and Rick Warren's *Purpose Driven Life* (2002). Through the 1960s, the industry was dominated by independent publishers, but since then several of these publishers were purchased by media conglomerates (Ferré 1990). Most notably, Zondervan is now part of the HarperCollins division of NewsCorp. A similar story describes the trajectory of Christian bookstores.[10] For decades, Christian retail was dominated by small stores that exercised an important gatekeeping function. When books and other products strayed too far from evangelical norms, they were subject to repudiation by the network of these small stores. For example, Christian booksellers boycotted a publishing company after it released a book arguing that abortion was immoral most of the time, but was nonetheless a humane practice for pregnancies with severe birth defects (Ferré 1990, 109–10). More recently, small Christian bookstores have lost market share to the LifeWay chain and, even more so, to mainstream chains like Barnes and Noble and Kmart, after the latter began stocking Christian books (Elinsky 2006; Hendershot 2004). This trend has facilitated rising market share for Christian publishing, but it has come at the expense of small Christian retailers.

Christian Contemporary Music

One of the most interesting new forms of Christian media culture is pop music, which parallels every conceivable secular genre and is known collectively as contemporary Christian music (CCM). The form originated in the late 1960s with Christian hippies, known as Jesus freaks (Romanowski 1990). This movement adopted the art forms, dress, hygiene, and many of the political and social ideas of the secular counterculture but also drew from evangelical Christianity a rejection of promiscuity and drugs and the notion of a life focused on an intense personal relationship with God. To reconcile their musical taste with their religion, the Jesus freaks played folk and rock music, but with lyrics that replaced images of debauchery with images of devotion. The defining moment in establishing CCM as a distinct genre came in 1968, when Larry Norman quit the band People after his record label refused to let him title his album "We Need a Whole Lot More Jesus and a Lot Less Rock and Roll."

Although CCM began musically as an offshoot of rock, it followed the singer-songwriter trend of the 1970s to develop a style known as contemporary praise, a type of soft rock with vaguely spiritual lyrics. This style was exemplified by Amy Grant, who was by some measure the biggest star in CCM in the late 1980s and early 1990s. As contemporary praise cemented its artistic dominance, a diverse set of artists interested in genre emerged. The first of these was DC Talk, a hip hop group formed in the late 1980s. In the 1990s, CCM bands proliferated and represent an eclectic array of styles, ranging from easy listening to hard sounds like rap-metal. This embrace of genre has been so complete that there is now a Christian equivalent to almost any secular artist. It would be hard to mistake the Christian hard rock band P.O.D. for Amy Grant. Furthermore the emergence of subgenres may explain increasing sales. In 1990, religious music accounted for about 2.5 percent of recorded music sales. Its market share rose steadily, peaking at 6.7 percent in 2001 and 2002, before declining to about 5.5 percent in following years (U.S. Bureau of the Census 2008).

Throughout its history, CCM has experienced tension between whether it is evangelism first and music second, or vice versa. Larry Norman and a few of his peers went so far as to cease charging for their music and instead solicited voluntary donations, on the model of a religious service. With the exception of the occasional free concert, this practice has not lasted, and CCM is now firmly on a commercial model. Nonetheless, the tension persists in terms of whether content will be explicitly and didactically religious or merely innocuous with references to religion concealed—a strategy especially favored for the release of singles (Hendershot 2004). Bands that seek crossover success tend to favor lyrical code words, which leads to accusations that they have sold out. At the other extreme is Carman, an artist with no aspirations to mainstream success and whose explicitly religious lyrics depict a world of sinners in the hands of an angry God. Many Christian artists would like to see themselves as evangelical, in the proselytizing sense. The problem is that nonevangelical audiences tend to avoid stridently religious messages. To reach these larger audiences, bands must deliver a less overtly religious message (for a similar dynamic at work in public policy discourse, see Klemp and Macedo, volume 2, chapter 7). Often the religious message becomes all but imperceptible. CCM songs that have received secular air play—like Amy Grant's "Baby, Baby" and Sixpence None the Richer's "Kiss Me"—almost require a cryptologist to be recognized as Christian. Thus in practice CCM, like all Christian media, is pastoral rather than evangelical. Ironically, cultural products explicitly intended to reach out into the broader culture and "fish for men" have such a limited mass appeal that they tend to reach only the subculture.

Christian Radio

Christian radio has traditionally favored an emphasis on evangelism, with talk programming known as preach and teach. Such programming goes back to the very beginning of radio, a medium that religion, in general, and missionary societies, in particular, saw as a natural tool for evangelism (Schultze 2003). Some preaching programs became very popular into the 1950s, but since then they have faded. Surprisingly, given the number of programs on the air, the evidence does not suggest that preach and teach radio has a large audience (Schultze 1990). This has to do with the peculiar economics of the format. Most radio stations are supported by advertising dollars, which are in turn based on ratings. Because radio stations with low ratings can make more money by switching to a more popular programming format, the number of stations in a format roughly tracks the number of listeners to that format. In contrast, preach and teach stations traditionally do not sell advertising but instead sell infomercial blocks of airtime to preachers, who in turn solicit donations, often using the show-based call-ins to build a direct-mail database (Diamond 1996, 107). Because the programming is perceived as evangelistic rather than pastoral, many donors do not listen to the broadcasts themselves and unlike a commercial sponsor investing in sales, these small religious donors do not use Arbitron ratings to validate their investment in souls. This gives the radio stations the character of an "existence good" in which supporters like the idea that they exist even if the listeners do not actually listen to them, much as environmentalists like the existence of remote wilderness areas they do not plan to visit. Thus, the supply of teach and preach programming can outstrip their actual audiences for it.

It is worth noting though that some preach and teach programming has devoted audiences. The best example of this is the syndicated radio program *Focus on the Family* (Gilgoff 2007). Following the therapeutic turn in American religion (Wuthnow 1988), this program is hosted not by an ordained clergyman, but by a Christian psychologist, James Dobson, who specializes in advice on child rearing. *Focus on the Family* is the keystone of a Christian media conglomerate (Hendershot 2004; Gilgoff 2007).

Christian broadcasting can also encourage political mobilization. This has been true at least since the early 1960s, when Christian radio stations mobilized against the nuclear test ban treaty (Friendly 1977).[11] More recently, Christian broadcasters have made "tell your congressman how you feel" type appeals on a variety of issues (Diamond 1996). For instance, Christian radio was largely responsible for mobilizing 800,000 phone calls opposing a bill that would have effectively banned home schooling (Diamond 1996, 42). Based on a content analysis, Sara Diamond estimated that about one-third of Pat Robertson's *700 Club* program was "overtly political" (1996). In 1993, Robertson gave the keynote address to the National Religious Broadcasters association in which he exhorted other broadcasters to follow his example by mobilizing support for culture war issues of abortion, homosexuality, and nonmarital sex. Although Robertson's influence has greatly declined in recent years, his role as movement leader and power broker was filled by another broadcaster, *Focus on the Family*'s James Dobson. Early on, Focus empha-

sized child rearing and other self-help content to the exclusion of explic-
itly political issues, but more recently it has added political content
(Gilgoff 2007). Dobson's influence was evident when President George
W. Bush sought and received Dobson's endorsement of Supreme Court
nominee Harriet Meiers to soothe the fears of social conservatives about
Meiers' reliability.

Class divisions are emerging in Christian radio. Since about 1980, the
increasing popularity and institutionalization of CCM gave Christian
radio a new way to program, particularly for stations in the FM band
(Schultze 1990). The CCM audience, which has a median age of thirty-
five to forty-four and household income of $50,000 to $75,000, is a more
valuable demographic than that of traditional religious radio, which has
a median age of forty-five to fifty-four and household income of $25,000
to $50,000 (Media Dynamics 2006). A sizable portion of Christian sta-
tions have begun playing CCM, often in their best time slots, and CCM
now reaches more listeners than traditional religious radio. In this respect, Christian radio is bucking a general trend in radio. AM radio has
been shifting to more talk since the end of the fairness doctrine in 1987
allowed that medium to become more explicitly ideological. Likewise,
since the early 1980s public radio has been trending away from locally
produced classical and jazz music programming and towards news and
talk syndicated by National Public Radio and American Public Media
(Stavitsky 1995).

Christian Television

Although there are many Christian television stations, these tend to
focus on preaching and so the Christian equivalent of secular television
tends to be found in direct-to-video, even if it is occasionally also broadcast. Much of this entertainment is aimed at children, in part because
many evangelicals fear that secular entertainment can corrupt children
(Hendershot 2004). The most successful of these product lines is *Veggie
Tales*, a computer-animated series for young children in which talking
vegetables learn moral lessons in the course of their various activities
and adventures. Although the series frequently mentions God, there is
nothing explicitly evangelical, or even Christian, about it. This ecumenical vagueness leaves nothing that a Catholic, mainline Protestant, Jewish,
or Muslim family would find offensive or apostate. This soft-pedaling interest in crossover may explain the series' high sales and widespread
availability in mainstream retail outlets. More didactic direct-to-video is
found with the action series *Bibleman*, in which a superhero who resembles a silver-clad Darth Vader fights super villains while quoting biblical
chapter and verse. Another example is the Focus on the Family sitcom
McGee and Me, in which a 'tween boy benefits from stern parenting. Not

surprisingly, these more distinctly evangelical series have much less crossover success and sales than *Veggie Tales*.

Videos aimed at teens are often in a Q&A or documentary format rather than the narrative format favored for children (Hendershot 2004). These videos, which are aimed more at youth pastors than at direct purchase by teens or their parents, tend to use the idea of extreme Christianity, which uses stylistic elements borrowed from southern California skateboard culture and frames evangelical Christianity as rebellious— not against parental authority but against the hedonism of mainstream popular culture. Typical of the trend are elaborately edited videos that intersperse skateboarding with filmed focus groups in which teens discuss their feelings about subjects such as chastity. Likewise, a line of "witness wear" clothing feature harsh slogans about how the unsaved face damnation or how Jesus endured tremendous pain on the cross for our benefit. Newer Christian clothiers like NOTW and One Truth tend to use skateboard fashion with religious references perceptible only to the wearer or others familiar with these brands (Stevenson 2007). There is some evidence that such oppositional framing of evangelical values and identity is more effective than traditional socialization. For instance, virginity pledges are only effective at delaying first intercourse when the number of those making the pledge is small enough for signers to view their pledges as countercultural, but large enough that they form a mutually affirming subculture (Bearman and Bruckner 2001).

Christian-Themed Films

Christian film traditionally involves low-budget independent films and often uses the Apocalypse as a theme. One of the things that many non-evangelicals tend to find odd about evangelicals is that many (but not all) of them subscribe to premillennialist eschatology. This doctrine, which became popular in nineteenth-century Doomsday movements like the Millerites, provides a detailed outline of the end of the world (Festinger, Riecken, and Schachter 1956). Most versions begin with the rapture, in which the saved ascend bodily into heaven, followed by the tribulation, a period in which postrapture converts are persecuted by the antichrist, and ends with the second coming of Jesus Christ and his millennial reign on earth. The first film to explore the dramatic possibilities of this prediction was *A Thief in the Night* (1972), which, as the title implies, focuses on how the rapture will come at an unpredictable moment (Hendershot 2004). This film was made for $68,000 and has been widely screened at Christian summer camps, often followed by altar calls or appeals to audience members that they publicly affirm their devotion to God. Although the Apocalypse is a backdrop, the film's emphasis is on the importance of making a personal decision for Christ, preferably before the rapture (that is, immediately), but if necessary after it, during tribulation.

More recent apocalyptic films have been directly or indirectly inspired by the bestselling *Left Behind* series of novels, which focus on tribulation and the efforts of postrapture converts to resist the one world government of the antichrist. These more recent films are less internal and more focused on politics and action. They are something like James Bond films but with more religion and much less sex, profanity, and lower technical production quality. Like the Bond films, these films focus on action and megalomaniacal villains. They also practice product placement, although in this case the plugs are for major televangelists, rather than vodka and sports cars. In the films *Apocalypse* (1997), *Revelation* (1998), and *Tribulation* (2000), Christian guerrillas fight the antichrist by hijacking television signals to broadcast tapes of several televangelists (specifically, the ones who had co-financed the films) (Hendershot 2004). Likewise in the film version of *Left Behind* (2000), the heroes discover a to-be-played-in-event-of-the-Apocalypse tape by televangelist T. D. Jakes.

Undoubtedly, comparable, or even superior, dramatic possibilities are present within the historical portions of the Bible. I have two speculations as to why Christian filmmakers are consistently more interested in Revelations and Daniel than in, say, 1st and 2nd Samuel. The NBC television drama *Kings*, which is based on 1st Samuel, is created by a secular company and primarily intended for a secular audience. First, historical settings would be more expensive than apocalyptic ones because the latter can use modern dress, locations, and even stock footage, whereas the former would require extensive sets and costumes. Second, the historical books of the Bible are morally ambiguous and exploring the foibles of such characters as Abraham (a classic trickster) or David (a bandit and a prodigious womanizer) lack a clear didactic message. Although the gospels are less morally problematic, they are also less inherently cinematic in that they are structured episodically. The lack of drama is even more severe in the epistles. Because of this, the two recent attempts to film the gospels, *The Nativity Story* (2006) and *The Passion of the Christ* (2004), focus on Christ's birth and death and ignore his ministry.

Conclusion

One of the implications of the exit-voice-loyalty model is that exit and voice work best in combination. If voice is used alone and there is no credible threat of exit, then a bargaining partner has little incentive to accommodate complaints. Voice alone is likely to be futile, particularly against media conglomerates as powerful as those that dominate the popular media. Likewise, exit is usually a difficult and expensive process. However, if there is a credible threat of exit, bargaining partners may have an incentive to accommodate voice. In the context of conservative Christian relations with popular culture, this implies that activism and the subculture are mutually reinforcing.

First, consider how voice supports exit. Imagine in the late 1990s, a conservative Protestant family with young children had been a heavy consumer of Disney products. However, on reading about Disney's various misdeeds in the *AFA Journal,* they resolved to join the boycott. The problem was that their four-year-old really enjoyed Disney sing-along videos, so the family substituted *Veggie Tales* for the Disney videos. Generally speaking, activism helps convince the constituency that the mainstream media is problematic, which (at the margin) leads them to seek substitutes provided by the subculture.

A more interesting and complex issue is how exit supports voice. The mainstream media is primarily interested in profit, and as such is happy to absorb or imitate successful competitors. Thus a successful subcultural organization may, by making money, influence the mainstream media as much or more than activism. Under the open systems business strategy, mainstream businesses are happy to incorporate niche products within their offerings (Lopes 1992). Indeed, one of the contentions of Christian Right critics of the media is that it is too interested in sex to serve its own financial interests. Of course, the best way to prove this is for subcultural investors to make super-normal returns on wholesome products which the mainstream market is currently undersupplying. Evangelicals are well aware of this dynamic, and Christian film marketing inevitably says that seeing this film (preferably on opening weekend) will send a message to Hollywood. At various times, the mainstream media have incorporated Christian culture either through mergers, or in a piecemeal fashion, one artist or property at a time.

Contemporary Christian music first came to the attention of the major record labels in the early 1980s, and the most important CCM labels were either acquired by, or signed distribution deals with, the major companies. Likewise, top CCM artists tended to cross over to secular genres, leading to accusations that they had sold out. However, even if it is true that CCM artists who did cross over to the mainstream media tended to dilute their evangelical message, a degree of Christianization of the mainstream culture is still implied. This is true for two reasons. First, some crossover artists do maintain an evangelical message, such as P.O.D., whose most recent album was called "Testify" (with the second letter *t* rendered as a large cross) and reached number nine on the (secular) Billboard Hot 200 chart. Second, even if a crossover band ceases to sing about God or Jesus, it is relatively likely though not certain to remain inoffensive. Because evangelicals' main objection to mainstream culture is that it is salacious, even watered-down CCM artists improve the palatability of the popular culture for conservative Christians.

In addition to incorporation, exit can provide a basis for imitation. The film industry experienced such a pattern starting in 2004 when *The Passion of the Christ* made $370 million in domestic box office on a budget of about $30 million. Although the film was made by a (schismatic) Catholic, evangelicals were largely responsible for the film's success, particularly the opening weekend, which relied heavily on group sales. That a depressing film with dialogue in Aramaic and Latin made such massive returns on investment got Hollywood's attention. The studios began trying to determine how to reach the Christian market, both through making films that would appeal to these audiences and through marketing them appropriately. The firm that most exemplifies this strategy is Walden Media, which often partners with Disney. Walden's business strategy is to produce G-rated films, often but not always with subtle Christian themes. Its most adult offering, *Amazing Grace* (2007), showed how the evangelical Christian William Wilberforce convinced the British to abolish the Atlantic slave trade. This films flattered evangelicals and did not offend secularists, given that there is no longer any constituency for slavery.

Aided by a growing field of Christian marketing firms, mainstream industries like Hollywood increasingly see evangelical Christians as an underexploited market niche (Stevenson 2007). The first major Christian marketing attempt after *The Passion* was United Artists' misguided attempt to market *Saved!* (2004) to evangelicals, a group the film portrays as judgmental, ignorant hypocrites. A much more successful evangelical marketing campaign centered on *The Da Vinci Code* (2006), a film that depicts a Vatican conspiracy to suppress a fertility cult dedicated to the descendants of Jesus Christ and Mary Magdalene. In one of media history's great feats of salesmanship, Outreach, a Christian marketing firm contracted by Sony, convinced 68 percent of its affiliated evangelical churches to encourage their congregants to see the film so that they could understand in detail exactly how it was heretical and ahistorical and then leverage that knowledge to explain the real story of Jesus Christ to their unchurched friends. A more direct bid for the Christian market was Disney and Walden's 2005 coproduction of *The Lion, the Witch, and the Wardrobe*, a Christian allegory by C. S. Lewis. As part of the promotion for the film, Disney engaged in pulpit payola by sponsoring a "drawing for pastors to win a trip to the Holy Land. To enter, a preacher only had to submit proof that he or she had mentioned *Narnia* in a recent sermon" (Stevenson 2007, 166).

Thus, exit and voice are complements. Voice convinces constituents that exit is appropriate and exit makes voice both a credible threat and a compelling example. In this light, it is not surprising to see convergence between the two. The American Family Association began as a voice organization dedicated to criticizing the mainstream media, but after a few years branched out into exit with American Family Radio, which is now the country's sixth largest radio chain, as measured by number of stations (American Family Association 1992; DiCola 2006). Coming from the other direction, Focus on the Family began with exit as a Christian multimedia conglomerate providing radio programming, books, magazines, and videos, but has lately gone into voice as a locus of evangelical politics (Gilgoff 2007).

Although the media is hardly as congruent with its values as evangelical Christians might like, its efforts to change the popular culture have had an influence. If we imagine a counterfactual world without the influence of the AFA or PTC, it is easy to imagine major advertisers being more willing to advertise on sleazy shows, the FCC gradually relaxing indecency enforcement, and movie theaters ignoring requirements to card for R-rated films. However, as demonstrated by systematic evidence on the increasing vulgarity of pop culture (Kunkel et al. 2005), evangelical Christians may be standing athwart the culture yelling stop, but the culture seems to be barely listening.

Ironically, though Christian media activism appears to have only a marginal and ameliorative direct influence on the mainstream media, one can see a more substantial effect on the mass culture, from Christian withdrawal to subcultural products. Withdrawal provides the conditions for the development of Christian talent in a protected niche. This talent can be thought of as a farm team for the mainstream media. A close parallel exists with Canadian cultural content restrictions. The Canadians have long been afraid of the cultural hegemony of America and as such have a variety of policies that privilege national performers on the Canadian airwaves. An unintended effect of this policy has been to create a protected niche within which Canadian artists can mature before crossing over to popularity in the United States. The effect of exit providing a niche has already had an influence on music with crossover by CCM artists. Since *Passion of the Christ*, this effect has begun to occur for film as well.

Thus Christians may have their greatest impact on the mainstream media when they give up on it and try to create their own alternatives. This way, they establish a pool of artists supplying content and an audience demanding it, making the mainstream media see them as a market to be exploited, rather than gadflies to be avoided. This dynamic implies that the mainstream media will increasingly supply products desired by conservative Christians, but will also continue to produce the wide range of thoroughly secular and often salacious products the majority desires, regardless of what Christian consumers think about it.

Notes

1. Note that the implicit demand here is for antiseptic entertainment, even if it is vapid, to the exclusion of more graphic material put to redeeming

purpose. For example, the American Family Association vehemently opposed the network television broadcast of the film *Saving Private Ryan*. In
so doing, they focused on their objection to the film's intense violence and
profane language, and ignored their sympathy to its themes of patriotism,
sacrifice, mercy, and the value of individual human life over ideological abstractions. The sort of Christian media criticism one rarely sees is exemplified by Gerald Russello's praise of the HBO series *Rome*. The series is satu-
rated with graphic sex and violence, casual dehumanization of slaves, and
a culture of shame rather than ethics. These sorts of things would drive the
AFA to apoplexy, but Russello praises these features because he finds that
their very vulgarity implicitly argues that Christianity, which was founded
fifty years after the series finale, was necessary to reform a heretofore
amoral Rome, and by extension, the West. Such an argument, which
was published in *First Things* and *National Review*, is notable primarily for
its lack of resonance with the characteristic attitudes of Christian media
activists.

2.   Although Ted Baehr and Michael Medved relied on anecdotal evidence
and summary statistics, peer-reviewed econometrics has verified that salacious films are less profitable than family-friendly ones (De Vany 2004).
This may or may not, however, reflect the preferences of media workers because conservative Christians who work in the mainstream media sometimes produce products that are just as violent, sexual, and even occult as
those made by their unchurched colleagues (Lewerenz and Nicolosi 2005).
This seems to reaffirm the old Frankfurt school position that artist agency
is nearly irrelevant in the face of genre conventions (Horkheimer and
Adorno 1944/1991).

3.   Obscenity, which is not constitutionally protected, was defined in *Miller v.
California*, 413 U.S. 15 (1973) and requires that the text in question violate
community standards, contain an enumerated "patently offensive" sex act,
and lack redeeming quality. In practice obscenity is usually taken to mean
things like child pornography or bestiality and not to include things that
are occasionally found in the mainstream media, such as profane language
or nudity. Under Pacifica, these moderately offensive expressions are usually described as indecent rather than obscene.

4.   The intrusiveness doctrine holds that unlike indecent printed matter,
which one must actively seek out, indecent airwaves enter one's home and
state regulation of indecency is therefore analogous to a homeowner defending his property from a burglar. The Supreme Court likewise held that
broadcasters have less First Amendment protection than print publishers
in *Red Lion v. FCC*, 395 U.S. 367 (1969), though in that case the problem was
not indecency but ideological imbalance and the reason for punishing it
not intrusiveness, but scarcity of useful broadcasting frequencies. In Action
for *Children's Television v. FCC I, II, and III*, 129 L. Ed. 2d 497, 114 S. Ct. 2445
(1994), the D.C. Circuit Court effectively scaled back the scope of Pacifica
by allowing a late night "safe harbor" for indecent material.

5.   One of the ironies of the boycott is that some of the products cited as casus
belli are quite obscure and in retrospect memorable primarily for their role
in provoking the boycott. For instance, the film *Priest* (1994) made less than

$5 million in the United States and several of the other complaints focused on small books published by Hyperion. On the other hand, some of the controversial products were major cultural phenomena, such as the *Ellen* program and the film *Pulp Fiction* (1994).

6. This decision followed a general trend of the Michael Powell FCC to base its decisions on the gist rather than keywords. The policy did not indicate leniency, but cut both ways. Shortly before the Bono incident, the FCC had issued several fines for content without profane words but with prurient themes such as the radio edit of an Eminem song.

7. *Goodridge v. Department of Public Health*, 798 N.E. 2d 941 (Mass. 2003) was a Massachusetts decision finding a right to gay marriage implied by the state constitution. *Lawrence v. Texas*, 539 U.S. 558 (2003) was a Supreme Court case striking down a Texas sodomy ban. Both cases raised social conservative fears that gay marriage would spread beyond Massachusetts. More broadly, many social conservatives feared a broader precedential impact of Lawrence following the warning in Justice Scalia's dissent that the majority's reasoning "effectively decrees the end of all morals legislation."

8. This section draws heavily on Heather Hendershot's excellent *Shaking the World for Jesus* (2004).

9. Publicly available circulation figures only cover the top 100 magazines (Magazine Publishers of America 2006). The estimate of *Christianity Today* being ranked around 250th comes from assuming that, like most measures of media product popularity, magazine circulations follow a scale-free distribution such that observing the right-tail of the distribution allows you to infer the unobserved portion of the density function.

10. Note that Christian bookstore is something of a misnomer because these stores distribute a wide array of products, including music and videos. As such, in 1996 the Christian Booksellers Association renamed itself simply CBA.

11. Democratic Party proxies attempted to suppress this criticism by harassing stations with fairness doctrine complaints (Friendly 1977). The most famous instance was when the radio preacher Billy Hargis used his syndicated radio show to accuse journalist Fred Cook of being a pink and a sloppy journalist. Cook then demanded free reply time from all of Hargis' affiliates. Red Lion broadcasting refused and Cook sued, eventually winning in the Supreme Court case *Red Lion v. FCC*, 395 U.S. 367 (1969).

References

Adler, Moshe. 1985. "Stardom and Talent." *American Economic Review* 75(1): 208–12.

American Family Association. 1992. "A Walk Through the Years." *AFA Journal* June(1992): 28–32.

Anderson, Chris. 2006. *The Long Tail: Why the Future of Media Is Selling Less of More*. New York: Hyperion.

Baehr, Ted. 1988. *The Media-Wise Family*. Colorado Springs: Chariot Victor.

Banerjee, Abhijit V. 1992. "A Simple Model of Herd Behavior." *Quarterly Journal of Economics* 107(3): 797–817.

Bearman, Peter, and Hannah Brückner. 2001. "Promising the Future: Virginity Pledges and First Intercourse." *American Journal of Sociology* 106(4): 859–912.

Board, Stephen. 1990. "Moving the World with Magazines: A Survey of Evangelical Periodicals." In *American Evangelicals and the Mass Media*, edited by Quentin Schultze. Grand Rapids, Mich.: Zondervan Academic.

Christianity Today International. 2007. "Christianity Today Readership Report." Carol Stream, Ill.: Christianity Today International. Available at: http://www.cti-advertising.com/files/publicationfiles/2007ChristianityToday-lowresr1.pdf (accessed March 1, 2007).

De Vany, Arthur S. 2004. *Hollywood Economics: How Extreme Uncertainty Shapes the Film Industry*. London: Routledge.

Dessauer, John P. 1982–2007. *Book Industry Trends*, 16 vols. New York: Book Industry Study Group.

Diamond, Sara. 1996. *Facing the Wrath: Confronting the Right in Dangerous Times*. Monroe, Maine: Common Courage.

DiCola, Peter. 2006. *False Premises, False Hopes: A Quantitative History of Ownership Consolidation in the Radio Industry*. Washington, D.C.: Future of Music Coalition. Available at: http://www.futureofmusic.org/images/FMCradio study06.pdf (accessed March 1, 2007).

Elinsky, Rachel. 2006. "Religious Publishing for the Red State Consumers and Beyond." *Publishing Research Quarterly* 21(4): 11–29.

Entman, Robert M., and Andrew Rojecki. 2001. *The Black Image in the White Mind: Media and Race in America*, 2nd ed. Chicago: University of Chicago.

Federal Communications Commission. 2004. "Complaints Against Various Broadcast Licensees Regarding Their Airing of the 'Golden Globe Awards' Program." Memorandum Opinion and Order # EB-03-IH-0110. Washington, D.C.: Federal Communications Commission. Available at: http://www.fcc .gov/eb/Orders/2004/FCC-04-43A1.pdf (accessed March 1, 2007).

Ferré, John P. 1990. "Searching for the Great Commission: Evangelical Book Publishing Since the 1970s." In *American Evangelicals and the Mass Media*, edited by Quentin Schultze. Grand Rapids, Mich.: Zondervan Academic.

Festinger, Leon, Henry W. Riecken, and Stanley Schachter. 1956. *When Prophecy Fails*. Minneapolis: University of Minnesota Press.

Friendly, Fred W. 1977. *The Good Guys, the Bad Guys and the First Amendment*. New York: Vintage Books.

Gilgoff, Dan. 2007. *The Jesus Machine: How James Dobson, Focus on the Family, and Evangelical America Are Winning the Culture War*. New York: St. Martin's Press.

Greeley, Andrew M., and Michael Hout. 2006. *The Truth About Conservative Christians: What They Think and What They Believe*. Chicago: University of Chicago Press.

Hamilton, James T. 1998. *Channeling Violence: The Economic Market for Violent Television Programming*. Princeton, N.J.: Princeton University Press.

Haveman, Heather, and Marissa King. 2005. "Hellfire and Brimstone: Religious Politics in the Rise of American Magazines." Paper presented to the American Sociological Association. Philadelphia (August 12, 2005).

Hendershot, Heather. 2004. *Shaking the World for Jesus: Media and Evangelical Culture*. Chicago: University of Chicago.

Hirschman, Albert O. 1970. *Exit, Voice, and Loyalty: Responses to Decline in Firms, Organizations, and States*. Cambridge, Mass.: Harvard University Press.

Horkheimer, Max, and Theodor W. Adorno. 1944/1991. *Dialectic of Enlightenment*. New York: Continuum.

Hunter, James Davison. 1991. *Culture Wars: The Struggle to Define America*. New York: Basic Books.

Kaiser Family Foundation. 2007. *Parents, Children, and Media*. Menlo Park, Calif.: Kaiser Family Foundation. Available at: http://www.kff.org/entmedia/up load/7638.pdf (accessed March 1, 2007).

Katz, Michael L., and Carl Shapiro. 1985. "Network Externalities, Competition, and Compatibility." *American Economic Review* 75(3): 424–40.

Kunkel, Dale, Keren Eyal, Keli Finnerty, Erica Biely, and Edward Donnerstein. 2005. *Sex on TV 4*. Menlo Park, Calif.: Kaiser Family Foundation. Available at: http://www.kff.org/entmedia/upload/Sex-on-TV-4-Full-Report.pdf (accessed March 1, 2007).

Land, Richard D., and Frank D. York. 1998. *Send a Message to Mickey*. Nashville, Tenn.: Broadman & Holman.

Lewerenz, Spencer and Barbara Nicolosi, eds. 2005. *Behind the Screen: Hollywood Insiders on Faith, Film, and Culture*. Grand Rapids, Mich.: Baker Books.

Lichter, Linda S., S. Robert Lichter, and Stanley Rothman. 1983. "Hollywood and America: The Odd Couple." *Public Opinion*, January 1983, 54–58.

Lopes, Paul. 1992. "Innovation and Diversity In the Popular Music Industry, 1969 to 1990." *American Sociological Review* 57(1): 56–71.

Magazine Publishers of America. 2006. "Average Total Paid & Verified Circulation for Top 100 ABC Magazines." New York: Magazine Publishers of America. Available at: http://www.magazine.org/circulation/circulation_trends _and_magazine_handbook/22175.cfm (accessed March 1, 2007).

Media Dynamics. 2006. *Radio Dimensions*. New York: Media Dynamics.

Medved, Michael. 1992. *Hollywood vs. America: Popular Culture and the War on Traditional Values*. New York: HarperCollins.

Montgomery, Kathryn. 1989. *Target: Prime Time: Advocacy Groups and the Struggle Over the Entertainment Industry*. Oxford: Oxford University Press.

Neuman, W. Russell. 1991. *The Future of the Mass Audience*. Cambridge: Cambridge University Press.

Parents Television Council. 2007. *The Ratings Sham II: TV Executives Still Hiding Behind a System that Doesn't Work*. Los Angeles: Parents Television Council. Available at: http://www.parentstv.org/ptc/publications/reports/Ratings Study/RatingsShamII.pdf (accessed March 1, 2007).

Romanowski, William D. 1990. "Contemporary Christian Music: The Business of Music Ministry" In *American Evangelicals and the Mass Media*, edited by Quentin Schultze. Grand Rapids, Mich.: Zondervan Academic.

Salganik, Matthew J., Peter Sheridan Dodds, and Duncan J. Watts. 2006. "Experimental Study of Inequality and Unpredictability in an Artificial Cultural Market." *Science* 311(5762): 854–56. Available at: http://www.sciencemag .org/cgi/content/abstract/311/5762/854 (accessed March 1, 2007).

Schultze, Quentin J. 1990. "The Invisible Medium: Evangelical Radio" In *Ameri-*

328   Evangelicals and Democracy in America

can Evangelicals and the Mass Media, edited by Quentin Schultze. Grand Rapids, Mich.: Zondervan Academic.

———. 2003. *Christianity and the Mass Media in America*. East Lansing: Michigan State University Press.

Shields, Todd. 2004. "Activists Dominate Content Complaints: FCC: Parents' Group Accounts for over 98 Percent of Indecency Filings." *MEDIAWEEK*, December 6, 2004, 4–5.

Stavitsky, Alan G. 1995. "Guys in Suits with Charts: Audience Research in U.S. Public Radio" *Journal of Broadcasting & Electronic Media* 39(2): 177–89.

Stevenson, Tyler Wigg. 2007. *Brand Jesus: Christianity in a Consumerist Age*. New York: Seabury Books.

Tepper, Steven Jay. 2001. "Culture, Conflict, and Community: Struggles Over Art, Education, and History in American Cities." Ph.D. diss., Princeton University.

Thomas, Cal, and Ed Dobson. 1999. *Blinded by Might: Can the Religious Right Save America?* Grand Rapids, Mich.: Zondervan Academic.

Turow, Joseph. 1997. *Breaking Up America: Advertising and the New Media World*. Chicago: University of Chicago.

U.S. Bureau of the Census. 2008. *Statistical Abstract of the United States*, 127th ed. Washington, D.C.: U.S. Department of Commerce.

Webster, James. 2005. "Beneath a Veneer of Fragmentation: Television Audience Polarization in a Multichannel World." *Journal of Communication* 55(2): 366–82.

Weyrich, Paul. 1999. "Untitled Open Letter to Conservatives." Alexandria, Va.: Free Congress Foundation.

Wildmon, Donald. 1997. "It Is Time to End Religious Bigotry." In *Religion and Prime Time Television*, edited by Michael Suman. Westport, Conn.: Praeger.

Wuthnow, Robert D. 1988. *After Heaven: Spirituality in America Since the 1950s*. Berkeley: University of California Press.

Zarkin, Kimberly. 2003. *Anti-Indecency Groups and the Federal Communications Commission: A Study in the Politics of Broadcast Regulation*. Lewiston, N.Y.: Edwin Mellen Press.

Chapter 11

An Almost-Christian Nation? Constitutional Consequences of the Rise of the Religious Right

ROGERS M. SMITH

STRANGE AS it may seem today, in the mid-1960s, the Harvard theologian Harvey Cox wrote a bestseller, *The Secular City*, advancing the thesis that the United States was in transition "from the age of Christendom" to a "new era of urban secularity" (1966, 235). The emerging new age might be so secular, he suggested, "that our English word *God* will have to die." It would perhaps give way to some novel expression for the continuing, if hidden, spiritual significance of human existence (232).[1]

In the last quarter century, the electoral, legislative, and litigative influence of resurgent, newly politically engaged Religious Right organizations has generated an environment in which the notion that the United States might be becoming overwhelmingly secular seems bizarre. Scholars often link the rise of a politically mobilized religious, predominantly Christian conservative movement in modern America to two great constitutional controversies: restrictions on officially sponsored prayers and other religious observances in public schools stemming from the 1960s school prayer decisions, Engel v. Vitale, 370 U.S. 421 (1962), and Abington School District v. Schempp, 374 U.S. 203 (1963), and constitutional limits on state powers to regulate abortions, first announced in Roe v. Wade, 410 U.S. 113 (1973) (Wuthnow 1989, 55; Brown 2002, 22–23; Hacker 2005, 2, 24). Those two issues have undoubtedly been seminal in many ways. My argument here, however, is that to understand and assess recent conservative religious constitutional advocacy we must pay heed to a different, more institutionally oriented set of cases. When we do so, moreover, we may well conclude that though Cox's prediction of an era of secularity was grossly overstated, modern religious activists are feeling compelled to accord with modern secular norms of pluralistic democracy, rather than to push strenuously for recognition of the United States as a Christian nation or even a fundamentally religious people.

A major source of the emergence and of the mission of Religious Right political activism generally, and litigation in particular, has been concern to protect and enhance the distinctive social institutions that Christian fundamentalists and evangelicals forged throughout the twentieth century, initially as alternatives to the predominance of mainline Protestantism in the United States up through the early New Deal. To preserve and propagate their own visions of Christianity, Christian conservatives created radio and television programs, book stores, publications, schools, social service programs, community groups, and other organizations. Though otherwise largely apolitical, these institutions often sought and received access to public facilities or governmental assistance in creating facilities of their own. Perceived threats to different forms of such access and assistance have often been the initial spurs to heightened Christian Right political and judicial involvement. Beginning as far back as the 1940s, accelerating in electoral and legislative politics from the mid-1970s, and adding a heightened stress on litigative strategies in the late 1980s, much of the activism of religious conservative groups has been devoted to trying to ensure that government policies do not hinder these social institutions but instead assist them.

This goal helps explain some of the limiting features of Religious Right litigation that analysts have recently noted. In the last quarter century, religious conservatives have won important changes in prevailing constitutional doctrines governing state-church and, more broadly, state-society relations; but the changes have been far less than many in the Religious Right, particularly conservative Christians, have wished. In establishment clause cases, they have had most success when they have argued for equal treatment of religious and secular groups, including equal access to public forums and governmental funds for charitable purposes. In free exercise cases, their greatest success has come when they have joined religious claims to broader free speech claims. In consequence, they have often preserved and sometimes expanded important traditional accommodations of religious groups, such as tax exemptions for religious charitable activities and facilities and fundraising through the sale of tax-exempt bonds, and they have also gained or most often regained access to public institutions and public funding on an equal basis with other organizations. In so doing, they have successfully countered those movements in contemporary American liberal thought and politics that have sought to keep religion out of public institutions.

But to be sure of winning this much, religious litigators have foregone seeking the full-fledged recognition of America as a Christian nation, or at least one in which religions generally receive special recognition, protection, and privileges, that many religious conservatives desire. The political challenges of defining positions that can win the support of coalitions powerful enough to protect their core institutional interests in the modern United States also indicate that religious conservatives are not likely to be able to go much further in these directions. Their distinctive social institutions are likely to survive and thrive, serving as a basis as well as a motive for influential political and legal mobilization. At times they may win policy victories that many secular liberals and other varieties of religious believers find disagreeable, even disturbing. But there is no danger of theocracy. Under the constitutional regime of equal treatment and broad freedoms of expression that religious conservatives have felt compelled to support, they are likely to remain only one set of voices among many, and a minority set, in modern America's pluralistic democracy.

The Spread of Conservative Christian Institutions

Let me first rehearse some well-documented but pertinent background circumstances. Although the American founders created the first national state in history without an established church, most Americans have always professed religions, and national, state, and local governments have provided many types of accommodation and assistance to religiously affiliated schools, hospitals, child welfare, and other social service agencies through much of U.S. history (Minow 2003, 10–11). In the nineteenth century, when the courts did not regard the First Amendment as restricting the states and when, in any case, most Americans thought it appropriate for governments to support broadly Christian values and endeavors, these kinds of aid were rarely challenged in litigation (Morgan 1972, 27–52; Monsma 1996, 13, 40).

Most of those forms of assistance have, in fact, never ended. They have only gone to a greater range of religiously affiliated organizations over time.[2] Since the mid-1920s, especially, and accelerating in the last third of the twentieth century, those organizations have included distinctly fundamentalist, evangelical, and recently Religious Right institutions. Most historians have long agreed that as the mainline Protestant establishment, represented after 1908 in the Federal Council of Churches, embraced a Social Gospel agenda of reform politics and more liberal theological views, many more traditionalist Protestants became disaffected. They favored premillennialist beliefs that, seeing little hope for progress, often blended with politically conservative or apolitical stances; evangelism aimed at personal salvation, not social reform; and greater biblical literalism. The turning point in their relationship to mainline Protestantism and American public life more generally is often said to be the Scopes Monkey Trial of 1925, in which John Scopes was convicted of violating Tennessee's Butler Act, which banned the teaching of "evolution theory" in public schools. Although Scopes lost the case, the widespread ridicule heaped on state's law and its evangelical defender, William Jennings Bryan, convinced many fundamentalists and evangelicals that they were no longer welcome in the nation's public spaces (Ahlstrom 1972, 909–10; Silk 1989, 280; Balmer 2006, xvi).

They did, however, continue to shape public policies and institutions in the many largely more rural locales where their members constituted the great bulk of the citizenry, and also began creating new institutional spaces of their own. Bible institutes tripled from 1930 to 1950, along with the proliferation of fundamentalist religious magazines, missionary agencies, publishing houses, book stores, and, perhaps most momentously for the funding and growth of these organizations, radio programs with charismatic, essentially nondenominational preachers and inspirational gospel music (Ahlstrom 1972, 913–14; Carpenter 1984, 6, 11; Hart 2001, 24–25, 41n21). With the advent of television and the spectacular Billy Graham Crusades of the 1950s, evangelicals were set on the path that would lead to modern televangelists who are national celebrities with tremendous fundraising capacities, and to megachurches that break from traditional liturgy, hymns, and formality in favor of comfortable dress, revivalist sermons, popular music, films and videos, and facilities supplying the shopping-mall conveniences of fast food franchises, fitness and recreation centers, and numerous family services (Silk 1989, 280, 282; Wolfe 2003, 26–31, 250; Diane Henriques, "Religion Trumps Regulation as Legal Exemptions Grow," *New York Times*, October 8, 2006, A1). From the 1930s to the present day, these still-burgeoning institutions have been the organizational backbone of modern conservative Christian movements, providing both money and members. More than many scholars have stressed, they have also provided a key motive for conservative Christians to become more politically active at the national level.

Writers have correctly contended that conservative evangelicals began organizing in the late 1930s and early 1940s in opposition to the more internationalist, more pro-labor, and less militantly anticommunist stances of the Federal Council of Churches (Schneider 1989, 110–11). Carl McIntire's American Council of Christian Churches formed in 1941 explicitly to attack Federal Council of Churches positions on virtually every theological and political issue. But it was the National Association of Evangelicals (NAE), founded the next year with the intent not only to resist religious liberalism but also to assist evangelical groups actively, that proved more enduring (Carpenter 1984, 12; Silk 1989, 278–79). By the 1950s, the Eisenhower administration had already begun to pay greater attention than ever before to the Christian conservatives who supported its main domestic and foreign policies (Matthews 1992, 135–36). The Federal Council's erstwhile policy spokesman, John Foster Dulles, had become secretary of state, but though he still met with them, he moved away from their positions (King 1989, 128–132).

Yet though domestic and foreign policy concerns as well as religious differences certainly helped fuel evangelical organizing in this period and won them greater political recognition, the primary "issue which helped galvanize and unite evangelicals" into forming the NAE was "access to air waves" (Matthews 1992, 39). In the early 1940s, the national networks were apportioning free broadcast time to Catholics, Jews, and Protestants, with the Federal Council of Churches treated as the sole representative of Protestantism. Network executives also resisted selling time to religious broadcasters, in part because their programs included extensive fundraising appeals. Establishing an office in Washington, D.C., and lobbying hard, the NAE sought successfully to preserve and extend evangelist access to paid and free radio and television broadcasting, strengthening this key organizational and financial instrument of evangelical groups. According to veteran evangelical journalist Arthur Matthews, the broadcast access issue was central to the NAE's formation and early agenda because it was "the point at which Bible-believing Christians throughout the country thought their freedom was most at risk" (Matthews 1992, 47; see also Ostling, 1984, 49 and Carpenter, 1984, 27, 44).

Evangelical broadcasts and revival crusades then expanded their numbers and institutional basis throughout the 1950s. Even so, in the 1960s Christian conservatives again found themselves out of step with many of the most vibrant domestic political developments of the day. The NAE and other conservative Protestant groups questioned the legitimacy of the Catholic John Kennedy's presidential candidacy, adding to their image as reactionary foes of a more pluralistic modern America (Silk 1989, 292; Matthews 1992, 138). The fading of strident 1950s anticommunism with which conservative evangelists like McIntire and Billy James Hargis were identified, and Hargis's eventual discrediting after a sex scandal, also worked against a strong conservative religious presence in public life (Pierard 1984, 163–65).

Perhaps most important, few conservative evangelicals embraced the civil rights activism of the 1950s and 1960s, and a number instead responded to school desegregation orders by creating new fundamentalist

Christian academies that tended to be overwhelmingly white. From the 1960s to the 1990s, and especially with the advent of court-ordered bussing for desegregation in the 1970s, these schools would grow to one-fifth of all private schools in the nation, with 90 percent of the conservative Christian private schools created after Brown v. Board of Education, 347 U.S. 483 (1954), and nearly 40 percent located in the south (Cremin 1988, 100; McLaughlin and Broughman 1997). Although these schools gradually became more racially diverse, they did so under governmental pressures that white conservative Christians resisted. Partly as a result of civil rights tensions, black evangelicals formed what became the National Black Evangelical Association in the 1960s, officially with amicable relations with the NAE, but clearly without a strong sense of a shared agenda (Matthews 1992, 143). As a result of these and related difficulties, the evangelical Christian right "was in a state of disarray" by the early 1970s (Pierard 1984, 169).

The Birth of the "Religious Right"

At this juncture, the U.S. Supreme Court decided Roe v. Wade, an event sometimes regarded as pivotal in the rise of the Religious Right (Brown 2002, 22). It certainly cannot be denied that opposition to abortion figures centrally in Religious Right agendas today. Also in this period, perhaps the most influential American liberal philosopher of the second half of the twentieth century, John Rawls, published *A Theory of Justice*, a work that gave elaborate philosophic expression to the egalitarian reform spirit of the 1960s. There Rawls argued that public institutions should be structured so that "the concept of right is prior to that of the good," a criterion that, as Rawls developed and modified his position, suggested that candidates and officeholders should moderate certain kinds of religious advocacy and always add secular arguments.[3] Some writers have suggested that at a deeper level, the "emerging movements in Protestant and Catholic circles" that sought to return religion to the public square arose in reaction to the spread in American culture of these sorts of liberal political and philosophic views, which they saw as dismissive and repressive of religious perspectives (Skillen 1998, 57, 61, 68–74; see also Carter 1993, 54–58, 216).

But though for some, both Roe and Rawls would become symbols of how, in their eyes, modern secular elites disregard traditional religious values, few would suggest that the Religious Right arose directly due to mass popular outrage with modern Rawlsian liberal doctrines, or even cognate legal advocacy by the American Civil Liberties Union (ACLU) and other organizations. More surprisingly, liberal evangelical Randall Balmer recently argued that when Roe was decided, "the vast majority of evangelical leaders said virtually nothing," while "many of those who did comment," such as W. A. Criswell, pastor of the First Baptist Church in Dallas and former president of the Southern Baptist Convention, "actually applauded the decision" (2006, 12). Balmer noted that at a 1990 conference, veteran Religious Right activist Paul Weyrich stated that he had "utterly failed" to prompt mass evangelical political involvement over the issues of school prayer and abortion, as well as the proposed Equal Rights Amendment (2006, 14–15).

But if not the school prayer or abortion decisions or more general liberal intellectual and cultural trends, what, then, spurred modern Religious Right political and legal mobilization? Perhaps the primary motivation was concern to protect public financial benefits for religious institutions, especially schools. The early 1970s were a period when the courts were less receptive to aid to religious schools than in any period before or since; and Weyrich contended that Religious Right organizing began to take off specifically when in these years the Internal Revenue Service denied tax-exempt status to Christian schools perceived as engaging in racial discrimination (Balmer 2006, 14–15). Steven Brown quoted Jerry Falwell as similarly saying that it was the IRS's new policy on tax exemption that "made us realize that we had to fight for our lives" (2002, 23). That level of anxiety may seem somewhat inexplicable, given that many evangelical religious institutions did not have racially discriminatory polices. But many favored fellow believers in hiring, had conservative religious content in their education programs, adhered to traditional gender roles, and had other practices that, they feared, might be viewed by secular liberals as a basis for removing the sorts of government privileges they had long possessed. To be sure, a broad and internally diverse movement such as the Religious Right is never caused by any single factor. Still, it seems fair to say that, just as the National Association of Evangelicals first coalesced around an effort to preserve access to the public airwaves for their profitable programming, at least one major source of concerted political action by modern Religious Right groups was their desire to maintain governmental policies that helped them to finance their schools and many of their other institutions.

Significantly for the development of this new political and legal activism, that goal did not easily lend itself to any claim of privileged status for religious institutions, much less Christian ones. When the Internal Revenue Service adopted the new tax exemption policy to which Weyrich and Falwell referred, it did so in the wake of recent Supreme Court decisions underlining that federal, state, and local tax exemptions could not be provided to religious groups per se. In the leading case, Walz v. Tax Commission, 397 U.S. 664 (1970), Chief Justice Warren Burger did rule, with only Justice William Douglas in dissent, that the New York City Tax Commission had acted constitutionally in granting property tax exemptions to "religious organizations for religious properties used solely for religious worship" (666). Burger noted that all fifty states had tax exemptions for places of worship, most by constitutional guarantees, and that the federal income tax had also always not applied to churches, part of an unbroken pattern of congressionally authorized exemptions that went back to the nation's origins (676).

He stressed, however, that New York had not given these exemptions to "churches as such." They were part of a "broad class of property owned by nonprofit, quasi-public corporations which include hospitals, libraries, playgrounds, scientific, professional, historical, and patriotic groups," all deemed "beneficial and stabilizing influences in community life." Qualification for such tax exemptions was, moreover, "not perpetual or immutable." It could be lost if the activities of tax-exempt groups took them "outside the classification" of publicly valuable entities (Walz v. Tax Commission, 673).

Burger also acknowledged that in practice, churches varied greatly in the extent of the social welfare programs or other "good works" they undertook. But he thought that for that very reason, government should not seek to evaluate the worth of each church's particular social welfare efforts. To do so would be a source of extensive "day-to-day" involvements and potential "confrontations" between religious groups and government agencies that the First Amendment sought to minimize. Similarly, elimination of the exemption entirely "would tend to expand the involvement of government by giving rise to tax valuation of church property, tax liens, tax foreclosures," and the conflicts that "follow in the train" of those legal processes (Walz v. Tax Commission, 674).

Pushed far enough, that argument might suggest that the exemption was in fact constitutionally required; but neither Burger nor the other justices who wrote in the case made any such suggestion explicitly. The chief justice instead cited a precedent (Gibbons v. District of Columbia, 116 U.S. 404 [1886]), in which the Court had overturned a real estate tax exemption for income-producing church property, though it also indicated willingness to uphold a lesser tax rate (Walz v. Tax Commission, 680). He also emphasized throughout that though churches could continue to receive this exemption, they did so not as an effort aimed at "supporting religion" or "sponsorship," but instead as a way to provide conditions conducive to the "free exercise of all forms of religious belief" and the similar flourishing of many other types of socially beneficial groups (673, 675, 678). As Justice William Brennan noted in concurring, the Court held only that "government may properly include religious institutions among the variety of private, nonprofit groups that receive tax exemptions, for each group contributes to the diversity of association, viewpoint, and enterprise essential to a vigorous, pluralistic society" (689). Justice John Marshall Harlan's concurrence similarly avowed that as long as the exemption "includes groups that pursue cultural, moral, or spiritual improvement in multifarious secular ways," including "antitheological, atheistic, or agnostic" groups, the tax exemption was consistent with what he saw as a constitutional demand for "neutrality," which "requires an equal protection mode of analysis" (697).

On the question of just how religious groups contributed to public life, there were differences in the reasoning of Burger, Brennan, Harlan, and obviously Douglas in dissent. Still, all four suggested that the tax exemption would have been questionable had it not extended equally to a wide range of other socially beneficial nonprofits. Christian conservatives and all other religious groups must have realized that they were far more likely to maintain their tax exemptions, winning support from judges and allies among secular nonprofit organizations, if they did not seek any exclusive or special treatment for religious bodies. They needed instead to present themselves as meriting the same status as other socially beneficial groups, in line with the conservative Justice Harlan's recommended "equal protection mode of analysis."

That conclusion was reinforced by a number of Supreme Court decisions over the next three years, both favorable and unfavorable to religious litigants. The favorable cases included upholding direct federal grants to religiously affiliated colleges and universities in Connecticut, Tilton v. Richardson, 403 U.S. 672 (1971), and a decision sustaining a South Carolina law that authorized a state agency to issue tax-exempt revenue bonds to assist in financing capital construction by higher educational institutions, including a Baptist-controlled college, Hunt v. McNair, 413 U.S. 734 (1973). Although in each case the Court perpetuated its historical pattern of approving most forms of governmental financial aid to religious institutions, it did stress that the institutions in question all served "secular education goals" and were not "pervasively sectarian" (Hunt v. McNair, 743–44). Again the lesson was that religious institutions were more likely to sustain their privileges if they stressed the contributions they made in common with nonreligious organizations, rather than claimed any special status.

Beginning with Lemon v. Kurzman, 403 U.S. 602 (1971), moreover, the Court embarked on a series of decisions through the 1970s that struck down many forms of financial aid for parochial schools, now seen as involving the sorts of "excessive entanglement" between church and state that Walz had held to be forbidden by the establishment clause.[4] These cases largely involved Catholic schools and did not spark any conservative Protestant political mobilizations. But they did reinforce lawyerly awareness that public programs seen as aids to religion were likely to be viewed by modern judges far more critically than they had been in most of America's past.

At the lower court level, the D.C. federal district court handed down a decision in 1971 initiating the developments that would make many conservative Christians particularly anxious about preserving their own traditional governmental privileges. In Green v. Connally, 330 F. Supp. 1150 (1971), African American parents in Mississippi sued to enjoin U.S. Treasury officials from according tax-exempt status to private schools in the state that discriminated against their children. In response to the suit, the IRS announced it would no longer allow tax-exempt status or permit deductions for contributions in the case of any private schools that practiced racial discrimination. They could not be viewed as "charitable" institutions, for they operated "contrary to declared Federal public policy," as embodied in the Civil Rights Act of 1964. The court recognized that "the promotion of a healthy pluralism" was one purpose of the tax exemption, but it held that the "declared Federal public policy against support for racial discrimination" overrode "any assertion of value in practicing private racial discrimination, whether ascribed to philosophical pluralism or divine inspiration" (33). Although the schools challenged in the case were not religious institutions, the court discussed the recent Walz ruling, holding that it did not prevent interpreting the First Amendment "in harmony with" the post–Civil War amendments by requiring religious institutions receiving the "indirect economic benefit" of tax exemption to operate in accord with federal opposition to racial segregation (52–55).

With this ruling, and with conservative Christian schools proliferating just as many federal courts were imposing aggressive desegregation orders, it was inevitable that the IRS would scrutinize the new evangelical institutions for practices of racial discrimination. Though Weyrich and Falwell later excoriated Jimmy Carter, an evangelical Christian whom Pat Robertson and many other evangelicals supported in 1976, for setting the IRS on this course, the case that most spurred them into action actually began before his election. Bob Jones University, founded in the first wave of new evangelical institutions in 1927 and located in Greenville, South Carolina since 1947, banned all African American students until 1971. In response to the IRS policy announced during the Green litigation, it then permitted married African Americans to enroll. The university also sought a ruling prohibiting the IRS from revoking its tax exemption, but in Bob Jones University v. Simon, 416 U.S. 725 (1974), the Supreme Court held that no action could be taken until the IRS did so. In 1975, the university permitted unmarried African Americans to enroll but continued its long-standing ban on interracial dating. The IRS then moved to revoke its tax exemption in January 1976, just before Carter's inauguration, with the change retroactive to 1970 (Martin 1996, 168–73; Turner 1997, 226–28; Balmer 2006, xvi, 14–16).

The university fought the IRS decision in court, winning at the district level, losing on appeal at the circuit court level, and then appealing to the Supreme Court. But though these efforts contributed to the first major mobilization of the Religious Right, with Jerry Falwell forming the Moral Majority in 1979, the main focus of conservative religious activism in this period was not litigation. It was on legislative lobbying, including congressional efforts to prevent the IRS from implementing policies that would deny tax-exempt status to "religious, or church-operated schools," and on the election of candidates favorable to evangelical Christian policy ideas, especially Ronald Reagan in 1980 (Pierard 1984, 169–70; Hacker 2005, 6; Balmer 2006, 15–16).[5] As president, Reagan tried to get the Justice and Treasury departments to drop the denial of the tax exemption, but a political outcry led the administration to reverse its position. Perhaps wary of the Reagan Justice Department, the Court then invited the distinguished African American lawyer William Coleman to file an amicus brief on behalf of the government. Finally it ruled against the university, with only Associate Justice William Rehnquist in dissent, Bob Jones University v. U.S., 461 U.S. 574 (1983). The university paid $1 million in back taxes and saw donations decline for a time (Turner 1997, 230–36). It seemed clear to many conservative evangelicals that their organizations were indeed at risk of losing forms of beneficial governmental treatment they had long enjoyed, whatever their other dissatisfactions with modern American life.

Although the main conservative Christian response to the threat of losing their tax exemptions was political, in 1975 the Christian Legal Society (CLS), founded in 1961 to promote fellowship among Christian lawyers, created a Center for Law and Religious Freedom, the first Christian Right litigation organization (Brown 2002, 31). When the Bob Jones case went to the Supreme Court, the center filed an amicus brief on behalf of the university, as did the National Association of Evangelicals, the American Baptist Churches, and Congressman Trent Lott. The ACLU, the NAACP, and the United Church of Christ, among others, filed briefs on behalf of the IRS decision.

For the Christian Legal Society lawyers, the Bob Jones case represented a challenge to the preferred litigation approach they were developing, a challenge they proved unable to meet to the satisfaction of the Supreme Court. From early on, informed by the Walz opinions and the school cases, they generally sought to argue that religious groups should have equal access to public programs and institutions, including tax exemptions for all publicly beneficial nonprofit organizations (Brown 2002, 69; Casey 2006, 7). But the IRS policy denied access equally to all racially discriminatory groups, so their brief stressed instead that the policy unduly burdened the free exercise of sincere religious beliefs and thereby threatened all religious practices (Center for Law and Religious Freedom 1981, 4–11). It added that Congress had not directly authorized the IRS to deny tax exemptions on this basis and that religious freedoms should not be impaired on the basis of inference (13). In Smith v. Wade,

461 U.S. 622 (1983), Justice Rehnquist's dissent agreed with the second argument—but, like all the other justices, he accepted that Congress could deny religious groups the exemption on these grounds if it did so decide, rejecting the claim that the free exercise clause gave them any special constitutional privileges in this regard. Thus the Bob Jones litigation underlined that conservative Christian groups were not likely to win in court by claiming that they as religious communities enjoyed any constitutionally preferred status.

The Turn to "Equal Treatment"

At the same time, conservative religious lawyers began to gain some signal judicial and legislative victories with the alternative equal access or equal treatment approach. In Widmar v. Vincent, 454 U.S. 263 (1981), with the NAE filing an amicus brief, the Supreme Court sustained a challenge to the decision of the University of Missouri at Kansas in 1977 to withdraw from student religious groups the same access to university facilities it provided to all other registered student organizations. With only Justice Byron White in dissent, the Court ruled that rather than avoiding a form of religious establishment, the university's new policy violated the free speech rights of the student group in question, which religious speakers possessed on the same basis all others (269, 274).

Building on this precedent, Christian Legal Society lawyers helped draft the Equal Access Act of 1984 (20 U.S.C. §4071–74), requiring public secondary schools that offered their facilities to noncurriculum student groups to do so on a nondiscriminatory basis. With the charismatic Messianic Jewish lawyer Jay Sekulow arguing on behalf of a student Christian club denied the opportunity to meet in a Nebraska high school, the Supreme Court sustained the act in Board of Westside Community School District v. Mergens, 496 U.S. 248 (1990). Since the passage of the Equal Access Act, conservative Christians have gone on to organize thousands of new student Bible groups that meet in public schools. But in an example of why many conservatives are dissatisfied with the equal treatment approach, the act has most recently been invoked chiefly on behalf of gay and lesbian student groups (Hacker 2005, 17–18, 24–27; ReligiousTolerance.org 2007).

Yet out of a combination of principle and pragmatism, the leading Religious Right litigation groups have since adhered overwhelming to equal treatment approaches to both establishment and free exercise issues. In 1982, former CLS lawyer John W. Whitehead founded the second major Christian litigation body, the Rutherford Institute. It has sought aggressively to initiate lawsuits broadening religious freedom rather than waiting for hostile governmental actions, in keeping with Whitehead's philosophy of Christian activism. But from the outset,

Whitehead has championed religious free expression not as specially privileged, only as a part of broad and equal liberties for all expression, professing not to aim "to have a Christian nation, but to enable religious people to survive" (Lienesch 1993, 167, 187–90; Brown 2002, 32–35). This position has helped sustain laws providing federal funds to religious groups on the same basis as secular ones. Notably, in Bowen v. Kendrick, 487 U.S. 589 (1988), the Court sustained the 1981 Adolescent Family Life Act (AFLA), which expressly included religious groups among those eligible for federal grants to organizations providing counseling on premarital sex and pregnancy. With the Rutherford Institute filing a brief, Chief Justice Rehnquist ruled that because the funds were available to nonreligious groups and financed essentially nonreligious services, religious groups were not rendered ineligible because their counseling might reference religious beliefs (Bowen v. Kendrick, 592, 607, 613).

The same subordination of religious free exercise claims to free speech arguments in order to keep religious groups eligible for public aid has also been the leitmotif of Sekulow's advocacy. He led his own small religious litigation firm from 1987 to 1990 and then became lead attorney in 1990 for the American Center for Law and Justice (ACLJ), founded by Pat Robertson to be a "Christian counterpart to the ACLU" (Brown 2002, 36; Hacker 2005, 21–23). In Mergens and subsequent cases, Sekulow and the ACLJ have consistently argued that religious groups are entitled to a "place at the table," but that free expression also extends to "the Satanists and the Nazis," despite predictable objections from others in the Religious Right (Hacker 2005, 25).

It seems likely that, scarred by the defeat of distinctive free exercise claims in Bob Jones University and many other cases of the 1980s involving organizational financial interests, most of those shaping Religious Right litigation in the past quarter century have concluded that they would risk losing essential protections if they undertook more militant litigation strategies, claiming privileges for Christian groups or even for religious groups that others could be denied.[6] Their concerns for "institutional maintenance" required them to adopt arguments that could actually win in court, especially given that they found they could not always rely on promised support elsewhere (Ivers 1992, 247, 265). Despite their enthusiasm for Reagan, many Religious Right activists felt that his administration provided them relatively little in the way of concrete improvements either in public policy or assistance for their institutions during the 1980s (Pierard 1984, 170; Lienesch 1993, 14). The aggressive lobbying tactics pursued by Jerry Falwell's Moral Majority also seemed to generate more controversy than benefits, and he dissolved his organization in 1989, though Pat Robertson created the Christian Coalition the same year to carry similar efforts forward.

But even as religious conservatives experienced disappointments in other political arenas, equal treatment arguments were providing protection and some new gains for religious groups both in establishment and free exercise judicial decisions. So, though the Religious Right's focus on electoral and legislative activities by no means disappeared, many in the movement came to agree that they should devote more energy than in the past to winning in court. Not only did older groups like the NAE begin to litigate more often in the 1980s; toward the end of the decade, new conservative religious litigation groups began to proliferate rapidly (Ivers 1992, 255–56; Hacker 2005, 7–9). In 1990, Matthew Staver founded Liberty Counsel, later associated with Falwell, which has also stressed free expression arguments, rather than specifically religious free exercise claims, in its litigation (Brown 2002, 55, 58; Hacker 2005, 39–41). Donald Wildmon's American Family Association (AFA), which had a network of 160 radio affiliates by the late 1980s, also created a Center for Law and Policy in 1990. It did so in part to counter a libel suit by *Penthouse* magazine, filed in response to an AFA boycott campaign, and to protect its newsletter from a separate lawsuit. The new center won both cases, though again on free expression rather than free exercise grounds (Hacker 2005, 93–96). Then in 1994, a number of Religious Right leaders, including Wildmon and also Bill Bright of the Campus Crusade for Christ, James Dobson of Focus on the Family, and James Kennedy of Coral Ridge Ministries, joined in creating the Alliance Defense Fund (ADF), in hopes of achieving coordination among the burgeoning conservative Christian litigation groups. In part because of controversies surrounding its initial leader, Alan Sears, the ADF has never succeeded in playing that role. Still, it has provided many grants to religious litigators, striving to insure that Religious Right activists file in every Supreme Court case on religion, as they have done unfailingly since 1990 (Brown 2002, 41–52).

The Qualified Triumphs of Equal Treatment Strategies

In the course of so much litigation, many Religious Right lawyers have not lacked for aspirations to win more resounding support for doctrines assigning religions in general, and Christianity in particular, the sort of preferred position Protestant Christianity enjoyed in practice during most of American history. Although for litigators like Sekulow and Staver, winning religious groups a place at the table equal to but not superior to others appears to represent a principled position, for others, the stresses on equal access, equal treatment, and equal freedom of expression for all seem to represent second-best positions, concessions to the political realities of a pluralist society. Exemplary here is Michael

McConnell, architect of some of the Religious Rights' greatest judicial victories and now himself a federal judge on the U.S. Tenth Circuit Court of Appeals. As an assistant professor at the University of Chicago Law School, McConnell argued in 1985 that the First Amendment's clauses banning religious establishment and protecting free exercise should both be construed to facilitate specifically religious liberty, often through giving religious groups special treatment in the form of accommodations not provided others (1985, 3, 5). Five years later in a major *Harvard Law Review* article, McConnell contended that the free exercise clause could plausibly be interpreted as compelling exemptions for religious groups from "generally applicable laws," but did hold that religious associations included groups concerned to raise doubts about religion (1990, 1415–416). In these years, McConnell was also becoming a favorite attorney for the Christian Legal Society and other conservative Christian groups (Brown 2002, 27, 66).

But the same year McConnell published his free exercise argument, the Supreme Court, in Department of Human Resources of Oregon v. Smith, 494 U.S. 872 (1990), delivered a devastating blow to efforts to win constitutionally privileged status for religious groups. Two members of the Native American Church sued to obtain unemployment benefits denied them by the state when they were fired from their jobs at a private drug rehabilitation center after their employers learned that they regularly used peyote as part of Native American Church ceremonies. Because few among the Religious Right identified with these religious claims to drug use, no Religious Right litigators participated in the case (Brown 2002, 77). But the Court's leading conservative, Justice Antonin Scalia, writing for a bare majority, not only refused to limit the state's powers to deny benefits to consumers of illegal drugs. He also denied that any "individual's religious beliefs" could ever "excuse him from compliance with an otherwise valid law" (Department of Human Resources of Oregon v. Smith, 878–89). Scalia also argued that free exercise claims should only receive "strict scrutiny" protection, with the Court determining if burdensome laws are justified as necessary for "compelling" governmental interests, when they were combined with other constitutional protections, "such as freedom of speech and press" (881).

The decision aroused a thundering chorus of criticism that included most liberal as well as conservative champions of religious and expressive liberties, the ACLU, and the ACLJ. With the CLS Center for Law and Religious Freedom again closely involved in the drafting, Congress quickly and overwhelmingly passed the Religious Freedom Restoration Act of 1993 (42 U.S.C. § 2000bb), signed into law by President Bill Clinton. It sought to restore the "compelling interest" test even when a case involved only religious free exercise claims (Casey 2006, 8). But in City of Boerne v. Flores, Archbishop of San Antonio, 521 U.S. 507 (1997), a case involving the freedom of a church to restructure its own historical landmark building, Justice Anthony Kennedy ruled for a plurality of the Court that Congress had no power to command the sort of scrutiny the Court should apply to constitutional claims (535–36). The Court was undeterred by numerous amici briefs for the church, including ones by Jay Sekulow for the ACLJ and Michael McConnell representing the United States Catholic Conference (510–11). The message remained clear: the Court was very receptive to claims that religious expression is strictly protected, like other forms of expression, but not more so. Religious Right litigants remained well advised to structure their arguments as general free speech claims, not as claims for distinctive rights of religious free exercise. Since 1994, they have done so in most of the cases they have litigated and in most of the cases they have won (Brown 2002, 78, 100).

And through the 1990s to the present, even as the Court has rejected strong free exercise claims, arguments cast in favor of equal treatment also have continued to win renewed and sometimes expanded access to public facilities and public funds for Religious Right organizations. The capacity of this position to build broad coalitions was evident in Lamb's Chapel v. Center Moriches School District, 508 U.S. 384 (1993), where the ACLJ, the ACLU, the AFL-CIO, the Christian Legal Society, the Rutherford Institute, and the National Jewish Commission on Law and Public Affairs all filed briefs on behalf of an evangelical church seeking to use school facilities to show a religious film series on family values and child rearing (386). With some differences in reasoning but no dissents, the Supreme Court addressed the issue strictly as a free speech matter and upheld the church's right of access to public facilities for its expression on the same basis as other community groups (387, 397).

The landmark case in this regard is generally seen to be Rosenberger v. The Rector and Visitors of the University of Virginia, 515 U.S. 819 (1995). The University of Virginia had denied to a new evangelical Christian student group, Wide Awake Productions, aid from the university's student activity fund. Michael McConnell argued on behalf of the students that their religious speech was entitled to equal status with nonreligious speakers, such as gay rights groups (1995, 5–7). For the majority of the Court, Justice Kennedy similarly treated the issue as fundamentally one of free speech for all, not protection for religious free exercise (Rosenberger v. University of Virginia, 828–29). Given that it was a 5–4 decision, the case probably could not have been won by arguments stressing special religious claims. Subsequently, McConnell argued before Congress and in some of his scholarship for equal rights of expression for religious and nonreligious speakers, foregoing in these writings any explicit advocacy of distinctive free exercise claims (1998, 38).

In the wake of Rosenberger, arguments stressing equal treatment, equal access, and free speech then won a series of further but often closely contested victories for public aid to religious schools, a cause that increasingly brought evangelical Protestants and their modern academies into alliance with Catholic institutions they had historically opposed. Overturning two 1985 precedents, Agostini v. Felton, 521 U.S. 203 (1997), held that the City of New York could send public employees inside parochial schools to provide remedial education to disadvantaged students. Justice Sandra Day O'Connor ruled for a 5–4 Court that such instruction did not amount to state religious "indoctrination" or "endorsement" and involved no excessive "entanglement," so there was no reason why disadvantaged parochial students should not also receive this public assistance (230–35).

Then, in Mitchell v. Helms, 530 U.S. 793 (2000), a 6–3 Court permitted the public schools in Jefferson Parish, Louisiana, to loan computer software and hardware to local religious schools (801). It did not matter that the institutions might be seen as "pervasively sectarian" as long as they served the community's educational objectives. Representing the petitioners, Michael McConnell argued that religious groups were entitled to "receive their fair share of neutrally available public funds" for such services, without having "to secularize their own speech as the price of receiving equal treatment." Even so, his brief firmly rejected any claim of privileged status for religion. It stated that "the Establishment Clause prohibits the government from expending money for religious purposes; it prohibits targeting public subsidies to religious groups, discriminating in their favor, or endorsing their messages; and it prohibits the government itself from promoting religion by supplying materials or personnel that advance indoctrinating messages" (1999, 15).

Again, to have sought more doctrinally would probably have resulted in the loss of Court approval in a context where important financial aid was at stake. The Mitchell case also helped pave the way to an even more significant decision, Zelman v. Simmons-Harris, 536 U.S. 639 (2001). There a 5–4 Court rewarded Religious Right litigants filing amicus briefs by sustaining Cleveland's voucher program that gave parents public funds to pay part of the costs of their children's attendance at parochial schools (649, 653). In contrast, when Alan Sears and Jay Sekulow sought to persuade the Court that the free exercise clause, especially, prevented the State of Washington from denying scholarship funds to a theology student, seven of the nine justices balked (2003, 15–16). Consistent with his opinion in the Bob Jones case that had so alarmed conservative Christians, Chief Justice Rehnquist ruled that there was no constitutional obligation to assist religious free exercise, even when the state was choosing to finance those pursuing other ways of life. Significantly, in Locke v. Davey, 540 U.S. 712 (2004), the justices saw no burden on the student's free speech rights or equal protection rights, which might have turned the tide. It remains true, then, that Religious Right litigants face serious risks of losing public access and public aid if they cast their arguments as religious free exercise claims alone, much less as contentions for the privileged status of Christianity.[7]

Charitable Choice

Equal treatment arguments have also continued to serve Religious Right advocates well on another front that many see as critical to the flourishing of their social institutions. Operating in legislative rather than litigative processes, Christian conservatives have built on the provisions of the Adolescent Family Life Act that explicitly included religious groups as recipients of public funds for social services, provisions upheld as facially constitutional in Bowen v. Kendrick. In 1995, Carl Esbeck, a law professor at the University of Missouri, sent draft legislation to conservative Christian Senator John Ashcroft designed to ensure that faith-based organizations could receive federal funds to provide welfare services (Esbeck 1998, 21–22; Sider 2005, 485–89). Those organizations were, moreover, to include not only social service bodies associated with religious groups. Congregations themselves were now also to be eligible to receive federal grants, so that churches too small to have affiliated nonprofits could still get assistance for their direct charitable work (Minow 2003, 12). The practice, in the 1960s and 1970s especially, of giving government funds to church-sponsored nonprofit service organizations, but not to churches, often made it both politically and legally easier for governments to impose restrictions on the bodies they were financing than would have been the case if the churches had received aid (Carlson-Thies 2001, 112). The flip side of greater liberty for churches was understood to be lack of eligibility for many sorts of direct public funding. Now that limitation was to end.

Supported by Religious Right advocates such as the Christian Legal Society, the idea, deemed *charitable choice*, caught on quickly (Casey 2006, 8). Congress enacted charitable choice provisions specifically requiring governments to include faith-based organizations when commissioning social services from nongovernmental agencies in the landmark Personal Responsibility and Work Opportunity Reconciliation Act that ended the Aid to Families with Dependent Children (AFDC) program in 1996. It went on to include similar provisions in the Welfare-to-Work Program in 1997, the Community Services Block Grant in 1998, and a substance abuse law in 2000. Both presidential candidates endorsed the concept in the 2000 election campaign, and President George W. Bush then established an Office of Faith-Based and Community Initiatives that further promoted federal aid to charitable religious groups, including churches (Carlson-Thies 2001, 117–23; Chaves 2003, 30; Sider 2005, 485).

The Supreme Court has not yet ruled on the substance of these charitable choice measures. But in Hein v. Freedom from Religion Foundation, Sup. Ct. Docket 06–157, decided June 25, 2007, Justice Samuel Alito ruled for a plurality that included Chief Justice John Roberts and Justice Kennedy, with concurring votes from Justices Scalia and Thomas, that taxpayers lack standing to challenge these programs as First Amendment violations. In briefs in the case, charitable choice proponents defended such programs as consistent with the modern equal treatment approach that provides "a level playing field" for religious organizations, without any preferences either way (Carlson-Thies 2001, 119; Sider 2005). The Court's ruling did not address those claims, but it may well be significant that both Alito and Roberts effectively sided with the programs said to embody them.

The sociologist Mark Chaves argued, however, that the need for charitable choice initiatives to counter exclusion of religious organizations from public programs has been exaggerated. He contended that instances of discrimination against religious groups in the distribution of social service funds were rare even before these enactments, and that in a 1993–1994 survey, only 11 percent of religiously affiliated, government-funded child service agencies reported "having to curtail religious activities" to retain funding (2003, 32). He also argued that only a small percentage of congregations actually engage in any extensive social service work, a fact that supporters of charitable choice acknowledge while saying that matters are slowly changing (Carlson-Thies 2001, 125; Chaves 2003, 33). For charitable choice critics, Chaves's claims suggest that these programs may actually be ways of giving special assistance to religious groups in public funding under the guise of equal treatment.

Controversy also continues over how the services provided by faith-based organizations compare to those of secular nonprofits. Critics again worry that what they see as false claims for the superiority of religious service providers might mean that these programs work in practice to privilege religious groups inappropriately (Chaves 2003, 33–34; Diane Henriques, "Religion Trumps Regulation as Legal Exemptions Grow," New York Times, October 8, 2006, A1). Undoubtedly, many religious conservatives hope such privileging will prove to be the case, in their eyes justifiably. But, educated by their experiences in modern litigation, religious advocates of charitable choice have been careful to insist that it remains based on a principle of "equal public treatment of all faiths, with none having the right, through control of government, to monopolize public policy and funding for its point of view" (Sider 2005, citing Skillen 2001, 298). Here as elsewhere, notions that these policy innovations are part of transforming modern America into a more explicitly Christian nation or even one that gives primacy to religion are steadfastly disavowed.

The Prospects for Religious Right Constitutionalism

The thrust of my argument at this point will be abundantly clear. Although modern conservative religious political mobilization in general and Religious Right litigation in particular have had numerous causes, the proximate sources of heightened activism have frequently been perceptions that governmental policies benefiting fundamentalist and evangelical institutions, especially their financing, were in danger of ending. Thus galvanized, contemporary religious conservatives have for the most part succeeded in preserving the forms of public assistance, such as tax exemptions, that Christians especially have had throughout U.S. history. They have frequently regained other types of aid, such as public funds for parochial schools, which had been temporarily limited from the mid-1960s through the mid-1980s, when courts were particularly concerned to advance the antidiscrimination goals of the modern civil rights movement. These sorts of aid and accommodation have always meant, and continue to mean, that American governments do give extensive practical assistance to the many of the nation's organized religious communities, sometimes in ways that are not available to nonreligious bodies, such as tax exemptions for clerical salaries, not provided to directors of secular ethical centers.[8] And religious conservatives have recently won support for expanding aid even to "pervasively sectarian" institutions doing educational and social service work in ways that go beyond what was common in the more distant past, when social service systems were far less elaborate. Let me add that one can also perceive in recent American liberal theory a growing tendency to reject the calls to qualify the expression of religion in discourses of "public reason" that characterized the heyday of Rawlsian liberalism (see, for example, Spinner-Halev 2000; Galston 2002; Dostert 2006; Swaine 2006).

Even so, the story of Religious Right litigation is far from one of unbridled success from the viewpoints of conservative evangelicals. Along with Steven Brown and Hans Hacker, I have argued that modern Religious Right litigators have relied more and more on arguments for equal treatment and freedom of speech, portraying fundamentalists and evangelicals simply as equal members of a pluralistic America and abandoning, at least in court, the aspirations that many have had to, in Jerry Falwell's words, "return America to her religious heritage" as a Christian nation (Brown 2002, 35, 78, 100; Hacker 2005, 2–4, 9). More than these authors, I have stressed how Religious Right leaders have felt compelled to do so in order to protect the funding systems and organizations that are the life's blood of their existence. But I also agree with these authors that as a result, many Religious Right leaders feel they are failing to achieve the kinds of change they really want (Brown 2002, 4, 118, 142; Hacker 2005, 7–9). By the same token, we might conclude that fears of the rise of premillennialist Christians to dominance in American life can be laid to rest, for all efforts to give extraordinary privileges to religions in general, much less to these forms of evangelical Christianity, are bound to have too little political and judicial support to succeed.

That is indeed my conclusion; but let me acknowledge a couple of points that may appear to tell in the other direction. First, as religious groups accumulate victories using equal access and free expression arguments, they also are acquiring a wide range of concrete forms of governmental assistance. In the fall of 2006, the *New York Times* ran a series of stories by Diana Henriques arguing, as the first installment contended, that since 1989, "more than 300 special arrangements, protections or exemptions for religious groups or their adherents were tucked into Congressional legislation," suggesting that under the guise of achieving a more level playing field, modern developments are actually strengthening religious sectors of society at the expense of secular ones ("Religion Trumps Regulation as Legal Exemptions Grow," October 8, A1).

Second, Jay Sekulow recently argued that throughout U.S. history and still today, judges have voted their religious beliefs. In his study *Witnessing Their Faith*, he canvassed religious litigation from the nation's founding to the present and contended that in "every one of the cases discussed in this book, the opinion of the justices coincided with the official positions held by the religious denominations that had influenced them" (2006, xii–xiii). If that pattern really has existed and holds in the future, secular Americans may have added cause for concern. In what is possibly a consequence of successful mobilization against Roe v. Wade, five of the current Supreme Court justices are Roman Catholics (Chief Justice Roberts and Associate Justices Scalia, Kennedy, Alito, and a convert, Clarence Thomas). Though conservative evangelical Protestants and Catholics have been often bitter opponents through most of U.S. history, in the modern era they are frequently found on the same side of issues involving governmental aid to and accommodation of religious groups. Perhaps, then, the pattern of greater and greater practical privileging of religion that Henriques perceives will get greater and greater support from the Supreme Court in the years ahead.

There is something to these arguments, and let me note that in the late 1990s I expressed strong worries that Religious Right advocates would win public funding through equal treatment arguments in establishment clause cases as well as preferred position status for their religious groups in free exercise cases, thereby ending up, on balance, unduly privileged (Smith 1998). I observed, however, that if free exercise claims were genuinely treated equally with other forms of expression, then even if courts treated all such claims as being in a preferred position, the number of individuals and groups who might claim exemption from various laws on free expression grounds would be so large that governments would often be found to have compelling state interests justifying denials of such exemptions (193–194). That is what appears to be happening in cases like Smith and City of Boerne v. Flores: the Court has not been willing either to uphold distinctive religious free exercise claims or to support broader exemptions from public laws and policies to all who might see otherwise illegal activity as part of their free expression.

Consequently, I think it is genuinely significant that the Religious Right has largely relinquished efforts to argue openly either in court or in legislative processes for a privileged status for religion in American life. As Henriques acknowledges and as the case law shows, for better or worse, most of the forms of governmental aid now being upheld have existed throughout U.S. history. In some cases, recent measures simply represent restoration of past privileges, and those that go beyond the past do not appear thus far to be fuelling any major expansion of Religious Right organizations or activities. Their most vital financial resource remains religious broadcasting, and even their broadcasting is constrained by concerns to maintain their nonpartisan, tax-exempt status (Brown 2002, 125).

In sum, whatever their deepest aspirations, nothing in recent litigation, legislation, or social experience suggests that Religious Right groups are likely to succeed in displacing secular social service providers, community groups, or broadcasters in law, public policies, or in social practices, only that they will exist alongside them within a highly pluralistic society. If Justices Scalia and Kennedy are any indication, the presence of Catholics on the high court is unlikely to alter those circumstances. Both have been very receptive to equal treatment and free speech arguments in religion cases, but both have frequently voted to reject claims made in the name of religious free exercise alone. Scalia is in fact the Court's most persistent champion of relatively minimal scrutiny of alleged burdens on free exercise. And though Catholics and Protestant evangelicals may be able to converge on arguments for giving religious groups "a place at the table" and on access to public funds for their schools, their notions of the Christianity that should prevail in a Christian America remain very different.

It is true, nonetheless, that Religious Right litigants have altered major constitutional doctrines over the last three decades, and that they have done so in ways that have directly assisted their institutions and programs. Religious Right activists and their political allies have also influenced numerous public policies to bring them in accordance with their religious convictions, particularly on topics seen as matters of sexual morality, including abortion and contraception. In the early 1970s, few would have predicted such success. So while at present I am more impressed with the limits on Religious Right constitutional advocacy than its potential reach, I still hesitate to forecast very precisely or confidently about what the future may bring. As an unconventionally religious American leader once remarked, "the Almighty has His own purposes."[9]

Notes

1. My thanks to Peter D. Hall, Stephen Macedo, Steven Brint, Jean Schroedel, and conference participants generally for their comments on an earlier version of this essay.
2. Stephen Monsma has noted that in 1993, even before the rise of recent "charitable choice" provisions that began with the Personal Responsibility and Work Opportunity Reconciliation Act of 1996, "65 percent of Catholic Charities' revenues came from government sources, as did 75 percent of the Jewish Board of Family and Children's Services' revenues, and 92 percent of Lutheran Social Ministries' revenues" (Monsma 1996, 1; Wuthnow 2004, 14).
3. John Rawls claims that "no one any longer supposes that a practicable political conception for a constitutional regime can rest on a shared devotion to the Catholic or the Protestant Faith, or to any other religious view" and contends that comprehensive "claims of religion and philosophy" should be "excluded" as "a condition of establishing a shared basis for free public reason" (1971, 31, 216; 1987, 5, 20). Rawls also contends that public reason involves a "duty of civility" that means political candidates should not seek to ensure the "influence and success" of their religious views (1999, 150, 174–75).
4. See also, for example, Levitt v. Commission for Public Education and Religious Liberty, 413 U.S. 472 (1973); Committee for Public Education and Religious Liberty v. Nyquist, 413 U.S. 756 (1973); Sloan v. Lemon, 413 U.S. 825 (1973); Meek v. Pittenger, 421 U.S. 349 (1975); Wolman v. Walter, 433 U.S. 229 (1977).
5. See Public Law 96-74, 96th Congress, H.R. 4393, enacted September 29, 1979, for provisions denying funds to efforts to deny tax-exempt status to religious or church-operated schools.
6. In addition to Bob Jones University, defeats for claims of special religious privileges under the free exercise clauses occurred during these years in Heffron v. International Society for Krishna Consciousness, 452 U.S. 640 (1981), denying special rights to solicit funds at a fairground; U.S. v. Lee, 455 U.S. 252 (1982), denying the Amish exemption from Social Security taxes; Alamo Foundation v. Secretary of Labor, 471 U.S. 290 (1985), requiring religious organizations to comply with minimum wage laws; Texas Monthly, Inc. v. Bullock, 489 U.S. 1 (1989), striking down a Texas tax exemption for religious publications because it did not apply to "a wide array of nonsectarian groups . . . in pursuit of some legitimate secular end" (2); and Hernandez

v. Commissioner of Internal Revenue, 490 U.S. 680 (1989), holding that payments made to the Church of Scientology for training purposes are not tax-deductible contributions, among other cases. These decisions all affected adversely the financial viability of the religious groups in question.

7. Even so, Religious Right litigants do seek to win interpretations of free speech guarantees that may effectively permit government to favor politically influential religious denominations. At this writing, the Supreme Court has agreed to review Pleasant Grove City, Utah v. Summum, Sup. Ct. Docket 07–665 (cert. granted 3/31/2008). In 1971, Pleasant Grove City permitted the Fraternal Order of Eagles to erect a monument with an engraved depiction of the Ten Commandments in the city's Pioneer Park. The relatively new church of Summum sought in 2003 to erect a monument in the same park that would display the Seven Aphorisms of Summum. The Tenth Circuit Court of Appeals ruled that the park was a public forum and that free speech guarantees meant that the government must be "viewpoint-neutral" toward private expression in that forum, so the city had to permit the erection of the Summum monument. Pleasant Grove City appealed, with its petition written by Jay Sekulow and other attorneys for the American Center for Law and Justice. They contended that the park was not a public forum and that the Ten Commandments monument was the government's speech, not private speech. They maintained the government had no obligation to open its park to clutter or to articulate all viewpoints itself. Their brief did not address the issue of whether, if the Ten Commandments monument was government speech, it represented an endorsement of religion in violation of Establishment Clause requirements, or instead conveyed an essentially civic message. The brief for Summum also did not raise this Establishment Clause question. It contended that both monuments were private speech in a public forum to which they were entitled to have equal access. Hence it is not clear at this writing whether the Supreme Court will consider whether the city's policies defended by Religious Right litigants threatens to privilege traditional forms of Christianity over other types of religion.

8. I am grateful to Professor Stephen Macedo, director of Princeton University's Center for Human Values, for this compelling example.

9. Abraham Lincoln, Second Inaugural Address, Washington, D.C., March 4, 1865. Available at: http://www.bartleby.com/124/pres32.html.

References

Ahlstrom, Sidney E. 1972. *A Religious History of the American People*. New Haven, Conn.: Yale University Press.

Balmer, Randall. 2006. *Thy Kingdom Come: An Evangelical's Lament: How the Religious Right Distorts the Faith and Threatens America*. New York: Basic Books.

Brown, Steven P. 2002. *Trumping Religion: The Religious Right, the Free Speech Clause, and the Courts*. Tuscaloosa: University of Alabama Press.

Carlson-Thies, Stanley. 2001. "Charitable Choice: Bringing Religion Back into American Welfare." *Journal of Policy History* 13(1): 110–32.

Carpenter, Joel A. 1984. "From Fundamentalism to the New Evangelical Coalition." In *Evangelicalism and Modern America*, edited by George Marsden. Grand Rapids, Mich.: William B. Eerdmans.

Carter, Stephen L. 1993. *The Culture of Disbelief: How American Law and Politics Trivialize Religious Devotion*. New York: Basic Books.

Casey, Samuel B. 2006. "Great is His Faithfulness: 45 Years of 'His-Story' at CLS." Christian Legal Society. Available at: http://www.clsnet.org/clsPages/history.php.

Center for Law and Religious Freedom. 1981. Brief of Amicus Curiae Supporting Petitioner, Bob Jones University v. Simon, 416 U.S. 725 (1974).

Chaves, Mark. 2003. "Debunking Charitable Choice: The Evidence Doesn't Support the Political Left or Right." *Stanford Social Innovation Review* 1(2) (Summer 2003): 28–36.

Cox, Harvey. 1966. *The Secular City: Secularization and Urbanization in Theological Perspective*, rev. ed. New York: Macmillan.

Cremin, Lawrence A. 1988. *American Education: The Metropolitan Experience, 1876–1980*. New York: Harper & Row.

Dostert, Troy. 2006. *Beyond Political Liberalism: Toward a Post-Secular Ethics of Public Life*. Notre Dame, Ind.: University of Notre Dame Press.

Esbeck, Carl H. 1998. "Equal Treatment: Its Constitutional Status." In *Equal Treatment of Religion in a Pluralistic Society*, edited by Stephen V. Monsma and J. Christopher Soper. Grand Rapids, Mich.: William B. Eerdmans.

Galston, William. 2002. *Liberal Pluralism: The Implications of Value Pluralism for Political Theory and Practice*. New York: Cambridge University Press.

Hacker, Hans J. 2005. *The Culture of Conservative Christian Litigation*. Lanham, Md.: Rowman & Littlefield.

Hart, Darryl G. 2001. "Mainstream Protestantism, 'Conservative' Religion, and Civil Society." *Journal of Policy History* 13(1): 19–46.

Ivers, Gregg. 1992. "Religious Organizations as Constitutional Litigants." *Polity* 25(2): 243–66.

King, William McGuire. 1989. "The Reform Establishment and the Ambiguities of Influence." In *Between the Times: The Travail of the Protestant Establishment in America, 1900–1960*, edited by William R. Hutchison. New York: Cambridge University Press.

Lienesch, Michael. 1993. *Redeeming America: Piety and Politics in the Religious Right*. Chapel Hill: University of North Carolina Press.

Martin, William C. 1996. *With God on Our Side: The Rise of the Religious Right in America*. New York: Broadway Books.

Matthews, Arthur H. 1992. *Stand Up, Standing Together: The Emergence of the National Association of Evangelicals*. Carol Stream, Ill.: National Association of Evangelicals.

McConnell, Michael W. 1985. "Accommodation of Religion." *The Supreme Court Review* 1985: 1–59.

———. 1990. "The Origins and Historical Understanding of the Free Exercise of Religion." *Harvard Law Review* 103(1990): 1409–1517.

———. 1995. Brief for Petitioner, Rosenberger v. Rosenberger v. The Rector and Visitors of the University of Virginia, 515 U.S. 819 (1995) (No. 94-329).

———. 1998. "Equal Treatment and Religious Discrimination." In *Equal Treatment of Religion in a Pluralistic Society*, edited by Stephen V. Monsma and J. Christopher Soper. Grand Rapids, Mich.: William B. Eerdmans.

————. 1999. Brief for Petitioners, Mitchell v. Helms, 530 U.S. 793 (2000) (No. 98-1648).

McLaughlin, Donald H., and Stephen Broughman. 1997. "Other Religious-Conservative Christian Schools." In *Private Schools in the United States: A Statistical Profile, 1993–94*. NCES 97-459. Washington: U.S. Government Printing Office. Available at: http://nces.ed.gov/pubs/ps/97459ch3.asp.

Minow, Martha. 2003. "Public and Private Partnerships: Accounting for the New Religion." *Harvard Law Review* 116(1): 1–41.

Monsma, Stephen V. 1996. *When Sacred and Secular Mix: Religious Nonprofit Organizations and Public Money*. Lanham, Md.: Rowman & Littlefield.

Morgan, Richard E. 1972. *The Supreme Court and Religion*. New York: The Free Press.

Ostling, Richard N. 1984. "Evangelical Publishing and Broadcasting." In *Evangelicalism and Modern America*, edited by George Marsden. Grand Rapids, Mich.: William B. Eerdmans.

Pierard, Richard V. 1984. "The New Religious Right in American Politics." In *Evangelicalism and Modern America*, edited by George Marsden. Grand Rapids, Mich.: William B. Eerdmans.

Rawls, John. 1971. *A Theory of Justice*. Cambridge, Mass.: Harvard University Press.

————. 1987. "The Idea of an Overlapping Consensus." *Oxford Journal of Legal Studies* 7(1): 1–25.

————. 1999. *The Law of Peoples, with "The Idea of Public Reason Revisited."* Cambridge Mass.: Harvard University Press.

ReligiousTolerance.org. 2007. "The Federal Equal Access Act: Student-Led Clubs in Public High Schools." Ontario Consultants on Religious Tolerance. Available at: http://www.religioustolerance.org/equ_acce.htm.

Schneider, Robert A. 1989. "Voice of Many Waters: Church Federation in the Twentieth Century." In *Between the Times: The Travail of the Protestant Establishment in America, 1900–1960*, edited by William R. Hutchison. New York: Cambridge University Press.

Sears, Alan E., and Jay Alan Sekulow. 2003. Brief for Respondent, Locke v. Davey, 540 U.S. 712 (2004) (No. 02-1315).

Sekulow, Jay Alan. 2006. *Witnessing Their Faith: Religious Influence on Supreme Court Justices and Their Opinions*. Lanham, Md.: Rowman & Littlefield.

Sider, Ronald J. 2005. "Evaluating the Faith-Based Initiative: Is Charitable Choice Good Public Policy?" *Theology Today* 67(4): 485–98.

Silk, Mark. 1989. "The Rise of the 'New Evangelicalism': Shock and Adjustment." In *Between the Times: The Travail of the Protestant Establishment in America, 1900–1960*, edited by William R. Hutchison. New York: Cambridge University Press.

Skillen, James W. 1998. "The Theoretical Roots of Equal Treatment." In *Equal Treatment of Religion in a Pluralistic Society*, edited by Stephen V. Monsma and J. Christopher Soper. Grand Rapids, Mich.: William B. Eerdmans.

————. 2001. "E Pluribus Unum and Faith-Based Welfare Reform." *The Princeton Seminary Bulletin* 22(3): 285–305.

Smith, Rogers M. 1998. "'Equal' Treatment? A Liberal Separationist View." In

Equal Treatment of Religion in a Pluralistic Society, edited by Stephen V. Monsma and J. Christopher Soper. Grand Rapids, Mich.: William B. Eerdmans.

Spinner-Halev, Jeff. 2000. *Surviving Diversity: Religion and Democratic Citizenship*. Baltimore, Md.: Johns Hopkins University Press.

Swaine, Lucas. 2006. *The Liberal Conscience: Politics and Principle in a World of Religious Pluralism*. New York: Columbia University Press.

Turner, Daniel L. 1997. *Standing Without Apology: The History of Bob Jones University*. Greenville, S.C.: Bob Jones University Press.

Wolfe, Alan. 2003. *The Transformation of American Religion: How We Actually Live Our Faith*. New York: Free Press.

Wuthnow, Robert. 1989. *The Struggle for America's Soul: Evangelicals, Liberals, and Secularism*. Grand Rapids, Mich.: William B. Eerdmans.

———. 2004. *Saving America? Faith-Based Services and the Future of Civil Society*. Princeton, N.J.: Princeton University Press.

Index